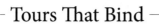 Tours That Bind

Tours That Bind

*Diaspora, Pilgrimage, and
Israeli Birthright Tourism*

Shaul Kelner

NEW YORK UNIVERSITY PRESS

New York and London

NEW YORK UNIVERSITY PRESS
New York and London
www.nyupress.org

Library of Congress Cataloging-in-Publication Data

Kelner, Shaul.
Tours that bind : diaspora, pilgrimage, and Israeli birthright tourism /
Shaul Kelner.
p. cm.
Includes bibliographical references and index.
ISBN-13: 978-0-8147-4816-9 (cl : alk. paper)
ISBN-10: 0-8147-4816-3 (cl : alk. paper)
1. Tourism—Israel. 2. Heritage tourism—Israel.
3. Jews—Travel—Israel. 4. Jews—United States—Identity. I. Title.
G155.I78K45   2010
338.4'7915694—dc22   2009044386

Excerpt from Yehuda Amichai's "Tourists," in *The Selected Poetry of Yehuda Amichai*,
translated and edited by Chana Bloch and Stephen Mitchell (1996), used with
permission of University of California Press.

Excerpt from Lydia Polgreen, "Ghana's Uneasy Embrace of Slavery's Diaspora," from
The New York Times, December 27, 2005. © 2005 The New York Times. All rights reserved.
Used by permission and protected by the Copyright Laws of the United States.
The printing, copying, redistribution, or retransmission of the Material
without express written permission is prohibited.

Some material contained herein originally appeared in *Contemporary Jewry*,
the journal of the Association for the Social Scientific Study of Jewry, volume 24,
copyright Springer, 2003–2004. Other material is adapted from a paper presented in 2004
to the Hebrew University of Jerusalem's Institute for Advanced Studies, and also appears in
Steven M. Cohen, Harvey E. Goldberg, and Ezra Kopelowitz, eds., *Dynamic Belonging:
Jewish Collective Identities in Israel and the United States,* Berghahn Books, forthcoming.

New York University Press books are printed on acid-free paper,
and their binding materials are chosen for strength and durability.
We strive to use environmentally responsible suppliers and materials
to the greatest extent possible in publishing our books.

Manufactured in the United States of America

10 9 8 7 6 5 4 3 2 1

For
Pamela
Where you go, I will go

Contents

Acknowledgments

Tourism is a social activity, shaped by travelers' relationships with people who guide and accompany them on their journey and also with those whom they meet along the way. So it is with authoring a book.

I was blessed with wonderful faculty mentors at CUNY. Sam Heilman helped me cultivate my inner ethnographer. Phil Kasinitz introduced me to transnational studies and showed me how to balance affection for my topic with critical distance from it. Paul Attewell, ever a voice of reason, grounded me solidly in statistical methodologies. Julia Wrigley helped me frame my research interests to speak to big questions. I also benefited from the guidance of Cynthia Fuchs Epstein, Juan Battle, Barry Kosmin, David Rindskopf, Herb Danzger, Egon Mayer z"l, and Mervin Verbit, among others. At the George Washington University my teachers Max Ticktin, Steven Livingston, Jarol Manheim, and Robert Eisen nurtured my budding interest in social science and Jewish studies. Yael Moses launched me on the path to Hebrew fluency.

When I had doubts about pursuing a career in academia, the vote of confidence given me by Larry Moses and the Wexner Foundation helped me overcome them. Bob Chazan helped me forge my own scholarly path. Cindy Chazan and Elka Abrahamson have helped me envisage my career not only in terms of what it means to me but also to the communities that sustain me. Among these communities is the alumni network of the foundation's Graduate Fellowship Program. To them, to Brigitte Dayan, and especially to the members of Class VIII go my enduring friendship. To Leslie and Abigail Wexner, and also to Maurice Corson, my admiration and gratitude.

During the first years of this research, I discovered how enriching is the camaraderie of fellow scholars. Ruth Abusch-Magder, Warren Bass, Scott Lasensky, Aaron Panken, and Rami Wernik inspired and taught me. At CUNY, Matthew Lindholm was a wise older brother. I owe my sanity to David Livert.

Brandeis University's Cohen Center for Modern Jewish Studies (CMJS) provided the context for embarking on this research. It also provided exceptional colleagues—Amy Sales, Larry Sternberg, Michael Rabkin, Fern Chertok, and Erez Yereslove, among others. At CMJS, I was fortunate to work with a talented team of field researchers who helped me see the Israel tours through their eyes, too. My thanks go to Benjamin Phillips, Matt Boxer, Mark I. Rosen, Minna Wolf, Meredith Woocher, Amy Adamczyk, Diane Purvin, Heather Shapiro, Rachel Canar, Jennifer Perloff, Rishona Teres, Craig Schneider, and Hal Ossman. Thanks also to Dana Selinger-Abutbul, Christie Cohen, Gloria Tessler, Claire Cohen, and Jim Kearney. With an abiding sense of loss, I call to mind the contributions of my intern, Shira Palmer-Sherman z"l.

At Taglit-Birthright Israel and at Hillel, thanks go to all who enabled this research. Barry Chazan showed interest in this work from day one. The "Israel experience" field bears his stamp, and it has been a privilege to engage in the dialogue with him. My gratitude also goes to Charles Bronfman, Michael Steinhardt, David Gedzelman, Yitz Greenberg, Gidi Mark, Shimshon Shoshani, Shelly Zimmerman, Bob Aronson, Liz Sokolsky, Andrea Hoffman, Clare Goldwater, Esther Abramowitz, and Ezra Korman. I recall fondly the support given by J. J. Greenberg z"l.

A deep debt of gratitude is owed to the members and staffs of the tour groups I observed, especially those in the three groups that figure prominently in these pages. They welcomed me eagerly and made my work fun. I hope they find this representation of our shared experiences to be fair, honest, and thought provoking. My promise to protect their confidentiality prevents me from giving them the individual recognition they are due. Were I able to thank them here in a manner befitting their contributions, these acknowledgments would take up most of the book.

I found support at Tel Aviv University's (TAU) Department of Sociology and Anthropology, where I spent the 2008–2009 academic year as a visiting scholar, and also at the Hebrew University of Jerusalem's Institute for Advanced Studies (IAS), where I had a fellowship in spring 2004. My thanks go to Harvey Goldberg, Ezra Kopelowitz, Dan Rabinowitz, Ofra Goldstein-Gidoni, and my other colleagues at TAU and in the IAS working group. Thanks also to Pnina Feldman and Seffi Shtiglitz.

Many people assisted with specific aspects of this research. On the history of Israel experience programs, special thanks go to Jules Gutin, Paul Reichenbach, and Susan Woodland, among others. On Israel-diaspora relations, thanks to Jonny Ariel, Elan Ezrachi, and the Kol Dor network. Sarah Bunin Benor served as consultant on linguistic issues, Saul Strosberg on Hassidic music, and textile artist Rachel Kanter on matters sartorial. Susan Bell directed me to the work of Andrea Louie. The PresenTense Group and Ari Kelman helped with web-related matters.

Friends and family have provided valued support. For their hospitality during my travels, thanks go to Jared and Debbie Kelner, Andrew Ely and Rachel Kanter, Jeff and Michelle Feig, David Umansky and Penni Morganstein, Rebecca and Danny Deutsch, Josh Mitnick and Lesley Benedikt, Amit and Doron Zehavi, and Tal Daniel. They have been valuable conversation partners, as have David Abusch-Magder, Moshe and Leslie Horn, and David Lewis. Alyssa Dolman, Alyse Lefkowitz, and Sara McDonough came to Pam's assistance while I was abroad. Mark Lefkowitz preemptively saved me from a computer crash. Danny Weinstock helped me measure progress. Ian Brecher, Sam Richman, and Beatrice Richman shared photos and insights from their own trips to Israel. Evan and Eric Ely helped me better understand potential participants' decision-making calculus. Jeffrey Schulman and Kristi Glasser provided consistent moral support.

This work owes much to my relationships with colleagues and friends. Conversations with Ted Sasson have crucially shaped my thinking at numerous points during the writing of this book. His penetrating comments on a draft manuscript reflect a first-rate sociological mind. From our first encounter, Steven M. Cohen has helped me grow as a scholar, encouraging my career development, challenging me intellectually, and modeling strategies for remaining intellectually dynamic. At our Upper West Side brunches, Bethamie Horowitz and I tackled issues of theory and practice. These conversations have been wellsprings of creativity for me. As I have tried to weave diverse research interests into a coherent whole, Riv-Ellen Prell has long been my north star. Noam Pianko and Marcy Brink-Danan have helped me think beyond my disciplinary boundaries. Noam also offered thoughtful comments on draft chapters. My treatment of tourism here is informed by conversations with Jonathan Wynn, Jackie Feldman, and Jenna Weissman Joselit. Both Lynn Davidman and Paul Burstein have provided valuable guidance.

To my teachers Charles Kadushin and Leonard Saxe I owe an enormous debt of gratitude for setting me on this journey, shepherding my work through its initial phase, and launching me to pursue these investigations further on my own. Charles has been a wonderful mentor, dissertation chair, colleague, and cherished friend. Through instruction, example, and oral history, he bequeathed the distinguished heritage of Columbia's long-lamented Bureau of Applied Social Research. Len energetically built an institutional framework at Brandeis's CMJS that has put this tradition into practice. As the first "graduate" of the CMJS incubator, I have tried in these pages to live up to the best of the intellectual tradition in which I was trained.

My 2005 move to Vanderbilt University placed me in a vibrant center for the study of the sociology of culture. My conversations with Jennifer Lena, Richard Lloyd, and Steven Tepper, among others, have fundamentally shaped the direction I have taken in this book. Lena provided invaluable feedback on a complete draft of the manuscript. My writing group—Allison Schachter, Tiffiny Tung, and Sergio Romero—helped me clarify my arguments and my prose. Tony Brown helped an ethnographer find his inner statistician. In sociology, Dan Cornfield, Karen Campbell, Holly McCammon, and Larry Isaac have been valued conversation partners and guides. So, too, have been my department and program chairs, Katharine Donato, Leah Marcus, Gary Jensen, and David Wasserstein. Laura Carpenter helped me gain sea legs in the world of academic publishing. Jack Sasson helped me reflect on Safed and the kabbalah. Lenn Goodman inspired the book's title. Carolyn Dever and Richard McCarty gave me the opportunity to think about my work in broader perspective by funding my participation in an Israeli and American Jewish tour of Holocaust sites in Eastern Europe, sponsored by the Wexner Foundation. The College of Arts and Science also gave me the opportunity to develop my thinking on tourism by providing a grant to develop a travel-based course in the sociology of tourism. My former teaching assistant, George Sanders, and my students in the spring 2007 "Tourism, Culture and Place" class honed my thinking on all matters tourism-related. Thanks also go to Ronnie Steinberg, George Becker, Mike Ezell, Richard Pitt, Martina Urban, Richard McGregor, Monica Casper, Jim Lang, and Sidney Halpern and to my graduate students Charles Bernsen, Ur Barzel, and Erin Rehel. Ari Dubin reflected with me on the Jewish involvements of travelers returning from Israel. Without Lynne Perler, Linda Willingham, Deanne Casanova, and Pam Tichenor smoothing the way, I would have accomplished little.

In working with Ilene Kalish at New York University Press, I quickly realized how well deserved is her reputation as a first-rate editor. She has helped me produce something that is far better—substantively and stylistically—than anything I could have written on my own. Ilene's assistant, Aiden Amos, has been a model of professionalism and a delight to work with.

In the life journey that led me to pursue a career in sociology and to author this particular book, I owe special thanks to two members of my extended family. My uncle, David Richman, the first college professor I ever knew, has long been among my most important role models and confidants.

My cousin, Stan Brecher, has been one of my most reliable and level-headed career advisors for a quarter-century now, ever since my high school days.

My deepest gratitude is reserved for my family. My father, Barry z"l, had a passion for learning that inspires me in all the work I do. My mother, Rhoda, is the model of caring generosity, having done more to support me in this work than I can ever describe. For all of it, large and small—from her words of encouragement and pride, to helping Pam with the kids while I was abroad, to giving me an ocean-view balcony from which to write, to schlepping my replacement computer to me in Israel—I thank her. Most of all, I thank her for channeling her mother, my grandmother, by giving me frank criticism that helped keep me on track. To my stepfather, Mort Schulman, for all these same reasons, go similar heartfelt expressions of gratitude and love. My in-laws, Gerry and Joan Ely, provided me a breezy beach library where I could spend summer days writing and, even better, a quiet slice of the Jersey shore where I could pack my computer away and just relax—at least until a raised eyebrow from Gerry called me back to the task at hand. The combination made for vacations that were both rejuvenating and productive. My children, Boaz and Shoshana, endured stretches of time when I was away in the field and many dinners without their father when I was cloistered in the office writing. To their credit, they only rarely taunted me with the chorus of "Cat's in the Cradle." Their restraint mitigated somewhat my own feelings of guilt, and for this I am grateful. Finally, the love and support of my wife, Pam, have been my strength and are valued beyond words. Pam has been living this project with me through all its ups and downs and twists and turns. When I went in 1987 to participate in USY Israel Pilgrimage, neither she nor I expected that diaspora homeland tourism would come to occupy a central place in both our lives for more than two decades. This book is as much hers as it is mine, and it is with gratitude and love that I dedicate it to her.

Preface

There was a time when researchers would have to defend the decision to take tourism seriously. Most of their audience, after all, had probably played tourist at some point and knew firsthand that this was a temporary escape from the matters of consequence that weighed on them in their daily lives. Fellow researchers could hardly have been expected to see things differently. For them, tourism was primarily a diversion to be enjoyed between semesters. Some hours baking in the sun, the company of family or friends, a little sightseeing. Maybe they would learn a thing or two about the local culture, but only—dare I say it—as dilettantes. Real scholarship, the knowledge that counted, would be produced in the stacks, or in the lab, or in the field, or at the desk. That was work. Tourism was just R&R.

Intellectual currents shaped tourism's reception, too. A modernist, prefeminist research agenda that enshrined labor and production could not help but marginalize the study of a consumption-based, symbol-driven, leisure activity. By the 1970s, however, tourism studies found more fertile soil in academia, as broader intellectual movements began staking claims for the centrality of symbolic consumption to self and society in market economies. At the same time that semioticians, postmodernists, and others were giving tourism a newfound respectability, those whose interest remained on the production side of the equation began to notice that tourism was becoming one of the major growth industries of the late 20th century. Now with international receipts representing more than one-fourth of global service exports and totaling over $850 billion annually, with an increasing number of developing countries staking their economic futures on the industry, with more and more cityscapes being transformed in the name of tourism development, and with today's tourists constituting the largest international population flow in human history (903 million arrivals in 2007 alone), tourism has become a favored object of study across disciplines from the social sciences to cultural studies to business management and more.[1]

In stark contrast to earlier conceptions of tourism as a peripheral curiosity, contemporary understandings locate it at ground zero of some of the most charged issues of cultural politics today. It is on the field of tourism that governments, multinational corporations, local businesses, citizens, and visitors vie for control of space and for the power to represent collective identities. It is on this field that the market penetrates local heritage and ancient tradition, transforming them into commodities for others to consume and altering locals' relationships to their own cultures. It is on this field that forces of globalization bring diverse populations into a direct contact that can breed mutual interest and understanding, as well as exploitation, resentment, and conflict.

In this book, I take up the question of the politics of tourism at that turbulent point where modern nationalism and postmodern transnationalism meet, for tourism features centrally here, too. First mobilized in the service of nation-building projects around the world, tourism has more recently become implicated in strategies of transnation- or diaspora-building. Drawing on nationalist assertions of inherent connections between people, culture, and place, these strategies seek to unite members of globally dispersed populations by fostering a sense of shared belonging in a common political community that is simultaneously territorialized and deterritorialized, rooted and uprooted. Nation-states and diaspora organizations, each for their own reasons, have recognized tourism's utility in furthering these transnational projects. Tourism is, after all, a medium through which people who do not live in a place can come to know it and, through a variety of practices, can actively position themselves in relation to it. The result of this recognition has been a proliferation of state- and NGO-supported international tours that represent countries as "homelands" to diaspora ethnics who are specifically brought to visit them. For governments, these homeland tours offer a means of developing ties to potential investors, political advocates, and migrants. For diaspora groups, they offer a means of strengthening collective identity and ethnic community around the world. Recognizing their mutual interest, the two sides have begun working in partnership to systematically develop tourism as a form of political socialization that fosters identification with a nation-state and a sense of belonging in a transnational ethnic community.

The case I examine here focuses on the efforts of the State of Israel and North American Jewish organizations to mobilize tourism as a means of cultivating diaspora Jewish engagement with the country. These efforts, which in recent years have come to include free tours of Israel for hundreds of thousands of diaspora Jewish young adults, represent the largest, most long-standing and most elaborated deployment of tourism for diaspora-building purposes in the world today. As I note in chapter 1, however, they are hardly unique and are being joined by an increasing number of similar efforts by other countries, polities, and diaspora communities around the world.

At the heart of this book lie three core questions:

- What is the nature of this cultural practice, tourism, that enables it to be mobilized to effect political socialization?
- What are the limitations of the medium and the contradictions that emerge through the attempt to deploy it?
- What is the nature of the socialization that occurs when tourism is used as a strategy for introducing diaspora ethnics to a national homeland?

As these questions suggest, this is a study in the instrumentalization of culture, examining how governments and diaspora organizations are systematically deploying tourism's distinctive set of place-engaging practices to shape political identities.

Something so ideologically pregnant tends to raise in many people's minds a host of intertwined questions about the ethics and effectiveness of using tourism in this way. In treating these questions, I make no assumption that travelers are passive objects on whom tour operators work. On the contrary, even as I emphasize the agendas that program sponsors bring to these efforts and the ability of program operators to assert substantial control over key aspects of the touring environment, I also place the tourists themselves at the center of the analysis. Far from treating official ideologies as determinative, I probe the ethnographic data to draw out the dynamism of the social processes at work. This dynamism emerges from the human agency that tourists never relinquish, from the sometimes-divergent visions of Israeli and diaspora Jewish program sponsors, from the gaps between organizers' intentions and staffs' implementation, and from the very contradictions that inhere within the medium of tourism itself.

In this approach, I locate diaspora homeland tourism at the intersections of structure and agency and of production and consumption. In so doing, I try to resist the temptation of mapping organizers and tourists onto opposite sides of these admittedly problematic conceptual divides. To be sure, there is some justification for associating the sponsors of homeland tours with the forces of structure and production on one hand and the tourists themselves with agency and consumption on the other. Even so, in much of this book, I explore the ways that tourists, through their active agency, enter into a collaboration with program sponsors and thereby position the parties as coproducers of the experience. Likewise, although tourists retain agency as individuals, the tour group as a collective emerges as an important structuring force that channels the experience of every person on the trip.[2] As for the sponsoring organizations, the pages ahead reveal them to be self-consciously responsive to the structural constraints that the tourists and their chosen medium impose on them. Ultimately, diaspora homeland tours are revealed as sites where ideology and rationalization collide with open-ended, collaborative, and contingent processes of meaning making.

This collision offers observers a window onto fundamental aspects of tourism that usually remain invisible. (I spare the reader any comparisons with atom-smashing physicists.) Diaspora-building homeland tourism is distinguished, in one sense, by program organizers' determined efforts to eke out of tourism its generally unrealized potentials. As organizers have learned how to use tourism to achieve effects, they have gained a practical knowledge of the nature of their medium. Part of my work involves reverse-engineering their process to identify the elemental features of tourism they are combining for use. Some of this involves scrutinizing tour organizers' own discourse about their efforts. Some of it involves scrutinizing those moments when the process breaks down. On the trips themselves, the collision between the formal plan and the emergent reality creates many opportunities for things to go "wrong." Such instances function as natural breaching experiments and reveal aspects of the social reality that are hidden when simply taken for granted.[3]

What I am claiming for homeland tourism, therefore, is that its instrumental approach of "applied tourism" affords it a privileged position for shedding light on the basic question, "What is tourism?" The answer I develop in the coming chapters is intended to be broadly applicable beyond the particular case. Tourism, I argue, can be understood as a collection of ways of knowing and relating to place. Some of these are semiotic, others interactional, others embodied, and more. Because tourism is not a singular practice, its various dimensions dynamically interact with one another. This complicates any attempts to bring it under control.

Even as I attempt to speak here to general issues of tourism and specific issues of its mobilization as an instrument of transnational community building, I also have something to say expressly about the particular case that was the site for my fieldwork. Jewish tourism to Israel is now deeply implicated both in the contest between Jewish and Palestinian nationalisms and in the ongoing political debates among Jews about the ideal forms of

Jewish political community and state-diaspora relations. The former tends to be more visible in light of its broad geopolitical significance. Among Jews, the latter can generate just as much passion (as intracommunal politics are wont to do). In addressing both sets of issues, my inclination is to complicate understandings so that those seeking easy answers will think twice before accepting any.

At various points in this volume, especially chapter 3, I turn my lens onto the ways that diaspora Jewish tours represent the Israeli-Palestinian and Israeli-Syrian conflicts. The tours I studied are expressly intended to generate sympathy for Israeli perspectives on these conflicts, recognizing that these perspectives range across a spectrum of views. At the same time, it turns out that the tours are easily capable of accommodating a complex discourse that acknowledges Arab counternarratives. The extent to which this complexity is given expression varies, however, from group to group and from guide to guide. What is consistent across the trips I studied is that these counternarratives, when they are voiced, remain addressed at the level of discourse only. By contrast, the embodied practice that is the heart and soul of the tour is thoroughly situated in an Israeli Jewish experiential context, and it is this holistic experience that lends the Israeli narratives much of their compelling emotional weight.

As to the debates between Israeli Zionists and diaspora Jewish non-Zionists, the tours confound partisans on both sides by refusing to choose either of the ideologically "pure" extremes that the two camps put forward. In the face of old-line Zionist aspirations to end the Jewish diaspora through an ingathering of the exiles, the tours quietly substitute round-trip visits for permanent one-way migration. Without drawing attention to the implicit ideological challenge that they represent to classical Zionism, they use Israel to sustain diaspora, not eliminate it.[4] Some non-Zionist critiques, by contrast, chide diaspora Jews for looking abroad to Israel for Jewish meaning rather than seeking such meaning in the communities in which they themselves live their Jewish lives. In the face of these charges of "vicarious" identity, the tours assert that the diasporic condition necessarily entails feeling implicated in a Jewish experience that extends beyond one's immediate circumstances in place and time. They also affirm the modern Jewish eschatology that integrates the Holocaust and the establishment of the State of Israel into the timeless biblical paradigms of exile and redemption, oppression and liberation, destruction and renewal.[5] In short, against claims by Zionists and non-Zionists alike, the trips deliberately refuse to resolve the tension inherent in maintaining connections to more than one place. On the contrary, they elaborate it, making it the de facto centerpiece of the model of diasporic identity that they are working to advance.

I say "de facto" because it is unlikely that program sponsors would express their goals in quite these terms. I am imposing a language and a set of conceptual categories here that differ from the native discourse used by those in the field. It is best to state this clearly up front. There are two key ways in which my framing diverges from those indigenous to the trips. First, I explicitly speak of these tours as a *diaspora-building* enterprise. Organizers, by contrast, speak of building connections with Israel. The directionality of their formulation emphasizes the closing of distance rather than the fact that the element of distance is the essential defining feature of the relationship. They also speak of strengthening Jewish identity without specifying that the nature of this identity is specifically diasporic. There are a host of reasons why diaspora is an assumed category that tour sponsors never raise to the level of principle, not the least of which, as I note in chapter 2, are the programs' ideological roots in Zionism. My decision to break from the indigenous discourse and to represent these tours as an effort in diaspora-building is intended not only to shed light on the hidden work that the programs are actually accomplishing but also to highlight the ways that these tours are part and parcel of the broader transnationalist trends that are gaining momentum worldwide. At the same time, my commitment to engaged scholarship leads me to hope that this formulation will enter the native discourse of practitioners and enable them to reenvision the enterprise in new and currently unimagined ways.

Second, I frame diaspora homeland tourism as an effort in *political socialization*. Organizers of the tours to Israel would be more likely to speak of ethnic or religious socialization—or, even better, Jewish education. Certainly it is all this, too, and I do not intend to diminish this fact. Yet I prefer to speak of political socialization because it offers a clearer window onto what I consider to be the key aspects of the phenomenon: first and foremost, the tours are efforts to foster identification with a nation-state. In this, they draw on and reinforce core nationalist tropes that identify a particular cultural group with a particular stretch of land. These efforts alone would justify the use of the term, but there is more. The tours, as a diaspora-building practice, take implicit stands in favor of multiculturalism in the countries where the diasporans reside: they assert the legitimacy of maintaining sentimental ties with foreign countries and reject the notion that citizenship alone should define the boundaries of political community. Add to this the active interest that national governments take in supporting the enterprise, and the tendency to view the tourists as potential goodwill ambassadors, and the utility of a political frame becomes even more apparent. All these claims refer to diaspora homeland tourism generally, regardless of the ethnic group or country in question. In the case of Israel, the notion of the trips as a form of political socialization takes on added meaning in light of the fact that the tours are tangled in the thicket of the Middle East conflict.

I, too, am tangled in this thicket, as all who choose to write on this issue eventually will be, even if they were not beforehand. My own entanglement has roots. I found work in New York for a time as speechwriter for Israel's Mission to the United Nations. These were the years of Yitzhak Rabin's premiership in the first half of the 1990s. I signed on a week after he and Yasser Arafat shook hands on the White House lawn and raised my farewell toast two short months before Rabin was gunned down in Tel Aviv by a Jewish opponent of territorial compromise. This assassination, particularly coming after I had dedicated two years of my life trying to help Israel realize Rabin's vision, defined my political coming of age. Even though the Oslo Accords have fallen into disrepute among Israelis and Palestinians alike, I remain proud of the work I did at the United Nations in support of them. Not that these were my best writings. Like most U.N. statements, they were painfully stilted. (Any place this book slips into jargon and overly careful formulations can be blamed on my years in Turtle Bay.) Nevertheless, they were my small contribution to a possibly quixotic effort to break the shackles of enmity that history has clamped on the region.

I have tried to be self-aware about my own biases and correct for them when writing. This includes seeking feedback from colleagues whose politics differ from my own. Such people are not hard to find. The Zionist left is an increasingly lonely place at the end of the 21st century's first decade. Only here in Tel Aviv, where I write these words, does it seem to possess a certain normalcy. (Maybe also on Manhattan's Upper West Side and some places in Boston.) If I have not been fully successful in controlling for my biases, readers may find this coming through in a mournful pessimism about the prospects that the two sides will opt for peaceful coexistence and in a certain exasperation with critiques that naturalize Palestinian nationalism while treating Jewish nationalism as a social construct. This latter stance is not solely a product of my politics but derives from my theoretical commitments as a determined social constructionist who balks at any notion that the approach should be selectively applied. The other area where I am aware that my theoretical and political predilections intersect regards popular critiques that portray the tours as a form of "brainwashing." I tend to be dismissive of these and hope that this stance stems from a principled resistance to behavioral models that smack of determinism rather than from an unwillingness to consider the political challenge embedded in the criticism.

Issues of Israeli-Palestinian politics aside, on the more fundamental issues that I deal with here regarding tourism's deployment as an agent of diaspora-building, I have a long and complicated history with my object of study that shapes the lenses I bring to it. It can be fairly said that when it comes to diaspora Jewish homeland tours, I am as much of an insider as one can be without actually having designed or run a program. I did once staff a synagogue youth movement tour of the United States (not Israel) when I was 21. It was a coast-to-coast kosher bus trek with some 40-odd hormone-raging 15-year-olds. We wrapped ourselves in white and blue prayer shawls to recite morning blessings in truck-stop parking lots, placed a velvet Elvis next to the Torah as we put ancient Hebrew words to the King's sublime melodies, and generally reveled in the absurd glories of America, adolescence, and the Jewish experience. The tour was the same one that I went on when I was a rising high school junior, and that was my initiation into the world of diaspora Jewish tourism. "Fine, sit alone on that couch and do nothing all summer! It'll be *your* problem. I'm done nagging you about it." The note of finality in my mother's voice as she shouted into the den from our suburban New Jersey kitchen convinced me that, this time, she really meant it. "Awwwright," I glumly conceded. "I'll call Ken and send in the application." My cousin Ken was the same age as me. He, however, was surrounded by girls. He was also able to hammer out on the keyboard any Billy Joel song you could name and had a piano-key skinny tie to prove it. Ken was active in United Synagogue Youth and had signed up for their 1985 "USY on Wheels" trip. I would ride in his wake.

Two years later, I was encouraging him to join me for USY's 1987 "Israel Pilgrimage," six-and-a-half weeks of touring fun. Like Wheels, but reputedly better. Although at 17 I had not yet read critiques of tourism as a form of neo-colonialism, I intuitively knew that I should be packing my Banana Republic wardrobe. (Back then, Banana Republic still specialized in reproductions of Edwardian-era British army- and safari-wear. What Lawrence of Arabia wore, before he went native.) I would indulge my Orientalist fantasies.

My high school sweetheart, Pam, whom I would later marry, had taken a summer job and would not be traveling with me. That would take some fun out of the trip. I would be pining for her while my traveling companions were scoring with each other. We were prepared for the separation as we both planned in any case to head off to different colleges. But neither she nor I was prepared for my catching what those in the field call "the Israel bug." Somehow, at some point during the tour, I developed an ache (there is no better word) to return to the country for a longer time. I spoke with my counselors, all in their early 20s, and like good mentors they told me their similar stories. If I really wanted to come back, I could do what they did, they suggested, and spend a year studying at an Israeli university.

I took their advice. With two semesters of conversational Hebrew under my belt, I bid a temporary farewell to the George Washington University and enrolled in the Hebrew University of Jerusalem's One Year Program for Overseas Students. It was a consequential decision. First, it introduced me to academic Jewish studies, something now central to my professional life. Second, it got me flirting with the idea of *aliyah*, or immigration to Israel, so seriously that it strained my romantic relationship and led to what my wife and I now refer to as "the Hiatus." As Pam went to New York to pursue her career, I returned to Israel to cut thorns off of date palms in the desert, teach mathematics to immigrant kids from Russia and Ethiopia, and sort live fish on a conveyor belt two stories above the kibbutz pond in which they had been farm raised. The year of volunteer service changed my thinking about where I wanted to make my home. I returned to the States to pursue graduate work in sociology and Jewish studies. Before I began applying to graduate programs, however, I put to use the Hebrew-language skills I had honed in the date fields and took a job at the Israeli U.N. Mission. The glamour of the position and the opportunity to serve were reason enough for my 23-year-old self to set aside a deep-rooted (and in retrospect utterly misguided) distaste for New York City and move into the metropolis I had always sworn never to live in. So it was, chasing Israel, that I ended up in an apartment across the street from Pam, and the rekindled romance achieved its happy ending. Now, we take advantage of the perks of academic life to go back and forth between the United States and Israel. Our children are bilingual and bicultural.

In short, when I think about diaspora Jewish tourism to Israel, I cannot help but think of my own convoluted personal history. Acquiring the critical distance needed to study it has had, for me, the sad effect of disenchanting my relationship to a formative influence in my own life. Yet it is in this sense of loss that I gain a measure of confidence in the analysis I offer here. I learned things I did not know, and that, on reflection, I would probably have been happier not to know. I still retain my affection for these programs and often while conducting my fieldwork felt a tinge of envy toward the tourists who were experiencing their trips for the first time, unburdened by the need to adopt a stance of analytic detachment.

This, of course, makes me aware of the danger of reading my own experiences into those of the people I studied. My history with diaspora Jewish travel to Israel began with a six-week summer tour but then continued with a year of university study and a year of volunteer work, all in the context of programs that placed me in groups comprised of other diaspora Jews. These long-term study and volunteer programs were of a different order and magnitude, and I tried to keep this in mind when doing the fieldwork. Knowing that my own experience could serve as blinders, and knowing that there is an innate tendency to want to see one's own experience reflected in that of others, I also made concerted efforts to examine *lack* of engagement.

The lenses I brought and the biases I had to control for were also shaped by the fact that this project, in the tradition of Paul Lazarsfeld and Robert Merton's Columbia School sociology, had roots in applied social research. My first years of fieldwork, from 1999 to 2004, were conducted under the auspices of Brandeis University's Cohen Center for Modern Jewish Studies (CMJS), both for an evaluation of a diaspora Jewish homeland tourism program called Taglit-Birthright Israel (described in chapter 1) and for a doctoral dissertation that I was writing at the City University of New York Graduate Center. In winter 1999–2000, I led a team of seven participant observers from CMJS to study the first round of Birthright Israel trips. Each of the seven accompanied a different group of 40 students for the duration of their 10-day tour. I conducted participant observation alongside each of them for one to two days apiece, giving some breadth to my team's depth. Afterward, I compiled, coded, and analyzed the hundreds of pages of field notes we had collectively generated. I repeated this again the following year with another team of seven researchers. The key difference was that, instead of joining each of them in their groups, I chose a group of my own and conducted participant observation in it for the length of the trip. Over this same period, and through 2004, I also helped design, field, and analyze annual surveys of Birthright Israel participants and applicants for the Cohen Center evaluations.

After completing the first draft, I independently undertook a second wave of fieldwork outside the framework of the program evaluation. Returning to conduct research in Israel three times between 2004 and 2008, I traveled with two Birthright Israel groups for the duration of their tours in two of those years and spent time in another year meeting with guides and observing selected program activities. Most of this occurred after I moved to Vanderbilt University. In the second wave of research, my strategy was to focus this new participant observation on attempting to disconfirm the conclusions I had drawn in "Almost Pilgrims." In essence, after having spent the first years of this study trying to understand how diaspora homeland tourism succeeds in accomplishing its sponsors' goals, I spent the latter years trying to understand how it fails to accomplish them. By placing the two approaches into dialogue with one another, I hope I have produced an analysis that is more accurate, more balanced, and more sensitive to the rich complexities of the diaspora homeland tourism enterprise.

—— 1 ——

Deploying Tourism

On the evening of June 6, 2004, the Israeli cabinet announced its intention to dismantle all Jewish settlements in the Gaza Strip, captured from Egypt on that same date 37 years earlier. Soon afterward, Prime Minister Ariel Sharon made the short drive from the Knesset building to Jerusalem's convention center, whose name, Binyanei Ha'umah—Buildings of the Jewish People—anticipated the crowd that had gathered to hear him. Packing the 3,100-seat Ussishkin Hall were college-age Jews from four continents whom Sharon's government, in conjunction with diaspora Jewish philanthropists and nonprofit agencies, had brought to Israel on an all-expense-paid tour. They were neither the first nor the last of their kind. During the first decade of the millennium, over 200,000 young diaspora Jews would travel to Israel on free tours that were billed as "a gift from the Jewish people" and their "birthright."

Flanked by four bodyguards, Sharon approached the podium: "Good evening to you all. I wish to welcome you to Jerusalem, the eternal capital of the Jewish people, and the united capital of the State of Israel forever." Whatever the cabinet's decision on Gaza, Jerusalem was not up for discussion, at least not then. Sharon went on to announce, first in Hebrew then in English, that by approving the "disengagement plan," Israel's government had declared its intention to exit the Gaza Strip by the end of 2005. Far more cheers than jeers arose from the audience. Still, Sharon's detractors were unabashed in expressing their opposition. Opponents of territorial withdrawal responded to his announcement with audible disapproval. At the other end of the political spectrum, some who might have been expected to look favorably on the dismantling of Jewish settlements found it difficult to resolve the dissonance engendered by the fact that the author of Israel's Gaza withdrawal was also the architect of its 1982 Lebanon invasion. A number of these people were not present for Sharon's pronouncement, having walked out when he took the stage.

Although these were foreign tourists spending only 10 days on a whirlwind visit to the country, the travelers had few qualms about expressing their support or opposition to government policy, even to the extent of booing Israel's prime

| 1

minister in the heart of Jerusalem. Some Israelis might have taken umbrage at the tourists' willingness to take sides in a divisive national policy debate. But perhaps these diaspora Jews were simply taking Sharon at his word. "Bruchim ha-ba'im ha-baytah!" he had greeted them. "Welcome home!"

Discovering and Deploying a Diasporic Practice

Home. In diasporic experience, no category is more unstable. Where is home, when, for members of a dispersed people, the term floats without a necessary connection to one's actual country of residence? Where is home, when the places that are assigned and that are denied that label, when both "homeland" and "host country," each share quotients of familiarity and strangeness? Surely it can come as no surprise that diasporic imaginings have been preoccupied with questions of spatial identity. From the Amoraim of the Talmud to scholars of the Birmingham School, intellectuals have attempted to think systematically about what almost everyone who has ever counted himself or herself a diasporan has been forced to do pragmatically: untangle the complexities that bind self, community, culture, and place—if not to resolve the tensions, then at least to find some modus vivendi. The ways in which this untangling has taken place have evolved over the centuries, being continually reshaped by each new technology of communication, travel, and symbolic mediation. Among modernity's contributions to this enterprise has been the insertion of tourism into the repertoire of diasporic practice.

Over the past half-century, many factors have enabled international tourism to become a point of contact between nation-states and their diasporas. These include the commercialization of jet travel, the expansion of a global tourism industry, and growing affluence in the Western world, to name but a few. All this has democratized international travel, opening to ever-greater numbers an experience once reserved for soldiers, pilgrims, some merchants, and the children of the elite. It has also affected the nature of state-diaspora interactions. With the rise of mass tourism, places sometimes conceived of as points of origin—"homelands"[1] from which people departed as emigrants, refugees, or slaves—are increasingly serving as destinations to which they and their descendents arrive as tourists, pilgrims, or some combination of the two.

Undoubtedly, much travel to ethnic homelands is embedded in familial, business, and social relations.[2] Emigrants return to visit friends, meet with suppliers, celebrate with relatives, and care for parents. Any of these activities might qualify the travelers as tourists under the expansive definition used by the hospitality industry for administrative purposes, whereby a tourist is simply "any person who stays away from home overnight."[3] In casting such a wide net, this definition has the advantage of highlighting just how diverse diasporic travel to ethnic homelands actually is. Still, it glosses over a crucial distinction. Tourism is not simply travel in the generic sense; it is a distinctive set of social and cultural practices, a way of traveling. Incorporating sightseeing, photography, souvenir shopping, and the like, and supported by a well-developed industry of airlines, hotels, museums, and more, tourism is a particular way of engaging a place, of coming to "know" it, and of forging a relationship with it. What is significant about tourism's entry into the repertoire of diasporic practice is precisely that it provides a means for diasporans to encounter their ethnic homelands, regardless of whether or not they have direct social and material ties there. Through the work of cultural entrepreneurs in the private, public, and not-for-profit sectors, nation-states commodified as diasporic "homelands" have been made available for mass consumption by diaspora tourists who use them as sites of memory and imagination, spaces to reflect on the perennial questions of diasporic existence and the individual's relationship to place. Tourism, accordingly, has become a crucial way to reestablish, maintain, or initiate a diaspora-state relationship, even when links between the two are attenuated.

It is not a foregone conclusion that states and diasporas would desire such a relationship. The idea could easily meet with challenges from elements on each side. Classical nationalist formulations have tended to unite countries of origin and destination in shared suspicion of migrants, equating emigration with abandonment, in the first instance, and homeland ties with disloyalty, in the second. Globalization has tended to mute (though not eliminate) objections to ongoing homeland-diaspora ties, however, drawing attention, instead, to the potential advantages that the ties might confer.

One reason for this stems from the way that globalization and mass migration have intersected. At the beginning of the millennium, the United Nations estimated that about one out of every 33 people on the face of the planet was living somewhere other than the country of his or her birth—a proportion that had doubled in a mere 25 years.[4] This upsurge in worldwide migration has taken place as globe-shrinking technologies of travel, commerce, and communication have been reshaping the migration experience. For today's emigrants, striking roots in a new place hardly means severing ties with the old. On the contrary, émigré communities are emerging as significant forces in new political configurations that link nation-states with their diasporas and "break down the long-held assumption about the isomorphism of places, nation, and culture."[5] In today's transnational moment, there is a growing realization that political and cultural identification and territorial location are only loosely coupled.[6]

At the same time, states' assessments of their interests are evolving to account for the fact that the economics and politics of globalization have conferred power on transnational actors such as corporations, nongovernmental organizations (NGOs), and decentralized networks.[7] How much this shift in power relations operates to the benefit or detriment of nation-states depends, in part, on how they adapt, resist, co-opt, or otherwise engage the situation. For states, the territoriality that is a central element in their strength is increasingly revealing its limiting character as well. It is this territoriality that confines them in their borders and tethers them in one and only one place. In an era of globalization, diaspora communities become a valuable (though not unproblematic) national resource. By claiming and co-opting their diasporas, nation-states achieve a certain liberation from the bonds of territoriality.[8] This brings to the political realm something not unlike the invention of mechanical flight, which extended the range of human action into a heretofore-inaccessible dimension. State-diaspora alliances command the prerogatives of both territorialization and deterritorialization, which in combination provide a wider array of options—for polities and for people—than either alone.

Against this backdrop, states and diaspora institutions have increasingly recognized the significance of mass tourism as a means of forging transnational community. They have found willing partners among individual diasporans, who more and more exemplify Zygmunt Bauman's contention that "if the *modern* 'problem of identity' was how to . . . keep it solid and stable, the *postmodern* 'problem of identity' is primarily how to avoid fixation and keep the options open."[9] For diasporans exploring questions of identity in a globalizing world and for nation-states seeking advantage in it, tourism has presented itself as a valuable resource. Both have sought to co-opt, develop, and systematize it, but their efforts are complicated by the fact that tourism entails multiple ways of knowing that are rife with contradiction.

What enables mass tourism to serve as a medium for constructing diasporic identities, and what contradictions in the medium undermine or limit attempts to put it to use? How do its social practices mediate the relationship between collective identities and the personal identities of those who travel? What is the nature of the knowledge that emerges? How does this shape peoples' understandings of themselves in relation to their ethnic and civic communities and to the places they imagine as homelands? To address the questions raised by the deployment of mass tourism as a medium of diasporic political socialization, I focus in this book on the setting in which the practice, as an institutionalized instrument of policy, was pioneered in the 1950s and where it has reached a thoroughly elaborated expression, the State of Israel.

"Israel Experience Programs"

In 2004, the president of the Arab American Institute, James Zogby, addressed a conference in Beirut on the relationship between Lebanon and its diaspora. As reported in the Lebanese *Daily Star*, Zogby expressed concern that an "entire generation or two of Lebanese Americans have grown to maturity having never ventured forth to Lebanon":

> Zogby offered two proposals for improving relations between Lebanese-Americans and the homeland . . . [one of which] was to develop a program to reconnect Lebanese-American youth to their motherland. Using an example rarely heard in this part of the world, Zogby described the Operation Birthright [*sic*] program operated by Jews in the U.S. to help young people develop an attachment to Israel. "We must do the same," he said.[10]

The program to which Zogby was referring is the one whose participants Ariel Sharon addressed in June 2004, and the one I examine in this book. "Taglit-Birthright Israel" is a half-billion-dollar joint initiative of individual philanthropists, the State of Israel, and diaspora Jewish organizations. Launched in December 1999, the program provides free 10-day pilgrimage tours of Israel to college-age diaspora Jews, primarily from North America but with significant representation from Western Europe, the former Soviet Union, South America, and Oceania. Since its inception, it has sent over 200,000 people to Israel, the majority coming from the United States and Canada. Taglit-Birthright Israel does not itself operate tours but functions as an umbrella organization financing, supporting, and licensing the operation of trips by approximately 30 different provider groups, one of the largest of which is Hillel, the organization serving Jewish students on college campuses. Tours are run semiannually in winter and summer sessions. Travelers are preassigned to groups of about 30 to 40 people each, frequently with fellow students from their university or with other people from their city. Each group has its own bus and driver, and each is staffed by an Israeli guide working alongside two or three counselors from the tourists' country of origin. Between 2000 and 2006, participation in Birthright Israel fluctuated between 9,000 and 23,000 annually and then in 2007 and 2008 rose to around 40,000, after a $70 million gift from the Jewish American casino magnate Sheldon Adelson enabled the program to expand its capacity. In the wake of the 2008 global economic collapse, the number of funded trips available in years to come is expected to drop from this peak.

Birthright Israel has been considered a model for using tourism to foster state-diaspora relations. Zogby's reference in Beirut was not an exceptional instance. A year earlier, officials from a nonprofit organization funded by the Hovnanian family, Armenian American real estate developers, met with Birthright Israel to exchange ideas in advance of launching a program that would coordinate the efforts of approximately one dozen organizations running youth trips to Armenia. One week before Zogby's address in Beirut, "Birthright Armenia / Depi Hayk" held its inaugural event in Yerevan—a gathering similar to the Jerusalem Convention Center gala, complete with an address by the foreign minister exhorting the visitors to "Believe in Armenia. Be committed to it. . . . stay involved . . . influence your governments, and become more engaged."[11]

Israel and the Jewish diaspora's mobilization of tourism as a medium of political socialization has gained recognition in recent years, partly because of Birthright Israel's unprecedented scale but also because the collapse of the Israeli-Palestinian diplomatic efforts of the 1990s raised awareness that the tours could be used to win the hearts and minds of a young generation of diaspora Jews just as the conflict was entering a period of renewed violence.[12] (The second intifada broke out in September 2000, some 10 months after Birthright Israel began.) Yet although public awareness of Jewish political tourism is recent, the practice is not. The ability and desire of Jewish communities around the world to invest so heavily in Birthright Israel stemmed in part from the fact that tourism's use as a medium of political socialization is deeply entrenched in the repertoire of modern Jewish practice. For immigrants to Palestine in the early years of the Zionist movement, tourism was a means of striking roots in an old-new homeland (chapter 2 in this volume). In the years after the establishment of the state, it served to introduce diaspora Jews to a country that was more a source of pride and wonder than of ethnic memory, few tracing any immediate ancestry to the place. Since the late 1980s, both the State of Israel and diaspora Jewish organizations have expanded their use of the medium beyond the borders of Israel, bringing Israeli and diaspora Jewish youth alike on "March of the Living" tours to Poland, where Holocaust sites are used to teach the moral imperative of Jewish empowerment.[13] In all instances, educators have taken the lead in crafting the on-the-ground practices that have developed tourism for political and cultural use. The result has been a substantial continuity between classical Zionist practices of nation-building and globalized practices of "diaspora-building,"[14] which are intended to strengthen Jewish cultural life outside of Israel.

Social scientists have taken an interest in diaspora Jewish tours of Israel since the early 1960s, when the first studies of these so-called Israel experience programs were conducted.[15] The bulk of this work (and it is voluminous) consists of market research and evaluations commissioned to document program impact on participants.[16] Only since the 2000s have researchers begun to show interest in deeper questions about the ideological work encoded in the enterprise[17] and about the nature of identity construction effected by the tours.[18] Like the evaluation studies, however, this newer research also tends to conceive of the trips as sui generis rather than as particular cases that partake in and shed light on more general phenomena. If there is any unifying characteristic of the research on Israel experience programs it is that it has largely been conducted without more than passing reference to scholarship on tourism generally[19] and without drawing insights from the studies of homeland tours of other ethnic groups.

Tourism: A Particular Use of Space

Diaspora homeland tours have been referred to as "ethnic pilgrimages."[20] The term has evident appeal. Pilgrimage can be thought of as a "journey undertaken by a person in quest of a place or state that he or she believes to embody a valued ideal."[21] Surely, diaspora trips undertaken out of a desire to explore one's roots should qualify as pilgrimages by this definition. Sponsors of diaspora homeland visits certainly intend them to be seen as such. At times in the pages ahead, I apply the lens of pilgrimage to interpret this form of travel. In general, however, I prefer to privilege the conceptual framework of tourism studies because of its power to reveal dimensions of the phenomenon that would otherwise remain hidden. For example, whereas the pilgrimage frame would foreclose analysis by presuming travelers' motivations and orientations toward their destinations, the lens of tourism lets us treat these as appropriately variable objects of inquiry. The diversity of motivations and orientations among the travelers I have observed convinces me that the humility inherent in the tourism frame is both empirically warranted and analytically fertile. Likewise, I find the lens of pilgrimage ill equipped to address the fact that the commercial tourism industry is the crucial enabler of the enterprise on a mass scale. The modern pilgrim is a tourist of a particular kind, whose approach cannot help but be informed by the ways that

commercial tourism teaches people normative practices of travel and structures their experience of it.[22]

Perhaps the most important advantage I see in the lens of tourism is its
ability to situate diaspora homeland trips in the broader context of the strategic mobilization of travel for purposes of political socialization. The culti-
vation of state-diaspora relations is not the sole political end to which travel
is put. If diaspora homeland visits are intended to foster in-group solidarity
among traveling co-ethnics, tourism is put to precisely the opposite use on
trips that foster intergroup relations by bringing blacks, whites, and others
together to jointly visit sites associated with the American civil rights movement.[23] If diaspora homeland tourism is used to subvert national identities by
fostering a transnational political consciousness, tourism is used to precisely
the opposite effect in American junior high and high school "civic education" tours of Washington, D.C. There is little if anything that limits the political ends to which tourism can be directed. The fact-finding and fundraising
missions of any number of nonprofit organizations attest to its ability to be
placed in the service of a variety of humanitarian, environmental, and other
causes. The framework of tourism enables the analysis of diaspora homeland
travel to speak to the political use of travel more broadly.

What, then, is the content of this framework? As noted earlier, tourism
is not simply travel in the generic sense. It is a particular form of travel. Its
particularities are what make it attractive to those who would put it to use
as a mechanism for fostering diasporic identification with the nation-state.
To distinguish these particularities, the phenomenon must be delimited.
Boundaries need to be drawn distinguishing tourism from what it is not.
Those who have set their minds to the matter have not been of a single opinion about an appropriate object of contrast against which tourism might be
defined. Definitional clutter has been the result. When defined against the
pilgrim's "movement toward the Center," tourism has become understood,
in Erik Cohen's words, as a "movement in the opposite direction, toward
the Other."[24] Defined through a contrast with the "lost art" of travel, tourism has been conceptualized, in Daniel Boorstin's critique, as a "diluted,
contrived, pre-fabricated" consumer experience, meaningless itinerancy par
excellence.[25] Defined in contrast to work, it has been discussed, in Nelson
Graburn's writings, as a "sacred journey" that is "morally on a higher plane
than the regards of the ordinary workaday world."[26]

Rather than add to this list, we might look for a common denominator.
The weakness in each of these descriptions is the attempt to specify or pass
judgment on the nature of the meanings that tourists attribute to their actions.

(Tourists seek the Other, not the Center. Tourists don't seek anything of significance. Tourists seek a break from the daily grind.) If we abandon such presumptiveness and treat the nature and quality of the meanings as something to be attributed by the actors themselves, with all the diversity and open-endedness that this implies, we will find elements of an underlying consensus: tourism, in each of these conceptions, is *a specific genre of travel, in which individuals construct meaning through the consumption of place.* Boorstin lambastes the quality of the meaning that is constructed. Graburn lauds it. Cohen passes no judgment but attempts to specify it. Stripped of these details, however, the substantive definitions reveal a formal one that is broad in scope yet sufficiently focused as to distinguish tourism from other forms of travel.

Tourism, in this conception, is a particular way of using space, a specific mode of experience, a particular set of knowledge practices—more aesthetic than instrumental, explicitly semiotic, and always experienced in an embodied context. People acting as tourists become, to a certain extent, readers of symbols. Their attention to sites and sensations engages them in attributing meaning to that which they see and experience. John Urry, taking a page from Foucault, labeled this entry into a semiotic relationship with surroundings, "the tourist gaze."[27] Although it can be faulted for placing too heavy an emphasis on tourism's visual dimension,[28] the concept remains crucial to any effort to distinguish tourism from other forms of travel. The tourist gaze implies that a site is not merely seen as it is. Instead, it is read as a symbol of something beyond itself. Its connotative meanings overwhelm its denotative ones. In Urry's example, "When tourists see two people kissing in Paris what they capture in the gaze is 'timeless romantic Paris.' When a small village in England is seen, what they gaze upon is the 'real olde England.'"[29] Without the tourist gaze, a kiss is just a kiss, even in Paris.

Anyone who lives in an area that plays host to tourists (and who doesn't nowadays?) will understand the difference between tourist and nontourist uses of space. The meeting of the two is at times a source of friction, often felt more acutely by locals than by visitors, and rooted not so much in a proprietary sense of turf as in an assumption that some uses of space are more legitimate than others. In the years I spent living on Manhattan's Upper West Side, the area of Central Park known as Strawberry Fields served me as a pathway connecting home to office while simultaneously serving legions of tourists as a memorial shrine to John Lennon, who lived and died a block away. Frequently, my use of the space (passage) and their use of the space (standing to photograph the Imagine mosaic and reflect on Lennon's legacy) came into conflict. Sometimes I would wait for them to snap their photos;

other times they would pause to wave me along. Sometimes I grumbled to myself about the crowd blocking my commute; no doubt, they sometimes grumbled to themselves at the New Yorker pushing his way through their group as their guide was speaking. One space, two different ways of using it.

Of course, there were times when I, too, used Strawberry Fields as a tourist (and pilgrim). I joined the crowds singing Beatles songs on the anniversary of John's death and on hearing the news of George's. I took visitors to see the mosaic. Tourism is not only done away from home, industry definitions notwithstanding. Even so, it is usually associated with travel, largely because tourism rests on a "semiotic of difference." Places, for tourists, take on meaning by virtue of the comparisons and contrasts they offer.[30] Whether the Center or the Other, what is experienced on a tour is somehow different from what is familiar in everyday life, and this difference is ultimately what makes the place worth visiting. Hence the pressure on cities and countries to differentiate themselves to capture their share of the tourism market.[31] If it were all the same, why not just stay put?

For diaspora communities, homelands are attractive as tourist destinations because they are not "the same." The differences that distinguish homelands from diasporic spaces are precisely what make travel there desirable. Homelands are imagined to offer consumable meanings that are unavailable, or less available, or differently available, elsewhere. Yet difference alone is not the entire source of the attraction, for homelands are also gazed on not solely as a signifier of the Other but also as a signifier of the Self. They hold out the promise of encountering difference within similarity, as well as similarity in spite of difference. In this dialectic resides homeland tourism's power as a locus for meditation on the meanings of diasporic identities. Yet the recognition of similarity is prevented from becoming a true experience of communion and full identification with the Other-which-is-Self because of the opposition that the tourist gaze establishes between the tourist as an observing subject and the homeland as an observed object. Tourism draws together people separated by geographic boundaries, but at the price of raising between them boundaries that are symbolic and cognitive in nature. It is a contradiction that lies at the heart of the enterprise.

Homeland Tours from Ghana to Taiwan

If scholars of diaspora Jewish tours to Israel have been neglectful of broader theorizations of tourism, they have also demonstrated little interest in the lessons to be learned from the homeland tours of other diaspora communities. In their defense, this is partially due to the fact that a literature on these other tours only began to appear in the mid-1990s, and even then, only at a trickle. The closest thing to a foundational text in this literature is a 1996 article by anthropologist Edward Bruner on African American tourism to the slave castles in Ghana. Drawing on central questions in tourism studies, a field whose agenda he helped to set, Bruner examined struggles over the meaning of the sites, control over them, and the politics of representation and display. The article highlighted a point that emerges directly from homeland tourism's Self/Other dialectic: African Americans who thought they were returning "home" were dismayed to find themselves considered by Ghanaians to be "obruni," a term meaning "whiteman" and "foreigner."[32] This would develop into a central theme in later scholarship on diaspora heritage travel—namely, that tours intended to bind diasporans to homelands and to their co-ethnics who reside there can have the contradictory effect of drawing attention to the differences that separate them.

By the mid-2000s, what little work there was on diaspora homeland tourism was addressing it primarily through the lens of globalization and transnationalism. The two most systematic treatments of the phenomenon to date, an edited volume on the subject and an ethnographic study of Chinese American tourism to China, both framed the core question as one of understanding how the forces of globalization are reshaping identities. Scholars of globalization have been preoccupied with the question of what the unprecedented mobility of people, information, and capital has meant for those social forms that traditionally have been rooted in particular places. Does an emerging transnationalism necessarily imply a weakening of the nation-state? Does it mean that local place becomes less important as the things that were once fixed to it are uprooted and made mobile? How does all this affect the way that people construct their identities? In diaspora tourism to ethnic homelands, researchers have found a way of studying the intersection of mobility, identity, place, and the nation-state. They have argued that transnationalism has not necessarily weakened the role of local place and the state: through tourism, transnationalism also has generated new practices that enable states to exert influence over people who are not their citizens and that enable people to construct new forms of identity that are rooted in multiple places around the world.[33]

The growth of diasporic tourism can be analyzed by focusing on both its producers and its consumers, although a strict separation of supply and demand would be misleading, as each is shaped by the other. A study of native-born American whites found that approximately one in 10 reported visiting an ethnic homeland. Noting that many of these trips occurred in the context of European vacations in which the ancestral stomping grounds were just one stop on a multicountry tour, the study was exceptional in that it did not imply that searching for roots was the sole motivation underlying the trip.[34] More often, demand-side analyses attribute diaspora homeland tourism to the quest for roots. This quest is sometimes said to be a reaction to the instability of identities in the postmodern context, but whatever its source, the roots-seeking phenomenon has become associated with heritage travel and genealogical research tours to ethnic homelands. Interest in the tours both generates and is generated by the development of a commercial infrastructure to support the practice, as well as governmental and NGO-based attempts to encourage it.[35]

This entry of governments and community organizations as promoters of diaspora tourism is of utmost significance, because it is this that transforms a market-based practice of individual consumption into a systematically mobilized agent of political power. In 2005, a *New York Times* reporter visited the slave castles in Ghana where Bruner had conducted his research a decade earlier. The story she was reporting: the country's attempts to capitalize on the flow of African American tourism in order to develop relations with the African diaspora:

GHANA'S UNEASY EMBRACE OF SLAVERY'S DIASPORA
CAPE COAST, Ghana—For centuries, Africans walked through the infamous "door of no return" at Cape Coast castle directly into slave ships, never to set foot in their homelands again. These days, the portal of this massive fort so central to one of history's greatest crimes has a new name, hung on a sign leading back in from the roaring Atlantic Ocean: "The door of return."

Ghana, through whose ports millions of Africans passed on their way to plantations in the United States, Latin America and the Caribbean, wants its descendants to come back.

Taking Israel as its model, Ghana hopes to persuade the descendants of enslaved Africans to think of Africa as their homeland—to visit, invest, send their children to be educated and even retire here.

"We want Africans everywhere, no matter where they live or how they got there, to see Ghana as their gateway home," J. Otanka Obetsebi-Lamptey, the tourism minister, said on a recent day. "We hope we can help bring the African family back together again."[36]

Imaginings of the homeland used to be the preoccupation of poets and philosophers. Now, they have landed in the portfolio of the tourism minister. A variety of motivations leads states and diasporas to take interest in encouraging the flow of tourists. At its core, diasporic homeland tourism is seen as a means of cultivating transnational relationships where such relationships do not strongly exist. This effort proceeds from an understanding of transnationalism that is broader than that which sees it as a set of ongoing cross-border contacts that thoroughly shape the life experience of émigré communities by engaging them in "occupations and activities that require *regular and sustained* social contacts over time across national borders for their implementation."[37]

As Andrea Louie argues in her study of Chinese American tourism to China, the efforts to use tourism to cultivate state-diaspora relations suggest that transnational practices are not limited to the emergent practices of "mobile transmigrants [who] easily negotiate national borders." Rather, they extend to include "highly mediated and indirect relationships between . . . populations that have been separated across generations and seldom interact directly."[38] We could push Louie's point further. She contends that tourism to China "forges" a relationship between the country and the second-, third-, and fourth-generation Chinese Americans who travel there. Even this argument, however, is premised on a migration-based link to a place in which recent ancestors once lived, a link that had been sustained by family practices over several generations.

The case of the Jewish diaspora's relations with the modern State of Israel enables us to further decouple the idea of transnationalism from its ostensible roots in migration. The vast majority of the 7.8 million or so Jews living outside of Israel tend to be either nonmigrants whose ties with the country, if any, are based on its status as a *symbolic* homeland, or migrants from countries other than the Jewish state. To the extent that these diaspora communities engage in a web of practices tying them to the State of Israel, this for the most part begins not with the emergent practices of individuals building on personal relationships in the country. Rather, it more typically begins with the efforts of the state and of diaspora institutions to deliberately cultivate cross-border relationships involving individuals who are not otherwise engaged in them.[39]

Because it mobilizes symbolic ties, tourism enables states and diasporas to forge transnational linkages even in the absence of migration-based social networks. This linkage opens an array of potential economic, political, and cultural benefits to countries and communities that otherwise might not have access to them. For Ghana, ties with the African diaspora hold out the prospect of tapping a global reservoir of intellectual and financial capital. Economic considerations also figure prominently in the Chinese government's development since the 1980s of a variety of heritage tours for foreign-born Chinese teenagers and young adults. The focus on youth is considered an investment in future business leaders and is based on the assumption that education and exposure to the homeland can activate latent feelings of connection to China.[40]

In contrast to mainland China, Taiwan's use of tourism to cultivate ties with the Chinese diaspora has been motivated more by political concerns than by a desire to benefit from economic globalization. In the mid-1960s, the government of Taiwan established the Chien-Tan Overseas Chinese Youth Language Training and Study Tour, which brings approximately 1,000 Chinese American 18-to-23-year-olds to the island each summer for six weeks of tours, Mandarin classes, and cultural programming.[41] Advertised as a program to "assist overseas Chinese youth to increase their ability to use the Chinese language, to understand Chinese culture and history, and to see at first hand the achievements of the Republic of China," the program is intended to create goodwill ambassadors for a country whose independence is not formally recognized by most of the world's governments.[42]

In Central and Eastern Europe, diaspora tourism has been intimately bound up with the nation-building efforts of new, postcommunist states. During the Soviet era, the ability of Lithuanian expatriates and their descendants to visit their "unwilling republic" was severely restricted, no doubt because diaspora Lithuanian nationalism and its fierce anti-Soviet sentiment was perceived as threatening to the regime. When independence gave Lithuania control over its visa policy, these restrictions were eliminated and diaspora Lithuanians began arriving as tourists, volunteers, entrepreneurs, and teachers.[43] In Croatia, diaspora tourism has been associated not only with the postindependence period but also with the battle for independence itself. Elements of "volunteer tourism" and "adventure tourism" could be seen in the travels of those diasporans who went to Croatia during its war for independence in the early 1990s to fight on the front lines or to support the war effort in other ways. After the fighting ended, the largest Croatian diaspora organization identified tourism as one of three ways (along with public relations and investment) that the diaspora could contribute to strengthening the newly independent country. For its part, the Croatian government has taken steps to this same end through a government-linked NGO that sponsors volunteer programs for visiting diasporans and educational summer schools similar to those run by China and Taiwan.[44]

Enthusiasm about diaspora tourism as a source of political and economic gain is not universal. One study attributes India's failure to significantly mobilize tourism to a deeply ambivalent relationship between state and diaspora and to the devolution of control over tourism policy to the regional governments. The religious and ethnic heterogeneity of its population, the anticolonialist distrust of foreign involvement, and a concern that nationals of Pakistan and Bangladesh would claim political rights in India have led the government to avoid a policy of engagement with its diaspora. Neither the national government nor the regional governments (which hold much of the actual responsibility for tourism management) have made significant efforts to foster diaspora tourism. One Indian state initiated a "Discover Your Roots" program, but it appears to have met with little success, in part because diaspora visitors generally have family connections and do not need governmental mediation of their encounter with the country.[45]

The lack of response from the Indian diaspora indicates that the mobilization of diaspora tourism depends on collaboration between both sides of the state-diaspora equation. Whereas states look to diaspora tourism largely for the economic and political benefits it offers, diaspora communities— although they often share a desire to advance the nationalist cause—are also motivated by consideration of the benefits that would accrue to them in the countries where they reside. These benefits are in large measure cultural. In the United States, across ethnic groups, diasporic discourse regarding the value of homeland tourism has centered (with varying degrees of alarmism) on the challenges that cultural illiteracy poses to ethnic continuity in the United States.[46] Viewing tourism as a partial "solution," organizations from a variety of diaspora communities—Chinese American, Irish American, Italian American, Jewish American, and more—have begun sponsoring programs to institutionalize the practice and exert a degree of communal control over it. Sometimes, after initiating tourism projects, they press homeland governments to assume a cosponsoring role.[47] The community organizations behind these travel programs consider them to be mechanisms of ethnic socialization—a means of providing cultural, psychological, and social resources to foster group continuity in diaspora.

The effectiveness of such programs is presumed to rest in both the symbolic and the social dimensions of tourism. In terms of the symbolic dimensions, tourism's value is perceived to rest in its semiotic of difference. Homelands are supposed to offer a contrast to diaspora life. They are imagined to offer a cultural breadth and depth—and perhaps authenticity, although this is contested—that is deemed to be unavailable elsewhere. They are valued for concentrating in a defined space a multiplicity of ethnic signifiers with pedagogical value that is both cognitive and affective. Against the backdrop of these signifiers, opportunities for social relations with co-ethnics and engagement in ethnic behaviors abound. That such opportunities may also exist in diaspora is beside the point. It is assumed that in the homeland they are more frequent, of better quality, less stigmatized, and hence more likely to engage the uninitiated. As a medium of socialization, the tours are valued not merely for fostering loyalties to the homeland and to the transnational community but for expanding the "cultural toolkits" that diaspora ethnics have at their disposal.[48] This mobilization of tourism envisages homelands as living museum, training camp, and playground all rolled into one—a place to send the uncultured to learn how to think, act, and feel. The intended result is "individual ethnic re-identification" among returnees who "carry back . . . the cultural material and personal knowledge" to help sustain and revitalize ethnic communities outside of the homeland.[49]

Studies of diaspora tourism programs have found that their effects on identity are more complex than their mission statements suggest. Reiterating the theme introduced by Bruner, researchers have found that feelings of primordial attachment (which can motivate homeland trips) often give way to an ambivalent sense of outsiderness. In Tim Coles and Dallen Timothy's words, "Tourism does not just represent a vehicle for straightforward, practically automatic voyages of self-discovery and identity affirmation. Visits to homelands . . . may result in troubling, disconcerting and ambiguous experiences as well as newfound ambivalences."[50] Both Louie's ethnographic research on Chinese American tours to China and Nazli Kibria's interviews with alumni of Taiwan's Chien Tan and a similar South Korean program found that linguistic and cultural differences made travelers increasingly aware of just how culturally American they were.[51]

A study of diaspora travel to Lithuania offers an important qualification to the conclusion that homeland tours tend to produce an ambivalent combination of identification and disidentification. There, feelings of distance were less likely to emerge among first-time visitors on brief tours because the tourists could remain relatively insulated from experiences that would challenge their idealized images of the place. Visitors on longer trips and on return visits were more likely to experience such feelings of ambivalence. Even in these instances, however, the outcome was not straightforward. Lithuania existed for these tourists both as a real place and as an imagined ideal. The collision of the two eventually revealed the contradictions between myth and reality. Those who had rooted their ethnic self-understandings in the idealized vision of the place were forced to reevaluate. This could lead to disillusionment and distancing, but it could equally lead to a revised identification with the homeland based on a less mythic, more nuanced understanding of the relationship between the self and its multiple places and communities of attachment.[52] Diaspora tours may serve to foster a form of transnational identification that affirms diversity, with Lithuanian Americans, for example, returning to feel both closer to and more distant from Lithuania, the United States, and the Lithuanian American community, each in its own way.

The tendency to produce complex effects on identities suggests limits to the ability to use tourism as an agent of ideology—that is, as a means of inscribing official discourses of identity on the self-understandings of tourists. Louie has argued the point most forcefully. Pointing to informal interactions that bind the tourists more to each other than to their hosts, "failed rituals" that assert similarity but convey an experience of difference, and the retention of the American ethnic experience as a continual point of reference, she contends that the tours' own dynamics prevent an easy adoption of a state discourse of unhyphenated ethno-racial identities expressed through patriotic support of the homeland. Instead, "Chinese-Americans create meanings out of their experiences in China that differ from those that the Chinese government intends to create and also departs from previous generations' understandings." The result is a new form of hyphenated diasporic identity, one that draws on cultural resources accessed through tourism but that is fundamentally a novel construction.[53]

The interplay of familiarity and strangeness, of feeling simultaneously "at home" and alien, is integral to the experience of diasporic homeland tourism. This complicates efforts to mobilize it for ideological purposes. More significant than the fact that scholars recognize these contradictions is the fact that states and community organizations recognize them as well and incorporate this recognition into the ongoing revision of their practices. What has become the conclusion of past scholarship on diaspora tourism is merely the starting point for those mobilizing it. For the social engineers who would use homeland tourism to forge transnational relationships, the aspects of tourism that establish social and symbolic boundaries between observer and observed are among the key dilemmas to be confronted. Much of the actual "work" of the tours is intended to overcome this. As a medium for constructing and deconstructing symbolic boundaries, tourism integrates an array of "knowledge practices"—semiotic, narrative, dialogic, ludic, embodied, aesthetic, emotional, and more.[54] These work in concert and exist in tension. Although they serve organizers as "tools of the trade" through which diasporic identities and connections to place and community are forged, they are a fickle set of tools.

Organization of the Book

In this book, I provide a study of the political mobilization of culture. At the broadest level, I ask how political actors deploy a meaning-making cultural practice in an attempt to inscribe collective identities on personal identities. Jews have been a diaspora people for millennia, but the ways in which this diaspora has been imagined and enacted has not remained constant. With the rise of the Zionist movement and the establishment of a Jewish state, Jewish understandings of their diaspora shifted in the 20th century from a decentralized (or symbolically centralized) model to a materially state-centered one. This shift was facilitated by the insertion of modern mass tourism into the repertoire of Jewish diasporic practice. This was less a spontaneous movement than the result of systematic effort. Agents of the state and of Jewish communities around the world developed tourism into a means of fostering a Jewish transnational identity in which feelings of connection to a nation-state-qua-homeland were an integral element.

In this Jews have not been unique. States and their diasporas have increasingly realized their confluence of interest in using tourism to develop and deepen their ties to one another. As a means of coming to know a place, and of entering into a symbolic relationship with it, tourism offers unparalleled opportunities to those who would use it to engage diasporans with national homelands. The deployment of tourism as a medium of diasporic political socialization, however, is fraught with contradiction and is replete with ethical dilemmas. It is also an increasingly important part of a globalizing world.

I explore the phenomenon of diaspora homeland tourism in the chapters ahead by asking how political actors mobilize tourism—a set of cultural practices centered on particular ways of using space—to shape diasporic identities. How do tourism's varied ways of creating knowledge—through semiotics, narrative, dialogue, play, embodiment, and emotion—interact to shape the ways that tourists understand the places they see, understand themselves, and understand the relationship of one to the other? How do their interactions simultaneously produce and undermine the conceptual and symbolic boundaries involved in the construction of diasporic identities? How do contradictions inherent in the medium of tourism complicate efforts to mobilize it? How do tour organizers and guides attempt to control these contradictions, and to what effect? How do they resolve to their own satisfaction the ethical questions that attend these efforts?

To answer these questions, I examine the case of Taglit-Birthright Israel. An intimate portrait of three groups is offered and analyzed to encapsulate nearly a decade of research that I undertook from winter 1999–2000, when the first trips departed, through summer 2008. At times, I supplement my own observations with ethnographic and survey data drawn from a program evaluation conducted by the Cohen Center for Modern Jewish Studies at Brandeis University, of which I was a part from 1999 through 2004. The first chapters set out the case. In chapter 2, I examine the historical evolution of Zionism's mobilization of tourism, the first American Jewish forays into this field, and the developments in American Jewish communal institutions in the 1990s that moved the issue of tourism to the center of the diaspora-state agenda. The creation of Birthright Israel and its implications for our understanding of this particular moment in American Jewish history are explored.

In chapter 3, I delve into political and ethical issues involved in representing contested histories and territories, as visitors tour a land embroiled in conflict. Through ethnographic portraits of visits to the West Bank separation barrier and to the Golan Heights, I examine the contradictions inherent in efforts to represent the different voices of Israel's conflicts with the Palestinians, Syrians, and Lebanese. I draw out the implications of the finding that efforts to represent oppositional points of view are limited largely to the realm of the discursive, whereas Israeli perspectives are extended into the realm of the nondiscursive. This case is used to set forth principles for the analysis of tourism as a set of contextually rooted and interacting knowledge practices by which people come to know self, space, and community.

In the next chapters, I investigate the practices themselves. I separate them out for analysis, but this reflects the necessities of writing and reading, not the actual character of tourism. In reality, these practices all operate simultaneously, in dynamic relation with one another. I begin with the central feature of tourism—the traveler's use of space. In chapter 4, I focus on the ways that places are used semiotically to signify meanings. I examine the tour guides' role in narrating sites and directing the tourist gaze, but I also look beyond the guide to consider how tourists themselves act as consumers of emplaced meanings. In chapter 5, I examine a key dilemma posed by these tourist uses of space: the alienation of tourists from the objects of their gaze. Taking as the starting point the oft-found paradox that homeland tours intended to create feelings of connection also produce feelings of estrangement, I examine the strategies that trip organizers use to undermine the symbolic boundaries that tourism interposes between an observing self (the tourist) and an observed other (the homeland). These strategies, which include site-specific rituals, consciousness-raising groups, and peer-to-peer encounters between tourists and locals, help to partially overcome the feelings of distance and alienation that the act of tourism itself generates.

In the next two chapters, I bring to the fore the intensely social and personal dimensions of tourism and examine trip sponsors' efforts to intervene in them. In chapter 6, I look at the individual traveler as a member of the tour group. I outline the ways that tour sponsors mobilize the small-group dynamics of the community of tourists both as a socializing *agent* that mediates the encounter with place and establishes norms around its interpretation and as a socializing *experience* of ethnic community in its own right. My consideration of tourist practices culminates in chapter 7, where I suggest that homeland tourism is not simply a way of coming to know state and society but a way of coming to know the self. Focusing on efforts to turn the tourist gaze inward so that tourists can apply to themselves the same interpretive frames they are using to make sense of the country, I analyze the nature and quality of the self-understandings that emerge.

In the conclusion, chapter 8, I reflect on tourism's particular characteristics as a medium and how these characteristics advance diasporic political socialization not in a generic sense but in particular ways that bear on crucial questions of nationalism, transnationalism, and the politics of state-diaspora relations. Through this, I direct specific attention to both the "diasporic" and the "political" in diasporic political socialization. Critiquing theorizations of diaspora in the literatures on transnationalism, cultural studies, and Judaic studies, I advance an alternative perspective that conceives of diaspora as an imagined political community in the Andersonian sense[55] and argue for open-ended inquiry into the myriad ways that diasporas are socially constructed through the different practices (including tourism) that are used to imagine them.

Striking Roots

"I want a hike to the death!"

Andrew's comment pierced the mountain air. It was not intended for me, but I turned back to offer a knowing glance. Our walk up the wooded trail to Mount Meron's peak was little more than a leisurely stroll. Hardly the climb we were led to expect when the tour guide, Ravit, told us she was canceling our visit to the industrial park to take us hiking up a mountain instead. It was the dawn of the 21st century, but she decided to have us encounter Israel's northern Galilee region 1940s style, by romancing the land, not by marveling at its dot-com-era entrepreneurship.

The dirt path up Meron was narrow enough that most of the group made their way forward in single file. We were 34 people—29 students from a private East Coast university, four staff members, and myself. Behind me, Andrew Meyer[1] walked alongside a fellow student, Nell Locurto, their conversation peppered with laughter. Andrew often made Nell laugh, frequently with dark humor.

"She's taking us to a mass grave," he ventured.

Did he know about the tomb of the second-century rabbi, Shimon bar Yochai, which tradition locates on Meron? Perhaps he was thinking back to our hike up Masada, where, hugging Nell and another woman close, he exclaimed on reaching the summit, "This is great! I'm on top of a mountain [where there was] a mass suicide, with my good friends." Or maybe it was just that Andrew's talk often tended toward the morbid, whether he was joking or describing his work as an intern at a Holocaust museum.

Although voiced as a joke, Andrew's call for a more strenuous climb was more perceptive than I suspect he knew. Our walk up Meron, intended to foster diaspora Jewish tourists' emotional attachments to Israel's landscape, was rooted in the classic Zionist practice of *tiyul*—hiking as a ritualized sanctification of space. In the first decades of the 20th century, the Zionist movement began using *tiyulim* (plural) to root immigrant settlers in the place they were claiming as their homeland. A fair number of these hikes were grueling trials, taking young pioneers to the point of exhaustion and dehydration. Among members of the pre-state youth movements and underground militias, such treks were common tests of Zionist character, opportunities to demonstrate commitment to the homeland and willingness to sacrifice for it.[2]

We did not know that our tiyul would be as leisurely as it turned out to be. We did know, however, that we would not be climbing to Meron's peak. The change in schedule had left us little time for the hike, and we needed to be back on the bus before dark. Eventually we reached a point midway up the hill where the narrow trail widened into a clearing looking eastward. People spread out to fill the space, the din of conversation growing louder. The sun had dipped behind the mountain, leaving us shaded and chilled in the Galilean winter breeze. I walked away from Ravit and the overlook, seating myself next to my new friend, Sam Pollack, on a low stone wall built into the hillside.

Ravit was positioned near the eastern edge of the clearing, standing where we would see the valley stretched out behind her. A few women had gathered around the young guide, but most of us remained absorbed in private conversations. I, too, paid Ravit little attention, more concerned with discovering what had erased Sam's perpetual smile. Sam, oblivious to Ravit and Mount Meron, was quietly pointing out Mark Gottlieb, who he said had been "stealing" his jokes.

In an Israeli accent even more leathery than her skin which was weathered beyond its years, Ravit called out, "You guys wanna come over?!"

Heads lifted. Someone sitting on the stone wall called back, "Is that a question or a command?" No one moved. Ravit, however, had captured our attention for that crucial millisecond. She seized the moment.

"Before I tell you about the view, look at *me*."

This was intriguing. As a group, there was nothing we found so interesting as ourselves, and Ravit's tone suggested an approaching confession. If the landscape alone could not command our attention, a personal story about *our* tour guide could. Some in the back stood up and approached Ravit. One wrapped his arm around her shoulder. "This landscape," she said, waving her free arm to indicate the valley below, "is my internal landscape."

For a few moments, we stared down on a green and brown panorama of farms, pastures, and scattered areas of denser human settlement. The kabbalists' city of Safed was discernible in the distance, as was the snowy peak of Mount Hermon on the Golan Heights.

From point to point, Ravit directed our gaze until we were looking at a small patch of land, unremarkable except for the fact that Ravit told us that she had purchased the plot and would be building her home there. Hers was a performance of roots and love of homeland, a model of nativeness for the visiting American Jews. In Ravit's presentation, topography and geography would not stand alone as dry facts. They could not if the external landscape was to become an internal one for the visitors, too. Declaring it to be a part of her, and herself to be a part of it—the place where she would plant herself, not by buying a house but by building a home—the Israeli tour guide wrapped the scene in a mantle of ideology and romance, imbuing a neutral patchwork of farms, hills, and towns with emotional resonance.

Ravit's presentation had shaken Sam out of his self-absorbed fretting. Still, he remained pensive. Turning to me, he said quietly, "In America, you have beautiful things and places and you appreciate it, but I don't feel like it's *mine*." He reached out to grasp the slender trunk of a nearby tree. "Here, this is mine. This is *my* tree."

A spontaneous gesture modeled after Ravit's, and enacting in miniature the very essence of tiyul as a ritualized affirmation of connection to place. Was Sam saying that he had a claim on the land, or that the land had a claim on him? Both, I suspect. Had the sponsors of the trip been there to witness it, they would have brimmed with satisfaction. You or I might ask how a country that Sam had experienced only as a tourist could feel more "his" than the place where he had lived all his 20 years. Or perhaps better, what was it about the particular way he was experiencing this place at this moment that elicited an assertion so pregnant with meaning?

These are outsiders' questions, though. They would have been lost on the program's organizers. The people who had made it possible for Sam to visit Meron and declare it his had created the trip, with its telling name "Birthright," out of their conviction that every Jew was entitled to claim an inheritance of history, culture, religion, community, land, and country. Encouraging the travelers to stake this claim—through the synecdochic act of asserting emotional attachments to Israel's land, state, and society and by maintaining these attachments even from the countries of the diaspora—was the program's express mission. Tourism was the medium by which it accomplished this.

Such a use of tourism to build connections between self, place, and community was not new, certainly not in the Israeli context. In reaching out to take hold of "his" tree, whose roots were planted in the side of Mount Meron in the Upper Galilee, Sam was doing more than echoing the claim modeled by Ravit. They both were enacting a script that had been set down in the 1920s, when Jewish educators in Palestine began systematically using ritualized travel as a medium of socialization. The only difference was that what the Zionist movement had developed for the purpose of state-building, Jewish organizations from North America and Europe had transformed to serve the very different purpose of Jewish diaspora-building.

Revolutionary Practice

In 1945, three years before Israel declared independence, a pioneer of Zionist ritual hiking named Zev Vilnay published a manifesto-cum-guide-training-manual titled, "The Tiyul and Its Educational Value." The modern practice of tiyul, Vilnay wrote, had deep historical roots stretching back to the biblical-era pilgrimage festivals and the travels of medieval rabbis and kabbalists. Vilnay's portrayal was hardly exceptional. Within the Zionist movement, touring and hiking have been imagined as a recovery of ancient Israelite practices and as the latest iteration of a Jewish pilgrimage tradition that has persisted over centuries.[3] Such an approach, however, reveals more about historiography than history. Invoking the past as precedent serves an important legitimizing function that imbues tiyul with the commanding aura of tradition.[4] It certainly informs the way that its practitioners interpret their actions to themselves. As analysis, however, it falls short, for in its key aspects the practice of tiyul is remarkable precisely for its discontinuities with the Jewish past.

Tiyul did not evolve out of the legacies of Jewish tradition. It was forged in the crucible of a diaspora nationalist movement trying to effect a social revolution by transforming a population of migrants into a nation rooted in a homeland. Modern Zionism, the movement for Jewish national liberation and self-determination in the land of Israel, had emerged in Europe toward the end of the 19th century. Bourgeois immigrants established Tel Aviv in 1909. Their socialist counterparts built the first collective farm, Kibbutz Degania, near the Sea of Galilee one year later. By the time the League of Nations in 1923 awarded the Mandate for Palestine to Great Britain, which had conquered the region in World War I, the Jewish population numbered some 87,000 souls, mostly immigrants from Europe and their children. The Arab population was eight times as large, and they, too, were asserting nationalist claims of their own to the former Ottoman territory.[5] In spite of its small size, the Palestinian Jewish community, known as the *Yishuv*, was large enough to sustain an independent institutional base that served it in a quasi-governmental capacity.

In the early 1920s, the Yishuv's educational establishment began to systematically develop hiking tours as a medium of nationalist pedagogy. "There can be no loving the land of Israel without knowing the land of Israel," a youth movement journal wrote, "And there can be no knowing the land of Israel without unmediated contact with it."[6] Schools, youth movements, and labor unions all treated the tiyul as a way of teaching new immigrants and their children about a place that was supposed to be a homeland but that was actually new and unfamiliar to them. Hiking tours were intended not merely to convey information but to generate affect, instill commitment, and accomplish the paradoxical mission of constructing an organic connection. "The tiyul's purposes," Vilnay explained, "are to mold the character of our youth and to make it an organic, inseparable part of the landscape of the homeland; to plant in its heart and soul, and to inscribe in its flesh and sinews the healthy feeling of deep-rooted, unseverable, valiant communion with the land, its stones, its waterways, its vegetation, and its entire history."[7]

Such a conception of tiyul was hardly cut from traditional cloth. As a form of Jewish education, the move outdoors to experience the environment broke sharply with the text-centered practices of traditional Jewish pedagogy.[8] Tiyul looked not to the yeshiva but to progressive educational theory, European youth movement culture, and the creativity of local educators as they improvised responses to novel circumstances. Even more decisive a break, however, was the "mystification of the Israeli landscape" that inspired the practice of tiyul and served as its ultimate justification.[9] Rabbinic Judaism of the diaspora harbored deep reservations about nativist claims of organic ties binding people and land, as well as about pagan-inflected notions of holiness inhering in physical places.[10] No such qualms characterized the Zionist movement. Quite the contrary. What had formerly been looked on with suspicion became a central principle inspiring the efforts to secure a Jewish national homeland.

In spite of Zionism's assertion that Jewish connections to the land of Israel were inherent and Jewish claims inalienable, in practice, the movement struggled against internal and external factors that challenged both of these points and threatened to cut Jews off physically, psychologically, and politically from the land they were trying to claim. The attempt to overcome these challenges was a major part of the nation-building effort in the pre-state period. Hiking tours served this mission by helping Jews strike roots in the land of Israel, stake their claim to it, and sustain their commitment to the movement's goals when it was not clear if and when they would be realized.

For the Yishuv's educators, the use of tourism to strike roots, stake a claim and sustain commitment was premised on the idea that *yedi'at ha'aretz,* "knowing the land of Israel," would breed *ahavat ha'aretz,* "love for the land of Israel."[11] This, in turn, would inspire loyalty to the nation-building effort.

Guides were trained to master details of local geology, history, botany, and more. This information they duly passed to their charges during hikes. The educational process, however, was never simply one of instruction inspiring emotion because the dichotomy between cognition and affect, knowledge and feeling, in truth never pertained. Tiyul was not so much an act of teaching information about the land of Israel (for which a textbook would have sufficed) as it was an act of sacralizing the homeland—affirming its importance through the ritual of "knowing" it.[12]

To "know," in the biblical sense, connotes an act of not only possessing and commanding but also communing, submitting, and giving up a portion of oneself in an act of union with another. Knowing the land of Israel was indeed a way of asserting control over the land. Knowing domesticated it, claiming the untamed from nature. Insofar as knowing also involved naming (for how can one know something without knowing what it is called?), the use of the Hebrew language to name the land and its features also claimed the territory for the Zionist movement from the Palestinian Arabs and from those before them—Romans, Mamluks, Ottomans, and others—whose own use of the power of naming had wittingly or unwittingly erased Jewish claims.[13] Beyond the power to control, however, knowing the land was an act of devotion to it and, by extension, of submission to the nation-building effort. Knowing proceeded not only from absorption of the facts mouthed by guides but also from the firsthand encounter with place. The more grueling the hike, the more a young Zionist strained and sweated to know the land, the more he or she performed a ritualized self-sacrifice that prefigured the ultimate one that the nationalist cause might demand.[14]

Institutionalizing Tiyul

In spite of its ritualistic dimensions, tiyul was framed by its proponents not as civil religion but as education.[15] This educational frame can be traced to tiyul's origins in 19th-century field trips in which Yishuv schools took students to explore the local environment around their settlements. By the 1910s, there were instances of longer excursions, such as the Gymnasia Hertzliya's 1912 trek to Masada.[16] This pedagogical tourism was a creation of the Jewish community of Palestine, emerging alongside rather than from within the growing commercial tourism industry that catered to Christian pilgrims from the West. After Israel gained independence and developed its domestic commercial tourism industry, the two would interpenetrate and blur. In the first part of the 20th century, however, European-based firms like the Thomas Cook Company and

Baedeker were ill equipped to serve the needs of the local Jewish population, largely secular-nationalist, residing in areas away from the circuit of Christian pilgrimage sites and interested in tourism for explicitly nationalist purposes.[17]

The decades under British rule between the 1920s and the 1940s were the key period that established tiyul both as a central medium of nationalist education and as a potent symbol of secular Zionist culture. In addition to entering the school curriculum, which increasingly emphasized "homeland education" and which made an annual field trip a highlight of the academic calendar,[18] the culture of tiyul found its institutional base in the labor unions, the newly established youth movements, and the paramilitary groups, especially the Labor-Zionist-dominated Haganah and Palmach.

The prominent role played by the labor unions might seem surprising until we recall the global context. Around the world, revolutionary socialism was engaging in a grand project of social engineering that treated political and cultural change as two sides of the same coin. The key institutions charged with responsibility for effecting these changes were the party and the union. In Jewish Palestine of the 1920s, Labor Zionism strove to effect a utopian revolution along both socialist and nationalist lines. The goal was not merely to create a Jewish state but to populate it with a "New Hebrew Man"—a free Jewish laborer ontologically at home in the new society. Like socialist movements in other countries, when the Labor Zionists established their General Federation of Labor, or Histadrut, in December 1920, they created a department to oversee the revolution's cultural dimensions. The Histadrut's Culture Committee undertook a variety of adult education programs, including what would soon become known as *yediʿat haʾaretz*. A handful of young "comrades," all men, were appointed as instructors and scattered across the country to lecture, present magic lantern shows, and lead tiyulim for workers in the agricultural settlements and road-paving crews. By the end of 1923, the tiyul was becoming the Culture Committee's preferred method for teaching *yediʿat haʾaretz*.[19] In these early years, teacher turnover was high, although a few, including Vilnay and Joseph Braslavi, made a career of it—the first of many to do so. They played important roles in institutionalizing the field, articulating its philosophy, exemplifying its practice, and training the next generations of educator-guides, including those who worked with the youth movements.[20]

For all of the ideological differences that divided the various Zionist youth movements, they all gave tiyul prominence of place in their repertoire of activities. This derived in part from their European genealogies. The Yishuv's major youth movements established themselves in Palestine between 1919 and 1933. Most had been founded in Europe and were transplanted as their members immigrated. Even those created in the Yishuv, such as Tzofim ("Scouts"), looked to European models. In raising the banner of tiyul, groups like Tzofim and Hano'ar Ha'oved ("The Working Youth") drew from two contradictory European youth movement traditions emphasizing nature and the outdoors. One was Lord Baden-Powell's Scouting movement, based in the United Kingdom. The other was Germany's Wandervogel. The Yishuv's youth movements, however, did not merely replicate European forms but developed their own distinctive practice, shaped by the imperatives of nation-building and by the particular conditions of Mandatory Palestine where, for example, to hike was to resist British colonial control over space. Tiyul reconciled contradictions between the Baden-Powell and the Wandervogel approaches to hiking. Although both venerated direct contact with nature, Scouting treated hiking as a means for building citizens of good character, whereas Wandervogel, in its romanticism, valorized hiking's potential to liberate the individual from social convention.[21] In developing tiyul as a practice of nationalist revolution, the youth movements reconciled the contradiction between socializing commitment to societal ideals and creating a space for youthful rebellion.

Zionism was a multigenerational struggle that united parents and children in opposition to the hegemony of traditional diasporic Jewish culture. Through the youth movements, the Palestinian-born children of the Jewish immigrants were socialized into the revolution and encouraged to reject the norms of the grandparents rather than of the parents. To the extent that the youth movements also fostered rebellion against parental norms, they channeled this in the direction of greater revolutionary fervor.[22] Tiyul quickly became implicated in intergenerational politics. Whereas immigrant parents had used tiyul as a means of striking roots in an unfamiliar place, their native-born children used it as a means of demonstrating the very nativeness that their parents could strive for but never achieve.[23]

Tiyul was embraced by the youth movements as a means of creating a nationalist subject. Activists were explicitly conscious of this, and they articulated this understanding in writings extolling tiyul and elaborating its contributions to the achievement of ideological goals. In contrast to a present-day tendency in the West to frame hikes and tours as a form of leisure, the Zionist youth movements since their earliest days conceived of peripatetic practice as "an educational, learning and social tool," "a major educational instrumentality," and even as "a tool for training the member toward a life of religious-pioneering self-actualization."[24]

Of the factors that established tiyul's importance in youth movement culture, one of the most important was the emergence of the hike to the desert mountain fortress of Masada, where, according to the ancient historian Josephus, nearly 1,000 Jewish rebels held out against a Roman siege and eventually killed themselves rather than be taken prisoner. Decades before the Herodian fortress in the Judean Desert would be excavated and developed for tourism, Masada had become a point of Zionist pilgrimage. The trek there was valued for its challenge, requiring several days of passage on foot through dangerous and unfamiliar desert terrain, deep in Bedouin territory and far from the areas of Jewish settlement. No simple route to the top existed. Throughout the 1920s and 1930s, tiyulim to Masada were sporadic affairs, suspended in 1927 after a hiker fell to her death, and again in 1929 as the simmering conflict between Arabs and Jews flared into violence.[25]

It was only in the 1940s that the youth movements began to embrace the Masada tiyul in earnest. This largely stemmed from the initiative of Shmaria Guttman, a student of Braslavi and a prominent trainer of educator-guides in his own right. Guttman worked intensively with youth movement leaders who were well positioned to shape movement practice and culture. In October 1941, he led 10 hikers from Hano'ar Ha'oved to Masada. Convinced of the power of the site for nationalist education, he then organized a week-long seminar three months later for 46 youth movement counselors from Hano'ar Ha'oved and two other socialist groups. Seminar participants, among them a young Shimon Peres, engaged in both the practical and the ideological work that helped make Masada a central point of Zionist youth pilgrimage throughout the 1940s, improving the trail to the summit, discussing Masada as a model of Jewish heroism and resistance, and considering the story's implications for themselves in the face of Rommel's advancing Afrika Corps.[26] The use of the site as a venue for drawing lessons about the present out of the memories of the past came to feature prominently in tiyul's nation-building work, a model that was extended almost everywhere that tiyulim went.

The vanguard who participated in Guttman's Masada trips took these understandings back to the youth movements that they led and also to the Palmach, established in 1941 as the elite "strike force" of the Haganah paramilitary organization. Through 1947, the trek to Masada was compulsory for all Palmach recruits.[27] These hikes were hardly the only instance of tiyul in the Palmach. In his study of the culture of the *sabra*—the native sons and daughters of the Yishuv—Oz Almog explored the ways that the Palmach developed hiking into a core component of its training, using it to develop a committed, cohesive, and effective fighting force. Known as "marches" (*masa'ot*) rather than "hikes" (tiyulim), these excursions were often grueling experiences that combined *yedi'at ha'aretz* with live fire exercises, simulation of combat conditions, and an explicit focus on teamwork. Beyond the training objectives, the act of sending the clandestinely armed units to hike in remote areas also served the strategic and tactical purposes of intelligence gathering, claim-staking, and deterrence. So important were these hikes and marches in the Palmach's activities that they became one of the important symbols of Palmach culture and a key status symbol in the fledgling Jewish state.[28]

Institutionally grounded in the schools, youth movements, paramilitaries, and labor unions, tiyul became established in the pre-state period as a principle of both formal and informal education for children, adolescents, and adults alike. The links across institutions—for example, the Histadrut educator-guides training youth movement counselors who would go on to become Palmach commanders—fostered a continuity in the culture of hiking that made it a unifying experience for many sectors of the Yishuv and especially for the Labor Zionists who dominated it.[29] During Israel's struggle for independence, tiyul brought together self, community, and space in a ritual of Zionist affirmation that enacted the nationalist idea in an embodied practice. It expressed *ahavat ha'aretz* through performances of *yedi'at ha'aretz* and of perseverance in the face of physical challenge. As a group activity, it fostered interdependence and mutual aid, socializing commitment not only to the land but also to the nation and the national movement. Its ritual dimensions were emphasized and elaborated. Biblical passages were read at the sites to which they referred. Nationalist slogans were inscribed against the night sky in letters of flame. Hikes were concluded with ceremonial presentations. In the pre-state era, tiyul served as a ritual of sanctification, a performance of nationalist identity, and a medium of political socialization, all at the same time.

In the decades since, tiyul has persisted as an important but contested element in Israeli culture. The state has absorbed many functions related to it, mandating tiyulim in schools and in the army, licensing guides, and monitoring for safety and security. Nonpartisan NGOs such as the Society for the Protection of Nature in Israel and the Avshalom Institute for Yedi'at Ha'aretz help sustain the infrastructure and culture of tiyul by training guides, maintaining field schools, and organizing excursions.[30] Commercial interests have also reshaped the practice, working with the public and nonprofit sectors to develop Israel's nature and heritage sites. The routinization and commercialization of tiyul have drained it of some of its ideological salience. Co-opted by the state and marketed by the tourism industry, today's tiyulim to places that have been secured under Israeli control—mapped, trailblazed, and developed for the tourist trade—may evoke memories of the pre-state practice, but they are altogether a different enterprise.[31]

This does not mean that the practice has been ideologically neutered. Anthropologist Tamar Katriel has shown how tiyul has become implicated in two of Israel's key societal conflicts—one over multiculturalism, and the other over the future of the West Bank and Gaza Strip. So much had the practice become identified with the Palmach and the youth movements that, even by the 1950s, it had evolved from a ritualized celebration of the land of Israel into a ritualized affirmation of secular, labor Zionist, Ashkenazi Israeli identity. When the new state confronted the challenge of absorbing hundreds of thousands of Mizrachi Jewish migrants from the Middle East and North Africa, army officers and educators looked to tiyul to refashion the new citizens in the sabra mold. Such efforts continued over the decades and often met with resistance.[32] Interestingly, the myth of tiyul's political neutrality, so evident in the assumption that sabra practice should naturally be embraced by all Israeli Jews, was shattered less by the reticence of Mizrachim than by the enthusiasm of religious settlers in the West Bank and Gaza. These settlers prominently embraced tiyul in the 1980s, both as a way of staking their claim to the territories that Israel had begun occupying in the 1967 Six-Day War and as a way of appropriating the mantle of Zionism from the secular socialists. The ensuing debate recast tiyul not as a unifying political symbol but as one that highlighted the fissures dividing Israeli Jews.[33]

Tiyul's ideological functions have persisted also in international pilgrimage tours that introduce diaspora Jewish visitors to the State of Israel. For over half a century, the precursors of Taglit-Birthright Israel have drawn on the infrastructures and pedagogical philosophies of tiyul to build diasporic Jewish identities in which affective and value-based ties to the nation-state hold an important place. Such programs have expanded the ritual and educational dimensions of travel beyond the nature hike to encompass almost all aspects of the tourist experience. Although pro-Zionist in character, most of today's educational tours of Israel are used by their sponsors and participants to construct diasporic identities, not Israeli ones. The Zionist nation-building practice of tiyul is not simply adopted, but adapted to become a Jewish diaspora-building practice that serves the interests and needs of Jewish diaspora communities around the world.

Origins of the "Israel Experience"

Organized diaspora Jewish youth tours to Israel began in earnest in the 1950s, shortly after the country declared independence.[34] Zionist youth movements in Western countries had been expressing interest in such programs since at least 1947, directing requests to the Jewish Agency, the Yishuv's quasi-governmental body.[35] Despite its favorable inclinations, the Jewish Agency did not succeed in creating a short-term program before the state was established. By 1950, however, it was running a summer institute for Jewish youth from Western countries, and by 1951 it was subsidizing and helping staff the U.S.-based Young Judaea youth movement's newly inaugurated "Summer-in-Israel Course," which sent 19 people that year.[36]

Diaspora branches of other Zionist youth movements also established programs around this time. The two largest American Jewish religious denominations, Conservatism and Reform, followed suit several years later, each establishing summer trips through their congregational youth movements. United Synagogue Youth (USY), founded by the Conservative movement in 1951, sent its first group of 10 to Israel in the summer of 1956 for an eight-week "Israel Pilgrimage" tour.[37] The Reform movement's National Federation of Temple Youth (NFTY) began its own "Bible Tour" and "Antiquities Tour" during the latter half of the 1950s as well.[38]

Whereas the Great Depression, World War II, the collapse of British rule in Palestine, and the ensuing Arab-Israeli war had effectively precluded the establishment of such programs in the 1930s and 1940s, by 1950, barriers to civilian travel to the area were removed and the factors that enabled the practice to take root among American Jews were put in place. A postwar boom in synagogues, schools, camps, youth groups, and other institutions serving Jewish youth helped create a number of the organizations that would eventually sponsor trips.[39] At the same time, the market for the tours was established with the invention of the "teenager." At the start of the decade, the term was only nine years old, having been coined in 1941 to refer to an age group that in previous eras might easily have been in the labor force; by the mid-20th century, however, those who could afford not to work were largely spending 10 months in school with summers free.[40] For many American Jewish teenagers, summertime was indeed leisure time, thanks to their suburbanizing parents' growing affluence.[41] Coupled with financial aid from Jewish organizations, the rising prosperity enabled many families to bear the cost of the trips, which in the 1950s ranged from about $750 to $900 for an eight-week program.[42] This price included airfare, which indicates the key technological development that made the programs feasible on a mass scale.

Sponsored by religious or ideological youth movements, run by educators, and targeted to the movements' leadership cores, the earliest trips were fashioned as mission-driven educational programs.[43] Such a framing echoed the Israeli conception of tiyul, although sponsors' motivations were different and their educational vision was broader. Hiking, sightseeing, and paying homage, while important, were only some elements in multifaceted curricula that included (depending on the orientation of the sponsor) prayer, study, group-building, physical labor, and meetings with Israeli counterparts. In spite of these differences, the Israeli culture of tiyul helped shape the diaspora programs from the earliest years. The main agent of diffusion was the Jewish Agency, which helped design curricula, supplied Israeli educator-guides, and organized tiyulim.[44]

Neither the Zionist-oriented Young Judaea nor the religiously oriented USY used travel with the intention of encouraging an Israel-centered diasporic identity. Young Judaea did indeed offer an Israel-centered program—engaging in "scoutcraft" with Israeli peers from Tzofim, picking olives on a kibbutz, and touring industrial and agricultural facilities—but with the intention of encouraging its members to abandon diaspora and immigrate to the nation-state.[45] USY, in contrast, attempted to craft diasporic identities that were Israel-oriented, though not Israel-centered. Pro-Zionist and often staffed by North American immigrants to Israel, USY certainly looked favorably on *aliyah* (Jewish immigration to Israel; lit. "ascent"), but it did not prioritize this as an educational goal. Instead, it treated the time away from home as an opportunity to refashion its young people in the image of their rabbis, crafting the tour group as an experiential learning community that immersed secularized teenagers in the religious practices prescribed by Conservative Judaism.[46]

For the most part, the vision of the tours as a conduit to aliyah has been an Israeli vision. It has found far more support in the diaspora communities of Europe, South America, South Africa, and Australia than it has in North America. In the United States and Canada, the dominant model remains one of using the trips to strengthen Jewish identities in North America. This receives strikingly explicit expression in the staff manual developed by Hillel for its Birthright Israel trip:

> Some models of the *Israel Experience* seek to bring the participant to Israel permanently. Some models of the *Israel Experience* seek to teach the participant about Israel.
>
> Our model of the *Israel Experience* seeks to create a Jewish Educational Experience by means of the use of Israel.
>
> Israel is a setting, a context, an opportunity. Israel is the means, not the end.[47]

Although most trips do not "seek to bring the participant to Israel permanently," Israel experience programs have not incorporated the phrase "diasporic identity" into their lexicon. Were the term to be invoked, it would likely be seen as a rhetorical thumbing of the nose at Israel's Zionist ideology, which rejects diaspora as a compromised form of Jewish existence and which holds out immigration as the preferred path. In practice, Israel experience programs have been shaping diasporic identities for over half a century, but the trips' sponsors have rarely pressed the ideological point. Instead, they have spoken of the trips as builders of "Jewish identity," stripped of any additional modifiers, and they have retained a determined openness to immigration to Israel as one of many legitimate paths to Jewish self-actualization.

The preference to define the Israel experience program's mission in the depoliticized language of generic Jewish identity-building has the effect of masking to practitioners and participants the broader political nature of the tours. Of course, there is a general awareness that the tours can cultivate partisans for Israel's cause, as well as a hope among many that it will. But on a deeper level, it draws attention away from the fact that the tours serve, in practice, as a means of socializing diaspora Jews into a particular way of imagining Jewish community. This way of imagining community accepts core nationalist claims that Jews are a political community with political rights, including the right to self-determination in an ancestral homeland. It insists that Jews around the world are bound to the nation-state that has been created in this homeland, but not exclusively so. As for Zionist claims that reject the legitimacy of Jewish communal life outside of the State of Israel, it holds these in tension by giving them a strong hearing while simultaneously denying them in practice and in principle. With regard to the political cultures of the countries where the diasporans live, it affirms the legitimacy of multiculturalism, hyphenated identities, and transnational ties. And, finally, it affirms the legitimacy of privileging ethnic identity over other identities for the purposes of community building. Each and every one of these stances has been challenged by Jews or by others vis-à-vis Jews at some point in history. Some of these stances remain in contention today. In simultaneously affirming them all, homeland tourism constructs a specifically diasporic identity that roots itself in multiple places.

Expansion and Self-Awareness

What began as an instrument of leadership development targeted to "those whose organizational background and educational background indicate that they will benefit most from the trip,"[48] has expanded over the years to embrace a broader market of teenage consumers. According to figures provided by the Jewish Agency, worldwide enrollment in short-term summer youth and young adult programs ranged between 1,000 and 2,000 persons annually before 1967. After the Six-Day War and through the end of the century, enrollment oscillated between 4,000 and 10,000 people. Annual fluctuations have grown sharper since the 1980s and generally move inversely with the severity of violence in the Middle East. With the outbreak of the second intifada in September 2000, enrollment in traditional programs fell to pre-1967 levels, although overall participation was higher due to the newly inaugurated Birthright Israel.[49]

The expanded participation is not simply the product of increased demand. Supply has mushroomed over the past half-century. From a handful of trips in the 1950s, over 100 organizations now sponsor programs that bring young North American Jews to Israel for visits lasting from a few days to the better part of a year. Many program organizers run more than one trip, having diversified their offerings to appeal to specific interests. By the late 1990s, for example, USY was offering five Israel trips in addition to its "classic" Israel Pilgrimage: London and Israel, Eastern Europe and Israel, Poland and Israel (emphasizing Holocaust education), Italy and Israel (with a "three-day sea voyage simulating the 'illegal' immigration to Palestine that took place in the 1940s") and "Etgar! The Ultimate Israel Challenge." Young Judaea, for its part, was offering three summer programs; B'nai Brith Youth Organization, 10 (including a combined "Israel and Safari in Kenya"); and the Orthodox Union's National Council of Synagogue Youth, six, including two separate-gender Torah study tours.[50]

Beyond the youth movements, organizations have emerged to serve niche markets. The Nesiya Institute runs arts-oriented tours. Shorashim emphasizes joint travel with Israeli peers. The Israel Basketball and Hockey Academy offers what its name announces, combined with touring and Torah study. Spotting potential in the growing market, companies that run Israel experience programs for profit have broken the nonprofits' monopoly on the industry. Potential applicants to any of these programs can decide among the abundance of choices by perusing professionally designed glossy brochures and web sites, and by studying comprehensive resource guides with checklists indicating which trips offer archaeological digs, European travel, army simulation, academic credit, and a variety of other special features.[51]

One offshoot of the Israel-oriented tours are youth pilgrimages to Holocaust-related sites in Central and Eastern Europe. These pilgrimages have emerged alongside Zionist tiyul, the Israel experience program, and the

United Jewish Appeal fundraising mission as one of the major new forms of contemporary Jewish political tourism. Holocaust-site pilgrimages share some of the infrastructures, personnel, and intellectual traditions that sustain the Israel experience trips. Israeli and diaspora Jews alike participate in the tours of the ghettos and death camps, sometimes traveling together. Often, the programs involving diaspora youth conclude by bringing the travelers to Israel for shortened Israel experience programs. Jackie Feldman's description of Holocaust-site pilgrimages as "a *ritual reenactment of survival* . . . [whose] ultimate purpose is to root the sanctity of the State in the experience of the Shoah [Holocaust]" is accurate not only of the Ministry of Education–sponsored trips for young Israelis, which he studied, but of the trips for diaspora Jews, as well.[52]

With the expansion of Israel experience programs has come a more self-conscious articulation of their rationale and method. What Vilnay's essay was to tiyul, a 1994 article titled "The Israel Trip: A New Form of Jewish Education" has been to the Israel experience program. Written by an American-born Israeli philosopher of education long involved with the trips, Barry Chazan, the essay was disseminated by one of the most prominent philanthropic foundations on the North American Jewish scene, a foundation that was leading a campaign to develop the Israel experience field. Building on more than four decades of practical knowledge amassed by Jewish educators working in this arena, Chazan outlines a pedagogical framework for conceptualizing the tours. He starts with the premise that modernity's erosion of traditional Jewish communities has transformed Jewish socialization from an organic, mimetic process to one accomplished primarily by deliberate communal intervention.[53] Arguing that youth trips to Israel should be developed further as a form of holistic Jewish education, Chazan identifies important ways that the experience of Israel as "a state, society and culture" might shape diasporic identity. Two main themes emerge: Israel as a forum for reflection on existential questions, and Israel as an inspirational model for individual and collective empowerment.

Chazan views Israel as a microcosm of the Jewish world—one that reflects the Jewish cultures of its many immigrant communities and creates a new "testing ground" for crafting Jewish responses to modernity. Because Israeli society brings all this together in one place, travelers who experience Israel are thrust into an encounter with defining tensions of modern Jewish existence such as those between diversity and unity and between universalism and particularism. Israel serves as a venue for reflecting on these tensions and, through them, on one's identity as a Jew.[54]

Whereas Israel's diversity and contradictions are used to provoke essential questions, its history, read in the heroic mode, is invoked to inspire feelings of belonging and empowerment. Chazan alludes to a particular construction of Israeli collective memory that can be summarized as follows: Zionism sought to accomplish the seemingly impossible task of gathering a people dispersed across the globe into its ancient homeland in order to forge a new society and an independent state. Against the odds, a vanguard of pioneers settled the land, established the foundations of a Jewish national homeland, fought victoriously for independence, and successfully defended their fledgling state against attempts to destroy it. Before they had a country of their own, Jews had been a victimized people with neither help nor refuge, but the establishment of a Jewish state has given oppressed Jews around the world a shield and a haven.

Chazan invokes this framing to represent Israel as an embodiment of core human and Jewish values. Jews who visit the country will encounter not merely a place but a "statement about the ability of human beings to reshape life according to a new vision . . . about the role of will, choice and human action in affecting history." They will experience "the collective principle in Jewish life" by touring a country that "boldly affirms the value of Jewish peoplehood and of the collective responsibility of all Jews for each other." Perhaps more than anything else, they will witness "an attempt to guarantee Jewish survival," for Israel, "established on the ashes of Jewish destruction" and engaged in "an ongoing struggle for self-preservation," both "symbolically and actually . . . reflects the Jewish will to live."[55]

Were the essay to leave it at this, we would have what amounts to a reasonable description of core themes that, in fact, do emerge in the portrayal of Israel to visiting diaspora youth. It does more, however. Chazan's critical move to establish the trips as pedagogy is to associate the core themes of place with specific dimensions of identity development. What appear at first to be important sociologically as collective representations are revealed to have a direct bearing on core psychological processes involved in identity formation. Chazan's representations of Israel position it as an impetus to reflection and choice regarding unresolvable existential issues, as well as a source of safety (by providing a sense of belonging), efficacy (by asserting the power of human agency), and self-esteem (by inspiring pride).[56] The vision is more humanistic, more theoretically grounded, and more generalizable than anything produced by the theorists of tiyul. It is also one that is clearly shaped with adolescents in mind.

Invoking Dewey, Chazan outlines the various teaching styles that Israel experience educators use to accomplish this. Experience and conversation, he suggests, are the main teachers. He does not ignore the transmission of cognitive information, but the absence of any specific discussion of didactic methods emphasizes the fluid, constructivist character of the educational vision.[57] These tours are to be voyages of self-discovery as much as they are opportunities to learn about Israel. The educator's prescribed role is therefore less focused on imparting information than on structuring experiences that enable independent exploration and learning.

Such an ambitious educational vision will obviously stand or fall on implementation. The philanthropic foundation and American Jewish educational agency that jointly published Chazan's piece were concerned with precisely this point, and they included an empirical analysis of best practices as a partner essay.[58] Chazan draws on the second article to offer his own recommendations for translating the vision into action. His list of best practices falls into two broad categories. The more technical of the two regards coherence in planning and implementation. The other is more ambitious. Chazan argues that the excellent trip will treat every aspect of the travel experience as part of the educational program. The itinerary will become a curriculum. Dynamics within the tour group will be mobilized. Informal activities, including free time, will be treated as crucial moments of learning. People-focused as well as site-focused, the trips will create opportunities to interact with Israeli peers. It will be, in Chazan's words, a "total experience."[59]

Chazan's essay emerges out of a tradition of scholarship on diaspora youth trips to Israel dating back to the early 1960s.[60] Most of these writings have been concerned with establishing whether the programs succeed in their identity-building missions. Dozens of posttrip evaluation surveys,[61] longitudinal panel surveys of program alumni,[62] community demographic surveys,[63] and studies of adolescent development[64] have demonstrated correlations between Israel program participation and subsequent indicators of Jewish identification.[65] More recently, ethnographers have begun exploring the processes that occur on the trips themselves.[66] Much of this newer work has been preoccupied with questions of the representation of Israel and of the relationship between internal group dynamics and the encounter with place.

One area of research that deserves mention regards institutionalized encounters with Israeli peers. Known as *mifgashim*, these meetings draw on theories of cross-cultural education to overcome the boundaries that tourism usually interposes between visitors and locals. Mifgashim emerged in response to a critique that the tours represent Israel as a symbol serving diaspora Jews' mythic needs rather than as a reality reflective of Israelis' lived experience.[67]

Beyond the scholarship, the educational theory of Israel experience programs has been developed also through practice. For some of the largest trip organizers, like Hillel, USY (Conservative), and NFTY (Reform), staff training is a formal process led by professional educators employed by the organizations themselves or by others established expressly for the purpose.

Tourism as a Diasporic "Solution"

Ironically, the most ambitious program of diasporic homeland tourism yet realized was not conceived with the homeland foremost in mind. A concern for Israel-diaspora relations was certainly one factor in the creation of Taglit-Birthright Israel, but the decision to mount the effort was made by North American Jews seeking to address dilemmas emerging out of the North American Jewish experience. Israel figured in their plan largely as an instrumentality to serve diasporic needs and only to a lesser degree as an end in itself.

Taglit took shape in the 1990s in the context of an American Jewish leadership increasingly concerned that its community was in decline and searching for ways to restore its vitality. In the preceding two decades, American Jews had understood themselves to be a vigorous community, galvanized by a clearly defined agenda of political activism to secure Jewish welfare against a variety of threats. By the early 1990s, however, the program of "sacred survival" had ceased to mobilize grassroots activism.[68] Soviet Jewry had been freed, the Holocaust memorialized, and barriers to American Jewish advancement largely eliminated. Political advocacy on behalf of Israel, once a great unifier, had become a matter of contention as American Jews found themselves divided over Israel's policies regarding the conflict with the Palestinians and the legal status of non-Orthodox forms of Judaism.[69] Flat fundraising campaigns merely added to the sense that the community was adrift.

Concerns over the erosion of community figured prominently in American public discourse during those years.[70] Different subcultures voiced it in different ways. American Jews' variation on the theme was expressed as a fear that group cohesion was weakening to the point where the very survival of the ethnic community was threatened. The malaise that attended the passing of the sacred survival agenda quickly turned to talk of an acute "crisis of continuity" after a major demographic study of American Jews indicated increasing interfaith marriage and weakened commitment to Jewish religious and ethnic norms.[71] Decrying these phenomena as portents of imminent demise, American Jewish activists had found a cause to rally around.

In the debate over how best to ensure the survival of the American Jewish community, no serious thought was given to abandoning or reshaping the American context. This was, after all, an American community given to thinking in terms of reform, not revolution. The proposed responses were premised on the belief that group cohesion in a situation of optional ethnicity rested ultimately on individuals' free choice to identify with the group and that efforts should therefore focus on influencing personal choices.[72] Building on existing institutions and patterns of activity, American Jews addressed their continuity crisis largely by funding educational interventions to foster Jewish commitment. They launched programs to expand enrollment in Jewish parochial schools, enhance Jewish summer camps, encourage adult Jewish learning, and bring generations together in family education. The largest single investment, however, sought to make the youth tour to Israel a universal rite of American Jewish passage.

Throughout the 1990s, local Jewish fundraising federations had become increasingly active promoters of youth trips to Israel, offering scholarships, seed money for program development, resource hotlines, and more. The key institutions advocating an expansion of the trips, however, were independent family foundations that were eclipsing the federations as the primary agenda-setting power in the North American Jewish community. Fueled by the booming economy, by the end of the decade more than 4,000 foundations were giving over $1 billion annually to Jewish causes, approximately $300 million of which came from about 20 individuals known colloquially as "the megadonors."[73] The community-based federation system at the time was still raising about twice the amount given by the foundations, but campaigns were flat, even declining after adjusting for inflation. As the Taglit-Birthright Israel initiative soon made clear, American Jewry's funding system was coming to rely less on consensual decision-making and more on entrepreneurial initiative.

Two foundations took the lead in presenting youth trips to Israel as a partial solution to the supposed problem of attenuated Jewish identities. Seagrams heir Charles R. Bronfman's eponymous, acronymous CRB Foundation, established in 1986 with a mission to enhance Israel-diaspora relations, was the first to take up the issue.[74] In the early 1990s, CRB initiated a program of research into Israel experience programs that investigated questions of impact, process, and market.[75] Finding that Jews who had traveled to Israel were more likely to affirm the salience of Jewish identity, the research helped convince an already sympathetic foundation of the value of nurturing Israel experience programs. Moreover, the "hard" data enabled CRB to make a case for greater resource allocation by the Jewish community at large. A foundation-supported review of the research written by Barry Chazan, then a consultant for CRB, declared emphatically that the Israel experience was "one of the most powerful resources that the North American Jewish Community has at its disposal to face the challenge of adult Jewish identity and involvement."[76] After several small projects, the foundation in 1996 unveiled Israel Experience, Inc. (IEI), a partnership between diaspora and Israeli NGOs and the Israeli government to market the programs to potential participants and potential funders.[77]

IEI was only several months old when its transformation into Taglit-Birthright Israel began. A partnership between CRB and another foundation, the Jewish Life Network (JLN), set the process in motion. JLN had been established in the early 1990s by hedge fund operator Michael Steinhardt to "revitalize Jewish identity through educational, cultural and religious initiatives that are designed to reach out to all Jews, with an emphasis on those who are on the margins of Jewish life."[78] Although it had been associated with high-profile projects in a variety of areas, Steinhardt's foundation was not at first identified with the effort to make Israel experience programs a top communal priority. Through its partnership with CRB, that would change.

The idea of using communal dollars to provide every Jewish teenager with a subsidized or free trip to Israel had first been suggested by Yossi Beilin during his tenure as Israel's deputy foreign minister in the early 1990s. At a 1994 Jewish Federation convention, Beilin proposed that "every young Jew [should] receive a birthday card from the local Federation on his or her seventeenth birthday with a coupon for travel and accommodations in Israel during the next summer vacation."[79] Such a visit would be considered every Jew's "birthright."

Although the idea was Israeli in origin, it was premised on a model of Israel-diaspora relations that neither rejected diaspora's legitimacy nor treated it as subservient to the state. Beilin's proposal stemmed from his position that a healthy Israel-diaspora relationship should be predicated on reciprocity, as opposed to the federation system's prevailing model of a unidirectional flow of aid from periphery to core. Arguing that American Jewish charity should be spent on American Jews rather than on Israelis, he suggested that the federation dollars traditionally allocated to social services in Israel be redirected to fund the trips.[80] Beilin's ideas aroused the ire of federation leaders who saw the prevailing model of Israel-directed charity as functionally necessary for American Jewry's system of fundraising and governance.

Federation opposition was rendered moot by the rise of megadonors not beholden to the traditional fundraising system. When the staffs of Steinhardt's and Bronfman's foundations gathered in 1998, they reconceived IEI along lines similar to those proposed by Beilin. Rather than market existing programs to high school students, they would bring together a variety of program organizers to provide college-age Jews with free 10-day trips run according to defined educational and quality-control standards. Any organization that met the standards could receive funding to deliver the program. To the young adults, the trip would be presented as a "gift from the Jewish people."[81]

These were significant departures from the earlier model of Israel experience programs. The target population was older, the duration of the trips shorter, and the organizational structure one of coordination rather than program delivery. To fund the new venture, a plan was worked out whereby the total cost, initially estimated at $210 million over five years, would be split evenly among three parties: the philanthropists, the government of Israel, and local Jewish communities via their central fundraising bodies.[82] Bronfman and Steinhardt each contributed over $10 million and began recruiting other philanthropists to commit at least $5 million apiece to the project. They also worked to convince the Israeli government and diaspora Jewish federations to follow their lead.

Opposition to the idea was present in both quarters. In Israel, critics questioned whether tax revenues should be spent to support luxury travel for affluent diaspora Jews. In diaspora organizations, opponents argued that the search for a "quick fix" to the problem of waning Jewish identity was misguided, that little of lasting value could be accomplished in 10 days, that college students would treat the trips as little more than a free party, and that scarce communal dollars would be better spent elsewhere.[83] The program overcame these objections and secured commitments from both the government and the federations, but in spite of this, funding from these sources has been intermittent and subject to continual renegotiation. Taglit has responded to its detractors' arguments: in the Israeli case, by highlighting the program's economic contributions to the tourism sector; in the diaspora's case, by commissioning an impact evaluation.

At the November 1998 Council of Jewish Federations convention in Jerusalem, Steinhardt, Bronfman, and the chairperson of Israel's Ministerial Committee on Israel-Diaspora Relations, former refusenik Natan (Anatoly) Sharansky, unveiled "Birthright Israel." After various literal translations of the name into Hebrew were rejected, the program's public relations department settled on "Taglit," a term that held none of the ideology-laden connotations of a diaspora Jewish "birthright" but meant, simply, "discovery."[84] Initially headed by a veteran Israel experience program educator, Taglit soon came under the leadership of a former director general of both the Jewish Agency and the Israeli Ministry of Education, a man who brought experience in education, knowledge of diaspora organizations, and connections among Israel's political echelon.

Recruitment began in autumn 1999 for the first trips, which were slated to depart later that year.[85] A $3 million advertising campaign promoted Birthright Israel in magazines, newspapers, and radio. One advertisement in *Rolling Stone* juxtaposed images of a baby boy about to be ritually circumcised and a young man floating in the Dead Sea: "Sometimes it's hard being Jewish. Sometimes it isn't."[86] Meanwhile, Hillel staff launched recruitment drives on campuses. Internet-based registration for the first trips opened at the beginning of September and closed a month and a half later with 12,000 applicants for 5,000 slots.[87]

In the final week of 1999, the first planeload of Taglit participants touched down at Ben-Gurion Airport outside of Tel Aviv. This was followed by a succession of flights that brought 6,000 young diaspora Jews from all over the world to Israel through February 2000. By the following June, the winter launch of Taglit had been completed successfully, spring trips were under way, financial commitments had been made to the program, third-party evaluations were positive, and alumni were speaking of their experiences in glowing terms. In the hot summer months that followed, however, developments beyond Taglit's control transpired in Israel to the detriment of many things, including Taglit. When Israeli-Palestinian negotiations broke down in a spasm of violence, Israel quickly became a less attractive destination to security-conscious travelers. Although applications doubled to 25,000 for Taglit's winter 2001 trip, enough people changed their minds in the intervening months that Taglit was able to fill only 8,800 of the 10,000 available slots for the program. By 2003, enrollment had picked up again, with annual participation ultimately peaking at 45,000 in 2008.[88]

The start of the second intifada in September 2000 led to a new framing of the program's purpose. Motivated originally by concerns over weakening Jewish identity in diaspora, Taglit increasingly came to be spoken of as a means of fostering political support for Israel in its intensifying conflict with the Palestinians.[89] At the same time, educators' visions for diaspora Jewish travel to Israel continued to expand in other directions outside of the

Birthright Israel framework. The massive investment in short-term trips led to a renewed push for longer-term programs, resulting in the creation of the Jewish Agency's Masa (Journey) initiative. In a significant conceptual innovation, in 2006, one of the former directors of the CRB Foundation's Israel experience efforts introduced a program that seeks to push the field beyond the paradigm of treating Israel as the primary destination. Kivvunim (Directions) is in essence an Israel-and-diaspora experience program in which diaspora Jews use Israel as a home base for a year of tours to explore the historical and contemporary Jewish experience in Morocco, Spain, Russia, and a handful of other countries in addition to Israel. Since the inception of Kivvunim, similar programs have arisen alongside it, including one sponsored by the same Young Judaea that in the 1950s helped pioneer the aliyah-oriented Israel experience tour.

Pilgrimage Instrumentalized

In January 2000, I stood in the departure terminal at Newark International Airport. The area had been converted to a campus quad. Students in sweatsuits stitched with university logos and Greek letters crossed a landscape of their peers parked on rows of plastic chairs and stretched out on the floor between piles of carry-on luggage. Some rested, worn down from the length of the check-in and lateness of the hour. Others milled about, bristling with anticipation. A flirtation here. A reunion there. With the entire wing of the terminal more or less to themselves, the students, over 400 strong, controlled the space. A small group commandeered the center of the circular hall to kick a hackeysack back and forth, ignoring a nearby Christmas tree until one of them accidentally kicked the beanbag into the tinsel. Where they were going, they could enjoy their game without having to contend with Christmas trees on the playing field. That was part of the point of the trip.

I had experienced scenes like this from the other side a number of times, the first being in 1987 when I headed off to participate in USY's Israel Pilgrimage. Yet, in some ways, the phenomenon had changed. "We didn't send kids to Israel in the '60s and '70s [in order] to 'inoculate' them prior to going off to college. Jewish identity wasn't in doubt in the way in which it is today," NFTY's Israel Programs Director Paul Reichenbach later told me. His words simultaneously reflected on and echoed the assumptions and medicalized policy language of "continuity crisis"–era American Jewish discourse. "It was about teaching them about Israel and Zionism and developing a love for Israel. . . . But the purpose and function for which Birthright was created, of course, could not have been understood 20 years ago."[90]

In fact, Birthright Israel was unlike the youth group–sponsored programs that had gone before. It differed also from traditional pilgrimages, as well as from leisure tours. Taglit was conceived as a social intervention, an "outreach to young people," which, if successful, would lead diaspora youth "to be more inquisitive and concerned about their identity . . . to appreciate and remain in the Jewish fold . . . [and] to understand the role that Israel plays in the Jewish dynamic."[91] Taglit was seen by its sponsors as a strategic investment in the Jewish future. It was pilgrimage instrumentalized.

Even my own presence in the airport on that January night had an instrumental cast. Notepad and pen in hand, I approached one of the men who had led the effort to create the program. Michael Steinhardt stood with his aides accepting handshakes and thank yous from a steady stream of students who had learned that he was one of the principal benefactors of their trip. I introduced myself, explaining that I was supervising a team of researchers that had been commissioned to conduct research about Taglit.

"For what purpose?" he asked. "Evaluation?"

Indeed, evaluation was a crucial part of the purpose and precisely the indicator that Taglit, for all its semblance to other mass movements of pilgrims and tourists, was something quite different. For in the end, this pilgrimage tour was being conducted in order to accomplish certain goals. If it failed, chances were that its funding would evaporate, its offices in New York and Jerusalem would close, and its potential pilgrims would spend their winter breaks engaged in other activities.

Anthropological studies generally treat it as given that pilgrimages have some effect on the pilgrims who undertake them. The reason for this is that they understand the act of setting out toward a sacred center to be, ipso facto, a performance of identity. Remaining closely tied to analyses of on-the-ground practices, anthropological inquiries tend to display little interest in questions of travel's long-term effects on individuals. Instead, they ask about the political and ideological agendas served by particular sanctifications of space[92] and about the contested meanings ascribed to specific sites.[93] They examine how pilgrimage breaks down barriers between people and groups, as in Victor Turner's classic studies, or they take issue with Turner to show how it builds barriers up.[94] They expound on the factors associated with the emergence, growth, and demise of particular pilgrimage centers.[95] They explore the relationship between setting out on the journey and arriving at the destination.[96]

To this tradition of pilgrimage studies, the discourse of evaluation is utterly foreign. To speak of a pilgrimage as being "effective" or "ineffective" is not merely a non sequitir, it is decidedly antagonistic to a perspective that sees the meanings of pilgrimages as contested and that charges researchers with the responsibility of accounting for this diversity rather than privileging the perspective of any one group.[97] Impact evaluation, by contrast, is essentially officialdom's tool for assessing conformity to particular definitions of effectiveness. This is not to say that research conducted in the course of a program evaluation cannot transcend its origins to speak to broader issues. Doing so, however, requires a willingness to move beyond the discourse of program evaluation and incorporate additional frameworks.[98]

I responded to Steinhardt's query by telling him that I was one of the researchers working with Brandeis University's Cohen Center for Modern Jewish Studies. I did not need to elaborate. He already knew that the center's evaluators would be bringing the tools of social science to bear as they studied the extent and nature of program impacts.

A Taglit executive standing next to him piped up: "You will only see wonderful things."

Steinhardt ignored him. "I want to hear about the bad as well as the good," he said.

I tried to imagine Victor Turner engaged in such a conversation, but the notion struck me as absurd. He studied pilgrimage. I was studying something that only resembled it.

Contesting Claims

[To: North Americans in Birthright Israel group #4386
From: Yoni Lefkovich, Corporal, Israel Defense Forces]
Sent: Thursday, August 17, 2006 2:59 PM
Subject: letter from yoni
  hi i came home from the war in lebanon. i was on the front
line 1,5 month. I wuld have been happy to find news from you
but never mind i am writing now. the fight was very hard. but
thank god, me and my friends are fine. during 6 weeks i wehad
three showers and the first two weeks we didn't take off any
clothes. we slept 2 or 3 hours every night whch was phisically
very hard. it was also hard not to see home all that time, seeing
bombs fall around you.
  you know that to defend yourself you kill some innocent
people because the terrorists hide among them and you feel very
bad about it. I hope that you know that all what you see in CNN
is very onesided. they only show the destruction in lebanon,
and not what HIZBOLLAH did to israel. it is very hard to fight
against terrorists. i hope to hear soon what you think about the
situation, how you are and what is going on in your life. i miss
you, yoni lefkovich, your israeli friend and soldier. [*sic*]

Three months earlier, on a bus parked on a quiet roadside in the
northern town of Kiryat Shmonah, near the Lebanese border, 40 students
from a Taglit group sat awaiting the arrival of eight Israeli soldiers, male and
female, who would be joining their tour. Like the American tourists, Yoni
and his comrades were also around 19 or 20 years old, but soldiering had
endowed them with a presumptive charisma. As they stepped onto the bus
for the first time, conspicuous in their olive fatigues, they were greeted with
applause, yelps and piercing whistles. The next several days of cross-cultural
exchange would be spent touring, hiking, talking, dancing, drinking, trading
gifts, and "hooking up." No one expected that, only weeks later, Kiryat Shmonah would be in flames and Yoni would be in combat.

In many ways, the trip had been preparing for such a moment. Its portrayal of Israel returned invariably to matters of Arab-Jewish confrontation, making this theme one of the primary lenses through which tourists came to view the country. The intent, in part, was to foster among visitors a sense that they have a personal stake in the conflict's outcome. Structuring opportunities to forge relationships with individual soldiers was one way of accomplishing this. The 2006 war in Lebanon was a moment of truth for the Israel trips, when the strength of the newly formed ties would be put to the test. Had the tours succeeded in fostering a sense of common cause, binding diaspora Jews to the State of Israel? Program evaluators found that, compared with a control group, those participating in the trips were "more likely to have actively sought news of the war, to have sought news from an Israeli source, to have supported Israel's position in the war, to have felt connected to Israel and Israelis, and to have taken action on Israel's behalf."[1] By contrast, the subtle rebuke Yoni emailed to the members of his Taglit group—"I w[o] uld have been happy to find news from you but never mind"—hints at the limits of the Americans' stake in Israel's conflict. In spite of the program's efforts to root American Jewish attachments to Israel in person-to-person relationships, few of those traveling with Yoni felt compelled to send any words of support to their "Israeli friend and soldier" as he went off to battle.

Politics of Tourism

State-sponsored diaspora homeland trips mobilize tourism, a practice of meaning construction, to encourage diasporans to see themselves not only as citizens of the countries in which they reside but also as members of a collective that transcends borders and yet is inextricably bound to a specific place. This type of transnational identity does not replace nationalist formulations but, rather, builds on them. The notion that diaspora trips represent a sort of "homecoming" rests on particular constructions—both of the human communities that are being engaged as tourists and of the stretches of land that they are being encouraged to visit. The Jewish diaspora visits a place posited to be "Jewish" (in multiple senses of the word), just as the Chinese diaspora visits a place posited to be "Chinese." By presuming a natural connection between a people, a culture, and a land, diaspora homeland tourism builds transnational community on the basis of the same nationalist claims used by nation-states to legitimize their sovereignty. The tours extend the presumed connection to encompass those who enact their relationship to the claimed territory in ways other than residing in it. At the same time, they reinforce the nationalist projects in the homeland states themselves by affirming the notion that the land has an inherent connection with a particular human group and its culture.

Israel experience programs advance a vision of diasporic Jewish identity in which Jews worldwide are stakeholders in Israel's state-building project. Their efforts are complicated, however, by the fact that the country is embroiled in a conflict with a rival nationalism claiming the same land for a different group. What complicates matters are not so much the military dimensions of this conflict as the ideological ones, for any challenge to Jewish nationalist claims also strikes at the foundations on which the transnational tourism project rests. In practice, this means that the representations of Israel shown to diaspora Jewish tourists can always potentially be met with a question: "But what about the Palestinian Arab counternarrative?"[2] The interests of the tourists, the ideology of the tour sponsors, and the power of tourism to constrain the interpretive schema that are applied in a given context all combine to limit the extent to which such a question is asked. Still, all involved in the programs are aware that there exists a rival perspective that would dispute many of the claims being made on Israel experience programs, from fundamental assumptions to specific details. When the tours directly engage issues related to war and peace, this awareness becomes pushed to the fore.

The reality of the Middle East conflict imposes itself on any tourist visiting Israel. It is something that diaspora-building programs like Taglit must inevitably confront. Doing so in a way that will be credible to independent thinkers even as it affirms (or at least does not undermine) the program's ideology is a central challenge to which the trips must respond. How do the tours convincingly represent the complexities of the Middle East conflict while remaining true to their goal of shaping Israel-oriented diasporic Jewish identities? While the question is interesting in its own right, it also bears on the theoretical issues at the heart of this book. Examining the tours' political work in an arena where it is most acute, explicit, visible, exposed, and contested will suggest a conceptual framework for addressing the broader question of how tourism operates as a medium of transnational political socialization more generally.

Toward a Practice-Centered Account

Both because they seek to represent a contested terrain and because they intend these representations to influence travelers' political identities, Israel experience tours are inevitably implicated in the charged politics of the Middle East.[3] As such, they have become lightning rods that attract partisan assertions about tourism's potential for shaping diaspora Jews' positions on the Israeli-Palestinian conflict. Sympathizers and detractors alike generally share the assumption that state- and community-sponsored trips can build support for Israeli positions in the conflict. The former laud this[4] while the latter decry it, but both take the trips' efficacy for granted. As for their explanations of this efficacy, those pleased by such an outcome sometimes speak of it as a natural result of seeing the country firsthand. Those less enamored can be heard at times attributing it to indoctrination, brainwashing, or other bogeymen.[5]

Research on the ethnic homeland tourism of other diaspora groups points to the inadequacies of such claims, both as purported explanations of the specific shaping of opinion about the Arab-Israeli conflict and, a fortiori, as attempts to account for the tours' deeper political work shaping homeland-oriented diasporic identities. Findings from China, Taiwan, and South Korea suggest that tours designed to bind diasporas to homelands have inherent contradictions that undermine their ability to impose their ideologies on tourists.[6] In addition to these findings, there are other good reasons to jettison the notion that Jewish diaspora tours of Israel shape political opinion by subjecting a captive, largely passive, audience to clear and consistent discursive messages from figures of authority who speak in one voice and who manage to quell the few murmurs of dissent. Tourists come to the trips having been exposed to iconic media images of the Israeli-Palestinian conflict, which are hardly flattering to Israel. Tour guides come to them from diverse positions on Israel's political spectrum. Both parties to the interaction possess critical knowledge, active agency, and the capacity for ethical reasoning. This must be taken into account when explaining how the Israel experience tours effect their work on political identities. The explanation I offer here draws from research in media studies (for tourism is, after all, a medium of communication) and is premised on four assumptions:

Tourism's discourses are multivocal and polysemous, not monolithic.
Political understandings emerge through the interaction of verbal representations and nonverbal contexts of experience.
Guides and tourists alike possess human agency.
Ideology is broader and deeper than a set of specific policy positions.

The approach I take eschews traditional cultural analysis in favor of a version that is more distinctly sociological. I see only limited advantage in deciphering the semiotic codes through which nationalist ideologies (in this case, Zionism) construct place and history. That type of analysis has some-thing to offer, but it also has the unfortunate tendency of divorcing symbols from the people who use them. Tourism's ability to serve as a medium of political socialization, however, rests heavily on the social practices of mean-ing construction that it enables and that it opens to strategic manipulation.

In this chapter, I begin to address these practices by examining them at the very point where they become most explicit and controversial on diaspora Jewish homeland tours—that is, in their representations of the Arab-Israeli conflict. Through ethnographic portraits of visits to the West Bank separa-tion barrier and to the Golan Heights, I examine how the actions of the pro-gram sponsors, tour guides, and tourists interact to create understandings of the Arab-Israeli conflict. The practices that generate these understandings tend to foster identification with the Israeli side, even as they allow for the fact that tourists are critical consumers of information, aware of rival per-spectives, and capable of evaluating any claims that are made.

I have chosen to focus the analysis on a group whose guide made delib-erate attempts to speak frankly about Arab perspectives. This is not to sug-gest that all guides on diaspora Jewish homeland tours are so forthright. Yet the approach is a common one that guides do adopt. (As discussed later in this chapter, it also is in compliance with Taglit's officially sanctioned but not always implemented policy that guides not impose dogma but, instead, pres-ent multiple perspectives.) My decision to focus on a guide who attempted to strike a verbal balance in his narratives is intended to show more clearly how the mechanisms of political socialization operate through both discursive and nondiscursive practices of representation. In revealing the importance of these ubiquitous nondiscursive practices, my analysis of the representation of the Middle East conflict introduces one of the key claims in this volume: in tourism, many different ways of knowing a place intersect in a dynamic—and, therefore, ultimately open—process of meaning construction. This sets the stage for the focused explorations of those ways of knowing that bear most significantly on the efforts to use tourism to shape diasporic identities.

Contradictions: An Afternoon by the West Bank

Nothing marks the empty residential street as a tourist attraction. There is no welcome sign, no ticket office, no official plaque, no parking lot. Our bus simply rolls to a stop beneath squat concrete apartment blocks and opens its doors onto a dusty rock-strewn field patched with the muted colors of some yellow-flowered desert shrub. Stepping forward 20 yards brings one to an outlook where the ground drops sharply to reveal a landscape of valleys and hills that stretch for miles. Areas of human settlement hug the terrain that rises and falls in the distance. All is quiet save for the whipping sound of a rough wind. It is the type of wind one expects at the edge of town. We are alone on the southern outskirts of Jerusalem, overlooking the West Bank.

Because the site is not marked physically, the construction of the tourist gaze will rest primarily on words—the tour guide's narrative and the ensuing conversation between guide and group. The *moreh derech* (educator-guide), Ra'anan, is a 33-year-old Israeli who speaks fluent English, gently accented. A former teacher, he has left the classroom to study *yedi'at ha'aretz*. His relationship with the visitors in this particular tour group has been cordial, but he has not become the object of "guide worship" that often emerges on trips like these.[7] This has surprised me. On looks alone—he is well tanned, well dressed, and well groomed, with thick black hair, green eyes, and a face whose round cheeks always rest in a smile—he could easily play the role of "our sexy Israeli." I have seen other groups build a relationship with their guides through exaggerated flirtation. This group has not. Instead, its members prefer to joke around with Gidi and Laura, their irreverent North American staff. As we arrive at that open field, though, people are beginning to see Ra'anan in a new light. We have just come from a hastily improvised visit to his sister's house in the artsy Jerusalem neighborhood where we had eaten lunch, and the backstage glimpse into the person behind the role has fostered a sense of intimacy that the relationship has previously lacked.

Ra'anan begins the process of verbally marking the site while we are still on the bus. "We're going to see the separation fence. Bring your cameras. That's about it," he announces over the microphone before disembarking. The details will come after we have it in view. We follow him out and walk across the dirt until we near the hilltop's edge. Then Ra'anan speaks. He begins by directing our gaze backward, not forward. "Guys! Okay! Okay, well, guys! Behind us, we are at the neighborhood in the name of Gilo." He shouts to make his voice heard over the wind. "If you came here in the year of 2000, you were in one of the most famous streets in Israel. Every night, you would have been in the news. Why?"

Those who are with Ra'anan, physically and mentally, venture answers to his question. "There were bombs?" someone suggests.

Not everyone is focused on Ra'anan, however. The rocky ground has provided about half a dozen men with something more interesting than listening to their guide discuss the politics of the Israeli-Palestinian conflict. They stand at the edge of the hill, throwing stones, first into the valley then at each other. Ra'anan points to the view several miles across the valley. "All the area there is Bethlehem and its suburbs." We look over to the areas of Palestinian settlement in the West Bank. Between us and it are the stone-throwing members of our group. Ra'anan admonishes them with a word: "People!" Turning back to the rest of us, he continues:

> It was actually October 2000. Palestinian neighbors from the houses on the other side of what today is the separation fence would have shelled those houses that are behind us every evening. Israeli tanks were standing on where we just parked our bus. All the houses you can see—I hope you can identify already the Arabic architecture—this is Bethlehem. And on top is a suburb called Beit Jallah, a mixture of Christian Arabs and Palestinian Arabs.

In his lexicon, "Palestinian" referred only to the Muslims. "The Palestinians, they basically took over the Christian houses, many Christian houses, and started with the last—Shhhh!" He hushed the stone throwers. "—with the last *intifada*. Okay, guys! It's really disturbing! If you don't want to stand here you can go back on the bus, you can take pictures on the other side, it's totally fine, but don't bother other people who want to listen."

Shamed, the men put the rocks down and moved closer to the group to hear Ra'anan ask, "What is an intifada?"

From the crowd, several people shout, "Struggle." This was not the first time they had heard of it.

Ra'anan affirms the answer:

> A struggle, a rebel[lion]. We had two intifadas here in Israel, one in '87 and one in the year of 2000. The last one had the consequences of lately building of the separation wall that you see to your left. In order to understand the reality today, I want to take you back, back to the [1947 United Nations] Partition Plan. We're going to deal with it tomorrow. The land of Israel was split into a Jewish state and an Arab state. This area is known as the West Bank, that we are just facing now, the mountains of—the Judean Mountains—[it] was given to whom?

"Arabs!" comes a confident response.

"Arabs," Ra'anan repeats for all to hear. "And they are still here. It stayed like this until when?"

"2000," comes a less confident response, which Ra'anan immediately corrects, saying, "1967."

People have started throwing stones again, and a pebble sails into the group, landing squarely on top of someone's head. People erupt in laughter, Ra'anan too, and he quips, "It's a dangerous area," which elicits even louder laughs.

I also laugh, even as my antennae are quivering. Should I be struck by the way that guide and group improvise a collaborative framing of the Israeli-Palestinian conflict, treating it as normal and nonthreatening, something that can evoke not only sorrow or rage but also humor? Should I be struck by the irony of American Jewish tourists using stone throwing, of all things, as a way of playfully ignoring a discussion of the intifada that is taking place while overlooking the West Bank? Either way, I am aware that my account of how understandings of the Israeli-Palestinian conflict are shaped will have to address convolutions like these.

After the laughter subsides, Ra'anan refocuses the group's attention. "It stayed like this until 1967 when Israel, in the Six-Day War, conquered all this West Bank. So all those villages, Bethlehem and other, many thousands of people, basically, around 3 million people today are living under Israeli occupation." He did not shy away from the term. "On and off there were rebel[lion]s from those people. In many towns there were good relationships between them and the Israelis, but in the year of 2000, the last event that they started rebelling against Israel, and shooting at this neighborhood of Gilo, a neighborhood of Jerusalem."

He directs our gaze back from Bethlehem to Gilo, behind us: "All the houses that you see behind you are houses of Israelis. The real estate here was really going down, and you can't—it's very hard to sell an apartment here today. Why? And all the windows that you see—look at the windows on the houses. You're going to see kind of bluish windows? Can you see blue windows on the houses? These are bulletproof windows."

People start murmuring, and one woman asks, "Then why are we standing right here?"

"What's that?" Ra'anan replies, not having heard her.

"Why are we standing here?!"

"Because it's, ummm, 'peacetime,'" he deadpans.

As laughter again erupts and people begin joking with one another, the rumble of the bus engine is heard, and another women shouts in mock fear, "The bus is leaving!"

In the face of the general mirth that has overtaken the group, Ra'anan tries to restore a semblance of decorum. "Okay! Guys! I'm going to try to present the two sides and then we're going to move to another more quiet place and try to discuss it for a few minutes. What are—Shhh! Guys!—Israel, after this intifada, after this fighting that [has] almost calmed down, Israel decided as a one-sided action, we decided that there are no partners for peace at the meantime, to build a separation wall-slash-fence." His verbalization of the punctuation would later become a running joke among some members of the group, but not yet, perhaps because his phrasing made sense in light of the scene before us. "You can look at the wall to your left. It is about 24 feet high. Do you, can you see it? And then it continues, and becomes a fence." At the edge of a town in the valley below, both were clearly visible, the one beginning where the other ended.

"First of all, technically, what does it mean to build this fence? Whose land is this?" When one man responds, "Israelis," Ra'anan quickly corrects him: "Palestinian land." He points down into the valley:

> For instance, look to your right at the houses and look to your left, you can see olive trees—all these plantations of olive trees belong to Palestinians that probably live on the other side of the fence. Which means, if you want to go to your own plantation [note whom the "you" identifies the Jewish tourists with] or the land that was basically yours before the State of Israel was established, you need to ask permission from—and I'm talking now only in Arab eyes. Okay? I'm going to present the two sides of the story. The reality today that if I'm an Arab farmer today, I want to go to my plantation, I need to go through a security checkpoint because of the security fence that those Israelis built to me.
>
> If I'm going to ask these neighbors here behind us in Gilo, they will tell you that before this fence was built, thousands of Palestinians, in order to—who didn't get permission to go and work in Israel legally, they were going and flooding in those fields, and basically smuggling themselves into the Israeli territory and to work in Jerusalem. They needed the money, if you ask the Palestinian side. And, so what is this fence basically blocking?

"Illegals," one person says, evoking in a single word an entire American discourse on immigration.

"Palestinians," comes another response.

"No, what is the physical border creating? What can it prevent?" Greeted by a confused silence, Ra'anan supplies the desired response himself, shifting suddenly from his framing of Palestinians as laborers to a framing of Palestinians as attackers. "Suicide bombers," he says, pronouncing the second B as well as the first: "Over 200 people injured in Jerusalem.[8] . . . In many cases on buses. How does it work? Many people are coming with dynamite. A bus here takes children from Gilo, like our bus that stands there. . . . A suicide bomber goes here without the fence, gets on the bus, about 20 kids are being injured. So this is the Israeli side."

At this point, people start peppering Ra'anan with questions about things like the route of the wall, why Palestinians don't simply cross at places where it is incomplete, why it is a wall in some places and a fence in others, and how Israeli law defines the legal status of Palestinians living in Bethlehem. Ra'anan responds to each in turn, then fields a question from a woman, Marnie Spitulnik, who often showed an interest in the politics of the Middle East conflict.

"I have a question," Marnie says: "'Cause I remember when it went up, like the media like really portrayed, like, I mean, like, didn't it portray, like, a big part, like, the Palestinian side? Like, I feel like a lot of people sympathize with the Palestinians, like, you know, and that 'Ohhhh, and the children, they can't get to school' [her voice drips with affected sympathy], you know, and all this stuff. So how does it, like, work—"

Ra'anan cuts her off to shout at the stone throwers, who have finally drawn a connection between their sport and the iconic images of the Israeli-Palestinian conflict. In addition to throwing stones, they have begun playing with the word "intifada," referring to it as "the enchilada" and then pretending to place orders at a Mexican restaurant.

While I am puzzling over the meaning of this, Ra'anan turns back to Marnie, who "like-you-knows" her question to its conclusion. The guide responds, addressing the whole group and tripping over his words:

Guys, a good person will not—the media is a lot of times showing the Palestinian—you see those pictures of the old lady that is stopped at a checkpoint, the woman that is about to give birth and is stuck at a checkpoint in an ambulance. The reality is much more complex than that. First of all, I'm going to bring you back to the Israeli side. Israel decided on this fence as a one-sided action, as a matter of no choice. We said, "We don't have a partner. We want to stop the suicide bombers right now. We don't want to wait anymore until a peace process, this or that will happen." If you ask the people here in Gilo, they say, "I don't care about the Palestinian plantations. I want my son to get safe to the school." So this is one side, the Israeli side.

On the other side, you ask a Palestinian farmer and he says, "It's not me! I was just working in my farms. Some Hamas people came here and took over my house, started shooting from this area. I'm afraid of them. And now I can't even make the little money I was making as a farmer."

The conversation, which has lasted for 10 minutes, goes on for another 15. As it winds to a close, Ra'anan solicits people's opinions: "Okay, I want to ask you now, if you were the Israeli government, what would you do about this fence? Would you build it? Not build it?"

People murmur their responses. The loudest voices say, "Build it."

Then Ra'anan asks, "Anyone think that this fence is problematic?"

At this point, Ken Wurtzel, who had alternated between throwing stones and asking questions of Ra'anan speaks up: "I do. I only think it creates more tension. And the fact that there are still open parts, such as you said, this part right here, would give me, if I were a Palestinian, would give me more reason to just come through the open parts and have more bombings because of the other fence." When one of the North American staff members asks if his answer would be the same if the barrier were complete, Ken reinforces his position: "I think it will create a lot of tension when it is fully completed."

I am surprised, for Ken was one of those who just moments before had been joking about "the enchilada." I had assumed, wrongly, that this would have reflected a different politics.

As a means of representing the Israeli-Palestinian conflict, the visit to Gilo was brief but not simplistic. Its contradictions—characteristic of the tours' political work generally—complicate the task of the researcher seeking to explain how Israel experience programs construct understandings of the Israeli-Palestinian conflict. One analytic approach could be to subject the guide's narrative to a close reading, paying particular attention to the silencing of rival discourses.[9] For example, work in this vein might note that Ra'anan referred casually to Gilo as a "neighborhood. . . . in Israel." It would then point out that such language, precisely because it seems innocuous, reinforces an ideological stance, masking and thereby denying the fact that Israel's capture of the area in 1967 leads most of the world's governments to deem Gilo an "illegal settlement" on occupied territory. However, one need only consider the interaction at Gilo to understand why such an approach fails to do what it purports to do: namely, to explain how the trips effect the political socialization of their tourists.

First, the search for rival narratives in the silences of the official discourse presumes that it is *in these silences,* and not elsewhere, that the alternative points of view are to be found. This presumption stems from the supposition that official discourse is monolithic and intent on suppressing alternative views. Situations like those at Gilo, where the guide represented Palestinian perspectives explicitly and at length, belie this notion. To emphasize the silences in the face of evidence that rival narratives are officially voiced would misrepresent the nature of the enterprise, suggesting a discourse that is hermetically sealed and consistent rather than porous and contradictory. Silences do persist, but they take on a different meaning when they occur in a context where oppositional positions receive a hearing.

Second, and perhaps more damning, the close reading hangs on the guide's words much more than the tourists ever do. When Ra'anan struggles to capture the interest of people who would rather throw stones than listen, it becomes difficult to sustain the position that the political understandings the tourists come away with result from the nuances of the guide's speech—nuances revealed only when the researcher sits down to review the transcript. The close reading substitutes literary critique in place of an empirical analysis of the social processes people engage in to construct meaning. Focusing on precisely what the guide says, it would treat the stone throwing and the humor as tangential rather than constitutive. Meaning, in its implicit model, emerges solely through narrative, and then only through the voice of the guide. The politics of the trip are explained by what the representative of officialdom says, not what the tourists hear or do.

Even a cursory reflection on the interaction at Gilo suggests that the political meanings there were constructed by a variety of contradictory practices. No single narrative was voiced exclusively. Palestinian perspectives competed with Israeli ones in Ra'anan's presentation, and both were marked as plausible points of view. The tourists asked questions and supplied answers that reflected a range of political views. At the same time, however, the experience of the separation barrier was situated in a particular Israeli spatial and social framework. The Jewish tourists stood alone on a hilltop next to an empty Jewish neighborhood in Jerusalem and gazed down on the separation barrier miles away. With no Palestinians present to speak for themselves, their perspectives were filtered through the voice of the Israeli guide who took the prerogative of representing them. The encounter with the separation barrier was "made strange" in the Brechtian sense, both physically and emotionally distanced so that the "fence-slash-wall" became an object of detached consideration rather than a spark to ignite passions.

The encounter did prompt laughter, however. Humor, improvised collaboratively by tourists and guide, did more than create a feeling of safety by acknowledging people's anxieties about violence. Joking about the dangers of the Israeli-Palestinian conflict served the contradictory function of simultaneously reinforcing and subverting official messages about it. The laughter undermined both Zionist and Palestinian ideologies by denying their implicit demand to be taken seriously. At the same time, the laughter proceeded from a sense of security that reinforced Jewish nationalist claims, identified the tourists with the Israelis, and engaged them in an oppositional relationship with Palestinian nationalism. When Jewish diasporans gazed down on the West Bank and joked about the intifada and attacks on Jewish civilians, they implicitly denigrated the claims that led Palestinians to take up arms. They also defied the Palestinian militants, showing that, in spite of the power of their attacks to take lives and generate fear, Jews retained hegemony over Jerusalem and could stand there laughing at the attempts to wrest it from Israeli control.[10]

Against this backdrop, Ra'anan's attempts to offer Palestinian perspectives can be read as a subversion of the anti-Palestinian messages encoded in the humor. His concluding remarks highlight the degree to which this was a self-conscious effort on his part:

> You're going to hear about this fence and wall again and again in the news and here and there. . . . Just remember that the reality is pretty gray rather than black and white. There are innocent people on the Palestinian side that are totally being hurt because of this action of Israel. And Israel, it is a matter of no choice, and it is a temporary action. It is building this fence in order to try to reduce, not to fully seal or protect itself, from the Palestinian actions. Hopefully, as it [was] said, it is going to be only temporary, but we know that the temporary things are the most permanent ones. Unfortunately.

Ethics and the Educational Frame

In light of the common assumption, shared by proponents and detractors alike, that state- and–community-sponsored tours of Israel are a means of enlisting diaspora Jews as partisans in the Israeli-Palestinian conflict, Ra'anan's decision to represent Palestinian as well as Israeli perspectives might seem surprising. Should we not expect the guides to ignore Palestinian points of view, to present only the Israeli government's perspective, and to discourage tourists from expressing dissent? Why would Ra'anan act differently?

The answer is found by viewing guides not simply as ideological functionaries but as decision-making agents who engage in processes of ethical reasoning. Ra'anan and his colleagues wield significant power to structure an experience that shapes diasporans' understandings of homeland. From the perspective of a guide as a practitioner, the questions of how this power should be wielded, to what ends, and within what limits are practical matters that arise moment to moment and demand actual decisions. The ethical dimensions of these decisions arise, in part, from the power to represent and, in part, from the power to structure the social environment. To understand ways that Israelis, Palestinians, and their conflict are represented on tours like those sponsored by Taglit, one must examine how tour guides and other program officials frame the ethical issues involved.

We begin by observing that the ethical frame has finite boundaries. Some aspects of the tours are made the explicit focus of ethical contemplation by those running the programs. Other aspects, however, are not. The latter case includes situations in which potentially problematic issues are treated as unproblematic—a phenomenon that has been labeled "depoliticization."[11] This is a reasonable term, yet it can imply a greater degree of intentionality than is often warranted. Depoliticization is most thoroughly achieved when it occurs beneath the level of consciousness—that is, when guides and tour operators themselves do not recognize that political or ethical questions might even be at stake. Outsiders who do not wear the ideological blinders worn by Israel experience practitioners may be better able than the insiders to discern the political character of various programming decisions. For example, outsiders are probably better positioned to see that the decision to conduct cross-cultural peer-to-peer encounters with soldiers like Yoni Lefkovich rather than with civilian noncombatants implicitly glamorizes the military, frames Arabs as enemies, and reinforces the global media's portrayal of Israel primarily through a narrative of conflict. Yet insofar as guides and sponsors remain unaware of what their ideologies prevent them from seeing, they cannot make it the object of ethical reflection.

We can distinguish between a representation that is depoliticized because the presenters do not recognize its inherent political dimensions and one that is depoliticized by a conscious decision not to convey these political dimensions to the tourists.[12] The line between the two is not always clear, however. I was traveling once with a group on a bus ride from Tiberias to Jerusalem. The fastest route goes south down the Jordan Valley and makes a sharp right after Jericho to climb the hills that approach Jerusalem from the east. Most of the trip takes place in land that was controlled by Jordan before 1967. Because there is no "Welcome to Samaria" sign at the military checkpoint on the Jordan Valley road to mark the entrance into the West Bank, an inattentive tourist with no understanding of the significance of the checkpoint might not notice that he has passed out of Israel proper.

Daniel Chernoff was more attentive than most, however. The slowing of the bus before the concrete barriers woke him from his sleep. His head was resting on the window, and he looked out to see why we were stopping. Two rows in front of him, Keren, the British-born tour guide, was telling the bus driver that for the previous nights' activity, they had screened *Yossi and Jagger*, a film that had won international acclaim and comparison with *Brokeback Mountain* for its portrayal of a homosexual relationship between two soldiers in an Israel Defense Forces combat unit. "Eizo shtifat moach!" the guide exclaimed in Hebrew. "What brainwashing! To show them we are open," she scoffed.

Daniel called up to the guide: "Is this a checkpoint?"

Keren looked at him and responded nonchalantly, "Yes, it's a checkpoint," but offered no further details and turned back to her conversation.

"Is it normal to have a checkpoint on the highway?" Daniel prodded.

"It is, because Jordan is over there on the left and the West Bank is over there on the right."

Daniel asks where the West Bank is, and the guide responds, "Over those hills."

A few minutes later, she made a similar statement on the bus microphone: "We are riding through the Jordan Valley. Just a little bit over these hills, the West Bank, the Palestinian areas of A-1," she said, invoking the technical designation given in the Israeli-Palestinian Oslo Accords.

The guide was not being inaccurate in saying that the West Bank was just "over those hills," but it was not the full truth. The West Bank was at that moment just as much under the wheels of the bus that we were riding in. Had Keren not just privately disparaged the tour for the subtle politics of its decision to show *Yossi and Jagger*, even tossing in the pejorative "brainwashing," the term critics and educators alike use to express their conviction that the tours should be beholden to certain ethical standards? If she recognized the existence of an ethical framework governing her work, what, then, was the source of her reluctance to tell Daniel that the checkpoint marked our entry into the West Bank and to tell the tourists that they were themselves traveling through it?

I asked her about this privately in a subsequent meeting with her, in response to her request that I offer some constructive criticism of her performance. I had thought she was going to tell me that she was trying to avoid making the tourists fear for their safety, but she said nothing of the sort. Instead, she seemed perplexed by the notion that she had been anything less than forthright. She said that she explained things to the group exactly as she understands them. When she thinks of "the West Bank," she thinks of it as the areas controlled by the Palestinian Authority, not the areas like the Jordan Valley and Jericho road that are controlled by Israel and that she expects will be retained even after a peace accord is signed.

Reflecting on our exchange, I weighed the contradictions. On one hand, Keren displayed a desire to uphold standards of professionalism by seeking out criticism that could help her improve her performance, and to all appearances she took seriously the question of whether her representation of the tourists' actual location had wittingly or unwittingly misled them with regard to a politically loaded issue. On the other hand, her protestations notwithstanding, it is hard to believe that the guide was unaware that we had left Israel proper. Yet the fact that she did not inform the tourists of this did not stem from a general societal inability to recognize the inherent political dimensions of the issue. Nor did it appear to stem from the guide's conscious decision to mislead. I suspect it resulted from her ability as a partisan to remain willfully oblivious to that which she did not want to see and therefore could not see. Perhaps she could feel confident that she was being entirely forthcoming, even as she misled the tourists, because she had first misled herself.

At various points throughout their tours, even guides like Keren recognize that they have the ability to choose between alternative ways of representing a site, each of which has different implications for the political understandings that tourists will be crafting. It is at these moments that processes of ethical reasoning become increasingly relevant, especially when the choice is consciously made to convey depoliticized representations of issues whose political complications the guides themselves recognize. In making such a choice, guides do not typically perceive their decision to be dishonest. Sometimes they see it as a choice made between competing values. Take, for example, Israeli tour guides' decisions about representing Masada's mass suicide story. The political messages to be derived from the Masada story are fiercely contested in Israeli politics.[13] Guides are not unaware of this. Nevertheless, some who harbor reservations about the standard narratives of Masada hide these feelings of ambivalence from the tourists and present the story as if it were uncontested. When asked how they arrived at this decision, these guides responded that presenting their own personal views would be a breach of professional ethics or that shattering myths would undermine the more important mission of fighting Jewish assimilation in the diaspora. In both cases, processes of ethical reasoning led to a decision to portray the story as one that enjoyed a consensus of interpretation.[14]

Some who have criticized the politics of Israel experience programs have adopted the position that a primary ethical obligation should be to represent politicized terrains as politicized, in order to enable tourists to make informed decisions about contested issues.[15] Debate over this position occurs within the tours themselves, as the contrast between the above-mentioned guides' representations of Masada and Ra'anan's representation of the separation barrier suggests. The day before the visit to Gilo, Ra'anan and I discussed the question of representing politicized terrains as the rest of the group took a bathroom break and bought ice cream at a rest station somewhere between the Dead Sea and Jerusalem. "Knowing that anything that you say is going to be interpreted [differently] by different people, depending on where they're coming from [politically]," I asked, "how do you deal with this minefield?" His response:

> I just present the faaac—the facts, and I'm trying to, to present the facts as objectively as possible from both sides. Like, I will talk about the security fence, so I, I'm going to speak in two voices. . . . And I'm just going to introduce to them of, like, what is it to be a Jew that lives in Gilo, for instance, and suffer from the shooting there, and what is it to be a Palestinian that hasn't done anything and has to go through a checkpoint to go to his field every day. Once again, the message will be a mixed message, which is the reality that the reality here is not black or white, and everything has mutual influences, and we make compromises and choices that are sometimes hurtful for us and for other people. It's part of the life here.

Ra'anan is not exceptional. Many guides adopt such an approach at various points in their trips, though not necessarily at all points. There are guides like Keren, however, who consistently avoid representing multiple perspectives, often deliberately. This has produced criticism from the Taglit organization itself, whose educational guidelines call on the programs to "respect the integrity and sensibilities of participants and . . . not attempt to missionize." Taglit monitors for political bias by sending third-party compliance officers to observe every group and survey its members.[16] Tourists informally monitor for this as well. Their criticisms are usually expressed privately but sometimes burst forth into open dissent (chapter 6 in this volume). In one group's concluding discussion circle, a woman who had debated for much of her trip whether to publicly air her discontent, decided finally to vent her frustration, accusing the staff before the assembly of making "unnecessary . . . irrelevant . . . [and] underhanded comments" that "demoniz[ed] every, like, the Muslim population anywhere." She then adopted a more cautious tone:

I feel like there's a little bit of political propaganda and that it, I don't know, it oversimplifies some of the situation. . . . I support Israel, but I think you might support Israel even more if you really, like, if people really, like— and I really hope that everybody and, like, myself too, like, goes home and does, like, serious research and not just take everything on this trip as completely one-dimensional, because we really, I mean, have only got one side of the story.

A posttrip survey of 2,476 Birthright Israel alumni found a roughly even split between those who felt that the trip staff were "reluctant to say negative things about Israel" and those who felt that they were not.[17] There was a wider consensus that the guides generally avoided forcing their opinions on the tourists. When asked whether "there was too much 'preaching'" on the trip, 70% disagreed (37% strongly, 33% slightly) and 30% agreed (7% strongly, 23% slightly). Significantly, those who felt that their guides were preaching to them tended to give the guides lower overall ratings.[18]

Within diaspora Jewish homeland tour organizations, the desirability of using heavy-handed representational practices, such as strident declarations and systematic exclusion of opposing viewpoints, is—at the very least—contested. I believe it is fair to go further and say that tour guides, tourists, and program sponsors themselves generally view such an approach as undesirable and even antithetical to the tours' mission. And yet the tours' acknowledged purpose is to forge diasporic identification with the homeland. What, then, prevents these ends from justifying any means?

An important part of the answer rests in the discourse of education that frames the program and shapes the ways that those operating it understand their actions. Israel experience programs, it should be recalled, are the products of Jewish educational institutions. This shapes their personnel, policies, and philosophies. It is the reason that a statement of principles rooting the trips in Deweyan pedagogy can be written by a philosopher of education,[19] that Birthright Israel can circulate written "educational standards,"[20] and that a "Center for Jewish Learning" at Hillel can design curricula for the tours.[21] It is also the reason that a Birthright Israel guide can write a master's thesis in Jewish education focusing on the tours, raising in it the same question we are addressing here: "How can [ideology] be prevented from overwhelming the educational process, turning it into indoctrination?"[22]

This educational frame determines the ethical bounds within which Israel experience programs are conducted. It helps establish the trips' ideological standpoints and also serves to mask them. It provides a normative basis for thinking about acceptable and unacceptable uses of power. Finally, it grounds tour personnel in a moral community of fellow professionals whose standards of practice bear on the educators' own self-understandings and provide a yardstick with which they can judge themselves.[23]

In his Israel programs manifesto, Chazan argues that no trip that takes pedagogy seriously can remain ideologically neutral: "The good trip is rooted in a 'curriculum' which reflects an underlying philosophy or ideology. . . . [It] is not simply an 'itinerary' or schedule of events. It is a carefully-woven scenario which reflects a world-view."[24] Yet he writes as one informed by a Deweyan philosophy of education that values the growth of the individual learner beyond any particular content points in the curriculum. This leads Chazan to advocate an approach, reflective of established practice, that treats a diverse and contradiction-laden Israel as an opportunity for raising questions. The effect is to create space for a liberal critique from within a Zionist framework, but not a radical one based on delegitimization of the state's existence.[25] The assertion that Jews are a people with a right to self-determination in the land of Israel is the starting point of a conversation that can be especially vigorous. It remains, however, a bounded conversation. The Deweyan frame serves to draw attention away from the boundaries themselves and toward the character of the learning that occurs within them. Ethical thought is thus focused not on questioning the "underlying philosophy or ideology" but on ensuring that, within this framework, the educational process remains learner-centered, open-ended, and humanistic.

On a practical level, one of the key ethical dilemmas that emerges in this context stems from experiential education's insistence that knowledge is constructed holistically, without separating cognition from emotion. Interviews with guides are revealing. When asked about the goals they set for themselves when guiding diaspora Jewish tourists, they often speak of creating emotions: "I want them to love Israel," an American-born male guide says. "I mainly try to create an emotional connection on the tiyul between the sites and each person individually," says another who himself was born and raised in Israel. A female guide who had emigrated from South Africa declares, "On Taglit, they really want to stir the emotions, to create an emotional experience."[26]

In contrast to secular school settings, where the objects of study are stripped of emotion in order to allow their dispassionate consideration, the guides advance the classic model of *yedi'at ha'aretz,* where the objects of study are constructed to be emotionally resonant.[27] The context of learning also embeds the individual's creation of knowledge in social processes that have inherent emotional dimensions. Emotion serves on the tours as both a means and an end. This approach clashes sharply with a Western rationalist tradition that has seen no legitimate place for emotion in the educational enterprise. As a form of knowledge, emotion has been considered imprecise and subjective, hardly a path toward universal truth. As a means of instruction, it has been reviled as manipulative and predatory, appealing to base instinct and allowing it to trump reasoned judgment. Dewey's philosophy of experiential education, however, offers the theoretical basis for rejecting a strict dichotomization of emotion and cognition. Rather than being expunged from the educational process, emotion emerges as integral to the process of human learning. Learning occurs when the whole person is engaged. By framing the tours as a form of experiential education, Israel program theorists and practitioners legitimize their creation of emotion-inducing situations even as they create a framework for thinking about the ethical use of the power at their disposal. In thinking about their work in Deweyan terms, they are constrained by the humanistic agenda inherent in the Deweyan approach. This acts as a check, albeit imperfect, on the unbridled use of power. It does not indicate precisely where to draw the line, but it raises awareness of the dangers that attend the pedagogical use of emotion.

Ra'anan offers a good example of how a tour educator thinks through these issues, balancing the desire to convey a message against the ethical awareness that teachers have a responsibility to respect their students' integrity. This is all tempered by a recognition that the amount of power he actually holds is rather limited in the greater scheme of things:

> SK: I have heard other guides "take the hammer," you know. "Move here! This is our last stand!" You didn't do that. . . .
>
> RA'ANAN: That's me. That's me. Because I totally believe in that. I don't think that all the Jews should come to Israel. And in general, it starts way deeper than that, that I don't think that any person in this world can be told what to do or manipulated what to do. And I believe—and that's the strongest thing for me that comes from Judaism—the belief in the free choice of [what is good] for us.
>
> Of course, everything we do in education is sort of manipulation, and I think, and sometimes I'm struggling with myself to do some manipulation and for the group that I am working with. There is a very, there is a very limited amount that I am willing to do it against my personal beliefs.
>
> What I believe in, it doesn't matter. If I told them, "People, it happened, and the Jews suffered here, and the Holocaust, and

you have to come to Israel, and you have to be Jewish!" Will it work?! We make our own choices. Like if I'll preach to them, because of my preaching will they?

And that's why there is a very thin line between not giving any tools at all, so I am, my major job is, as I said, is asking questions and exposing, and saying—and this is going to be my final message to them—I say, "Listen, you got, you were born into it, you got this huge, amazing baggage of history, culture, and values, from what you were born into, and it's, the only thing I want to tell you, it's yours, that it's yours to choose and the only thing I'm going to ask you to do and I want you to do is not to drop it. And to keep asking the questions. And to carve your path, to find your path. But don't throw it [away]." That's what I—if there's going to be one manipulation or one message that I'm going to say, "Don't throw it away. Because you don't like the ultra-Orthodox?! Or these people, or that people, or that historical time period?! Don't throw the whole package. Like, 'Don't pour the water with the baby,' as we say in Hebrew."

Juxtapositions: A Day on the Golan Heights

If questions about the ethics of representation become especially visible at a place like Gilo, it is due in part to the structure of the visit there. The trip to Gilo was undertaken solely to address the politics of the separation barrier. Its boundedness in space and in time carved out an environment in which politics were considered in isolation. There, the tourist gaze was focused on the "wall-slash-fence," something that lent itself to being read almost exclusively in political terms.[28]

The venues in which understandings of the Arab-Israeli conflict are formed on diaspora Jewish tours are not limited to situations like these, however. Even more common are excursions that do not isolate politics but juxtapose them with other areas of focus (sometimes in an integrated manner, sometimes not). In situations like these, guides are relatively free to decide whether to ascribe political or apolitical meanings to the things they show. The ambiguous boundaries of the political are crucial to the diaspora tours' ability to serve as a medium of political socialization, as becomes clear from a consideration of a trip Ra'anan's group made to the Golan Heights, the plateau captured by Israel from Syria in 1967 and a battleground in the 1973 Yom Kippur War.

The day's itinerary indicates the diversity of experience that characterized the group's encounter with the Golan: a walk through a nature reserve, a visit to a biblical-era archaeological ruin, shoe shopping at a kibbutz factory outlet, R-rated ice breakers with the newly arrived Israeli soldiers, lunch in a town square, a tour of 1970s-era army bunkers overlooking the Syrian and Lebanese borders, a facilitated group discussion about land-for-peace and the future of the Golan, rafting on the Jordan River, an alcohol shopping spree, dinner at the kibbutz hotel, a daily wrap-up meeting, and a retired army officer's late night lecture on "the security situation in the North." To select any one as "the" representation of the Golan Heights would be misleading. The contested ground was as much the setting for a consideration of the Israeli-Syrian conflict as it was an environment for learning about nature as it was a playground for hedonistic 3-S tourism (sun, sea, and sex). Understandings of the Golan, and, more broadly, of Israel generally, were constructed not out of a crisp linear narrative but out of the tour's juxtapositions, intersections, and disjunctures.

Nowhere is the pastiche of meanings more evident in a concentrated time and place than in the walk through the Tel Dan Nature Reserve that begins the day. The sweet-smelling reserve, declared a "rainforest" by one effusive student, protects the Dan River, the largest of the three sources of the Jordan. Water figures prominently in the guide's discussion there of the significance of the Golan Heights, just as water is the centerpiece of our afternoon recreation when we strip to our bathing suits and climb, four by four, into the inflatable rafts that take us floating down the not-so-mighty Jordan. The theme first emerges, however, on the bus ride from our kibbutz hotel to the reserve.

Gidi, one of the North American staff people, takes the microphone and announces, "We're going to do an Israeli fact every day. And this is something that has been intriguing to most of you—why [do] your [Israeli] toilets have two handles?" He pauses for effect, then explains:

In Israel, water is a serious—water *shortage* is a serious issue. And so when you brush your teeth, you should really get in the habit to turn off the water tap. It's a really serious issue. And what they've done to accommodate for this—and I think it's actually a really brilliant idea that we should probably use in the U.S. as well—is that the toilets have either two buttons or two handles. The shorter handle [which flushes half the water in the tank] is if you do "Number One," and the longer handle [which flushes all the water] is for "Number Two." And sometimes they actually do have numbers on them and sometimes they even have pictures.

Although Gidi's joke is greeted by groans and mock laughter, in his light-hearted approach he has broached the idea that water is a serious matter, not to be taken for granted. The mundane, the toilet, has become an object of the tourist gaze and used to signify a theme of consequence. While the explicit message is that water shortage is a problem in Israel, the implicit message is that there is nothing in Israel that can be deemed insignificant. Even the toilet handles are implicated in matters of national import.[29] This blurring of the line between the consequential and quotidian has implications for understandings of the political situation.

When Ra'anan draws people's attention to water at the Tel Dan reserve, he, too, chooses to frame it as a matter of dire significance. We are listening to the percolating sound of mountain streams trickling over rounded stones as we breathe in the cool, damp air, but Ra'anan does not address the aesthetic appreciation of nature when explaining the "meaning" of the water around us. Thoreau's Walden Pond is not his chosen trope. Rather, he presents the water's relevance as strategic. It is bound up in the conflict with Syria over the Golan Heights. Whatever other meanings the nature reserve might have for us, Ra'anan teaches us to see it as a place of military significance.[30]

"Okay, where are we, and what is the theme of the day?" he asks at our first stop on the walk through the reserve. Surrounded by vegetation, we sit on log benches and rocks in a semicircle around Ra'anan, who stands in front of a burbling brook, map in hand: "The two major issues that we're going to be dealing with today are *security* and *water*. Okay?" The days are each structured around themes, per the approach recommended in Chazan's manifesto. Our itinerary lists today's theme as "Nature and Security in the Galilee and Golan."

He unfolds the laminated map, orients us in space by tracing our route from the airport the day before to our present location at the base of the Golan Heights, and points out the geographic features that will figure in his discussion: the Golan's location at the borders of Israel, Syria, and Lebanon; its great height relative to Israel's Jordan Valley below; the snowy peak of Mount Hermon, the tallest mountain in the region; and the water sources that flow down into the Sea of Galilee and the Jordan River. The orientation accomplished, he turns to his theme: "So, Mount Hermon, the Lebanese border, the sources of the Jordan River. How many major sources does the Jordan River have?"

"Three," comes the attentive response.

"Three. Good. We're next to the most important one of them, which is the Dan. The Dan provides half of the water for the Jordan River that flows all the way to the Sea of Galilee. And this is the major water source for Israel. So we're in a very strategic point from the aspect of the water consumption of Israel. Okay?"

To help the tourists "understand the complexity of the present," he goes on to provide a brief history of the British, French, and United Nations boundary drawing, which assigned the Golan Heights to Syria. Then he draws out some implications of this: "The Syrians are sitting above this valley, above the kibbutz that we are staying in, above many other kibbutzim and moshavim that are underneath them in the valley. . . . What are the Syrians doing? . . . For 19 years, from 1948 to 1967, the Syrians are sitting up there. Think Syrian. You don't like the Israelis. What can you do to them if you sit up there?"

People suggest ways that the Syrians might use the topographical advantage to attack Israelis in the Jordan Valley below. Ra'anan repeats their responses: "Shoot missiles, shoot on the kibbutzim from above. And another thing, if you look closely here"—he points to the map—"What flows here?"

"The sources of the Jordan," people respond, grasping where Ra'anan is taking the story.

The themes of the day, security and water, thus converge. Ra'anan affirms the response: "The sources of the Jordan. This one, the Dan was in Israeli hands. The two others, one of them started in Lebanon, and one of them was totally in Syrian control."

Then, Ra'anan asks them to again think as if they were Syrian policymakers hostile to Israel: "What can you do if you are a smart Syrian?" People assume the role, responding appropriately, and Ra'anan repeats their answers:

> Block the water. Try to dry out the Jordan River and through that dry out the Sea of Galilee, the major source of water for Israel. This is what the Syrians actually were trying to do. They were starting to dig a canal in the '60s. This one, the Dan, was in Israeli hands, so they couldn't do anything about it. But the two others, they wanted to divert the water from here through the Golan Heights, which was theirs, to pour it somewhere between Syria and [the Hashemite Kingdom of] Jordan. Which means basically to dry out the Jordan River. . . . Israel blasts the Syrian workers and stops this attempt. But, the water, and the security issue that they're bombing the Jewish settlements underneath them is one of the major reasons for Israel to open the frontier in the Golan Heights in the Six-Day War, which was in 1967. OK? Questions?

"How long was the Six-Day War?" someone jests.

"It's funny," Ra'anan replies with an ironic laugh: "Only in Israel, a war is six days, and we had the [1982 invasion of Lebanon called] 'Operation [for] the Safety of the Galilee,' which lasts three years—and actually 20 more years after that, when Israel stayed in Lebanon. An 'operation' is 20 years, and the 'war' is six days."

He then prepares the group to move on to the next stop in the Tel Dan reserve:

> Okay, if you understand this, you have enough foundation to deal with what we're going to discuss later. . . . Toward the end of the day we're going to have a discussion with the soldiers about recent issues, relevant issues, what can be done today, what should be done today with this area. . . . You ask any Syrian, "What's the situation, or what is your condition to make peace with Israel?" What would they tell you? "Give back the Golan Heights!" If I'm Syrian, I'm going to say, "This is mine! It was given to me by the United Nations legally. You conquered it from me." Okay? . . . And we're going to have to ask ourselves what are the, what are the outcomes of doing this and not doing it. . . . The most important water sources of Israel are here, basically responsible for a third of the water consumption of Israel, and strategic points, and I'm even putting aside the nice area and the national parks that we have here. Questions? Okay, so we're going to continue now.

As we wind our way through the trails, the conversations ignore Ra'anan's presentation. I speak with one student about her sorority. Laura, the North American staff person, discusses Japanese animé and college majors with another student. We collect around a giant pistachio tree on an outcropping that provides a view of the Golan Heights above and the valley below. Ra'anan orients us but then directs our gaze to the tree, which already has half a dozen people sitting on its branches. Water, security, and Syria drop out of the narrative entirely, to be replaced by a lesson in the connection between botany, the Hebrew language, and Israeli naming customs.

"This is one of the most popular natural trees in Israel, and I am going to [also show] you another," Ra'anan says, and then begins introducing the trees' names by asking, "How do you say 'God' in Hebrew?"

There are many names for God in Hebrew, and the ones that the students suggest are not those that Ra'anan is looking for. Eventually they arrive at the answer.

"El!" Ra'anan declares. "'El' is 'God' and the name of those trees—there are a few names of trees that preserved the name of God. This is one of them. It is called 'elah.' It is also a common name for a girl today in Israel, Elah. 'Elah' is a 'goddess.' If you want the botanic name it is *Pistacia atlantica*."

Ra'anan is speaking over the laughter of the group, because once he said that Elah is a popular girl's name, Laura leads her students in screams of "Ella! Elllllaaaaa!" The chatter around the joke does not mention *A Streetcar Named Desire*, but *Seinfeld*'s reference to it in the episode where Elaine, doped up on muscle relaxants, imitates Brando screaming "Stella!" With the Golan Heights in view, they are far removed from Israeli-Syrian politics and Hebrew naming customs alike, amusing themselves in a virtual reality that references a reference to a quotation from a film of a play.

Ra'anan concludes quickly, freeing the students to take pictures of their friends in the elah tree. He then leads us several meters down the path to an oak—"alon" in Hebrew, also incorporating the name "El," he says, and also a popular name for boys in Israel. He picks up an acorn and begins explaining the interesting symbiosis between plant and animal that enables the tree to reproduce:

Mice and rabbits are eating the acorns. . . . But if they eat the whole thing, nothing will last to create another tree, so the oak invented a nice mechanism. . . . The seed itself is, like, half tasty and half bitter, so the animals start eating, chew, chew, chew, and then it gets to the bitter part. It spits it out and then the important part of the seed is in the bitter part, so it opens for rain in order to go in, and a new oak can grow up.

Whether this is true or not, I do not know, but it is interesting, and I take him at his word.

As with the discussion of the names, Ra'anan blends culture with nature so that in learning about trees we also learn about Israeli society. He tells us that it is common for Israeli children to make Hanukah menorahs (candelabra) from the acorns. Then, with a smile, he adds that "troublemakers like to make [their teachers] crazy" by using the acorns as whistles. "Just take an acorn and try to—" he places an acorn to his lips and blows across it, making an ear-piercing shriek.

"It's Laura's mating call!" one of the men in the group jokes. People pick up acorns from the ground and try to produce the whistling sound. Most fail miserably, prompting much laughter.

When Ra'anan leads the group to the next stop, the theme again shifts, this time to archaeology and the Bible. In front of the restored ruins of an ancient stone wall, a student reads from a plaque on which a biblical passage referencing the place is inscribed. Ra'anan thanks her and elaborates:

> This is from the Book of Joshua. And we heard that one of the twelve [Israelite] tribes, the tribe of Dan, is coming here and conquering the city from someone. If you open the book of Joshua before that, when the twelve tribes inherit the land of Israel, you're going to hear that the tribe of Dan was settling in another place next to Jerusalem, and actually in the area of Tel Aviv today. By the way, until today, the whole metropolitan [area] of Tel Aviv is called *Gush Dan,* "the Dan area." Why did they move here?

"Because it's higher?" a woman offers, possibly thinking in terms of the earlier conversation about the strategic advantage of the high ground.

"Well," Ra'anan jokes, rejecting her response, "as we are going to be in Tel Aviv, you're going to see, you [won't] want to leave Tel Aviv so fast. But that's recent." Just as nature and culture intertwined in his discussion of the trees, the Israeli present and the scriptural past flow into one another. Ra'anan then provides the answer he had wanted to receive: "Someone pushed them from there. The Philistines.... They [the Danites] moved here and they conquered [this] city." The ruins, he said, date back 4,000 years.

We move on to the ruins of what were the city gates, where Ra'anan discusses the types of activities that would typically have taken place at the entrance to an ancient city: moneychanging, judicial proceedings, petitions to the king, and so on. He then speaks of the biblical references to two Israelite kings who ruled in the city of Dan—Jeroboam and Ahab— providing a brief summary of the Bible's historical narrative of the split of the Davidic kingdom into the Israelite north and the Judean south.

In the middle of his story, Ra'anan stops abruptly to ask about the veracity of the claims he is making: "How do we know, by the way? How will *you* know? Okay, *I'm* telling you, this is the city of Dan. How do *I* know? I read. Okay. How do *the archaeologists* know? What evidence can you have?" Step by step, he traces the knowledge claim back along the chain of authority and questions its basis: "How do you know that this is the city of Dan that is mentioned in the Bible?"

When a student suggests that the archaeological artifacts can serve as evidence, Ra'anan seizes on the response. "Okay, so you use the artifacts.... Here it's pretty easy because an inscription was found here. Someone was dedicating something to the 'goddess in Dan.'[31] So they actually give us the address of the place. Some other places, it's harder and you have to make assumptions and geographical connections. But here it's pretty trivial."

Insofar as contemporary Jewish claims to Israel rest in the notion of a homecoming to the nation's ancient birthplace, mentioning the archaeological confirmation of the biblical place name serves an important legitimizing function. Ra'anan never draws the connection explicitly, but the issue is clearly a matter of importance to him. He ends this part of the tour on the topic:

> There is a whole group of historians that claims that the House of David . . . did not exist. Here outside at this yard, an inscription was found that is today in the Israel Museum. And it said that some Syrian king from Aram said, "I defeated the king in Dan," this and this and this, "from the dynasty of Beit David [the House of David]." The first time outside of the Bible that we found an inscription that actually mentions King David. It was found outside here, okay? So it's a very important recent artifact that uses historians to claim against those who say that the House of King David did not even exist.

In other words, the scriptural-historical foundations of contemporary Jewish claims to sovereignty in Israel remain solid, in spite of efforts to challenge them.

Laura and Gidi, the North American staff, take charge of the group at the final stop. They conclude the visit to the Tel Dan Nature Reserve with a 10-minute orientation session to prepare the students for meeting the soldiers who will be joining their group. "They are your age," Laura tells them:

> They are 19, 20, 21. They are in the army, and we all know that Israelis have to serve in the army, right? Y'all are aware of this? So I just wanted to have a minute, or take a couple of moments to really think about what you want to get out of [the meeting]. I know some of you want a little smoochin' action. But others of you want to, like, really know what it's like to be an 18-year-old Israeli. Like it's completely different than what you do. Their focus is on securing the country and not, like, getting drunk. You know, I'm not knocking what your focus is. I fully support it.

The laughing students knew that she was sincere about this, and their faith in her support was not disappointed. Laura arranged that afternoon for the bus to stop at a rest stop where the students could buy alcohol to drink in their rooms later that night.[32]

As much as this extended description can convey a sense of the diversity of experience on the Tel Dan tour, it omits far more than it portrays. Even so, it better enables us to draw conclusions about the political work accomplished on these types of trips. Without suggesting that this is the sum total of what could be said on the topic, I want to highlight three aspects of the trip to Tel Dan that exemplify general processes by which diaspora tourism shapes understandings of war and conflict in the homeland: the politicization of the normal, the normalization of the political, and the decentering of the conflict narrative.

In the context of the trips, the politicization of the normal emerges from the semiotic character of tourism. Tourists gaze on sights as signifiers of broader meanings. The particular meanings that are signified, however, do not inhere in the objects of the tourist gaze but are imposed on them. A tour group of watershed managers considering the Dan River might come to a completely different understanding of what it "means" than would a group of religious pilgrims interested in its connections to scripture. Although the water at Tel Dan could be framed in any number of ways, Ra'anan chooses to represent its significance in military terms. It is presented as a strategic interest, the object of hostile enemy action, and a reason for going to war. The choice to frame objects of the tourist gaze in terms of the Arab-Israeli conflict is, in fact, a choice. Choices like this occur repeatedly on Taglit trips, when visiting forests, archaeological sites, shopping malls, and many other places. This recurrence helps establish the conflict as a primary interpretive frame, creating the expectation that things which elsewhere would be overlooked or considered in other terms will in Israel be seen as elements of the ongoing struggle between Jews and Arabs.

The effect of politicizing the normal is to normalize the political: that is, to portray Israel as a place where wartime mobilization is the natural state of existence. This is evident in Laura's words preparing the students to meet their Israeli peers, who not by chance just happen to be soldiers—people whose "focus," ostensibly, "is on securing the country and not, like, getting drunk." It is also evident in the way that Ra'anan's narrative of the conflict over the Golan Heights begins with the assumption that Israeli-Syrian hostility is the natural context against which the story should play out. Hence, his command to "think Syrian" obviously implies adopting the perspective of an enemy bent on harming Israel.

At the same time that these semiotic practices of tourism create an understanding of Israel as a country that is thoroughly defined by its conflict with its neighbors, other aspects of the tourist experience undermine such an understanding. The rapid juxtaposition of different sights and narratives reveal the conflict to be only one of many possible interpretive frames. The disjunctures between the formal program and the informal interactions are another aspect of tourism that help to decenter the Arab-Israeli conflict as the primary lens through which the country is viewed. In the visit to the Tel Dan Nature Reserve, tourists move from talking about the dispute with Syria to a discussion of Hebrew botanic nomenclature, to joking references to popular culture, to a nature lesson, to biblical archaeology—all while simultaneously incorporating picture taking, hiking, and side conversations about animé. If this is how the tourists form their understandings of the Golan Heights, what does the site end up meaning to them? Perhaps all we can say is that the meanings they ascribe to the Golan cannot be reduced solely to those related to the Israeli-Syrian conflict. The dynamics of tourism—with its juxtapositions and disjunctures—complicate any attempt to construct a single coherent narrative of place. Multiple meanings abound and inform one another.[33] Yet the decentering of the conflict narrative that results from this is itself a significant political achievement. For one, the multiple frameworks of interpretation establish a sense of normalcy and thereby depoliticize a hotly contested terrain. More important, they take an implicit ideological stand, challenging positions that claim that the sole proper way of understanding the country is through the lens of the Arab-Israeli conflict.

Speaking in Shades of Gray, Experiencing Israel in Technicolor

The power of diaspora homeland tourism to serve as a medium of political socialization rests largely in the fact that it operates not simply at the discursive level but deeply beneath it as well, through embodied, emotional, and interactional experience. Ideas and values are enacted in practice before they are raised to the level of consciousness, if ever. Because the tourists themselves often initiate these behaviors, such as, in the Israeli case, by flirting with soldiers or joking about the dangers of Palestinian attacks, the travelers tend to be more aware of their own feelings of agency than they are of the tours' structural features that facilitate and encourage their behaviors. The tourists' awareness that they retain control over their own actions and opinions is crucial to their willingness to listen with an open mind to the officially voiced political discourse. This serves as one of the incentives for guides to incorporate multiple perspectives into their representations, to avoid creating the impression that they are attempting to compel adherence to a party line.

None of this precludes the possibility that normative environments will emerge, either through the actions of the staff or of the tourists as a group. As noted in chapter 6, Taglit's consciousness-raising discussion circles foster a culture in which it becomes normative to assert that one's Jewish heritage is experienced as personally meaningful. Whether group norms make specific political positions unvoiceable is less clear. I have witnessed situations on the Israel trips in which facilitators set a tone that validated diverse opinions, just as I have witnessed group discussions where leading questions made clear that the staff had a sense of "right" and "wrong" answers. Participants' reactions to the latter situation varied. In some cases, would-be dissenters held their tongues. In others, they became more motivated to make their voices heard. On the diaspora Jewish homeland tours, the only area in which a normative political stance appears to be universally present is the one that could be deemed the most banal or the most consequential: the tours do not create a sympathetic space for a categorical delegitimization of Jewish national aspirations in the land of Israel. Beyond this common denominator, however, the political conversation on the tours tends to accommodate a diversity of opinion. There is no firm basis for proposing that the creation of a normative environment is the source of the tours' effectiveness as mechanisms of political socialization.

In this chapter, I examine the complexities of discourse and practice evident in the visits to Gilo and the Golan Heights in order to offer an alternative account of the politics of homeland tourism—one that is not hobbled by a portrayal of discourse as monolithic, a bias in favor of the verbal, a denial of the tourists' and tour guides' human agency, or a conception of ideology as a set of specific policy positions. In the account offered here, I acknowledge that guides vary in the ways they choose to represent politicized issues. More important, I address the questions raised by the observation that individual guides can weave open-ended narratives that represent multiple positions and that do not foreclose interpretive possibilities. In this account, I show that political messages are conveyed through nondiscursive practices, such as the rapid juxtapositions that decenter and normalize the Arab-Israeli conflict as an interpretive frame. No less important, I examine the complementary and contradictory ways that these relate to verbal discourse. I consider guides and tourists not as ideological functionaries or dupes but as thinking human beings. The guides and other program staff are theorized as moral actors engaged in ongoing, bounded processes of ethical decision-making. The tourists are considered not only as audiences consuming tourism through active, critical processes of meaning construction but also as coproducers of the touring experience. Likewise, I show that ideology operates here as it does in society generally: not by imposing specific positions but by quietly establishing the boundaries of legitimate disagreement.

With this in mind, let me reconsider the questions asked at the outset of this chapter: How do the tours convincingly represent the complexities of the Middle East conflict while remaining true to their goal of shaping an Israel-oriented diasporic Jewish identity? How do the actions of the program sponsors, tour guides, and tourists interact to create an understanding of the Arab-Israeli conflict in a manner that fosters identification with the Israeli side, even as it recognizes that all involved are critical consumers of information, aware of rival perspectives, and capable of evaluating any claims that are made?

For a host of reasons—sincere sentiment among guides, professional ethics, educational philosophies, a desire to maintain credibility in the face of critical consumers of knowledge—Arab perspectives often complement Israeli ones in the presentations of tour guides like Ra'anan, who lead diaspora Jews on Zionist homeland tours. The attempts at verbal balance help tourists understand the debates of Middle East politics from a variety of perspectives. This may foster an appreciation for the complexity of the issues at stake and may also generate a sympathetic understanding for people on both sides of the conflict. Because they are exposed to a variety of viewpoints and can evaluate them for themselves, tourists generally relate to the tours as a form of education. The trips' credibility as education depends in large measure on the tourists' perceptions that they are being exposed to multiple points of view and are free to use this information to form their own opinions.

The significance of the presence of Palestinian and Syrian perspectives on tours of places like Gilo and the Golan Heights is not only that they are present, and not only that Israeli tour guides express them sincerely, but that they are *voiced*. That is, when Palestinian and Syrian perspectives are conveyed, they are conveyed only through discourse, not through experience. Some groups' itineraries do include a presentation by a Palestinian speaker, but, more typically, such voices are absent and any Arab perspectives that are conveyed are mediated through the voice of Israelis who assume the right to speak for them. Ra'anan speaks of the Palestinian farmer who cannot get to his olive trees because of the separation barrier, but this is related from a distance through an Israeli intermediary. The tourists do not go into the West Bank for a mifgash encounter with the farmer's family and a tour of the place where the barrier blocks the path to the plantation.

Contrast this with the holistic manner through which Israeli perspectives are conveyed. Palestine and Syria are discussed, but Israel is experienced— cognitively and emotionally, personally and interpersonally, with the senses and the body fully engaged. Tourists do not only hear an Israeli tour guide explain Israeli positions regarding the conflict. They encounter these ideas through narrative techniques that go beyond straight exposition: story and song, video and museum. They engage with them on an emotional level, as Ra'anan's group did at a military cemetery in Jerusalem. There, the guide orchestrated a participant-led graveside reading of a heartrending children's story written by a bereaved mother to memorialize her son who was killed in battle. The tourists also come to understand Israeli perspectives through their many informal interactions with Israelis. The soldiers who are combatants in the conflict join the tour groups, weave cloth friendship bracelets as gifts for the diaspora visitors, and write them emails about their wartime experiences.

The tourists' immersion in an Israeli frame of reference penetrates to the deepest level of the experience of space and the structuring of time. In the name of protecting them against terrorist attacks, freedom of movement is limited, leisure time is constrained, and pubs are declared off limits, as is the Arab market in Jerusalem. The need for protection is accepted, even demanded, by the tourists.[34] Indeed, in the presence and absence of fear, whose triggers can be learned so thoroughly that the bodily reactions they generate become instinctive, we can discern the habitus that locates tourists squarely in an Israeli frame of reference.[35] For the tourists, the Israeli soldiers are never objects of fear, not as they would be if the tourists encountered them from the perspective of Palestinians. Rather, it is the specter of the Palestinian attacker that generates apprehension, questions about safety, and calls home to reassure parents.

Fear appears to be prompted more by the Arabs who are imagined than the Arabs who are actually present in the flesh. In part, this is due to the controlled circumstances in which Arabs are encountered. Typically, and in contrast to the way that many of the Israeli Jews are met, Arabs are encountered in planned meetings where they are presented as objects of the tourist gaze. The Bedouin who host groups in their tents serve as specimens of "authentic" Bedouin culture (similar to the representation of ultraorthodox Jews). The Druze, loyal to the state and serving in its army, attest to Israeli multiculturalism. In the rare occasions when tour groups meet Palestinians, the encounters tend to be framed exclusively in terms of the Israeli-Palestinian conflict, with the Palestinian interlocutors serving as representatives of "the other side." Only the Israeli-Arab hotel workers are encountered informally, but their service position tends to render them invisible to tourists' eyes.

By virtue of their particular combination of discursive and experiential learning, diaspora Jewish tours of Israel are able to expose travelers to Arab perspectives on the Middle East conflict and yet still foster identification with the Israeli side. At the level of verbal discourse about the conflict, the tours hold the potential to readily acknowledge complexities, rival points of view, and the lack of a monopoly on truth and righteousness on either side of the political divide. Often, this potential is realized, but not always. Even in this most balanced of scenarios, however, when the discourse paints both Israelis and Arabs in shades of gray, the *experience* of Israel, and Israel alone, occurs in 3-D Technicolor with Surround Sound. Palestinian and Syrian perspectives may be understood and appreciated intellectually, but they cannot command the authority of emotion and firsthand knowledge that is produced by the immersive experience in Israel.

Were we to presume a mutually exclusive dichotomy between sympathies for the two sides in the Israeli-Palestinian conflict, we would be forced to argue that the pro-Zionist political socialization that occurs on the trips is inherently and inevitably antagonistic to Palestinian nationalist claims. We need not be bound by such dichotomous thinking. Indeed, we have identified representational practices on the tours that may help the tourists themselves escape the trap of seeing the conflict as a zero-sum game. By decoupling discursive and experiential representations, the tours are able to incorporate sympathetic portrayals of Palestinian perspectives into a decidedly pro-Zionist framework. They can acknowledge and even affirm Palestinian viewpoints without fear of undermining feelings of attachment to Israel, because whereas the former are being generated discursively, the latter are also being supported by a wealth of experiences that engage the travelers' hearts, minds, and bodies. From the tourists' vantage point, as the connection to Israel comes to transcend the particular framework of the Arab-Israeli conflict, and as emotional attachments therefore become more robust, the travelers gain an increasing ability to think about the conflict in *both-and* rather than *either-or* terms. Sympathy for Palestinians and critiques of Israeli policies need not entail disaffection but can exist comfortably alongside a deep attachment to the country.

The dynamic need not foster sympathy for Palestinians, however. It can also accomplish precisely the opposite and may even be more likely to do so. One effect of tourism's juxtapositions, as noted, is to decenter the Arab-Israeli conflict as a lens through which Israel is viewed. By virtue of their diversity and their immersive character, the tours' experiential aspects also reinforce an awareness that Israel is a multifaceted society that cannot be reduced to the conflict with its neighbors. No such awareness emerges with regard to Palestinians. Represented solely through an Israeli-mediated verbal discourse that focuses on the clash between two peoples claiming the same land, Palestinians come to be understood only as actors in the conflict. Even the ability of the Jewish tours to acknowledge that the conflict is painted in shades of gray and that Arab perspectives have a certain legitimacy may work to Israeli advantage and Palestinian disadvantage. The combination—an Israel that is experienced as complex and that is seen as capable of acknowledging its enemy's point of view—makes any narrative of innocent Palestinian victims versus malevolent Israeli aggressors appear simplistic, if not disingenuous. Further, this unsubtle narrative is made an implicit foil against which Israeli perspectives can be contrasted as being marked by liberal open-mindedness and reasoned moderation. On the tours, only Israeli narratives are shown as possessing an ability to recognize that all is not black and white, that there is legitimacy in the Other's point of view, that the situation is fraught with moral ambiguity, and that the conflict is a tragedy, not a morality tale. It is perhaps the greatest irony and greatest political success of the tours that in those instances when they attempt to acknowledge the legitimacy of Palestinian perspectives, these very attempts serve to delegitimize the most strident anti-Zionist positions.

To explain how diaspora Jewish tours to Israel shape travelers' understandings of the Arab-Israeli conflict, I have sought in this chapter to move beyond the discursive level to address interpersonal, emotional, and embodied dimensions of tourists' experience. Likewise, a thorough accounting of tourism's role in shaping diasporic identities will require a consideration of the intersecting knowledge practices that tourists employ to develop understandings of the homeland and their relationship to it. In the remainder of this volume I explore these, beginning with the semiotic practices that are at the heart of the tourist gaze.

4

Consuming Place

An ancient teaching warns that one should not begin studying the Zohar, the central text of the kabbalah, until one reaches 40 years. Any earlier would invite misunderstanding and court madness. Touring once with Birthright Israel in the the city of Safed, where the Jewish mystical tradition achieved its fullest refinement, none of us, save for our 47-year-old guide, had reached the age for unlocking the Zohar's mysteries. Nor, to the best of my knowledge, were any of us—guide included—versed in the mystical practices that might gain us some privileged knowledge of the Divine. We did, however, have command of the tourist practices that offered some knowledge of place, and if Safed was at first a mystery to us, its otherness was far less radical than that of the kabbalists' God. We as tourists could make some meaning of Safed, and in the process, we could position ourselves as diaspora Jews in a particular relationship to the city, to Israel, and to Jewish culture.

That we were strangers to Safed was evident in the facts of our arrival. We came there from elsewhere. A kibbutz hotel about a half hour's drive north, close to Israel's northern border with Lebanon, served as our temporary residence for that leg of the trip. In the morning, before the clouds had burned off, we had left it and driven to Safed on a private tour bus that was our true home away from home, the only space that was consistently ours for the duration of our stay. Of the 40 or so people on the bus, none of us, not even the tour guide, Michael, could claim ongoing involvement in the life of the city. His use of the microphone to share with us interesting facts about Safed, however, positioned him as the knowledgeable insider on whom our ability to understand the city depended. Safed has no traffic lights, only traffic circles, he told us. It was an economic center during the Ottoman period. It has a large textile industry. No one engaged in any independent fact checking, and I chose to hold my tongue when later the limits of the guide's knowledge became clear to me.

Whatever inklings of outsiderness our approach to the city had given us, we became painfully aware of it immediately on our arrival to Safed when, for some unknown reason, we were denied access to the bathrooms at City Hall. In Hebrew cadences that grew louder and more fervent, Michael argued on our behalf with the building's security guard. His tour groups had never been turned away before, he insisted, using all of his imposing 250-pound, six-foot-two-inch frame to make his point. But the guard held his ground. Standing across the street by a small, decommissioned "Davidka" cannon from the 1948 Independence War, we watched as the guard granted entry to locals. Our status in the 28,000-person town was such, however, that finding a place to go to the bathroom became the major challenge of the morning. Later, after the guide encouraged us to follow the local custom of spitting on the wall of a prominent mystic's house (said to ward off the evil eye), one member of the group decided to empty his bladder on the side of a collapsed building. Some found restrooms in local eateries, while others ended up having to wait several hours until we had left the city and had driven to a highway rest stop.

Not all places were closed to us, however. On city streets, in centuries-old synagogues, in souvenir shops, art galleries, and restaurants we gained some access to Safed. Through sightseeing, storytelling, shopping, and eating, we constructed understandings of the windswept mountaintop city.

As our tour bus climbed the winding road to Safed, which Michael referred to by its Hebrew name, Tzfat, the American-born guide flitted from topic to topic on the microphone. He pointed out a large army base with its commanding view of the surrounding region, explained that the name Tzfat derives from the Hebrew word meaning "to view," and directed our gaze to the Sea of Galilee which had become visible in the distance below. He spoke about the threat that Hezbollah missiles could pose to Safed. He told us of the neighboring town of Rosh Pinah and surprised us with a story about a nearby spa whose specialty massage is "a therapeutic treatment while snakes slither across your body." Eventually, however, he relegated everything he had told us to secondary importance: "But Tzfat, of course, what is important for us today, what we're going to be marking, what we're gonna be talking about, is that it's the third most holy city in all of Judaism . . . because of its connection to the mysticism, the Jewish mysticism."

To the extent that Safed was represented as a city of Jewish mysticism, this was accomplished not by any direct experience of the kabbalah. We did not pore over the text of the Zohar, meditate on divine names, or engage in any other practices for achieving ecstatic communion with the Divine. Instead, a collaboration between locals and visitors ascribed this meaning to the city through the production and consumption of multiple, interlocking signifiers of the mystical tradition.

Mysticism in present-day Safed is as much a part of the city's tourist economy as the city's tourist economy is a part of it. They are not merely overlapping fields; they have thoroughly interpenetrated one another. On our late morning tour of the city, we experienced this and contributed to it in many different ways. One of our first stops was the Sephardic Ari Synagogue, named for the great kabbalist Rabbi Isaac Luria who helped lead the flowering of Jewish mysticism in 16th-century Safed that gave the city its reputation. The synagogue is a functioning house of worship, but it is also set up to accommodate a steady flow of tourists whose donations are an important source of revenue. Visitors typically use the space not to pray but to sightsee. We were no exception, using the site as an architectural gem to be appreciated aesthetically, as a springboard for talking about the kabbalah and its practitioners, and as a venue for taking a group photograph and socializing with one another.

We began in the synagogue courtyard where Carla, one of our two American staff members, read an apocryphal story with mystical overtones (and political undertones) about a Palestinian Muslim who came to Safed and embraced Judaism after discovering through a series of unlikely coincidences that he was actually the descendent of one of Luria's colleagues. Michael then rose to tell us another story of strange coincidences, this time tied directly to the synagogue itself:

> When you see the *bamah*, [the raised central pulpit] where we read the Torah scroll from . . . you'll see a hole in it. In the 1948 war one of the bombs fell over here, from the Arabs. And while they [the Jews in the synagogue] were in the midst of prayer . . . just as they bend over and they say, you know, "We bow down before God," . . . just then . . . the bomb landed and a piece of shrapnel flew in and busted a hole in the *bamah*. . . . A miracle they call it. And that, too, is a place of pilgrimage.[1]

With these stories in mind (or perhaps already out of mind), we entered the synagogue. We admired the architecture, joked about a piece of matzoh in a glass box on the wall ("In case of Passover, break glass"), dropped coins in the donation box, and exited—all in less than a quarter of the time than we had spent outside sitting in the courtyard. On our heels came another tour group streaming in for their five minutes.

We walked along the winding streets outside. Michael directed our gaze not to the clothing stores and cafés but to the graffiti scrawled across their limestone outer walls. "The Messiah is here! Where are you?" he read, his voice booming and full of energy. Even the walls, he implied, testified to the culture of ecstatic religion that Safed was said to embody:

> Man! I tell ya! . . . It almost sounds like a Bible-thumpin' evangelistic Christian preacher-pastor on TV, right? From the South. Right? "The Messiah is here, where are you?" And they talk about it for an hour and people get excited, and they start screaming. Well . . . you may not experience that kind of enthusiasm in your Judaism, but there are a lot of people in this country and around the world that do.

It was not only through Michael's guiding—his choice of sites and his editorial decisions to frame them in particular ways—that the representation of Safed as a city of Jewish mysticism was accomplished. We spent as much time in Safed away from the guide as with him. Even after he had sent us off on our own to shop and eat, we continued to engage in an encounter with a "city of mysticism." The nature of this self-directed encounter, confined to Safed's tourist district, was largely continuous with the one orchestrated by Michael.[2]

Both with the guide and on our own, one of our primary modes of encountering Safed as a kabbalistic city was as consumers. Safed's tourism industry can be said to center on the commodification of mysticism. Signifiers of la vie mystique could be consumed visually at the synagogues-cum-museums. They could also be purchased in tourist shops in the form of amulets and charms, glowing candles, and religious wear inscribed with kabbalistic phrases. Some of my traveling companions seemed aware of Safed's urban brand even before we began our tour. As we waited by the decommissioned cannon across from the city hall, a college junior named Tori Fischman told me that she planned to buy a "flowy skirt and a *hamsa*," or hand-of-God amulet.

"How do you know that you can get those here?" I asked.

Safed seems "free and flowy," she said. Besides, she had friends who had bought these when they had visited here. Tori was not the only one who bought a hamsa that morning.

The commodification of mysticism was not solely a function of the goods available for purchase. Beyond any material objects that might be acquired, what we were consuming in Safed's tourist district was primarily an "experience" that involved sights, smells, tastes, sounds, conversations, activities, and more. Together, these encouraged us to imagine that we were interacting with the contemporary bearers of Safed's mystical tradition. We wandered along stone alleyways and through an appropriately orientalized covered market, entering small galleries where painters, weavers, and scribes created ritual objects and religious art. Some of the artists and shopkeepers were women in long sleeves, headscarves, and the same type of "flowy" dresses Tori was looking to buy. Others were bearded men in loose cotton shirts and white knit skullcaps, more similar to the large kufis worn by observant Muslims than to the small disc-like yarmulkes perched atop heads in American Jewish synagogues. The dress, male and female alike, suggested a fusion of Jewish orthodoxy with 1960s counterculture. Of course, not all the artists dressed as devout Jews or as leftover hippies. Regardless, the strong presence of artists in Safed's tourist district reinforced the city's image as a place of mystical retreat. It did so by playing on the cultural trope of bohemia as a place where people come to renounce material concerns and pursue a life of art and truth.[3]

The owner of a local restaurant and kabbalah reading room suggested as much when a middle-aged husband and wife from California asked if they could convince him to come back with them and open a restaurant in the United States. Not Taglit participants, they stood next to a small group of us in a stone alleyway, eating a frozen green sherbet made of plants that the Israeli chef playfully suggested may or may not have had consciousness-altering properties. He bantered with them from behind a streetside counter, lined with round wooden platters, bowls of spices, and a brass Bedouin coffee pot. As he talked, he ladled batter into two small cast iron frying pans. "Lahuhe," the sign above him read, a Yemenite pizza made with tomato, hyssop, and an egg cracked on top. He had spent some time living in New York and had been successful there, he told them in a high-pitched, accented English. But why go back? Life was better in Safed. Dressed in a sleeveless gray pinstripe robe worn over a loosely belted ankle-length white tunic with an embroidered yoke, and wearing a brown velvet brocade kufi on his head, the lahuhe chef hummed a hassidic prayer melody as he worked. The music was familiar to me—Rabbi Shlomo Carlebach's jaunty tune to the Sabbath hymn, "El Adon": "God Is Master of All His Works." Black sidelocks that reached to the end of his long beard swayed as he moved. Hamsas and pictures of rabbis adorned the walls. The refrigerator behind him was covered with bumper stickers all bearing the same mystical expression, "Na nach nachma nachman meuman," a mantra said to have been revealed by the spirit of the 18th-century hassidic master, Rebbe Nachman of Breslov. Near the low tables in the adjoining room, kabbalistic literature lined the display racks. It was an iconic performance on a perfectly set stage, and it made the 20-minute wait for the meal a pleasure in itself. In truth, the 20 sheqels (about $5.50) were not being spent for the lahuhe alone, but for the entire atmosphere that the chef created around it. We photographed him, photographed the tableau, photographed ourselves eating the lahuhe. This was not just a consumption of food but a consumption of experience.

The mountaintop views and winding alleys, the synagogue sanctuaries and studio galleries, the pious artists and singing chefs, the souvenir amulets and flowing robes, the messianic graffiti and kabbalistic bumper stickers, the miraculous stories and recited mantras—all were elements in a set of iconic representations that pointed to one another to depict Safed as a city of Jewish mysticism.[4] There were other parts of Safed that did not speak to this image of the city. We even saw some of them. But they were less useful to us, because we were engaged in the enterprise Jonathan Culler was referring to when he wrote, "To see the world is to grasp each culture as a series of signs of itself."[5] We were tourists, and our goal was to understand Safed as distinctively "Safedian." We accomplished this as tourists do, by treating the city as a theater of thematically coherent signifiers that testified to a unique local culture.

Writ large, this is the way tourists on Israel experience programs approach the country as a whole, scouring the homeland for symbols that attest to its uniqueness as a Jewish space. The tours enact a form of diasporic engagement with Israel that is built not on religious observance, political action, or philanthropic contributions but on symbolic consumption. The state is a symbol and a container for symbols of which the diasporans are the consumers. Trip organizers have attempted to harness tourism's engagement of people in a semiotic relationship with place by asserting control over the meanings that are ascribed to Israel.[6] But even as they seek to accomplish this by thematizing the trip itineraries and the tour guides' presentations, representations of Israel emerge in other ways that are rooted more in the tours' structure than in their content.

In this chapter, I delve into this semiotic dimension of tourism, examining how the acts of ascribing meaning to Israel end up mapping culture onto place and place onto culture. I consider how structural elements of tourism, including sight-marker transformations, semiotics of difference, and themed environments all contribute to the territorialization of Jewishness in Israel and to the creation of a consumption-based form of diasporic engagement with the ethnic homeland.

Symbolic Encounters in the Borderzone

Perhaps more than most cities, Safed can accommodate a wandering Jew. Its reputation as a center of mystical contemplation brings it a steady stream of religious seekers and has spawned a cottage industry of proselytizing programs that, for months on end, generously provide room, board, work, spiritual instruction, and caring community. In most ways, however, Safed is a city like any other. Locals and quasilocals have their places to go and things to do. Outsiders have no set places of their own to hang their hats and spend their days. With little familiarity with the urban geography and few if any contacts, outsiders are not integrated into the temporal and spatial routines of the locals. They may not even speak the language. How then, are they ever able to encounter the city?

Writ large, this question is one that Jewish organizations have contemplated as they have sought to cultivate nation-state-oriented diasporic identities. In spite of the rhetorical trope of "homeland," Israel is precisely not "home" for Jews living elsewhere, at least not in any individual sense. The very foreignness of this would-be homeland deprives most diaspora Jews of the basic cultural competencies and social capital necessary to effect a quick immersion on their own.

In the face of such barriers, tourism seems an obvious bridge. For one, it solves the problem of physical absence by drawing on an existing infrastructure for bringing visitors from abroad. This infrastructure also solves the problem of being a stranger in a strange land by accommodating the visitors during their stay and structuring their use of time while they are there. Israel's tourism industry provides travelers with homes away from home (in the form of hotel rooms, private tour buses, and the like). It also enables them to access and use certain public and private spaces. The social space created by this infrastructure is neither a tourist "bubble," hermetically sealed off from Israeli life, nor a complete penetration into every nook and cranny of residents' daily existence. Rather, it is what anthropologist Edward Bruner calls a "touristic borderzone," a social space that is very much a part of local life and that is structured as a meeting site where visitors and some categories of locals come together to interact.[7]

In this borderzone, tourists behave according to routines that are structured to enable outsiders to make use of local spaces. These clichéd tourist activities are familiar to us all. They involve ascribing meaning to the place through sightseeing and other applications of the tourist gaze, participating in leisure activities that engage the body and its senses, and consuming other commercially available goods and services. Of course, there is often overlap among the three types of activities, particularly because the tourist gaze is often applied when engaging in the other two. For instance, visitors to the Negev Desert enjoy camel rides around Bedouin tourist tents, not only because they provide a novel (though somewhat painful) physical experience but also because they play into orientialist fantasies that would imagine Israel as part of an exotic world of Arabian Nights. The camels emblazoned on souvenir t-shirts also represent the country in this manner.

To those seeking to foster diasporic Jewish connections with the State of Israel, tourism is especially attractive because its key practice, the tourist gaze, engages people in an active process of ascribing meaning to place. Insofar as this process can be directed to privilege some meanings over others, tourism becomes a deployable medium. In Israel experience programs, a variety of interested parties—government, community organizations, educators, and even private-sector businesses—intervene to assert control over meanings ascribed to sites and thereby to influence the ways that diaspora Jewish tourists come to understand the country that claims to be a national homeland for them, too. By setting up Israel as an object of symbolic consumption for gazing tourists, the homeland tours engage non-Israeli Jews in an essentially semiotic relationship with the nation-state. To the extent that they are successful, these diaspora-building projects foster a symbolic identification with Israel as a foundation on which pro-ethnic actions and relationships can then be built.

Place Differentiation

Homeland tourism finds much of its justification in the assertion that a nation-state is a different type of ethnic space than that in which diasporans live. It is precisely this difference that makes the homeland worthy as a destination and valuable as a resource for diaspora-building projects. When diasporans are taken on a tour of a homeland, they are promised an encounter with facets of ethnic culture and history that are said to be unavailable to them where they live, or available only in attenuated, adulterated, or otherwise altered forms. The sponsors of homeland tours hope to use the cultural resources of the nation-state to invigorate an ethnic consciousness that is at once diasporic and homeland-oriented.

Having promised difference, sponsors of diaspora homeland trips must then deliver. They must place this difference on display. For Israel experience tours, this requirement entails more than simply highlighting things that would distinguish Israel from other places around the world. Their diaspora-building mission necessitates that the travel programs represent Israel as a different type of Jewish space from those in which diaspora Jews exist.

In research on tourism, place differentiation is typically understood through the lens of economics. It is a central element of any strategy of tourism development, addressing the fundamental question, "Why come here, rather than go someplace else?" Among the contradictions of globalization is that the increased homogeneity of places has led cities, regions, and countries to try to differentiate themselves in order to compete for tourist dollars. One of the primary strategies for place differentiation is the identification, development, and promotion of potentially distinguishing aspects of local culture.[8] This tends to reduce complex places to a "series of formulaic images" that serve as "both an attraction for potential tourists and as a cultural framework for authenticating the tourist's experience once they arrive."[9] Predictability is a key desideratum in the tourist economy. Places should conform to expectations, lest travelers be disappointed and not return.

Place differentiation in the context of diaspora homeland tourism is not primarily an economic strategy, however, but a political one that both precedes the tourist economy and intersects with it. The claim that places have inherent attachments to peoples and cultures is certainly an economic move that lies at the core of place-branding strategies. Yet before this was recognized by businesses and civic boosters, it was already a key political assertion of nationalism. Vis-à-vis diasporic spaces, the assertion of a homeland's distinctiveness rests on claims of an essentialized relationship between a space, a people, and a culture. Only in a homeland are these three imagined to overlap perfectly.[10] In homeland tourism, the economic and political imperatives of place differentiation converge. An industry that is structured to produce and display place difference is mobilized to accomplish the nationalist work of representing a country as a unique ethnic space, a homeland that is different from ethnic spaces elsewhere in the world.

Sites and Themes

In the printed itinerary, our visit to Safed was given a title, "The Spiritual Search." The entire day's program, in fact, was listed under the thematic heading, "Jewish Searching." This was apparently intended to suggest some conceptual coherence to what was actually a disparate set of activities. The itinerary also presented themes for the tour's other days: Day Six presented our visit to Tel Aviv as an encounter with the "First Hebrew City." The visit to the Holocaust memorial museum Yad Vashem and the military cemetery at Mount Herzl took place on the day devoted to "Memory and Renewal." "Day Nine—The Struggle for Survival" included a hike to the top of Masada and what, in the context of the theme, could only be seen as a non sequitur or as a reward for a hard-earned victory: mud treatments at a Dead Sea spa.

In the thematization of individual attractions and of different days of the tour we see evidence of a systemic effort to assert control over the meanings that are used to differentiate Israel and its sites from diasporic spaces. Taglit-Birthright Israel has gone as far as to codify this as Educational Standard 3.02 (rev. 2001): "In developing their programs, Trip Organizers are encouraged to use a thematic approach."[11] Theming, in this sense, refers not to the use of unifying motifs in the built environments of symbol-laden commercial spaces (such as one finds in Disneyworld and the Hard Rock Cafe),[12] but to the weaving of site narratives with coherent storylines that converge on a common message. (Theming in the Disneyesque sense is addressed later in this chapter.) The use of themed site narratives follows the well-established principle in the Israel experience program field that itineraries should be conceived of as curricula.[13] Rather than leave decisions about the representation of sites solely to the idiosyncratic and possibly ad hoc choices of tour guides, this crucial power is assigned first to educational policymakers who can wield it strategically to serve the tour's overall diaspora-building goals. The key effect of this rationalization of control is to allow for what in pedagogy is called "backward design."[14] Instead of starting with a list of popular sites and then attempting to figure out how these can be invested with relevant meaning, program designers can begin with a set of curricular themes and proceed to identify sites that might be useful for representing them.

Of course, educators' rationalized control over the itinerary is never fully realized. Among the contradictions inherent in the medium is that tourism is simultaneously semiotic, spatial, and embodied. Each one of these dimensions competes with the others as governing principles for itinerary development. Thematic coherence may prescribe that a trip to Masada be followed immediately by a trip to Yavneh to contrast opposite choices made by two very different groups of ancient Jews facing destruction at the hands of the Romans.[15] But the drive to Yavneh would take several hours. The Dead Sea is less readily made to speak to themes raised on a trip to Masada, but it has the advantage of proximity.[16] It also has the advantage of allowing for some recuperation in its spas, a welcome relief after what can be a difficult mountain hike under a sweltering desert sun. The balancing act that itinerary planners and tour guides must engage in is captured nicely in the words of Clare Goldwater, a leader in Israel experience education. Even though her own scholarship emphasizes the power of theming,[17] when I asked her in a 2005 interview how she planned the tours that she led, she called my attention to "the element of logistics, which is no less important":

How many hours are you going to be out in the sun? When are you going to have a swimming break? And what's your pacing level? And where are the bathrooms? And how old are the people? I worked a lot with family groups in the summer. You have to stop to swim every single day. You just have to with kids. . . . It doesn't matter how fabulous the site is, you just have to stop to go swimming. So those kinds of things . . . are no less important, and if you don't do them then you end up sacrificing everything.[18]

Still, theming is a crucial and consciously applied element of itinerary planning, and its use to achieve some measure of backward design sheds light on the particular character of Israel experience itineraries. Many Birthright Israel groups visiting the Sea of Galilee will spend time in a 100-year-old kibbutz cemetery unknown outside of Israel. By contrast, they will never set foot on the famous Mount of Beatitudes, where according to Christian tradition, Jesus delivered his Sermon on the Mount. Nor will they take in another of Israel's major tourist destinations, the seaside Church of Loaves and Fishes, which believers say marks the site where Jesus performed a miracle of feeding 5,000 followers. Although it may seem an obvious point, it bears stating that tours like Taglit are intended not to show Israel (an impossible task in any case because every representation is by nature selective) but to show "Israel," a tailored depiction for a targeted audience intended to accomplish defined identity-related goals.

Visits to Christian sites are not necessarily antithetical to these goals. Some Israel experience groups do go to see such places, and talented educators sometimes integrate them into theme-driven curricula by portraying them as indicators of Israeli diversity or religious tolerance or Roman-era Jewish history. However, in the greater scheme of things, the kibbutz cemetery where some of the Zionist movement's early pioneers are buried can be more easily used to represent the key diaspora-building theme of passionate Jewish commitment to the land of Israel. When program planners are allocating precious time slots on a relatively brief itinerary, the choice to see the cemetery and skip the mount is an easy one.

In theory, the themes associated with individual sites should tie into a "larger meta-narrative, which connects and synthesizes the disparate pieces of information into a single unified story that can make sense of the whole experience."[19] Birthright Israel's educational guidelines hint in this direction, requiring trip providers to represent Israel as a "modern Jewish society" that reflects "core ideas and values . . . of Jewish life" and that embodies what program organizers call "the narrative of the Jewish people." Clues about the content of this narrative can be found by considering the list of places Birthright Israel insists be included on the itinerary: the Western Wall, an ancient Jewish historical site such as Masada, a site related to early Zionist history such as Independence Hall, a Holocaust-related site such as Yad Vashem, and a "state national site" such as the Mount Herzl military cemetery.[20] Observers of Taglit and other Israel experience programs have argued that, in practice, the core metanarrative is that of ashes-to-redemption, in which the modern State of Israel is represented as the resurrection and restoration of the Jewish people after a 2,000-year exile whose persecutions culminated in the slaughter of six million. A symbol of the Jewish will to live, it is also represented as an answer to what are said to be ongoing threats to Jewish survival, such as antisemitism, assimilation, and loss of ethno-religious identity in diaspora.[21]

The choice of themes and the relative ease of using Israeli sites to convey them should hardly come as a surprise. Diaspora Jewish tours are not creations ex nihilo. Rather, they operate in ideological and touristic fields whose meanings are constrained and often overdetermined. Israel experience planners draw on and reinforce understandings of Israel that the local tourism industry and the government have already configured into built environments and commodified for consumption. For example, Masada, a pilgrimage site that Zionists had been using to meditate on themes of threat and survival since the early 1940s, became a centerpiece of diaspora Jewish homeland tours after the state invested significant sums in the 1960s to pave roads to the isolated fortress, excavate and reconstruct its archaeological treasures, and develop a modern visitors' center with a cable car to the summit.[22] When place meanings are underdetermined, such as in Tel Aviv and Eilat, the representational work of tour guides becomes more challenging and the efforts at theming appear more manifestly contrived.[23]

In the move from "site-driven" itinerary planning to "theme-driven" planning,[24] we see a recognition among Israel experience programmers that tourism involves the ascription of meaning to place and an awareness that it is possible to exert some control over the semiotic processes that ascribe meaning. Still, the intentions that curriculum designers write into printed itineraries must be realized in practice, and it is here that guides play a crucial role.

It is by now a commonplace in tourism studies that sites become sights (i.e., tourist attractions) not by any property inherent in them but by socially structured practices that mark them as gazeworthy. In his seminal book, *The Tourist*, Dean MacCannell developed this very Durkheimian notion by decomposing into its constituent stages the transformation of unmarked sites into marked attractions. This process of "site sacralization" first distinguishes something as a potential attraction by *naming* it and then differentiates it further by placing it on display (*elevation*) and by setting boundaries around it to protect and enhance it (*framing*).[25] While elevation and framing may include alterations to built environments, such as the post-1967 clearing of buildings to create a plaza in front of the Western Wall, they are simultaneously practices of symbolic boundary construction that are accomplished by establishing discourses that proclaim a site's distinction and shape the ways it is seen.

To illustrate the process, consider how our tour guide Michael transformed an unremarkable wall in Safed into a tourist attraction and thereby represented the city as a place of ecstatic Judaism, a place where one might embark on "The Spiritual Search."[26] Before we had even stepped off the bus in Safed, Michael had named the category of site we would be seeing, saying, "While you're in Tzfat, we're going to see a lot of mystic symbols written on walls, graffiti spray-painted by ultra-Orthodox [Jews]." Tours of graffitied walls in other cities might be situated in discourses of urban blight or urban art, but not here, at least not in this instance. Michael's naming—"mystic symbols written on walls"—located Safed's graffiti in an entirely different universe of meaning.

Having named the sites, Michael, still on the bus, immediately began setting them up for display through verbal instructions that would direct our gaze. "Keep your eyes open" for the graffitied walls, he told us. On the streets, he elevated specific walls as gazeworthy by having us come to a full stop and face them, standing at a reasonable distance that would allow us to see the wall writings clearly. At the first such wall, he began his verbal marking of the site by naming the inscription, which was spray-painted in gold and blue Hebrew letters. "Na nach nachma nachman meuman," he read. The words of this inscription were themselves elevated and framed by being made the object of a verbal performance that interpreted them: "A reference to Nachmanides. Okay?" Although substantively this explanation was both incomplete (who was Nachmanides?) and inaccurate (the phrase is actually a reference to Rabbi Nachman of Breslov), structurally, it advanced the transformation of an ordinary wall into a tourist attraction.

Michael elaborated further: "And [the people who write this phrase] believe that if the entire world were to say this one statement at the same time, 'Na [nach] nachma nachman meuman,' okay, if we all said it at one time, the Messiah would come." In Michael's transformation of common graffiti into a sight worth seeing was contained an implicit, but clear, message: because the graffiti's inscription signified Jewish messianism, the graffiti's presence on the wall signified the existence in Safed of a subpopulation of Jewish messianists whose religious fervor plays a role in the city's public culture.

Someone shouted, "Let's do it!" and Michael said, "All right. On three. Those people who want to say it. 'Na [nach] nachma nachman meuman.'" Our ritualized performance before this messianist graffiti served to further elevate it as an attraction. It also engaged us as coproducers of the mysticism-themed representation of Safed. Guided by Michael, we used the graffitied wall synecdochically, as a part that stands for its whole. We selected one small piece of Safed, elevated it to the status of tourist attraction, situated it in a discursive frame centered on Jewish mysticism, and arrived through this at a representation of the broader city of which the graffitied wall was a part. As the wall testified for Safed, so Safed testified, in turn, for Israel. As this process of looking at parts to signify wholes was repeated day after day, site after site, a sometimes coherent and sometimes contradictory representation of the country was built up through the accumulated meanings of many layers of synecdoche. At the most basic level, the meaning making that was occurring by the graffitied wall was simply an act of arranging various signifiers and signifieds into relationships with one another. Gestures and sounds that elicited shared meanings in people's minds were associated with markings on a wall, first to denote meaning (What does the graffiti say? "Na nach nachman"), then to connote it (What does the graffiti mean? "The Messiah would come"). In this way, our acts of tourism in Safed created signs, in semioticians' sense of the word—meaningful unions of a signifier and a signified.

To draw out the implications of this, we can look to MacCannell's general semiotic of tourism, which specifies the relationship between visual fields, or *sights*, and the information about them, or, in MacCannell's terms, *markers*. In his elegant formulation, a tourist attraction (sign) is the meaningful unity of a marker (signifier) with its sight (signified). As MacCannell notes, however, the interchangeability of signifier and signified is a basic principle of semiotics. We might just as easily speak of the sight as the signifier and the marker as signified.[27] We would be on firm empirical ground if we did.

On our spring morning in that Galilean hilltop city, representations of Safed and mysticism swirled around and around each other in a dance whose partners kept switching lead. By using discussions about Jewish mysticism as signifying markers to interpret the novel sights before us, Michael helped establish (or reinforce) a link between the place and the discourse. This provided us with cultural tools that we could draw on to read Safed's sights for ourselves as signifiers of an entire cultural field of Jewish mysticism.[28] As we thought of mysticism we could imagine Safed, and as we thought of Safed we could imagine mysticism. Each, in turn, became a sight as the other became its marker.

This "sight-marker transformation"[29] is one of the crucial practices that diaspora tourism uses to differentiate the homeland as a place whose relationship to the ethnic culture is intrinsic. Cultural elements that transcend place (e.g., "Jewish mysticism") are territorialized as signifying markers to inscribe meaning on the geographies of Israel (e.g., Safed). In the transformation from sight to marker and marker to sight, the geographies of Israel come to represent these elements of Jewish culture, but in distinctly place-bound ways. This ends up creating a semiotic field in which a national homeland and a place-transcending transnational culture are positioned as mutually referencing objects of tourist contemplation that can be encountered together by traveling to the homeland and engaging its physical spaces as symbols. This dual inscription of Jewish cultural meanings onto Israeli spaces and vice versa is structurally rooted in the core dynamics of the tourist gaze. It is mobilized to powerful effect when tour educators use themed itineraries to represent Israel as a place whose sights offer opportunities for sustained reflection about core questions of Jewish existence.

Semiotic of Diasporic Difference

In their advocacy of theming, tour planners have approached the representation of Israel primarily as a matter of specifying the meanings that are to be ascribed to the country. What is less understood is that both the representations of Israel and the tourists' understandings of the country emerge not only through tourism's thematic *content* but also through its semiotic *dynamics*. It will not do merely to say that tour educators make Israel meaningful by making ideologically informed choices to privilege certain interpretive schema over others. This is true, but it misses the point. One could easily sit at home reading Leon Uris's novel *Exodus* and encounter a similar ideological narrative of place. Sightseeing, however, is a situated practice and it is this—not the ideological discourses that exist prior to and independent of tourism—that we need to account for if we are to make sense of diaspora homeland travel.

We have seen already that tourists' awareness of Israel as a bearer of Jewish meanings is rooted in the dynamics of sight-marker transformations that turn signified places into signifying symbols. There are also other ways in which tourism structures symbolic engagements that specifically inform the construction of diasporic relationships to place. One involves a *semiotic of difference*. Another involves *consumption of themed environments*.

Regarding the first, we begin with a self-evident principle: sights are worth seeing because of their distinctive features. To speak here of "distinction" implies that the tourist gaze positions its objects relationally in a field of contrasts.[30] Some tourist encounters, Urry points out, involve seeing objects that are differentiated by being one of a kind. Others establish contrast by showing "unfamiliar aspects of what had previously been thought of as familiar." Still others accomplish this by showing ordinary activities being "undertaken in unusual contexts."[31] We could extend the list, but the various forms of difference will always reduce to one or more of the following three: absolute difference, difference within similarity, and similarity within difference.

When people tour internationally, a primary field of contrast emerges from the juxtaposition of the foreign country with home. In diaspora tourism, another layer is superimposed, contrasting the ethnic space of the homeland with the ethnic spaces outside of it. The contrast may be implicit or explicit, but its existence is assured because it is structurally rooted in tourism's relational construction of sightworthiness. Not only is diaspora homeland tourism premised on the notion of a difference between homeland and diaspora lands, it actively differentiates the two by engaging diasporans in repeated acts of comparison and contrast. The meanings that are ascribed to the homeland also help construct travelers' understandings of the places from which they came.

In Israel experience travel, the semiotic of difference guides tourists' gazes toward aspects of Israeli Jewish culture that seem notable for their differences (again, of the three forms mentioned above) from the Jewish culture travelers know from home. Understandings of Israel emerge as much from these structurally rooted contrasts as they do from program organizers' explicit efforts to represent Israel in particular ways. To a large degree, specific lines of contrast proceed from an overarching distinction between Jewishness as a minority subculture outside of Israel and a majority culture in it. Viewed in terms of the semiotic of difference that they mobilize, the diaspora tours of Israel can be said to foster a representation of the Jewish homeland as a place where Jewishness is, among many other things, indigenous, public, collective, embattled, empowered, and consequential.[32]

Indigenous Jewishness

The notion that Israel is distinguished among Jewish spaces as a site of Jewish origins and foundational history does not begin with tourism, of course. Tourism does engage people in practices that affirm this key tenet of Jewish religion and Zionist ideology, however. In framing places like the Temple Mount and the Valley of the Shadow of Death as sightworthy because of their "one-of-a-kind" character (i.e., their "authenticity" in the sense of being "original, as opposed to a copy"),[33] tourism differentiates this stretch of land as the one that is *actually* referred to in the biblical narrative.

Taglit's tourists commonly spoke of Israel in terms that highlighted its uniqueness as a site of ancient Jewish roots: "When [the tour guide] mentioned that Abraham and Isaac and David were part of the history of the city," one person said during a visit to Jerusalem, "it felt like it was everything I was taught as a kid coming to life. This is where Judaism really happened— beyond any textbook."

This interpretive frame was made all the more powerful by a landscape that appeared "authentic" in a second sense, meaning that it achieved "historical verisimilitude" that was "credible and convincing."[34] In other words, the landscape conformed to expectations of what a "Land of the Bible" should look like. In fact, the Judean Desert looked so much like a film set for a cast-of-thousands Panavision epic that, on scanning the scenery, one tourist commented, "I can see Moses leading the Jewish people through the desert here." In the Bible's telling, Moses never actually crossed over into the land of Israel, but this made little difference. The tourist gaze had the power to give wings to the imagination.

Public Jewishness

Outside of Israel, the public cultures of the countries where Jews live may incorporate some Jewish symbolism in certain times and places. By and large, however, diaspora Jews are accustomed to seeing Jewish symbols predominate only in their minority subcultural spaces. When these Jews visit Israel, the ubiquitous presence of Jewish cultural elements in Israel's public square becomes one of the most striking features in the field of contrasts that differentiates Israel from the tourists' diasporic spaces. Hebrew signage is one of the most commented-on aspects of this, as exemplified by an exchange that took place next to me one morning at breakfast.

"Everything is special when it's written in Hebrew," Patricia Portnoy told Tori, who was sitting across from her at the table in the dining room of our Jerusalem hotel.

Tori Fischman, of the flowy skirts, smiled mischievously and replied with a skeptic's delight: "So the bathrooms here are special because they are in Hebrew?"

Patricia stood her ground but joined in the joke. "Yes! They are *special.*" She enunciated the last word, and then added with feigned earnestness, a broad smile, and an emphatic nod of the head: "They are Special Bathrooms."

Collective Jewishness

Participants in diaspora tours of Israel are brought into repeated encounters with Israelis whose professional roles engage them in working on behalf of other Jews. They meet Jewish educators, government officials, soldiers, social welfare workers, and more. In addition, they tour sites associated with the government (e.g., Independence Hall), army (e.g., the armored corps memorial museum at Latrun), kibbutz movement, and social service sector. All of these represent Israel as a collective Jewish project in which Jews act together for the greater good of the Jewish people. The role of the state in collective Jewish action is especially evident and stands in sharp contrast to diaspora Jewish environments where the state does not assume this role and, instead, relegates it to the volunteer sector.

Embattled Jewishness

One of the ironies of diaspora Jewish tours to Israel is that they represent the Jewish homeland as a site of danger where the threat of physical attack is possibly greater than that which tourists face as Jews in the places where they live. The tours accomplish this not only through their discourse about Israel and their display of its war- and terrorism-related sites, but, even more important, through a program structure that is pervaded by attention-grabbing security measures that tour operators highlight rather than mask. These security measures turn the tourist gaze inward so that the touring process itself becomes a form of representation. They also add valence to the portrayal of Israel as a dangerous place for Jews by creating a vicarious experience of Israeli Jewishness in which tourists are helped to feel themselves to be potential targets of Arab or Islamist violence. This is not to say that Jews in diaspora are not targets of such violence. The wave of attacks on Jews and Jewish institutions in Europe and South America during the 2009 war in Gaza reflects the globalization of anti-Israeli violence that represents an increasing danger for Jews worldwide.[35] It is, however, in the omnipresence of security-mindedness and in the perceived immanence of the threat of attack that the tours foster a contrast between Jewish life inside and outside of Israel.

In creating a sense among tourists that they are potential targets by virtue of being Jews in an embattled Jewish state, tour operators engage in a complicated balancing act that simultaneously tries to convey the contradictory messages "We are in danger" and "You are safe." The rifle-toting medic-guards that accompany the tour groups wherever they go, the restrictions on wandering freely during free time, the avoidance of populated Palestinian areas, the requests that travelers call parents to calm their fears after news reports of any attack, and the assurances about the trip's security arrangements given during the first night's orientation—all serve to amplify a sense of underlying threat even as they try to diffuse concerns about its immanence.

The contradictory message was given explicit voice, for example, by one guide on the first afternoon of a Taglit tour. The group had reassembled after dispersing to shop in the tourist district of a northern town. When one person asked how big Israel was, the guide said "rinky dink" and then drew attention to its borders:

> We're surrounded, all right? . . . Five Arab nations are surrounding us completely. . . . We're gonna be very, very close to our borders. Same border we were attacked from, by the way, in 2006. By the way, there were missiles that landed *here*. . . . But . . . we're in a safe, safe time, and no one should be worried about any of that.

Empowered Jewishness

Representations of Israel as a site of danger are countered by representations of it as a site of safety. It is a commonplace to say that the Yad Vashem Holocaust memorial frames the necessity of a sovereign Jewish state by portraying diaspora as a site of collective powerlessness. There are few other locations in Israel where the contrast is so overtly made. Most of the time, the tours draw the contrast implicitly by bringing tourists into contact with symbols of Jewish empowerment that are generally absent in diaspora. The most obvious of these are the soldiers and their guns, which are universally commented on and frequently photographed. The encounter with Jewish hard power is generally celebrated by tour staff and tourists alike as a source of pride and confidence. Israel experience programs for high school students often bring tourists to army bases for weeklong simulations of Israel Defense Forces basic training. On Taglit, one of the most popular souvenirs in recent years has been an olive green t-shirt emblazoned with the words "Israel Defense Forces" in Hebrew and English over the army logo. The symbols of public and collective Jewishness discussed above also contribute to a representation of Israel as a country whose Jewish majority is capable of wielding for themselves all the power that a state can bring to bear.

Consequential Jewishness

When Laura, the American staff person on Ra'anan's bus, told her students that the life of an 18-year-old Israeli is "completely different than what you do. Their focus is on securing the country and not, like, getting drunk" (chapter 3 in this volume), she was giving exaggerated voice to a contrast that emerges repeatedly throughout the trips: Jewishness—as a status, an identity, and a culture—is observed to have consequences in Israeli society that it does not have in diaspora communities. Meeting Israeli peers in uniform is one reminder of this. Others emerge from the encounters with the public, collective, and empowered dimensions of Jewishness in Israel. The turning of the tourist gaze onto ideologically and religiously committed Jews—particularly immigrants from Western countries, settlers in the Golan Heights, mystics in Safed, and Orthodox Jews in Jerusalem—also helps to differentiate Israel as a place where Jewishness will not be made invisible or relegated to irrelevance. Just as Laura's contrast of drunk American students with self-sacrificing Israeli soldiers implied a moral hierarchy, so, too, do the encounters with passionately committed Jews serve as morally loaded reminders that an invisible and irrelevant Jewishness remains a viable option for tourists living in countries of the West.

Not out of the Israeli environment alone but out of its imagined juxtaposition with diasporic spaces emerges this conversation about Jewishness centered on dichotomous categories like indigenousness versus foreignness and consequentiality versus irrelevance. The ability to define the terms of the conversation is part of the socializing power of homeland tourism. Yet, in this conversation there will always remain room for movement, maneuverability, and renegotiation. The initial understandings of diaspora that emerge by applying a semiotic of difference on the tour are only opening gambits.

Consumption of Themed Environments

When diaspora Jews debate the merits or shortcomings of using Israel experience programs to foster ties with Israel, the phrase "a Jewish Disneyland" often makes its way into the conversation as shorthand for everything that is supposedly frivolous and inauthentic in tourism.[36] Critics and boosters alike agree that the programs should strive to make the encounter with Israel more than just a trip to a Jewish Disneyland (whatever that may mean). They argue only over whether the programs actually aim to do so and whether they succeed if and when they try. Invoked to accuse rather than analyze, the charge and the insistent denials it elicits tell us less about the trips than about the anxieties that attend tourism's deployment in "serious" matters.

If we refrain from using the term "Disneyland" to denigrate and instead use it to indicate a model of structuring tourist and consumer experience, we will find that the term's application in relation to Israel experience programs is both more and less apt than those who casually invoke it would suspect. Mark Gottdiener has observed that Disney's model of themed entertainment is increasingly coming to characterize many types of consumer spaces, more and more of which are incorporating overarching symbolic motifs into their built environments. Labeling this trend, "The Theming of America," he identifies the economic logic driving it: it has become so easy to mass-produce quality goods at low cost that many businesses see more potential to grow profits not by competing to further lower their already low production costs but by developing unique brand images and charging a premium for them. The shift away from trading on a product's use-value to trading on its sign-value emerged with the onset of brand marketing in the 1870s and was certainly evident in the early postwar era when advertisers sold automobiles as a ticket to freedom and not simply as a means of transportation.[37] By the last quarter of the 20th century, however, the realization that economic value could inhere even more in a product's image than in its functionality led increasingly to the Disneyesque theming of restaurants (e.g., Hard Rock Cafe, Planet Hollywood, NASCAR Cafe and Sports Grille, Rainforest Cafe), retail outlets (e.g., Niketown, American Girl Place, Hollister, the Apple Store), and even entire shopping malls and corporate offices. These fabricated fantasy environments attract customers by serving as destinations in their own right. They enable businesses to charge higher prices than nonthemed competitors because in addition to the consumption of food, goods, and services, they sell the consumption of symbols and the consumption of a novel experience.[38]

Diaspora Jewish tours of Israel occur today against this backdrop of a leisure culture that makes increasing use of themed consumer entertainment environments. Like many other local tourism industries, Israel's has commodified several thematic motifs to differentiate the country and position it as a desirable tourist destination. Yet it would misrepresent the nature of Israeli theming to say that "Land of the Bible," "Mediterranean Paradise," "Arabian Desert," and "Modern Jewish Homeland" are to Israel what Fantasyland, Tomorrowland, Adventureland, and Frontierland are to Disney. As Gottdiener takes pains to note, not all instances of theming are Disneyesque. What distinguishes Disney's approach is its use of theming as an economic strategy that is deliberately applied in "controlled commercial spaces

practices to be enacted is also reflected in the tourists' other major form of engagement with this religious tradition: the purchase of its material culture. A far, far greater number of people in Michael's group bought yarmulkes, hamsas, mezuzahs, and other Judaica as gifts and souvenirs than attended Sabbath morning services. Their overwhelming preference at that moment for a Judaism of purchase over a Judaism of prayer did not simply reflect the tour group's demographics—young and largely secular, with minimal Jewish education. It also reflected the fundamentally consumerist context of modern tourism in which they were operating.

Diaspora of Consumers

The semiotic dynamics of tourism in a themed environment enact a diasporic relationship to homeland that is built around consumption, positioning Jewish tourists as consumers, and positioning Israel as a marketplace of consumable signifiers of itself and of Jewish heritage generally. In a discussion circle held immediately after the visit to Safed, Tanya Muller, a member of Michael's group, hinted at the centrality of symbolic consumption: "Compared to the U.S. . . . if you drive around here, everything has something special, like when you go . . . somewhere completely random and it shows up that, you know, just everything seems to have meaning, *everywhere*, which is so much different than [home]." Tanya imagined that this was an inherent feature of Israel, but, in fact, the experience of Israel as a place where "everything seems to have meaning, *everywhere*" is purely a function of how she was consuming the space as a tourist, supported, of course, by a tour guide and tourism industry that did a thorough job in marking Israel's sites and turning them into signifiers. Still the ease with which she misrecognized the nature of the dynamic and imagined that a product of her own and others' actions was really a product of some fundamental characteristic that inheres in the physical place is crucial to the understandings of the homeland that emerge from the tours. Homeland trips fetishize their destinations and in so doing imbue them with a symbolic power that can live on after the tour.

It is not only the generic perception of Israel as a meaning-laden environment that is significant here. The specific meanings that the country is understood to bear have crucial implications for the formation of diasporic identities. For one, these meanings enter into the field of comparisons and contrasts that help construct understandings of diaspora against an Israeli foil. Meaning is relational, such that if the other end of the pair were changed from Israel to, say, Poland or the Lower East Side, the relational field would be entirely changed and so, too, therefore, would the specific meaning-generating comparisons and contrasts that would be made. The choice to use Israel as the opposite pole in the relationship bestows on it a certain power to set the terms that inform the way travelers reflect on the meanings of their diaspora. (By the same token, tourists' understandings of Israel are inevitably shaped by their use of their own countries of residence as points of reference. One expects that American, Argentine, and Russian Jewish tourists will each see a different Israel by virtue of their different national lenses.)

Second, Israel experience tours territorialize Jewish heritage, placing Jewish culture and Israeli geography in a semiotic loop so that understandings of one inform understandings of the other, and so that attachments to one evoke attachments to the other. Tour sponsors hope that the encounter with Israel will translate later into heightened interest in Jewish cultural life in diaspora. But just as equally, the encounter can have the effect of reshaping the meanings travelers ascribe to their Jewish cultural involvements there, recasting them as performances of a transnational identification with the homeland.

There is reason to believe that the primary effects of homeland tours lie more in the second category than in the first, altering the meanings that program alumni ascribe to their Jewish involvements rather than increasing their propensity to participate in them—a qualitative change rather than a quantitative one.[42] Although some of the Birthright Israel participants do become intensely active in Jewish communal life after the trips, the trips generally have not met with unbridled success in translating the enthusiasm they generate into sustained, broad-based participation in Jewish religious, organizational, and political organizations. Even though I am doubly wary of offering a post hoc explanation of a nonfinding, I would venture a proposition that is consistent with the data and therefore at least plausible: the tours primarily engage people in—and hence prepare people for—a narrow Jewish behavioral paradigm centered on consumption. Between this form of practice and those that constitute the core repertoires undertaken in synagogue sanctuaries, Jewish community classrooms, federation boardrooms, and American Israel Public Affairs Committee (AIPAC) parlor meetings is a fundamental disjuncture. Such institutionalized forms of diaspora Jewish practice find few analogues on Israel experience trips. Prayer may be the only exception, but its centrality as a practice is dwarfed by that of symbolic consumption, which is the centerpiece of homeland tourism.

Precisely because it builds on the repertoires and infrastructures of modern mass tourism, Israel experience travel encourages the construction of diasporic Jewish identities as consumer identities to be realized through the consumption of symbols, products, and experiences that are commodified in an Israeli market. The tours create an environment for expressing and developing an identification with the Jewish homeland and with Jewish culture through consumer acts like purchasing souvenirs, eating foods, viewing films, visiting museums, shooting photographs, and so on.

This is clearly not the set of behaviors that rabbinic tradition prescribes as the preferred mode of Jewish ethno-religious practice. As such, it raises a host of normative questions that devotees of tradition may wish to ponder. From the perspective of the sociology of culture, by contrast, the finding that homeland tourism encourages consumption-based ways of "doing Jewish" poses little difficulty. Studies in the sociology of culture have long proceeded from the premise that consumptive practices are fundamental building blocks of modern social identity—key ways that we construct our individuality and express our affiliations.[43] (Skeptics are invited to consider where modern advertising would be if this notion did not contain a kernel of truth.) Similarly, social historians have shown that modern religion is commonly realized in and through market-based practices that people use to actively consecrate their special times, places, and relationships. A classic example is the set of contemporary rituals around the Christmas tree: the family outing to purchase it, the retrieval from the attic of the box of decorations accumulated over the years, the transformation of the home's look through the placement and decoration of the tree, the Christmas morning gathering around the tree to open the gifts placed under it, and so on. Through all these market-enabled practices, Christians create sacred time, sacred space, and sacred memories with one another.[44]

From one perspective, we might interpret the tourists' acts of photographing synagogues and buying gifts of Judaica for loved ones in a similar vein. Yet even as we recognize the consecrating power of rituals of consumption, we can also acknowledge that the tours' penchant to position the travelers as consumers tends to privilege an aesthetic engagement with the homeland over a moral engagement with it, making it "a matter of taste, not responsibility."[45] Herein lies one of homeland tourism's great contradictions, for even as the tours derive from nationalist ideologies that demand moral engagement, the aesthetic stance that they foster represents an inherent denial of that claim on the self. Zionism becomes something to be appreciated and enjoyed, not acted on. But as noted in chapter 5, tour organizers take measures to overcome the distancing that aesthetic contemplation breeds and to foster a moral engagement with Israel and its ideology of home. The result is a tension that remains unreconciled.

However one judges the moral worth of this tourism-generated Jewish consumer identity, the one charge that cannot be leveled at it is the charge of inconsequentiality. In constructing diasporic identities as consumer identities, homeland tours activate one of the most elemental dimensions of the modern self and turn it to the service of transnational ethno-religious community building.

Jews have been defined in many ways over the millennia: as a religious group, as an ethnic community, as a political nation, and even for a time as a race. The notion of Jews as a consumer market and Jewish identity as a set of consumer lifestyle preferences finds little precedent in traditional Jewish self-understanding, but it does situate contemporary Jewish experience in terms of what is arguably the defining trend of modern life—namely, the rise of mass consumer society.[46] One small part of a broader array of global forces that have for more than a century been reconstructing Jewishness as a consumer identity, diaspora Jewish homeland tours have emerged as a venue in which this modern mode of Jewish being is given, perhaps for the first time in people's lives, free rein to achieve full self-actualization. In the words of the Nike knock-off Israeli souvenir t-shirt whose slogan epitomizes this novel type of Jewish selfhood, the tours become an arena where diaspora Jews can "Just Jew It!"

5

Collapsing Distance

"I miss Wal-Mart," Michael said as he stood holding the microphone by his seat at the front of the bus.

We were about 20 minutes into our ride from Ben-Gurion Airport to the ancient Roman beach town of Caesaria, our first stop in Israel. Michael was addressing the group, making introductions, warning us about dehydration, and preparing us for what lay in store. People were surprised to find that their guide was an American immigrant and not a native Israeli.

Victor Barabash, a member of the group who himself had come as a child to the United States from Odessa, asked Michael how it felt to have made the move: "Do you miss the States?"

"I miss my family," Michael answered. "I miss Wal-Mart. . . . Our food costs 25% or 30% more in this country than it does if you buy it in the States. Clothes. I still buy all my clothes back in the States."

The response was banal. It was probably intended to be, because a probing exploration of the stresses of international migration, at least in this initial hour of the trip, would have accomplished the opposite of what Michael was trying to achieve. His goal was not to widen the conceptual gulf separating diaspora Jews from Israel but to narrow it; to make the country feel familiar and comfortable, not strange and disorienting. He immediately dismissed the significance of any feelings of loss or longing and used this dismissal to make the ideological point:

> I miss some things, you know, some small things. But really, this is home,
> guys. I have no doubt in my mind that, you know, I was meant to be here
> and will always be here. My kids and my grandkids will be here. . . . I have
> to tread softly. I'm not supposed to convince you to make *aliyah* or to come
> to this country, live in this country and join the army. But I'll tell you, my
> last group—and I didn't [try to convince them] . . . but eight kids, you
> know, I'm sorry, eight young adults, eight Taglit members, wanted to make
> *aliyah* or join the army at the end of that tour. I hope I don't push you to

that extreme, but I can't help it. I'm super Zionistic! I love this country! I love everything about this country. And you can look around. Look at the road systems we're building. We got traffic jams in Israel! You're in a traffic jam in Israel! [A country] that didn't even exist 60 years ago! It's a country of 7 million people, 5.5 million Jews in it. This is home! You guys are finally home! Okay? This is your home away from home, and I hope throughout this 10-day tour you're going to feel that attachment even more.

Home, of course, is the key trope in these types of tours. In its particular usage in Israel experience programs, home is not just a swath of territory claimed by the ethnic group but something that is supposed to manifest itself on an individual level through a person's emotional relationship to place. Experienced as the feelings of ownership, belonging, obligation, and implication that tie a person to a territorialized ethnic community, home is not to be defined by biographical details of residence or legal technicalities of citizenship. In the framework of a diaspora nationalist ideology, diasporans should feel at home in a country where they do not live and should feel a modicum of otherness in the countries where they do.

This diasporic definition of home blurs the symbolic and social boundaries erected by national citizenship. It asserts that political identity, political community, and the nation-state do not map precisely onto one another. This challenges any monopolistic claims that nation-states might make to command people's political allegiances and to define membership in their polities. For Jews outside Israel, the problematics of the transnational challenge to state sovereignty have been evident in the "accusations" of dual loyalty sometimes leveled against them. (The very notion that multiple loyalties should be cause for accusation rather than celebration exposes the monopolistic thrust of statist morality.) In Israel, these problematics have been at the core of highly charged debates over the country's very self-definition. Should Israel be the *Judenstaat* that Herzl envisioned, a national state in which the Jewish diaspora holds a stake that is not shared by the country's own non-Jewish citizens? Or should the special stake of a transnational Jewish community be denied so that Israel can redefine membership in its polity solely along lines of citizenship and not also along lines of ethno-nationality?

Many diaspora Jews are motivated to travel to Israel because of transnational ethnic and religious bonds. Yet many participants on Israel experience tours embark on the trips without feeling strong ties to the country. For example, the pretrip survey conducted during Taglit's second year shows that fewer than one-half (44%) of the participants said that, to them personally, being Jewish very much involved caring about Israel. Even though diaspora Jewish homeland tours find much sympathy among their audience, tour organizers and guides conceive of their work as an attempt to *generate* feelings of ownership, belonging, obligation, and implication in the State of Israel. This understanding that the emotional connection is something to be accomplished rather than assumed is evident in the responses of several Taglit guides to the question, "What are your main goals when you guide groups from North America?"[1]

I mainly try to forge an emotional connection on the tiyul between the sites and each individual person.—*Yariv, a veteran guide working with Taglit since its inception*

I want them to love Israel. I want them to see how much I love Israel. I want them to see my Israel. . . . I don't want them to feel like tourists. That's one of the reasons volunteer work is so important. . . . You're not tourists. This land belongs to you the same way it belongs to the Israeli soldiers and your *madrichim* [tour educators]. . . . When you can feel at home enough to give to other people, then it is really yours.—*Avi, an Orthodox Jewish immigrant from the United States who works primarily with an Israel experience program built around voluntourism*

It depends a lot on the group. On Taglit they want to arouse emotion, to create an emotional experience. You go up Masada before sunrise, spend two and a half hours. With Christian groups [from abroad] you spend maybe an hour. On Taglit you stir up conversation, participation, involvement. In groups of Christians the guiding is more information-based.—*Hagit, a veteran guide who works with Christian tour groups as well as Jewish ones*

The basic dilemma of the diaspora Jewish homeland tour is that the very medium used to encourage people to "feel that attachment," in Michael's words, and see a foreign country as "home" contains within it forces that create distance and estrangement. Intended to break down the social and symbolic barriers that prevent diaspora tourists from claiming Israel as a personal homeland, the tours also confront travelers with evidence of the cultural divide that separates them as foreign nationals from the place they are visiting. Studies of diaspora-building tours for Korean Americans, Chinese Americans, and Lithuanian Americans have all found that the firsthand encounter with the ethnic homeland leads tourists to realize, often with a degree of surprise, just how much they have been shaped by their American environment. Rather than make South Korea, China, or Lithuania feel like home, these trips often lead to a novel sense of at-homeness in an American society that tourists had previously perceived as a place of enforced otherness.[2]

Diaspora Jewish travel to Israel is subject to the same contradictions of tourism. Over the course of 60 years, the organizers of Israel experience programs have come to an inchoate but indigenous understanding of this fact and have developed institutionalized responses. Through a host of strategies—including discourses of home and otherness, role modeling, consciousness-raising discussion circles, rituals, embodiment, and interactive cross-cultural encounters—they attempt to use the potentials inherent in tourism to bring the enterprise under control so that it might serve diaspora-building goals rather than undermine them. Before exploring these strategies in depth, I consider the boundary-raising obstacles that these strategies are designed to confront.

Tourism as a Distancing Agent

Forces of estrangement are at work on Israel experience programs from the very moment of the tourist's arrival. The official welcome to the homeland takes the form of an encounter with an agent of the state who stops the tourist at a border-control booth. Culminating (hopefully) in the soft thud of a stamp hitting a passport, the encounter asserts not the diaspora Jew's homecoming but his outsiderness. The passport that must be displayed testifies to membership in a different political community. The entry visa, which restricts both the time that can be spent in the country and the things that can be done while there (e.g., no paid work), testifies to the rights of citizenship that are not being extended.[3]

Once access to the country has been granted, many tourists find that language barriers and cultural incompetencies make them dependent to a greater or lesser degree on the mediating infrastructure of the tourist borderzone. This grants them controlled access to and helps them navigate certain types of Israeli spaces. Experienced tourists are accustomed to such dependency and even come to expect it.[4] Although the support systems in the borderzone do not provide tourists with the necessary skills for complete self-sufficiency in the local culture, they provide a base from which tourists can make brief forays to explore on their own. This supporting infrastructure is by no means the hermetically sealed "tourist bubble" of popular imagination. It does, however, reinforce social boundaries between tourists and locals by engaging travelers in more sustained interactions with other tourists than with most of the locals they meet, save perhaps the tour guide.

Tourists are generally aware of the mediated nature of their foreign encounters. This raises among them anxieties that they are seeing staged and hence "inauthentic" representations of the country. For instance, seeking validation of his tour's authenticity, one participant in the group Michael led asked the guide pointedly, "So have we seen mostly touristy stuff or mostly everyday Israeli kinda stuff?"

Tourists' anxieties about the validity of their experiences as ways of coming to know a place are central agents of estrangement. The irony is that these anxieties do not stem from a failure of tourism to realize its promise but, rather, from the internal contradictions of a medium that creates distance even as it seeks to collapse it. As a semiotic act in which sightseers use sites as symbols to be consumed, the tourist gaze establishes the tourist/toured relationship as one where an agentic Self confronts and acts on an objectified Other. Tourists acknowledge the inherently alienating character of their enterprise on only the most superficial level when they seek to avoid the "touristy" in search of a more "authentic" experience. Their penchant to invoke a discourse of authenticity only exacerbates the distancing effects, primarily because their working definition of authenticity is "that which occurs when tourists are not there to look." Conceived in this way, an encounter with the "authentic" culture of a destination can be approached asymptotically but never reached because the tourist's own presence negates the possibility. But even if tourists dispense with the concept of authenticity—whether because they are sophisticated enough to realize that it is a category they use to structure their thinking rather than a characteristic that actually inheres in sites themselves, or because in true post-tourist fashion they simply "delight in the inauthenticity of the normal tourist experience . . . [and] find pleasure in the multiplicity of tourist games"[5]—their construction of sites as symbols continues to objectify them and hence breeds distance.

Essayist Walker Percy once lamented that "it is almost impossible to gaze directly at the Grand Canyon under these circumstances and see it for what it is . . . because the Grand Canyon, the thing as it is, has been appropriated by the symbolic complex which has already been formed in the sightseer's mind."[6] Early critiques of tourism shared Percy's view that tourists substitute the consumption of symbols in place of an unmediated encounter with reality.[7] Largely discredited among tourism studies scholars,[8] the idea retains force in popular imagination and also among planners of diaspora Jewish homeland tours, who are especially concerned that the symbolic resonance of Israel's biblical past will blind tourists to daily life in the country's present. On Hillel-sponsored Taglit tours, staff often engage participants in a study of Israeli poet Yehuda Amichai's poem that raises the issue explicitly. Written in proselike verse and included in resource books distributed to all participants, the poem is titled "Tourists":

> Once I was sitting on the steps near the gate at David's Citadel and I put down my two heavy baskets beside me. A group of tourists stood there around their guide, and I became their point of reference. "You see that man with the baskets? A little to the right of his head there's an arch from the Roman period. A little to the right of his head." "But he's moving, he's moving!" I said to myself: Redemption will come only when they are told, "Do you see that arch over there from the Roman period? It doesn't matter, but near it, a little to the left and then down a bit, there's a man who has just bought fruit and vegetables for his family."[9]

Not recognized as symbolic of anything, the man with the baskets is ignored by the onlookers. The poet wishes that the value of this man's life would be affirmed by the tourists, but, paradoxically, this can be accomplished only by inserting him into their semiotic field. Only as a signifier of Individual Life writ large can the man with the baskets represent the privileging of the present over the past, the personal over the political, and the mundane over the symbolic. But herein lies the contradiction, for Amichai's hope cannot be realized in the tourist framework. The tourist gaze inevitably objectifies, transforming its objects into symbols. Any notion of escaping this through a tourism without semiotics is chimerical.[10]

Bridging Strategies

Many of the distinguishing features of Israel experience tours, including the central position assigned to "experience" itself, can be understood as strategies to lower the barriers that tourism itself raises between gazing subjects and the country that is the object of their contemplation. Of the strategies commonly deployed—discourses of homeland belonging and diasporic otherness, role modeling, group discussion circles, site-specific rituals, embodied experience, and cross-cultural peer-to-peer encounters—most draw on tourism's nonsemiotic knowledge practices (dialogic, ludic, etc.) to counteract the distancing that is effected by the semiotics of the gaze. With the possible exception of role modeling, all co-opt and formalize processes that are simultaneously emerging in an unsystematic manner through the tourists' own efforts to engage the place they are visiting. Internal contradictions in each strategy prevent them from achieving their ends perfectly, but together they constitute a powerful set of tools that Israel experience organizers have become increasingly adept at utilizing.

Discourse of Belonging and Home

Tour guides exert enormous control over the discursive field that emerges on the trips. Although theirs is not the sole voice that is heard, it is the dominant one. Invested with the authority of the expert, the power to control the microphone, and the right to speak for Israel and its sites, the guides establish the interpretive frame through which the encounter with Israel will be filtered in the public discourse of the group. It is a matter of no small importance, therefore, that guides almost universally adopt a discourse of belonging and home when representing Israel to diaspora Jewish tourists. Of all the bridging strategies designed to foster feelings of ownership, belonging, obligation, and implication in a country where the tourists do not live, none is more straightforward than simply asserting outright: "This is home!" "This land belongs to you the same way it belongs to the Israeli soldiers and your madrichim."

This discourse can be established in a matter of fact way as the foundation from which conversation proceeds. A recurring theme in Goldwater's study of Israel experience guides is the shifting referent of the pronoun "we" in guides' narrations:

> When [one of the guides] uses "we" to mean "us—Israelis" and "us—Jews,"
> he blurs the distinction that exists between him and the group, and man-
> ages to include them in his Israeli reality, giving them access to a culture
> that they are otherwise excluded from. . . . When [another guide] says that
> [the ancient Jewish freedom fighter] Bar Kochba "stood up for everything
> that we hold dear to us" he speaks as a representative of the Jewish collec-
> tive, and rather disingenuously includes his group in the joint "we."[11]

A discourse of belonging can also be established by drawing explicit attention to the very effort to establish it. Michael took this approach when he told his newly arrived group, "I'm not supposed to convince you to make *aliyah* . . . but I can't help it," and then raised his voice to declare, "You guys are finally home!"

Exhortations like Michael's are not the norm on Taglit, or at least are not perceived as such. When a survey of the 2000–2001 North American winter cohort asked if there was too much "preaching" on the trip, a solid majority of the respondents, 70%, said no. Of these, 37% were emphatic in their response. On the other side, of those who did agree that there was too much preaching, 23% agreed slightly and only 7% agreed strongly.[12] One might suspect that heavy-handedness like Michael's would generate resistance. Here, the survey data offer mixed evidence. It appears that being perceived as preachy lowers the esteem in which tour guides are held, possibly undermining their ability to wield moral authority. A total of 94% of people who felt strongly that there was not too much preaching rated their Israeli tour guide as very good or sensational, compared with 71% of those who said definitively that there was too much. But although this percentage is substantially smaller, it still represents a sizable majority giving the tour guide a vote of confidence.

A better indicator of resistance to overt moralizing might be found by looking at the correlation between perceptions of being preached at and professed feelings of "connection" to Israel after the tour's end. We find no significant relationship between the two when we limit our focus to those who entered the trip feeling somewhat or very connected to Israel, but we do see such a relationship when we look at people who entered the trip feeling not at all or only a little connected.[13] Here, the more preachy the staff, the less connected to Israel the participants later claimed to be.[14] In other words, preaching to the choir does not undermine diaspora-building goals; preaching to would-be converts does.

Regardless of how the discourse of belonging and home is established, this discourse fosters a normative environment that tourists themselves commonly affirm, even in casual speech. I recall an exchange I had in Jaffa with one member of Michael's group at the mid-point of our 10-day tour. Lyle Messinger was standing on the steps near a landscaped limestone ledge across from a public restroom that our groupmates were using. I walked over to wait next to him because the spot had a bit of shade and the sun was already high in the late morning sky.

"People think I'm Israeli," Lyle opened, turning to me.

I had noticed that when Lyle would speak, he would often sound hesitant and nervous. Many times, although not in this instance, he prefaced his words with disclaimers and apologies. I found out later that, at 18, he was the youngest person on the trip and the only one who had yet to start college. I was not sure why he chose to begin a conversation in medias res, and I responded with a bewildered look. He backtracked and told me that people had been coming up to him and speaking to him in Hebrew. I looked him over. Medium height, slight build, olive skin, jet black hair close cropped in a style I had seen on teenage Israeli boys. Yes, he could pass, I thought to myself.

"I might move here," he said with a shrug.

His voice was flat, with as much conviction as if he were telling me that he had eaten scrambled eggs for breakfast. I had heard him mention moving to Israel once before in much the same way—a non sequitur that filled an awkward pause in conversation. I never heard him say anything specific to indicate that he took his words seriously, and I got the impression for a second time that Lyle was saying what he thought he was supposed to be saying. At the time, I took it as something that bespoke the normative context established by the trip rather than any intentions Lyle may actually have had.

How effective at bridging the divide between tourist and toured is this establishment of a discursive context? Of all the bridging strategies employed by diaspora Jewish homeland tours, this is the one where an answer is the most elusive. On one hand, there is no doubt that the power to control language is the power to constrain thought. Moreover, the immersive, liminal environment of the tours creates a "plausibility structure" that gives this discourse a potency it might not otherwise have.[15] On the other hand, as I attempt to demonstrate repeatedly in the thick descriptions of the goings-on at Mount Meron, the Golan Heights, and Gilo (chapters 2 and 3 in this volume), tourists have a remarkable capacity to tune out the guides and get caught up in worlds of their own making. They also have capacities for lip service and resistance (on the latter, see chapter 6). The question of effectiveness is thus one that pits structure against agency. My inclination in this study, for reasons both epistemological and empirical, has consistently been in the direction of the latter.

Discourse of Jewish Otherness

With its citizenship checks, language barriers, and reliance on mediating agencies to overcome cultural incompetencies, international tourism is structured to reaffirm that tourists are outsiders whose homes lie elsewhere. A discourse of belonging attempts to erode the boundaries that tourism raises between diaspora Jewish visitors and Israel. So, too, does its counterpart, a discourse of outsiderness-in-diaspora. Even as Israel experience programs encourage Jewish tourists to feel at home in Israel, they simultaneously encourage them to disidentify—partially, never entirely—with their countries of residence by emphasizing the othering of Jewish minorities abroad.

The notion that minority existence is inherently precarious for Jews emerges with greatest force at the Yad Vashem Holocaust memorial museum. Yad Vashem's centrality as a site of Israeli self-representation to visitors from abroad—from prime ministers to wandering backpackers—is well known and continues to inspire debate over the role that Holocaust memory plays in Israeli nationalism and collective identity. The museum is built at the base of a Jerusalem hill known as Har Hazikaron, the Mountain of Memory, whose other side contains the Mount Herzl military cemetery. As one ascends Har Hazikaron, one symbolically moves from the depths of annihilation to the sacrifices made to secure the state and finally to the triumph of a free and independent Jewish people in their homeland, symbolized at the summit by the tomb of Theodor Herzl, the founder of modern Zionism. The hill's architecture powerfully inscribes in Jerusalem's landscape a narrative whose ashes-to-redemption, exile-to-home, death-to-resurrection motifs draw from the deepest wells of human myth.

Even if one visits Yad Vashem only and foregoes the military cemetery, the space is configured to convey the sacred story. The museum of death exits onto a panoramic view of Jerusalem's hills, a view intended to demonstrate sovereignty and, by this, security and home. On the El Al flight back to the United States, Patricia Portnoy shared the impression it made on her. Her comments echoed those I had heard from countless other Birthright Israel participants:

> I finally understood that there would be nothing that would have separated me from them [the Jews who perished in the Holocaust]. Had I been born however many years before I was. Nothing. And that really hit home and I started crying. . . . It blew me away. But the most—the best part of the museum was walking out and seeing that beautiful view of Jerusalem. It brought me to tears again, because that's all they [the victims] wanted, to see the Jewish faith thriving without persecution. It was beautiful. It was absolutely beautiful.

The events chronicled at Yad Vashem are distant from the experience of Jews today, both temporally and, for those living outside of Europe, geographically. In this situation, Israel experience programs try to make the Holocaust relevant by encouraging Jewish tourists to treat it paradigmatically, as the ultimate object lesson in the inherent insecurity of living as a dispersed minority. Tourists are prompted to consider contemporary manifestations of antisemitism and to reflect on whether these could escalate to the level of genocide. Michael blundered through the issue as he addressed his group on Mount Herzl:

> The Holocaust continues to go on in many different ways and antisemitism still goes on. The most recent *aliyah,* the most recent influx of immigrants, has been coming out of France over the past [several] years. Why? Because on a weekly basis—and guys, I am not exaggerating—on a weekly basis in France, some Orthodox, some Jewish person is attacked, okay. His home is spray-painted with neo-Nazi symbols. Jewish graveyards are littered, tombstones kicked over, synagogue windows busted out. *Every week. . . .* We have to say to ourselves as a people, whether you live here or not, "Never again!" *We* are not going to allow it to happen, those of us living here, but we hope to God that *you* are not going to allow it to happen ever again from without.

As the notion of feeling at home as a Jew outside of Israel becomes problematized, tourists are encouraged to reflect on ways that they personally experience the outsiderness that Jews can face as members of a minority ethno-religious community. In structured group discussions designed to elicit autobiographical stories and make them objects of collective consideration, travelers share tales of becoming the object of antisemitic taunts or of Christian proselytizing. Sitting on a shaded lawn on a hillside park in the ancient port city of Jaffa, members of Michael's group offered such stories as they responded to a question that their American staff person, Janet, had read aloud from her staff manual: "What about being Jewish makes you feel special or unique, and what about your Jewish identity makes you feel normal . . . in relation to other people?"

"Goyim or other Jews?" one man asked.

"Either way," Janet answered without batting an eye.

The first person to take up the question was Victor Barabash. He had been refusing to eat lunch after having discovered that there were beggars on Israel's streets. He insisted that it was immoral for tourists to dine at restaurants while locals starved. Janet was at wit's end trying to convince him that for his own health he needed to eat something during our marathon days under the Mediterranean sun. Still, she allowed him to take the floor first, perhaps because he was the only one who showed more interest in her question than in the gaping hole in Derek Goodman's pants that had seized the rest of the group's attention.

As ever, Victor spoke in deliberate, formal English: "I feel perfectly at home and comfortable and absolutely at ease saying that I'm Jewish, telling a little bit about how I practice Judaism . . . and so on and so forth, in the community of Christians," he said. "I feel absolutely accepted, welcome, and I feel a really wonderful, educational, meaningful exchange with all."

Adi Zilbershtein, a South African–born Israeli soldier who was traveling as a member of the tour group turned to him: "Can I ask you a question? Do you think that that situation—your confidence that you feel—is something temporary, or is something which can last for your lifetime?" A skepticism about the durability of such Jewish-Christian amity was implicit in her question.

Her sentiment was shared by Natalie Unger, a student at the same college as Victor. "I went to an Episcopal school when I was little," she said. "And I remember in third grade I said that I didn't believe that Jesus, um, rose from the dead—like the whole Easter story, I didn't believe that that was true. And I had my art teacher tell me that she thought I was gonna go to hell because I said something that, like, blasphemous or something."

"You should've said you don't believe in hell," one man responded.

"I just sorta like awkwardly didn't say anything back," responded Natalie.

"That's probably the right response," Janet said.

Natalie continued: "Even at college, I've sort of felt that there's, like, antisemitism. And it's like, I had a friend try and convert me last year by saying like, that, like, 'What you believe, like, it's not real. Like, Christianity's the Truth.'"

Other people told of similar incidents, which prompted a debate about the proper response to proselytizers' denial of Jewish religious legitimacy. In the midst of this, Jake Woloshin broke in to supplement this discussion with an example of intolerance of another kind. Squat, stout, stubbly, and red-nosed, he dominated the public space of the group in the crassest ways. At a memorial to a platoon of soldiers killed in the line of duty, he shattered any hope Michael had of creating a somber mood by interrupting him with a primal scream, "Aaaarrrrgggghhhh!"

"You all right?" Michael asked.

"No. He hit me in the balls! But it's cool." A day earlier, with his hairy belly hanging out from under a pink, hooded women's sweatshirt four sizes too small, he seized the bus microphone and told of meeting a reality-TV sex idol: "I freaked out. I was like, 'What do I do? What do I do? Do I whip my junk out? I gotta do something big.'"

His tone was grave, however, as he spoke on the lawn in Jaffa about a friend in the United States who contacted him on his cell phone while he was on the trip:

Yesterday as we were coming to Jerusalem, a girl kept texting me and she kept insulting me and through her insults she would throw in the fact that I'm Jewish. She'd be like, "You're dumb. You're ugly. You're stupid. You're Jewish." And I was like, "Please don't insult my heritage." And she said, "I'll do whatever I want, you dumb kike. . . ." It just made me feel, like, closer to every Jew I've ever met, because, like, that's never happened to me before. I've never been, like, that offended about anything.

The discussion veered off to consider the etymology of the slur, after the man who had unabashedly said "goyim" declared that "'kike' is not even an insult. . . . It comes from when we went to Easter Island—or what was that island? Ellis. Ellis Island. Sorry. . . . Esther Island."

"Yeah, like the N-bomb didn't start, like [as a slur]," someone else added.

Janet tried to rein in the spiraling conversation. "So how do you think, or *do* you think, that a relationship with the Other, however you want to define Other, can make us stronger as individuals or as Jews?"

Victor was the only one to respond directly to the question. He had the last word:

I don't view it as, "Oh, they're trying to convert me." I appreciate it. I appreciate that they have such a love and passion for their faith and for me, that they care about me enough to share something meaningful from their life with me and try to bring me into that. I'm not *going* to [convert]. But I appreciate the concern and consideration, and every time a Christian person interacts that way with me I tell them how much I value that.

While the discussions made room for a range of viewpoints, the exchange was premised on calling into question the acceptance of Jewish difference in situations where Jews live as a minority. Without any prompting from me, Patricia picked up this theme during our conversation on the flight home. She first raised the issue when talking about Yad Vashem, saying that after seeing "how the Germans would portray Jews . . . I don't want to hear the jokes when I go home. I never liked the 'Oh, you have a big nose' jokes or 'Oh, you're cheap' jokes. . . . It was never really funny to me, but it's just like, I don't—to me that would be like German propaganda that never went away." Later, she returned to the topic in a way that rarely gets raised in public forums like the group discussion circle, addressing the sexual othering of Jews, and of Jewish women in particular:[16]

> Being at college in Northern Florida, everyone is blonde, Southern, and it was, you know, personally, it's hard to find people to be interested in you when you look different. You have dark features, and you don't look like a cookie cutter. . . . When I look at myself, I see a very Jewish look, and I was very at peace with that there [in Israel]. I felt beautiful there. And now . . . I want to go home and be very proud of it. I want someone to think I'm beautiful and lovely because I'm Jewish and intelligent and I'm a good Jewish girl and I'm in touch with my faith. It's actually important to me now, and it doesn't matter so much now that I'm not like everyone else, because I like the way that I am even more.

The elaboration of Jewish otherness in diaspora is offset by two counterforces. One is the attention drawn to existential threats to Israel. Any efforts to portray Israel as a safe haven where Jews can escape the persecutions of diaspora crash squarely into the message that even Jews in Israel are unsafe and, perhaps even more than diaspora Jews, live under a cloud of potential annihilation. Ben Hovav, one of the Israeli soldiers who took part in the conversation in Jaffa, expressed it by saying, "What's unique in this country is that we get to have a normal life, but under constant danger. I mean, now there's the Iranians with the nuclear weapons, and in a day, everything here can be vanished."

The other element offsetting the efforts to foster a sense of Jewish otherness outside of Israel is the intention of diaspora-based organizations to use homeland tourism to strengthen their communities. In an earlier era, these interests conflicted more directly with those of their Israeli partners who saw Israel experience programs primarily as sources of potential immigrants. As the ideology of *shelilat hagolah* (negation of diaspora) has waned in Israel, and as the value to the state of thriving diaspora communities has increasingly been affirmed rather than grudgingly accepted, few still consider immigration to be the primary justification for making sizable investments in the enterprise. Israeli officials who address Taglit groups still ritualistically call on the tourists to make aliyah, but this is little more than lip service.[17] More indicative of the program's real intent is the chant that Taglit's cofounding philanthropist Charles Bronfman leads when the participants gather together in their thousands at the semiannual "megaevent" held in the Jerusalem convention center: "I'm Canadian [or American, or French, or Argentine]! I'm Jewish! And I'm proud!"

Role Models

The essential limitation of a discourse-based bridging strategy is that it does not operate directly on the private sentiment that is its ostensible target. Rather, it works to shape a public culture that, as we know from Ann Swidler's work, is selectively adopted and adapted by those who put it to use.[18] For tour organizers, the challenge is not to establish a discourse of belonging and home. Guides can do this easily, though to uncertain effect. Instead, the challenge is to help participants internalize a feeling of belongingness that is experienced as a set of emotions and normative commitments. To accomplish this, tour organizers look to other bridging strategies that use interaction, embodiment, and praxis to elicit the active cooperation of the travelers in their own socialization.

Of these strategies, the one that demands the least of the tourists is the one that demands the most of the staff: Israeli guides and American counselors are to act as paragons of *ahavat ha'aretz,* love of homeland. Through a relationship between tourist and staff, it is hoped, a public discourse of belonging will be converted into individual feelings and value commitments. All the travelers need do is identify with their tour leaders, even in a small way, for this identification enables the guides and counselors to function as models for "imitation and emulation."[19]

Role modeling mediates the relationship of tourist and toured through an emotional attachment to the mediating agents themselves. Consider the episode described in chapter 2, when Ravit stood on Mount Meron and pointed out the place in the distance where she was building her home. At first, she struggled to corral the tourists at the overlook point. They had spread out along the hillside and had immersed themselves in a dozen separate conversations. When Ravit called them over, most initially ignored her. Their interest was piqued only when she made clear that she would first be talking about herself: "Before I tell you about the view, look at *me*. . . . This landscape is my internal landscape."

Although I frame role modeling as a "strategy," I would be misrepresenting the actual experience of the trips, as well as doing an injustice to the people I studied, were I to allow this to imply that remarks like Ravit's were the product of cool calculation rather than heartfelt sentiment. A belief that tour leaders should function as role models is now commonly accepted among Israel experience planners and is evidenced in staff manuals and orientation seminars. But this belief can be traced as much, if not more, to the value commitments of educators trained in the spirit of Dewey as to an instrumentally rational search for effective means of fostering a love of homeland. Role modeling manages to work as a strategy only when it is treated not as a strategy but as matter of professional ethics. Sincerity is all. In the words of one long-time scholar of the Israel experience, the tour leader's responsibility "is to be him/herself, to act authentically, to present him/herself to the participants as he or she is. . . . [Their authority] is derived primarily from the extent to which their personality and actions are congruent with the messages they are delivering as representatives of the program."[20] (In this regard, the choice to hire tour guides who themselves are immigrants is particularly significant.)

Sincerity was on ample display when Laura and Gidi, the American staff members on Ra'anan's bus, took the prerogative of inserting their own voices alongside Ra'anan's as the group encountered the Golan Heights. To preface a group discussion circle, they told the story of an Israeli spy who, before he was caught and executed in 1965, managed to convince the Syrian military to plant eucalypti to provide shade and cover for their fortifications on the Heights: "Two years later, the Six-Day War breaks out, and what's the first thing Israel does? They bomb all the eucalyptus trees and gain access to the Golan Heights very, very quickly."

To frame the story, both staff members spoke of their own feelings about it, Gidi even breaking his narrative to reiterate his own sentiments with audible excitement:

LAURA: We have a story to set the mood for our conversation. So please, pay attention to [Gidi]. He has a five-minute story, maybe seven, don't yell at him if it goes that long. And, uh, it's actually one of the coolest stories that I've ever heard when I was here, so I know that you all will enjoy it.

GIDI: This is amazing. This is really inspirational when you think about Israeli heroes. . . . Israel, in the early 1960s recruited, through the Mossad, which is the Israeli secret service . . . a man by the name of Eli Cohen. I don't know if you've heard of this man or not—this is a *great* story. I think it's one of the most powerful stories to me about commitment to Israel and commitment to just incredible, incredible, amazing things that can happen in Israeli society.

The impression Gidi and Laura conveyed was one of tour leaders speaking from their hearts because they themselves were inspired by the places they were showing and stories they were telling. Although Gidi made very clear that "commitment to Israel" was a value he hoped to inculcate, it was as if he and Laura were offering this as a gift—something that touched them that they were excited to share so that others might be enriched by it, too. The more the tourists identified with their trip leaders (and Gidi and Laura were widely revered), the more they would be willing, in theory, to receive the gift.

Group Discussion Circles

If we view tourism as a communicative process about the meaning of place, we can quickly recognize the key weakness of discursive strategies for bridging gazer and gazed. The organizers of diaspora Jewish homeland tours seek not merely to formulate, encode, and transmit the message that, by virtue of being Jewish, tourists have a personal connection to Israel; they want to help travelers internalize this message and feel it as a personal truth. Tour guides' efforts to articulate a discourse of belonging act only on message creation and delivery, though, leaving all issues of reception, decoding, and processing to chance. It is for the purpose of intervening here that formal group discussions have been instituted as a regular part of diaspora Jewish homeland tours. Birthright Israel has codified its policy:

> All programs must include at least three group tie-in/discussion sessions. These tie-in discussions should be conducted every few days. *Their aim is to enable participants to reflect on and process experiences they are having, and to link them to their own lives.* These sessions need to be led by staff skilled in the area of group dynamics and inter-active discussion.[21]

The frequency and formality of these discussion sessions vary from tour to tour. Sometimes they are confined to sharing personal reactions to the places visited. At other times, set curricula are used to address issues that extend outward from the site visits to encompass broader themes. Hillel, the Jewish campus organization and one of the largest operators of Birthright Israel trips, adopts the latter approach. Its education department has designed a program of "conversations" that it bills as "The Educational Model for Our Ten-Day Experience."[22] Staff and participants are provided with background material for discussions on topics like "How I Relate to Israel—How Israel Relates to Me," "My Relationship with Jewish Memory," "Spirituality: Wrestling with G-d," and "Special and Normal," the title of the discussion Janet led in Jaffa.[23]

This material includes over 60 readings, from one sentence to one page in length, drawn from traditional religious texts, as well as from an array of distinguished personalities including Rebbe Nachman of Breslov, Immanuel Kant, Theodor Herzl, Mark Twain, Elie Wiesel, and comedian Lenny Bruce. Tour leaders are given written guidelines for facilitating discussions, including suggested introductory lines, talking points, open-ended questions linked to the readings, and recommendations for structuring the conversations. The staff manual explains the philosophy driving the curriculum:

> There are two educational goals for Hillel's Birthright Israel trips:
>
> - Enhance the participants' connection to the greatest living laboratory of the Jewish people, the State of Israel.
> - Strengthen the participants' connection to the Jewish community.
>
> Note that the Jewish content of this trip is to be transmitted through conversation, and not through lectures or conventional classroom techniques. All conversations begin with the participant and build on the participant's values, memories and perceptions.
>
> The methodology is simple:
>
> - Step one is to introduce the conversation by asking personal questions of the participants.
> - Step two is to use that knowledge of individual experiences and apply it to the collective experience of the Jewish people.
> - Step three is to bring that experience back to the participants to help individuals articulate where they stand in this new context.[24]

The group discussion circles formally institutionalize the types of conversations that occur casually as tourists talk about the things they are seeing and doing together. They are, in the words of performance studies scholar Barbara Kirshenblatt-Gimblett, "among the ways that interior processes of reflection are exteriorized, monitored, and regulated."[25] The discussion titled "How I Relate to Israel—How Israel Relates to Me" is hardly the only one that opens for public consideration people's private feelings about their relationship to Israel. All of the conversations do this in some way, even as they touch on other major themes that emerge at significant sites on the tour.

The discussions take various approaches to their subject matter. In some cases, conversation leaders ask people to speak from their own experience, as when members of Ravit's group were convened atop Masada, having just witnessed a glorious sunrise over the Dead Sea, to discuss what "spirituality" meant to them and how Israel and Judaism related to it, if at all. In other cases, they ask people to reflect on the world at large, as when members of one group who had just visited the Yad Vashem Holocaust memorial were asked whether "it" could happen again. Then there are instances when discussion leaders use sites to pose moral dilemmas. For example, the night before their predawn hike up Masada, Ravit asked her group to share their thoughts about the morality of the Zealots' choice to take their own lives rather than submit to the Romans. Similarly, at the Tel Aviv plaza where a Jewish opponent of territorial compromise assassinated Prime Minister Yitzhak Rabin in 1995, Adi, the South African–born soldier traveling with Michael's group, led a discussion in which she asked people to debate the line dividing legitimate from illegitimate forms of democratic dissent.

The use of sites to pose moral dilemmas is a special case because it has the tourists imagine themselves into the site narrative and talk about how they might act in such a situation. This approach repositions the tourists and the site narratives alike. Tourists are encouraged to move from readers to protagonists as the presentation of site narratives shifts from static and foreclosed to unfolding and open-ended. This engagement with sites by imagining oneself as a protagonist in its stories is an example of tourism as a ludic practice—one that uses play to construct some understanding of place, self, and the relationship between the two. Here, the fantasy role playing occurs in the mind and is spoken but not acted out. In other instances (considered later in this chapter), the mobilization of tourism's ludic practices also encompasses its embodied dimensions.

What all the discussions have in common is that they treat episodes in Jewish history as bearers of eternal questions that demand personal engagement on the moral, intellectual, and emotional levels. By using the sites as springboards for reflection, participants in the discussion circles take action to implicate themselves in the meanings attributed to the sites; in so doing, they enter into a relationship that bridges the gap between subject and object. Not everyone participates actively in these discussions, however. Nor do those who choose to take part necessarily find that the conversations enable them to penetrate deeply into the questions they raise. I give greater consideration to these issues in chapters 6 and 7, where I examine how the discussion circles help shape group dynamics and individual identity construction.

Site-Specific Rituals

In the predawn hours of a January day, the members of Ravit's group climbed an ancient Roman ramp to the top of Masada. We had discussed the ethical dimensions of the Masada story the evening before and were now on our way to see the site that had inspired the conversation. Stars filled the sky as we started our ascent. By the time we reached the top, only the brightest remained visible. Because the ramp leads up Masada's western side, we had to make our way quickly to the mesa's opposite edge to see the sun rise. People were subdued but jocular. "We sacrifice the virgin cat at sunrise!" one prankster, Fred Jaffe, exclaimed.

When we arrived to the place from which we would watch the new day break, Ravit pointed out the wide, flat valley below us that contains what is left of the Dead Sea. It is "the lowest thing on Earth," she told us.

Hearing this, Sam Pollack, who, like Fred, prided himself on his comic prowess, called out in a deliberately squeaky voice to a friend, "See, Beth! I'm *not* the lowest thing on Earth." He would soon turn serious, as he would later do when he claimed his tree on Mount Meron.

As the joking subsided, people went alone or in clusters of two or three to face the mountains of Moab to the east and wait in patient silence for the sun to rise. Time passed, and some people wandered further away from the group to sit by themselves closer to the cliff's edge. Most seemed to be trying to make the moment special. Ravit left the group to do Tai Chi on a ridge above. A few people joined the staff to recite the morning prayers, the men wrapped in prayer shawls. When members of a different Taglit group several hundred meters to our south began shouting to people even further away, derogatory comments were made about them for disturbing the peace. It was about 6:10 a.m.

A half hour later, the ridge of the mountaintops to the east, which until then had appeared a diffuse brown on powder-puff blue, became a pencil-thin black line sharply defined against the narrowest band of radiant gold. People started whispering excitedly, "It's coming! It's coming!" At 6:50, as the sun finally crested the mountain, we heard the piercing blast of a shofar. Heads snapped left toward the sound. Silhouetted against the morning sky was Sam, standing alone on a stone wall. To his lips he held a two-and-a-half-foot ram's horn, streaked charcoal gray and curved in a helix. The shofar had been purchased as a souvenir by someone else in our group, but as Sam was the only one able to sound strong blasts with any consistency, he had taken control of it. He made the decision to bring it to Masada, although he pawned it off on me to carry in my backpack up to the summit.

Lucas, the American staff person, called loudly to Sam and told him to sound the shofar again. Sam struck another single note, then a string of several medium-length blasts, recognizable as the traditional sounds of the Jewish New Year prayer services. Some people sat in silence. Others snapped photographs. Two birds chirped as they wove quickly from behind us on the left to disappear in front of us below Masada's edge. When the sun was fully over the mountains of Moab, Sam let out one long final blast, a *tekiah gedolah.*

A maintenance worker saw him on the wall and yelled at him, "Down! Down!"

Sam ran over to me, smiling. He had confided that he was nervous that he would "screw up" when it came time to blow the shofar at sunrise. But he had succeeded in marking that first flash of golden light in the way he had hoped, and people were appreciative.

Brimming with enthusiasm, Lynne Cassel, an international affairs major who would be spending the next semester learning Arabic in Cairo, came up to me to announce, "That was definitely a *moment!*" She had taken to updating me regularly about which activities she felt moved by and which not. Later she told me that when she heard Sam blow the shofar, she cried. I do not doubt it, but I saw no indication of this at the time. After her quick report to me, she ran back to her friends and screamed Leonardo DeCaprio's signature line from the film *Titanic:* "I'm king of the world!" She was only half-joking.

Diaspora Jewish homeland tours regularly engage tourists in embodied rituals that perform a relationship to the sites they visit. Sam's use of the shofar to mark daybreak on Masada was exceptional in the degree to which a lone tourist took initiative to ritualize the encounter with the site, in the degree to which it positioned the group as spectators to one man's performance, and in the degree to which its meaning was left relatively open-ended. Yet Sam would not have been able to do what he did had it not been for the itinerary planners' decision to have his group engage Masada through the classic tiyul-inspired tradition of the predawn hike to the summit. This in itself is a ritual performed to the site, and even without shofar blasts it is a powerful one.

There is an art to constructing emotionally gripping site rituals. Not taught in the certification courses that train Israeli guides, it is passed along informally as new guides learn from the examples of experienced morei derech steeped in the tradition of tiyul.[26] Guides who have mastered the art know intuitively that a site ritual is most powerful when staged as a climax. First the site is introduced. Then it is engaged on a cognitive level as the guide offers a narrative that ascribes meaning to it. Finally, the tourists use ritual to affirm their own involvement with the site and with its meanings. As Goldwater shows in her study of guiding practices on Israel experience trips, the process maps directly onto the stages of site sacralization described by MacCannell, with the conduct of the ritual corresponding to the stage of *enshrinement*.[27] The ritualization of the Masada visit, for example, typically continues so that at the end of the tour, after the guide has elaborated on the Zealots' "live free or die" story, tourists shout over the side of the mountain to a resounding echo the words "Sheinit metzada lo tipol" (Masada will not fall again), "Am Yisrael chai" (The Jewish people live), or "Shalom" (Peace).

In certain cases, control over site rituals has been assumed by organizations that have routinized their conduct. The visit to Independence Hall in Tel Aviv is a case in point. After screening a 15-minute video about the history of the building and its connection to the founding of the State of Israel, visitors enter the room where David Ben-Gurion declared the country's statehood on May 14, 1948. The room has been reconstructed to look as it did on that day. A docent offers more details about the declaration ceremony and then plays an audio recording of Ben-Gurion reading the declaration of independence. At this point, sheets of paper containing the transliterated and translated words to Israel's national anthem are distributed, and all assembled are asked to rise to conclude their visit with the singing of "Hatikvah" [The Hope]:

> As long as deep in the heart
> The soul of a Jew yearns
> And forward to the East
> To Zion, an eye looks
> Our hope will not be lost
> The hope of two thousand years
> To be a free nation in our land
> The land of Zion and Jerusalem.

Like the singing of "Hatikvah" at Independence Hall, the entry into Jerusalem is also typically structured to give ritual affirmation to the Jewish bond to the homeland. In sharp contrast with the passage into Tel Aviv, which usually goes unmarked, the first view of Jerusalem is carefully staged. Ra'anan ritualized his group's first view of the city by playing "Jerusalem of Gold" on the bus stereo. Known by Jews around the world, this love song to Jerusalem became an instant classic when it was released just before Israel's reunification of the divided city in the 1967 Six-Day War.

Michael, for his part, used narration rather than music to ritualize the entry into Jerusalem. His group was approaching the city from the hills of Judea in the West Bank, which meant that the first view of the Old City would come as the bus exited a long tunnel. "As soon as we get through this tunnel," Michael says, "I want you to look right to the left-hand side and have your eyes fixed on your first view of Jerusalem. Excited?!"

He is answered by cheers.

The end of the tunnel is visible before us, and Michael uses it for a metaphor: "It's about being born. We're coming out of the womb right now. We're coming out of the womb of the Judean Desert. We are about to be born, and if you want to cry, too, you can cry, you know, as you look over to Jerusalem. . . . The capital city of our country, Israel." And then a whisper, "Jerusalem. Welcome, welcome, welcome."

Soon, the bus stops at a small amphitheater on a terraced hillside overlooking the Old City. As is its custom, Hillel has organized an official ceremony for the three groups arriving at that hour in Jerusalem. With festive religious music blaring from a loudspeaker on a tripod, Naomi, an American immigrant in her mid-40s working as one of Hillel's Israel-based representatives, takes the microphone and shouts, "Welcome to Jerusalem!" Answered with scattered applause, she tries again. "Welcome to Jerusalem! A little louder!"

This time there are cheers as attention comes to focus on the proceedings:

We are here for a very special occasion. It is called a *shehechyanu*. When you do something for the first time you say *shehechyanu*, you say that we're blessed to be at this place in this time. So I want everyone to turn to their right and everyone to turn to their left. This is the person that you will always be sitting next to the first time you saw Yerushalayim [Jerusalem], so remember that person.

She then invited one member of each bus group to offer words of thanksgiving. In equal measure, the remarks conveyed the speakers' heartfelt sentiments and their awareness that they should say something situationally appropriate.

"Being here is a dream come true. . . . I am finally home," one woman said. "At the beginning of the trip, Jeanette, our staff, asked us if we felt at home in Israel, and I wanted to say I did, but I didn't really feel like I did. But now, I know that Israel is in my heart and soul."

Her remarks were followed by those of a man who said, "I was not really raised religiously, but since I've been in Israel I've acquired a Hebrew name, I'm having a bar mitzvah, and I can honestly tell you that I am happier than I have ever been in my entire life today. This is our city. This is our capital. Jerusalem."

Sweet Concord grape wine and challah were passed around. "So, when King David, *hamelech David,* would come to Jerusalem, he would greet his guests, his dignitaries, with wine and with bread," Naomi said. "And you guys are our guests into Jerusalem today, so we are greeting you with a lot of love, with wine and with bread."

Representatives of the three groups pronounced the Hebrew blessings, including the *shehechyanu:* "Blessed are you, God, king of the universe, who has given us life, sustained us, and enabled us to reach this time." Then the music was turned up, a hora was started, and people either joined in the swirling dance circle or watched it from the sidelines.

Site rituals use strategies of embodiment to erase boundaries that tourism interposes between observing tourists and observed destination. They establish a relationship between tourists and site by engaging travelers in actions that perform a communion with places and with values that places are said to represent. Travelers sing Israel's national anthem at Independence Hall. They dance the hora when entering Jerusalem. They stand in reverent silence at the Mount Herzl military cemetery. They recite memorial poetry at Yad Vashem. They plant real trees and symbolic roots at Jewish National Fund nurseries. These rituals are a form of praxis that realizes ideals by enacting them. They circumvent the distancing effects of an intellect that observes and considers and, instead, enable sites to be known in an immediate way through the feelings and emotions that are experienced while there. In the process, the rituals reestablish Israel's geography as an object of Jewish devotion, echoing an ancient pilgrimage tradition but realizing it through contemporary tourist practices whose hallmark is their novelty.

Embodied Experience and Embodied Action

At lunch in a cafeteria overlooking grottoes on Israel's northern Mediterranean coast, I was sharing a plate of hummus with Lynne Cassel, Misha Velinsky, and Mickey, all members of Ravit's group. ("Mickey" was a nickname. He was identified on the official roster as Joshua Goldman, but he had been called Mickey since he was a teenager, when someone decided that his large ears resembled those of a certain mouse.) Our talk had turned to previous travels. Mickey, characteristically, took center stage in the conversation. He was one of the most vocal members of the group—alternately funny and profound. He played a role akin to that of a Greek chorus, and people generally listened when he spoke. He was liked and respected, and none used his name in a teasing sense.

"Acapulco was probably the best week of my entire life," he started. "Except for this. This tops it. . . . I haven't thought about weed at all this entire trip—"

"Mazel tov!" joked Lynne sarcastically. She got on well with Mickey, in spite of the fact that his close friends in the group tended to be those of whom she had said, "If I were alone in an elevator with them, I wouldn't feel comfortable."

Mickey tried to explain what he meant. "But that's what Acapulco was all about. . . . You don't need to [think about weed on this trip]. This takes care of all the senses." He enumerated the sights, smells, and tastes of the past week. Lynne, mentioning the shofar blast on Masada, told him not to forget sounds.

Tourism is an embodied engagement with place. Its defining feature, as Kirshenblatt-Gimblett observes, is "precisely one's physical presence in a location and experiences that are above all sensory and proprioceptive, or having to do with the body's orientation in space."[28] Premised on the actual placement of physical bodies in tangible locations, tourism's materiality ensures that the conceptual distancing of tourist and toured can never be absolute. Israel experience programs find much of their justification in their ability to temporarily collapse a geographic divide by establishing a physical copresence of diasporic bodies and homeland spaces. On the trips themselves, tourism's embodied character is further mobilized to overcome the distancing effected by other dimensions of the medium.

Mickey's assertion that the Birthright Israel trip "takes care of all the senses" points to an important aspect of tourist experience: the monitoring that travelers' engage in is directed not only outward to destinations but also inward to their own selves. Feelings, both sensory and emotional, are also a dimension of tourist consciousness. This embodied self-awareness is not divorced, however, from the broader context in which tourists find themselves physically situated. Places are engaged as settings for out of the ordinary sensations and as stimuli that prompt them. This form of engagement bypasses discursive awareness and is experienced as an embodied knowledge of place that is not as much a knowledge of place-as-object as a knowledge of an emplaced self. Participants on diaspora Jewish homeland tours come to know what it "feels like" to be in Israel. Or, more precisely, each tourist knows what it feels like for himself or herself to be in Israel in the context of an Israel experience program.

Whereas the bridging strategy of role modeling mediates a connection to the homeland through a relationship with another, the bridging strategy of embodiment mediates it through sensory perceptions of a situated self. This situated self both perceives and acts (or consumes and produces), and organizers of Israel experience programs attempt to engage it in both these ways. They structure activities to generate uncommon or intense bodily sensations. Some of these activities involve movement and sometimes physical challenge, particularly in nature: camel and donkey rides, rafting on the Jordan river, predawn desert hikes.[29] Others, like the megaevent and shopping in Middle Eastern open-air markets, involve what Kirshenblatt-Gimblett refers to as spectacle.[30] Some combine the two to barrage the senses: hassidic dancing at the Western Wall, disco cruises on the Red Sea, pub and club nights in Jerusalem or Tel Aviv.

As the last examples hint, while attempting to avoid the appearance of providing official sanction, the programs also enable tourists to carve out times and spaces where they on their own can experience the highs of intoxication and sex. (One key informant—who would later go on to rabbinic school—told me, "Everyone knows, like, what the understanding is, that people hook up [with each other and/or with Israelis] on the trip. And they sort of feel like they haven't had a real Israeli experience until they have. You know, it's like another stop on the tour.") By structuring the tourists' encounter with Israel as a barrage of physical and emotional highs, the tours foster an embodied knowledge of Israel as a place where one can acutely feel what it is to live with gusto.[31] For Mickey, this meant that Israel could "top" even Acapulco, and even manage to do so without "weed."

At the same time that Israel experience programs engage the self that perceives, they also engage the self that acts. The trips allow tourists to try different types of Jewish or Israeli behaviors that they may not commonly engage in or even know of at home. People who have never read from the Torah are helped to do so in bar and bat mitzvah ceremonies organized by trip staff. Men approaching the Western Wall are spotted as tourists by Lubavitch hassidim who schmooze them up in rapid-fire New York or London or Johannesburg Orthodox Jewish English and then encourage the befuddled visitors to wrap on leather-strapped *tefillin* [phylacteries] and pray.[32] ("Whereyafrom?" *"New Jersey."* "What, the whole state? Where'nJersey?" *"Scotch Plains."* "Scotch Plains, ahh. Y'aYankeefan?" *"Sort of."* "Yeah? Haveyawrappedtefillintoday? Y'know howtawraptefillin? Come!")[33] Here is tourism as a ludic practice—a bounded environment that offers a chance to experiment with new behaviors and try on different identities. It operates primarily in the realm of religious ritual—a dimension of Jewish experience that can remain relevant to the tourists when they return to their homes in diaspora—but it is evident outside the religious sphere as well. When I spent two months on an Israel experience program the summer before I turned 18, I played soldier on an army base in the basic training simulation where I dressed in fatigues and learned to fire an M-16. (It remains the only time in my life that I have ever fired a gun.)

The self is a dynamic formation constantly evolving as it is coproduced moment to moment by embodied actors and their social environments. Through their acts of experimentation and play, Jewish tourists use Israel to change themselves. The gulf separating traveler and destination becomes collapsed as the two are fused in the new selves that are coproduced by Jewish tourists and their Israeli environments. These selves that are created during the tours may be evanescent, but, once they exist even for a moment, they become facts of biography and hence raw material for the creation of future selves.

Cross-Cultural Peer-to-Peer Encounters

Israel experience organizers' most ambitious strategy for breaking down the barriers that tourism erects between touring subjects and toured objects is a program of cross-cultural peer-to-peer encounters known in Hebrew as *mifgashim* (sing. *mifgash*). Intended specifically to counter the objectification of locals that is one of tourism's most pernicious tendencies, mifgashim strive for a mutuality of gaze by integrating Israeli Jewish peers as members of the tour group. When locals enter into the tour bus as full and equal participants, they cross and thereby subvert a spatial boundary that powerfully signifies tourists' separation from the country around them. No longer will the bus window allocate the categories of foreigner, local, tourist, and toured across the two sides of its pane. Through the mifgash, Israel will be inside the bus as well as outside it, locals will be tourists as well as toured, and foreigners will be objects of the gaze as well as subjects applying it.

Just as important, the presence of local tourists will provide foreigners with greater opportunity to encounter Israel dialogically, through interaction. On one hand, this holds the potential to introduce greater pluralism into the discursive field by ensuring that the guide's voice is not the only one invested with the authority of the local. On the other hand, organizers often select and prepare Israeli mifgash participants with the intention of deploying them as expert communicators who will voluntarily reinforce the program's core messages. Evaluation research suggests that Israeli participants in Taglit mifgashim generally understand their role in these terms.[34]

In design and implementation, mifgashim have grown increasingly sophisticated over the years. Peer-to-peer encounters have been used in Israel experience programs since the earliest trips of the 1950s,[35] but it took three decades before educators began thinking of them as an organizing principle for structuring the tours.[36] By the mid-1990s, mifgashim were being proposed as the best way to address educators' and researchers' concerns that Israel experience programs represented a "mythic" Israel that was divorced from the daily realities of its citizens, that did little to break down stereotypes that diaspora Jews held about Israelis, and that encouraged visitors to treat Israel instrumentally as a "setting or backdrop for an American teen adventure."[37] A support and advocacy agency was established to seed programs and fund research. Drawing on studies of intergroup contact, a variety of structures for cross-cultural encounters of different durations were developed and evaluated.[38] For its part, Birthright Israel settled on the model of integrating five to 10 Israeli soldiers as co-tourists for several days of the trip only after trying different models and finding the others lacking.[39]

As a strategy for overcoming the structural barriers that tourism erects between tourist and toured, Birthright Israel's mifgashim meet with considerable success. Meaningful exchanges about cultural difference are frequent and extensive. Israelis and diaspora Jews alike speak of gaining deeper understanding of the other through the encounter. Diaspora Jews who extend their stays beyond the 10 days are often hosted at the homes of their new Israeli friends. They reciprocate the hospitality later when the Israelis traveling on their post-army treks around the world come to visit them. When they are not together, many maintain contact with each other through social networking websites and, to a lesser extent, email and telephone.[40]

Even as the mifgashim meet with a significant degree of success, they are prevented from fully realizing their goals by tourism's own structural dynamics. For one, the person-to-person encounters unfold in the context of a group tour, which means that the ability of any particular Israeli to befriend any particular diaspora Jew is constrained by the tour group's social dynamics. Although a fair number of foreign tourists on Taglit have the opportunity to become close with their Israeli counterparts, the five-to-one ratio of diaspora Jews to Israelis ensures that many do not. A social network survey that asked members of Michael's bus to identify whom they felt closest to as the trip approached its end found that, of the 40 Americans, 25 either mentioned some of the eight Israeli soldiers or, conversely, were mentioned by them—a glass half full, glass half empty finding.

Language barriers are a contributing obstacle to friendship formation in the mifgashim, but even more important are the dynamics of gender and sex. From the first piercing whistles when Yoni Lefkovich and his fellow soldiers climbed aboard Ra'anan's bus, to the rafting trip on the Jordan River when people pulled me aside and told me to pay attention to who ended up switching into who's boat midstream, I was well aware that the mifgash encounter was a highly sexualized one. I was also aware that this sexualization did not structure all interactions equally. Strongly heteronormative, it primarily shaped the interactional field through which Israeli men and American women related to one another. On boxy lounge chairs in a Jerusalem hotel lobby on the last night of the trip, Hailey Farber and Jenna Eisenstein, two well-liked sorority sisters, offered firsthand accounts. I had managed to interview these virtually inseparable friends individually, but as is befitting their actual relationship, I weave their comments together below:

HAILEY: There was talk . . . starting at the airport, like, "Oh, are you going to hook up with an Israeli soldier? . . ." It was a huge deal. People were, like, making pacts about it. . . . "Okay, we're going to kiss Israeli soldiers. . . ." I think, the soldiers [for their part], come in with a mentality like, "Oh, American girls! Let's hook up with them." So they are very flirtatious also. It's not like one-sided.

JENNA: I think almost everyone has heard the anecdotal . . . "American college girl goes to, you know, Israel and hooks up with a hot, you know, Israeli soldier." You know, like, "Oh, cool! Like, I want to do that!"

HAILEY: We were excited for [the soldiers] to come. . . . But we knew at the same time that there is going to be this, like, competition, for like, who can—because there was a limited amount of soldiers. There's like 16 girls, 14 girls, and only four guys, you know. . . .

JENNA: I remember, we pull up to the bus station [where the soldiers are waiting to join the group]. . . . Everyone is peering out the window. "Oh, what does that one look like? What does that one look like?" Calling dibs almost. . . . Within an hour of them being on the bus, you could already tell, like, "Oh, who's interested in this one, because, well, I'm going to lay off, and maybe I will go over there a little bit and try to talk to this [other] person. . . ."

HAILEY: As soon as—I think Shimon was the first [soldier] to come in—
like, someone got kicked out of their seat—I think it was Bauer.
Or he—people were like, "Someone has to leave so the soldier can
come sit back here." I think Bauer just volunteered to go somewhere else. . . .

[Shimon] sat down, and literally, like, these girls—I feel like
the claws came out. Like everyone was like, "Oh my God! I need
to be the one to talk to him. He needs to like me. I need to look
the prettiest. . . ." I tried talking to him for the first, like, three
minutes, and then I was like, "This isn't worth it right now. This
is *ridiculous*." And then, I was sitting next to [another soldier],
Rami, for a little bit and talking to him, and it was fine and like—
but then someone else, like, stole my seat. . . . I personally thought
it was a mess. Like I didn't realize that there was going to be such,
like, competition between the girls. . . . People were getting angry
at each other about, like . . . "She just asked me who I like and I
told her and now she's flirting with him." So it's just ridiculous.

JENNA: There was a lot of competition, especially among the females to
talk to the Israelis. . . . "Oh, who is he going to sit next to on the
bus?" And this and that, and like, "Who are you going to walk
with? And who are you going to have lunch with? And who are
you going to hang out with tonight?"

HAILEY: I felt really bad because the next day, I think, I moved from the
back of the bus because I couldn't handle it anymore. And I sat
next to Nora, and we were talking about how it's really hard. . . .
She is not the kind of person who is going to go and, like, try to
compete with these other girls to flirt with them. But she was saying how she just wanted to get to know them, but she didn't even
get a chance. . . . And I think a lot of people didn't get the chance
to get to know them because other people were just bombarding
them. I mean, granted, I might've been one of them, but I think it
was hard [for] people who didn't want to put themselves out there,
you know, and flirt with them just to get to know them.

JENNA: I was also talking with some of the other girls on the bus who
are maybe less aggressive in terms of, like, pursuing of the males
in general, for whatever reason, and a couple said it is really
frustrating that, like, the soldiers wouldn't even give a lot of girls
the time of day, because maybe the soldiers weren't necessarily
interested in having, like, relations, at all with these girls. . . . It's

just unfortunate that it's, once you've removed that potential possibility of hooking up, it's like, it's almost, people are just, "I'm not interested."

SK TO HAILEY: Were they able to make friends with the female soldiers?

HAILEY: The girls? I don't think so. Meital was really sweet and I think that [of the three female soldiers] she made the most friends, but the two other girls kind of kept to themselves more. . . . I think it would have even been hard for someone, anyone really, to try to move in with those two and try to get to know them really well.

SK TO HAILEY: The female soldiers don't seem as interested in the American guys.

HAILEY: We asked [Meital] about it, because Bauer liked her . . . and she said that she doesn't do meaningless relationships. Understandable, respectable. But, yeah, I don't think that the other two girls were interested.

On tours for adolescents and unmarried young adults, the hypersexualized character of the meeting between Israelis and diaspora Jews is one of the mifgash program's most powerful contradictions. At the same time that it intensifies cross-cultural learning for some through an intimacy that transcends the physical aspects of sex, it also limits the ability of many tourists to experience meaningful cross-cultural encounters. More significantly, it testifies to the entry of the mifgash into the very semiotic field that the encounters are intended to undermine. As with other forms of sex and romance tourism, the cross-cultural liaisons on diaspora Jewish homeland tours are rooted in fantasies of eroticized exotic Others.[41] Unlike other forms, there is a mutuality of objectification, as male Israeli soldiers and American women fantasize each other as embodiments of macho sensuality, on one hand, and feminine sexual aggressiveness and promiscuity, on the other. The desire to "hook up" with a "hot Israeli soldier" or with an "American girl" even prior to the trip, and the frantic search to realize that desire with someone, anyone, to whom that label might be applied, testify to the determination of mifgash participants to relate to each other as members of categories rather than solely as individuals.

This is symptomatic of the broader contradiction inherent in the mifgash. Even as it forges people-to-people relationships, its mission of fostering cross-cultural understanding ensures that it does so in a way that leads mifgash participants to relate to each other not simply as individuals but also as symbols of their respective societies. Structured programs engage them in representations of cultural difference. For example, the icebreaker game that Michael's group conducted consisted of a series of statements. After each, everyone who agreed with the statement would run into the center of the circle. Among the statements offered by staff were, "I am willing to die for my country." On clear display to all was the fact that every Israeli soldier had stepped into the circle, but almost none of the North Americans.

In spite of their successes, mifgashim can never fully respond to the critique that the tours reinforce myths and stereotypes, for what these critiques really take issue with is not the nature of Israel's representation but the fact of representation itself. Ambivalent about the very essence of the medium they deploy, educational tour planners offer critiques of tourism's semiotic character that are latter-day variants on Daniel Boorstin's classic charge that tourism substitutes symbols for reality.[42] As such, they do precisely what Jonathan Culler, in a seminal tourism studies article, warned against when he suggested that scholars should adopt a "semiotic perspective" so that they might avoid the trap of "thinking of signs and sign relations as corruptions of what ought to be a direct experience of being or of the natural world."[43] Mifgashim cannot do the impossible and reconfigure tourism as a nonsemiotic enterprise. Their use on diaspora Jewish homeland tours is significant, however, not just for what they do accomplish but because they testify powerfully to the ambivalences surrounding a medium premised on representation. In their efforts to forge diasporic connections to a homeland, Israel experience programs are ever and always suspended in the tension that results from being drawn simultaneously toward the opposite poles of mythmaking and mythbreaking.

6

Encountering Community

The night air was crisp and the January sky ablaze with stars. At 4:20 a.m., all was stillness and silence, save the tour bus blasting disco as it barreled through the Judean Desert toward Masada. On board, the atmosphere was electric, an inversion of the collective half-sleep that marked the wake-up at the hotel in Arad an hour earlier. Bleary-eyed college students, unshowered and clad in university-logo sweatsuits, had trickled into a common room whose fluorescent lights only brought out the dingy yellow of the walls. On a table near the stairs were slices of a bone-dry brown cake that may have been chocolate or may have been honey. Next to it was something even less appetizing, which Lucas, the lead American staff person, described as a "holiday fruit cake." Lucas was one of the only people cracking jokes at that hour. Most stood around making small talk in low voices or sipping coffee in silence. I prepared myself a cup of tea.

Ellen Galperin, the youngest member of the group and a person who talked incessantly about drugs, stood by a pillar and lit a cigarette. Someone nearby snapped, "Can you do that somewhere else?!" People had been growing impatient with her, and what had begun as snide comments behind her back was giving way to more direct expressions of disdain.

By 3:50, most of us had made our way out into the cold winter night to look for the bus. From the front entrance of this sleepy desert town hotel, we could see the road leading off into blackness. It was not immediately clear which of the buses parked there was ours and which would be carrying the other Birthright Israel groups on their 45-minute drives to Masada. Eventually, we all found our way to the right place. Our bus was the one throbbing with the rhythms of Earth, Wind and Fire.

As I arrived, Ravit stepped down from inside the bus and started dancing. She tried to get some of the half-dozen members of the group standing with Lucas to dance with her. "Come on, guys! This is my generation," she said. Todd Adler, as usual reeking of cologne, teased Ravit about her dancing.

I approached Lucas and gestured as if to say, "What's going on here?!"

He smiled and pulled me aside. "It's the last thing they expect at 3:00 a.m.," he confided, adding that it gets people excited and has the extra benefit of tiring them out so that by the time they are atop Masada watching the sunrise, they can enjoy it quietly. Lucas was only about 10 years older than the students, but he had been doing this sort of work for years and was skilled at fostering a positive group dynamic.

As I climbed aboard, I saw that the bus had been transformed into a dance club filled with dozens of revelers. I twirled down the aisle and found a seat in front of the rear staircase. Others came on, each wearing the same expression of amused bewilderment, and each miming dance moves as they walked to their seats. Soon, the doors closed and we sped off into the desert night.

People continued dancing as the bus began to move. Didi Sandler and Isabel Pankow stood up from the seat that the two of them usually occupied together near the back of the bus, and with Todd pressed tightly between them, the three started grinding their pelvises in unison. They were cheered on by people nearby. Behind the trio, two fraternity brothers rapped to the beat.

Hearing them, someone screamed out, "Let's get Jesse to freestyle for us!" Jesse Benjamin was a South Philadelphian with a crew cut and a menacing scar on his cheek. After demonstrating his talent for free-form rapping, he was often given the bus microphone, although he used it only to lead the count off that staff had instituted to confirm that all were present. Jesse was also the owner of the shofar that the men in the group were trying to commandeer.

"Play your shofar!" someone called out to him.

Hearing this, Sam Pollack shouted across the bus, "Hey Jesse, bring your shofar up to Masada."

Shouts went up when Daphna, the tongue-pierced, rifle-toting Israeli medic, stepped out into the aisle and started grinding with one of the American men. Before that moment she had shown little interest in befriending the Americans, in spite of the fact that they were close to her in age. She usually spent the bus rides in the front seat huddled with her Meir Shalev novel.

Occasionally, the dancers would be thrown to one side or the other as the bus careened down mountain curves visible only to the driver. The side windows could have been made of polished ebony for all the view they afforded. The only light came from the bus itself—a faint blue glow in the ceiling that ensured that those who wanted to gaze into the desert night would see only their own reflections and those of the dancers. I felt as if I were in a submarine or a spaceship, a metal capsule sealed off from surroundings that whipped by at speeds I did not want to contemplate. The ride had an otherworldly feel to it. The veil of sleep that lingered from the 3:00 a.m. wake-up call was violently torn off by the assault of noise, rhythm, speed, motion, darkness, and blue light. The limited visual field focused people on the only thing they could see: the party around them. It was a distinctive sensory experience that enhanced the feeling of a distinctive social experience.

People were acting on the bus in ways that they had never acted there before. The aisle, normally an empty path during travel time, had become a stage alive with movement. Seats still faced forward, but many people had positioned themselves to see in front, across, and behind them—wherever the action was. Some social lines that had not been crossed before were. At the same time, it was clear to anyone who cared to observe that, with the exception of Daphna and her dance partner, most of the action was taking place— in a cliché straight out of the 7th grade—in the back half of the bus. They were the rowdy ones standing and dancing in the aisles, shouting to Lucas, making their comments loudly for all to hear, rapping across the aisle, and talking to each other across the seats. Those in the front stayed seated, and when they participated in the revelry it was primarily by taking it in as an audience.

As we got closer to Masada, Lucas turned off the music and took the microphone. "We should thank Ofir," he said, acknowledging the bus driver, "for handling the curves, Ravit for shaking her groove *thaanng,* and the Bus 194 dancers who sometimes bordered on the inappropriate." Then he reminded us to wear hats and drink plenty of water during the hike. "Ravit suggested we should play drinking games," he joked. Lucas put the microphone down and turned the music back on. When the disco mix ended, people asked for more. Lucas told them that the other side had Israeli disco.

"No! No! No!" came the shouted replies. "Rewind the tape!"

Lucas did not accommodate their request. Instead, he handed the microphone to his junior staff person, Julie Beth, a mousy-haired woman in her late 20s who carried a prayerbook in her backpack. I knew what was coming. After dinner at the shopping mall in Arad the previous evening I had accompanied Julie Beth to a bookstore where she purchased a stuffed cat as a mascot. "They're going to name it Sababa," she declared confidently. "Sababa" was Hebrew slang, lifted from Arabic. It translates roughly to "groovy." Ravit had taught us the word early in the trip, and many people had been peppering their speech with it. Usually, they shouted it simply to hear its sound irrespective of whether it made any sense in context.

As Julie Beth took the microphone, she kept the stuffed cat hidden. "We need a bus mascot. And I thought, a camel? No, because we haven't seen any camels. So what about a donkey? Because we are going to be riding donkeys. But that wasn't good, either. And then I thought, 'What animal do we have a connection with?'" She produced the surprise.

People laughed, immediately catching her reference. On Shabbat at the Western Wall several days earlier, our pensive mood had been broken by the sight of two cats copulating in a flurry of fur, shrieks, and arched backs. The group had erupted in peals of laughter, flashing cameras, and topical jokes ("It's a triple *mitzvah!*"[1]). At the time, Julie Beth had tried with a mixture of dismay and chagrin to shuffle the group along, disappointed that their memory of the holy site would be colored by such an unholy sight. Now, though, she seemed not only to have relented but to have decided to co-opt the moment and use it for group building.

In point of fact, the sight of the cats in heat was ignored by a number of us. But as Julie Beth stood at the front of the bus and asserted that this was something "we," meaning all of us, "have a connection with," she reinforced the connection where it already existed and helped to forge it where it did not. Then, having decided for the group that they would have a mascot and that it would be a stuffed cat, she gave the tourists an opportunity to take part in creating their collective symbol. "We need a name for it," she said, and turned the decision over to them.

From the back of the bus someone shouted, "Chavchalash," a frequently referenced nonsensical word from a movie I was never able to identify.

Within seconds, though, several people, including Mickey Goldman, called out, "Sababa!" As Julie Beth had predicted, the name was chosen by acclimation.

As a unifying symbol, the stuffed cat was an imperfect one. Mickey took possession of the mascot much more than others in the group, both physically and symbolically. In a social network survey I fielded, he even wrote down "Sababa" as one of the "people" he felt closest to in the group.[2] His fraternity brother, Todd, did the same. In contrast, Mark Gottlieb, who fancied himself a part of Mickey and Todd's crowd but was never really accepted as such, tried to no avail to get people to call it "The Bus 194 Pussy." For her part, Ravit began referring to the group as "Sababa Cats," but the term remained hers alone. Most others continued to refer to themselves simply as "Bus 194." In short, the mascot was commandeered by one person. Another contested its name and offered an alternative that retained a numeric designation for the group. Only Ravit made the Durkheimian leap and called the group by the name of its totem. But in spite of the authority she commanded, no one followed her example.

As they rode toward Masada, Bus 194's collective attention was directed not outward toward the icon of Zionist collective memory that was their destination but inward toward their friends' grinding hips and then toward their new stuffed cat. This was a product of Lucas's and Julie Beth's deliberate choices to structure the bus ride in a way that seemed to use Durkheim's *Elementary Forms* as an instruction manual, first creating conditions that gave rise to collective effervescence and then creating a collective representation to give symbolic expression to the emergent feelings of group solidarity. Lucas showed no concern that directing attention inward toward the group would detract from a full engagement with Masada. On the contrary, he thought that the physical exhaustion brought on by the 4:00 a.m. disco party would help the tourists achieve the inner quiet he wanted them to have as they sat on the mountaintop watching the sunrise. More important, Lucas, like the organization he worked for, Hillel, also considered group-building among diaspora Jews to be an end in itself.

One of the dimensions of tourism that makes it attractive as a diaspora-building medium is the small group context in which it typically embeds the encounter with the homeland. Trip sponsors deem this valuable for two reasons. First, because it allows them to mobilize the peer group as a *socializing agent* that mediates the encounter with place and establishes norms around its interpretation. The individual tourists will see Israel not only with their own eyes but also through those of their peers. Second, because it allows them to mobilize the encounter with fellow diasporans as a *socializing experience of ethnic community* in its own right. It is hoped that such an experience will lead tourists to seek out ethnic community after the trip ends. Hence the efforts to foster a constructive group dynamic. As with the efforts to enlist other structural dimensions of tourism, the efforts to mobilize its group context are riddled with contradictions. Tour group dynamics may draw travelers closer to the object of their gaze, but they can also distance them from it. Likewise, these dynamics can breed solidarity, but they can also establish the tour group as an arena of differentiation and status competition. Notwithstanding the efforts of trip staff, these tensions are never quite resolved.

Mediating the Encounter with Place

One of the commonly noted contradictions of tourism that complicates efforts to mobilize it for developing diaspora Jewish attachments to Israel is the tendency for the shared group experience to focus attention inside the tour bus rather than outside it. In his study of a summer-long high school tour, Samuel Heilman observed that of the group's list of "top ten moments in Israel," nine had nothing to do with "actually being in Israel" but, instead, involved things like "Tim and Leo's love affair" (#5) and "Melanie stepping in shit" (#1).[3] He concluded that Israel served more as a "venue or backdrop" for an American teen group experience than as a focus of collective attention.

One could argue that any tendency for the social experience to draw tourists' attention away from a singular focus on the symbolic engagement with place depends on the particular makeup of the tour group. Those of whom Heilman wrote, after all, were unmarried adolescents (the primary target population for many homeland tours, not only Jewish ones). Birthright Israel tour guides who have worked with both high school and college students have reported that they find the older groups somewhat more place oriented and less group focused. Somewhat. When the college students on Ra'anan's bus were given the choice to go to a bar that had been rented out for a private Hillel-Birthright Israel party or to take a nighttime tour of the first Jewish neighborhoods built outside the walls of Jerusalem's Old City (icons from the birth of Zionism in the 19th century), only nine out of 48 chose the tour. Just as Taiwan's Chien Tan program has come to be known as "The Love Boat," Birthright Israel participants have sometimes spoken of "Birthrate Israel" in light of its active hook-up scene (and also in light of their awareness that trip sponsors hope that the tours will make them more likely to marry other Jews).

Tourists avidly follow the soap opera–like convolutions of their groupmates' relationships. Who does he like? Why did she dump him? He hasn't made a move on her, do you think he is gay? Should we tell his girlfriend at home that he hooked up with someone else? I found myself here at the limits of my observational powers. Having no need to navigate this dating scene, I had difficulty recognizing cues that were patently obvious to the college students. And as a 30-something-year-old married male professor, I was not privy to much of the information they shared with one another. Among themselves, however, there are few secrets.

I discovered just how much this was true when, on the plane ride home, some people from Ra'anan's bus showed me what they could do with all the knowledge they had amassed. I was wandering the aisles, when someone called out, "Hey, Shaul, come here!" Ten group members had congregated in one of the flight attendant stations and were huddled around Jessica Harman and Martin Greenstein, who were holding a sheet of paper between them. Jessica and Martin had a lot in common. They both seemed to be poised for success, with handsome looks, outgoing personalities, mischievous senses of humor, brains, ambition, money, friends, and connections. I walked over to them.

Jessica indicated the paper they were holding and said, "Shaul, you'll be interested in this." It was a social network map, like the friendship network maps that I was gathering information to draw (and which appear later in this chapter). But theirs had a crucial difference. "It's the hook-up network," she announced with a broad smile. I laughed. Jessica flashed the paper to allow me to eyeball the diagram but not read names. If each person had a liaison with only one other, the map would feature a series of pairs, with no pair connected to any other. The map did not look like this. Instead, it showed two large webs, one smaller chain, some pairs, and a series of isolates. Evidently, some people were having more than their share of fun.

"We gotta connect the map," Martin said. He grabbed Jessica, kissed her full on the mouth—a long, wet kiss—and then stepped back. She took a pen and drew a line connecting two points on the paper. "Did it taste like tuna?" he asked her with a grin.

Adolescence can explain only part of the tendency for tourists' gazes to be directed inward to the community of travelers itself. Structural properties of group tourism are also at work. For one, in a situation where people are continually moving "through an ever-changing landscape," the tour group is, as Heilman has observed, "the one constant to which the campers and staff [can] cling."[4] The tourist borderzone's infrastructure of buses, hotels, heritage sites, and shopping districts also tends to restrict tourists' interactions so that they occur primarily (though not exclusively) with each other. The challenges of independently navigating a foreign environment and the anxieties these raise also lead tourists to seek one another's support such that unstructured forays to encounter the local culture tend to occur in small groups rather than alone.

Other contributing factors derive from those aspects of mass tourism that limit personal autonomy, standardize experience, and subordinate individual needs to those of the group. These are especially evident on Birthright Israel. Itineraries are presented as faits accomplis, binding on all. No one has the option of deciding to stay an extra day in a place they especially liked or to abandon the hotel for a cousin's apartment. Privacy and personal space are extraordinarily rare. The trips afford almost no opportunity to be alone and keep travelers in the public eye almost constantly throughout the tour. The hours spent traveling from one place to another are not spent in private automobiles but on a bus that is a single public space. Off the bus, the same applies. Sightseeing is a group activity. Meals are eaten together. Hotel rooms are shared.

All this helps establish the bus group as a "total institution," albeit more temporary, more benign, and more explicitly committed to humanistic values than the asylums, prisons, and army barracks that Erving Goffman described when coining the term. Still, the four defining characteristics of total institutions are decidedly present on diaspora Jewish homeland tours:

> First, all aspects of life are conducted in the same place and under the same single authority. Second, each phase of the member's daily activity is carried on in the immediate company of a large batch of others, all of whom are treated alike and required to do the same thing together. Third, all phases of the day's activities are tightly scheduled. . . . Finally, the various enforced activities are brought together into a single rational plan purportedly designed to fulfill the official aims of the institution.[5]

The seeds of the trips' character as total institutions rest not in the particularities of diaspora Jewish homeland tours but in mass tourism generally. What distinguishes the homeland tours is that they realize potentials that remain dormant in other travel contexts.

There are a number of reasons for this. Generally speaking, restrictions on tourists' ability to tailor their own experiences are functional responses to the financial and logistical challenges of managing the movement of large numbers of people. Beyond this, Israel experience tours tend to locate themselves on the more restrictive end of the continuum due to the influence of three factors particular to their case: organizers' concerns about security and liability in the face of terrorism and their desire to allay similar concerns among parents and potential travelers; awareness of their responsibility for the behavior of their young charges, coupled with a modest skepticism about the willingness of youth to behave responsibly;[6] and a self-understanding that they are not engaged in the business of leisure but in the crucial mission of education.[7]

The same factors that lead individual buses to function as total institutions are also implicated in the quasi-Fordist character of the Birthright Israel enterprise. In order to take diaspora-building homeland tourism to scale, the planners of Birthright Israel adopted a model of licensing partners to mass-produce package tours that offer consumers a choice among a small menu of preset options but whose variation is limited by quality-control regulations that ensure a standardized product. Applicants may select whether they want to travel on an Orthodox-sponsored trip that includes religious text study or on a secular-sponsored trip that highlights outdoor activities, for example, but participants in both will end up making the circuit of Israel's iconic attractions (Western Wall, Masada, Yad Vashem, Mount Herzl, Independence Hall,

Golan Heights, Dead Sea) and will take part in the standard menu of Taglit programs (e.g., Shabbat celebrations, mifgash, discussion circles). Beyond choosing their group, opportunity for further customization is minimal.

The mass production of a standardized group tour is one of the central factors giving rise to the dialectic of attention and distraction that characterizes Israel experience participants' engagement with Israel. There is no doubt that the group tour lays the groundwork for an intensive, sometimes rousing, sometimes oppressive collective experience that can draw attention away from the semiotic encounter with the homeland and direct it, instead, toward the social encounter with other tourists. This groundwork is developed by key policy decisions regarding group size (limited to one or two buses), group assignment (tourists and staff are assigned to a specific bus group rather than allowed to float freely from bus to bus), and program duration (trips are long enough for people to get to know one another).

Nevertheless, the collective character of a group tour also forms the basis for shared encounters with place. Two hours after the disco bus ride ended, Lucas's group was sitting silently on Masada's eastern edge waiting for the sun to rise (chapter 5 in this volume). Spread over a wide area, most sat in clusters of two or three. Some had wandered off to an adjacent section of ruins, but every member of the group was within the field of vision, and with the exception of one grounds worker, no other people were in or near the space we had claimed for ourselves. In two cases, people who stood alone became a focus of group attention: Ravit, the guide, who wandered off to move her limbs gracefully in the meditative martial art of Tai Chi; and Sam, who went to find a raised area from which he could stand and blow the shofar when the sun rose. Both encapsulated the simultaneously private and public, individualistic and collective character of the experience. Ravit and Sam separated themselves from the group, but in conspicuously public ways. Although from their vantage point they could not see themselves framed against their respective backdrops, I suspect they knew the shots they had established even before other people's cameras began preserving their poses for posterity—Ravit with arms extended and leg raised; Sam profiled on a ruined stone wall with a ram's horn raised to his lips. Each stood apart from the group, but neither was truly alone.

So it was with all of us. Sitting in relative silence, we were still able to hear the whispered oohs and aahs and to see the looks on each others' faces as the sun rose. We could also observe those around us as part of the scene we were taking in. No matter how hard we might try to be alone with our thoughts as we contemplated the sunrise, the awareness of others' presence invariably colored perception. The experience on top of Masada was one of *collective solitude*—its solemnity a product of a social context that echoed and amplified each person's silence.

Ravit and Sam were not the only ones to separate from the group. We ended up spread out on the mountain's edge rather than clustered together because people were trying to gain some measure of space for themselves. The more intrepid began climbing down the cliffside in order to place the group behind them, out of sight. Such efforts reveal one of the ironies of mass tourism. Precisely because tourists feel that a standardized group tour impedes their ability to have a personalized encounter with place, they try to carve out individualized experiences whose uniqueness endows them with an aura of authenticity.[8] This usually does not involve tourists' active separation from the group but merely their attentiveness to particularities of their own interactions with shopkeepers and other locals who populate the borderzone.

Meeting in our kibbutz hotel conference room at the end of a long day touring the Golan Heights and rafting on the Jordan River, for example, Gidi asked the members of his group, "Who wants to share something that was really great about the day? . . . Highlights?"

Ken Wurtzel, a wiry, energetic person whose raft I shared as we went down the Jordan, raised his hand and told the story of an encounter we had had with Israeli children who were rowing next to us. "Uhh, in our raft—Jeff, Ben, and Shaul—we were going through and these little kids—they didn't really know English or anything—but they said, 'Tom Cruise?' And then, like, all of us were like, 'Yeah, Tom Cruise! Tom Cruise!' . . . It was hilarious."

People laughed with Ken as he told the story. When he finished, Gidi complimented him:

> That's awesome. You made a connection. . . . Those experiences are really kind of authentic. They are outside of the bubble. What makes me really nervous . . . is that you end up staying inside the bus and the bus becomes this really kind of mini-U.S. and that you don't get to experience anything in the cultural aspect of [Israel]. . . . But that [encounter with the Israeli children] is something that you can't schedule. You don't plan. . . . And that was an interaction that was authentic, and I think that's priceless.

A further irony of mass-tourism's self-generated impetus to experience site encounters that are not mass-produced is found in the fact that such experiences, when they do occur, do not long remain the private possessions of those who experienced them. Instead, they are quickly transformed into collective properties as people come back and recount their stories to their friends. The personalized experiences that offer a means of escape from the group end up also binding people closer to it, winning them status in it, and reinforcing group solidarity by forging shared stories. These shared stories mediate the group's encounter with place by enabling tourists to fashion understandings that are based not solely on their own firsthand experience but also on their vicarious participation in the experiences of others.[9]

As suggested by the example of Ken's Jordan River tale, group discussion circles become important venues where the public, retrospective, and sometimes even prospective mediation of site encounters occurs. Here again, we see tour organizers attempting to take emergent dynamics, encourage them, and direct them systematically to serve program ends. The discussion circles ensure that the processing of site encounters will not be simply a private matter but a collective endeavor, accomplished publicly, as well. Tourists will be able to see the sites through the eyes of their peers, and they will find their own sentiments subject to the monitoring of the group.[10] Focused on "highlights" and things "that [are] really great," these discussions mobilize the peer group in ways that create a normative environment that both supports and challenges the tours' goals of fostering diasporic attachments to the homeland. On one hand, the sharing of stories offers powerful firsthand evidence to travelers that their friends are attentive to their Israeli surroundings and derive pleasure from encountering them. On the other hand, the social pressures that are thusly created demand only that tourists engage Israel aesthetically, as pleasure-seeking consumers.

Tour organizers strive also to foster a moral engagement that includes a sense of obligation and responsibility, but on this matter—which is less directly relevant to the immediate context of a situation centered on aesthetic consumption—peer group dynamics do not in themselves generate any clear or immediately actionable behavioral norms. There is peer pressure operative at that very moment to find an iconic souvenir and to taste falafel, but nothing of the sort demanding that people phone in a donation to Hadassah, recite the prayer for the welfare of Israel, or write to a congressperson in support of a foreign aid bill.

The tour group mediates the encounter with place not only by encouraging individualized encounters, by making the processing of sites a collective act, and by fostering normative environments. It also makes its influence felt at the sites themselves as people look to one another for assistance in navigating the foreign environments. This is especially evident during free time when people go to shop and eat. Both the unfamiliarity of the setting and the desire for social acceptance generate anxieties that limit people's willingness to leave the group and explore on their own. It is uncommon to see people alone during free time, in large part because being alone can signal lack of standing in the group.[11] Hence, at the beginning of free time, one can observe a general scramble as people try to ensure that they are not left to wander by themselves. Once they have formed their small groups, these groups often look to one another and end up converging on the same one or two restaurants. Decisions about which streets to turn on and which shops to enter depend less on individual preference than on small group dynamics. In some cases, dominant individuals impose their will. In others, decision-making is consensual. In others, people wander aimlessly as each waits for someone else to assert authority. In others, authority is delegated to someone thought to have expertise.

I learned about the latter two cases on a lunch stop at the pedestrian mall in the gentrified section of Zichron Yaakov, a coastal town on the slopes of Mount Carmel. It was the first day of my trip with Michael's group, and I was walking with a couple, Adam Epstein and Naomi Reingold, and with Hannah Umansky, whom they had just met. The three agreed only that they did not want to waste time standing in line at the shawarma stand where most of the others had gone. I knew a Yemenite restaurant around the corner but did not feel it my place as a participant observer to take the lead. We wandered into a café, looked at the menu, stood around waiting for someone to make a decision, and then left when someone eventually said they were not in the mood for salads. We walked up the road. We walked back down the road. Finally, Naomi and Adam asked if I could recommend something, considering that I had been here before. I suggested Hateimaniyah Shel Santo, which was off the main strip, tucked in a courtyard accessible via a narrow alleyway. As we sat at an outdoor table, my lunchmates asked me to recommend dishes, to translate the menu, and to ask where the bathrooms were located.

Conscious that I was instrumental in shaping this experience and somewhat uncomfortable with the fact, I scrutinized the role I was playing. They were looking to me as a local expert who could use insider knowledge to gain them access to Zichron Yaakov in a way they would not be able to do on their own—a pathfinder, or Original Guide in Erik Cohen's terminology.[12] As the trip wore on, I noticed that our interaction was hardly out of the ordinary. Tourists were constantly seeking and receiving from each other guidance in navigating places and activities. Any knowledge that tourists had gained could be placed at the disposal of their travelmates. This included place-specific information (eat here, don't shop there, you can find this cheaper somewhere else), translation skills, and consumer expertise. Souvenir and gift shoppers often asked other people for their opinions before making purchases and for their affirmation after it. Shopping for a gift for my wife, I looked to Renni Horn for advice about a pair of silver earrings I was considering. A few minutes later as Renni shopped for a necklace for herself, she asked Melissa Feig to help her choose between two options. Earlier she had shown me a limestone mezuzah she had bought for her parents and asked if I thought it would be appropriate for a beach house.

Normative Environments

In Israel experience travel, tour groups join tour guides and staff as active agents of diasporic political socialization. One of their key contributions to the effort is the creation of normative environments that support sponsors' official goals. Directing attention to the semiotic encounter with the homeland is the least of this. With regard to the politics of Israel, Palestine, and the Middle East, the peer environment mitigates against strident critiques of Israeli policies and of the ideological underpinnings of Jewish nationalism. It is not that critiques of both are unvoiceable but that certain norms govern the ways in which they may be expressed. Critiques may be made from a stance of caring concern, third-party neutrality, suspicious skepticism, bemused resignation, and principled conviction. Critiques rooted in moral outrage or righteous indignation, however, bear too much resemblance to anger, the taboo emotion in a group oriented first and foremost toward pleasure. In the rare instances that anger does emerge, it is usually sparked by matters pertaining directly to the group (interpersonal conflicts or staff's failure to respect people's time or sensibilities), and even then its expression causes visible discomfort among many who witness it. To invest a political critique of Israel with such emotional valence risks incurring social disapproval while serving no immediately socially relevant end. The group's hedonism is thus one of the most effective checks against a determinedly critical politics, shunning not merely the emotions that energize it but also a broader concern for politics generally. In a group committed to fun, politics is a downer and a politics perceived to be "angry" is toxic.

As Taglit participant Kevin Healy put it to me in a plane-ride interview, "I was here to have fun. And that's not fun. I hate talking about politics. It's not something where you're making friends by talking politics. . . . I came here to travel, and have fun and make friends."

One of the important ways peer groups help shape diasporic understandings of self is by creating a context that is broadly supportive of the tour's message that diasporans should identify themselves ethnically, valuing their cultural inheritance as Jews, valuing their connections to the State of Israel, and embracing these in ways that are personally meaningful to them. The normative environments that affirm this stance emerge through a combination of nondiscursive and discursive practices. As tourists enthusiastically partake in the opportunities to engage with Jewish and Israeli culture, the fun and good feeling created around their collective experience has the consequence (unintended from the perspective of the travelers but not necessarily from the perspective of the sponsors) of bringing peer pressure to bear in support of program goals. Peer pressure, to be clear, is "less a push to conform than a desire to participate in experiences that are seen as relevant, or potentially relevant, to group identity."[13] That is, it is internally generated, not externally compelled.

These emergent norms gain reinforcement and also take on a more constraining character when translated into discourse. Discussion circles are the key venue in which tourists articulate to one another normative positions regarding the value of finding personal meaning through an engagement with Israel, Judaism, and Jewish heritage.

Lucas and Ravit's group wound down its visit to Masada with a discussion circle devoted to the topic of spirituality. Staff asked the group to split in two. The half that went with Julie Beth found a large rocky clearing toward Masada's southern edge and sat on the ground. To the south, behind Julie Beth, the cliff face of the neighboring plateau could be seen, the colors of its strata washed out by a brilliant sun in a nearly cloudless blue sky.

Julie Beth opened the conversation by asking whether we had "had spiritual moments here" in Israel. It was a leading question that implied that such moments would not be out of the ordinary, that Israel was a place where diaspora Jewish tourists should expect to experience spiritual epiphanies.

Fred Jaffe responded first: "Being up here so high, stepping back to see the world and get some perspective," he declared. It was the only thing he would say during the conversation.

Others joined him in mentioning the visit that they were still in the midst of. Ellen Galperin spoke of Sam's shofar blast at dawn and received Mickey Goldman's vocal assent.

Ron Geller, Mickey's closest friend in the group, said, "Sunrise this morning was the most spiritual I think I've ever felt in my entire life."

All who spoke affirmed the premise underlying Julie Beth's question, raising the stakes for those who might have been inclined otherwise.

Mark Gottlieb, the accused thief of Sam's jokes and the advocate of the vulgar name for the stuffed cat, mentioned "feel[ing] the power" in Jerusalem.

Perhaps aware of the emerging dynamic, Julie Beth felt it necessary to give permission, as it were, to those inclined to dissent. She intervened to say that many people often feel upset at the Western Wall because they do not experience the feelings they expect they should feel there.

At first, no one took the bait. Instead, Mickey began describing his experience at the Western Wall, saying, "I was rubbing the Wall, I pushed my head up against it. I felt like I was speaking directly to God."

When Julie Beth responded by saying that his comment was a good lead-in to what she wanted to say next, Mickey burst out enthusiastically, "Score! The segue!"

Next to him, Ron pumped a fist in the air in support. If they were able to treat the discussion circle as a game, it was because they recognized that it was, in fact, governed by implicit rules.

Their friend, Isabel Pankow, also recognized the rules but chose not to play along. Tall, haughty, stunning Park Avenue progeny who would just as easily discourse on Roman conceptions of glory as drop the names of socialites whose parties she frequented, Isabel was also a graduate of a Jewish day school and a speaker of near-fluent Hebrew.[14] Yet when Julie Beth tried to broaden the discussion to frame the Jewish religion as a locus of spiritual experience, Isabel refused to affirm the direction in which she was taking the conversation.

"Does Judaism have the power to bring you spirituality?" Julie Beth asked, mentioning the *Sh'ma* prayer, Judaism's central affirmation of faith: *Hear O Israel! The Lord is our God. The Lord is One.* "How do these words make you feel?"

"It makes me think of being a little kid," Isabel responded. "My parents would make me say the *Sh'ma* every night before I went to sleep. As I got older, I realized they were words that meant nothing to me." She then steered the conversation into a technical discussion about Hebrew grammar in the *Sh'ma*. For five minutes her diversionary tactic succeeded, until Julie Beth reined the conversation in.

Throughout these exchanges, Jeffrey Shain remained silent. Jeffrey was a pallid, lanky man who made few close connections with his groupmates. He typically did not hesitate to voice his opinions strongly, even when they went against the grain. After Isabel spoke again, this time saying, "I'm really jealous of people who can feel [a sense of God]. At the Kotel [the Western Wall] I felt nothing," he finally spoke up, echoing some of the sentiment she had voiced. "I'm not feeling spiritual," he said. "I didn't feel spiritual at the Wall." But rather than leave it at this, as Isabel did, Jeffrey expressed interest in learning why Judaism, which he said meant little to him, was meaningful to others. At that moment, as in others during the trip, he seemed honestly bewildered by the interest and excitement that things Jewish generated among his peers.

He adopted a tentative and questioning tone: "When I read a book that speaks to me . . . is that what it is to have a spiritual experience? When something strikes a match inside of you?" (For all his professions of ignorance, he knew the appropriate metaphors.) His open-minded skepticism challenged others, "Convince me!" Although it was in one sense oppositional, its effect was to reinforce the emerging normative environment by inviting people to rearticulate norms and make explicit efforts to quash or co-opt his dissent.

Mark, who had developed a generally confrontational relationship with Jeffrey, immediately jumped in. "I disagree," he said, cutting Jeffrey off.

"What do you mean 'you disagree'?!" Jeffrey shouted back. "It's the way I *feel!* You can't disagree.'"

Ellen Galperin and Beth Dolman gave Jeffrey some support. Beth said, "That book could be someone else's Western Wall. You can't know when it's gonna come over you."

Mickey leaned up off his hands, dusted the dirt off of them, and said, "For me, it's math. When you look at something and it completely makes sense."

"Will Hunting!" Ron exclaimed. "That's who you are." People smiled at the reference to the fictional math genius played by Matt Damon in the Oscar-winning film.

Mickey shrugged off Ron's joke and waxed poetic: "On this trip, my view of God has totally changed. God is the universal connection of everything. . . . In my opinion, it's a more mature view of God." He said he began thinking seriously about his view of God after hearing a lecture on "the pillars of Jewish identity" delivered by a South African–born Israeli educator on the first night of the trip.

As Mickey continued, a plane flew overhead, the sound of its engines drowning out his voice. The faint scent of suntan lotion wafted in the breeze. Fred leaned back and tilted his head toward the sky, eyes closed, basking in the sun. Judy Berson passed around her bag of pretzels.

Jeffrey waited for Mickey to finish, then responded, "I don't really believe in God. But I see that some of you [do]. At what moment were you convinced?" It was an invitation to others to help him empathize with their feelings.

Ron, Mark, and another man each responded with some variant of "There is always doubt" but that it can be reconciled with belief. Julie Beth echoed the sentiment, prompting Jeffrey to respond, "I marvel at the amount of dedication. I can't be so dedicated."

"Did you ever do a what-if?" Mickey asked, perhaps trying to encourage him.

Jeffrey responded by saying that he had wrapped the pair of tefillin on his arm and forehead at the Western Wall, where a booth for that purpose had been set up and staffed by two long-bearded Orthodox men with thick Brooklyn accents. He felt uncomfortable, though, he said. This was not him. He went up to the Western Wall with them on but did not—could not—pray. Instead, he just thought.

"I did the same thing," Mickey responded in affirmation.

Most of the men in the group had gone together to the tefillin booth and so shared the experience. Now they were getting a chance to encounter it again, this time through the eyes of others. The women who were not allowed to be present because the authorities enforce strict gender segregation at the Western Wall were also brought in vicariously through the tales that Jeffrey and Mickey were making public possessions of the group.

As the discussion wound down, Mark also offered uncharacteristic words of support: "You've got to find your own way."

More than once in this exchange, Julie Beth tried to offer validation, announcing that all feelings were legitimate. Many times during the trip she and Lucas would return to this refrain, which was inscribed in Hillel's staff manual: "Give students permission to dislike things without being condemned."[15] The policy appeared under the heading, "Creating a Safe/Non-Judgmental Environment" and was a core ethical principle that was taken seriously by the tour staff I observed. In this instance, though, Julie Beth's protestations were superfluous. Jeffrey's dissent was already being engaged respectfully. True, people were trying to offer him a path toward normative conformity, but, then, Jeffrey had asked them to.

Channels of Dissent

Jeffrey's decision to place his skepticism up for collective consideration as the centerpiece of a group conversation was exceptional. With regard to the homeland tour's assertions that Jewish heritage, community, and connection to Israel should be experienced as personally meaningful, the strength of the normative environment is such that opposition is more often channeled away from highly public stages like group discussion circles and directed into more private expressions.

The couple Naomi and Adam, for example, frequently but quietly voiced their discontent to each other, as well as to a few others whom they had come to trust. At a dinner table in a kibbutz hotel dining room one evening, Adam confided that he found the guide's use of the term "we" to be presumptuous. Being Jewish was marginal to Adam's identity, he said, but on this tour he felt as if he were being categorized by others in an essentialist way that denied his right to define himself differently.

Private dissent is not always expressed with gravity. The use of humor is a popular way for people to signal their lack of wholehearted commitment to the program's identity-shaping ambitions. It is a "safe" form of dissent in that it allows criticism to be made obliquely, provides plausible deniability, maintains a sense of proportion, and enables people to distance themselves only partially rather than entirely.

Evan Walsh, an Irish American Jewish American who prefaced his discussion circle confession of ambivalent feelings about being Jewish with the words, "I don't want to sound like a traitor," often used this tactic. Arriving at the Temple Mount in Jerusalem, he gazed on it with a friend who was surprised to find it nowhere near as large as he had expected.

"Are the mountains here all so small?!" the friend asked.

Evan's response—"I hope Mount Sinai isn't such a piece of shit, or it might really shake my Jewish identity"—elicited guffaws from those nearby, even as it mocked the tour's goal-oriented character.

Something similar was evident at the megaevent, where thousands of cheering Birthright Israel tourists at the Jerusalem convention center were treated to a laser show, rock concert, and prime ministerial welcome. Evan walked toward a small cluster of friends and held up a small plastic Israeli flag that he had been handed at the entrance: "I never was given a flag at a political event before. I feel like we're at a Cuban rally." With a mischievous smile pasted on his lips, he waved the flag and started chanting: "Fi-del! Fi-del!"

Of the ways people channel their dissent to avoid overt public confrontation, the most difficult to analyze are the retreats into silence and the withdrawals of participation. These may be motivated by things other than opposition and are easy to misjudge. I recall a Sabbath meal in which several hundred Taglit participants were crowded into the large dining room of a Jerusalem hotel. Two singers from the Israeli army choir tried to lead the assembled in song. Entire tables joined enthusiastically in the singing, but not the one where I sat, not even when the songs were *niggunim,* repetitive wordless melodies that one could easily learn in less than a minute. The table's occupants, including Evan, Ellen, Misha Velinsky, and three others, sat in complete silence. Although I knew and liked the tunes, I kept my lips sealed because I did not wish to model an alternative behavior, nor did I relish the thought of being the only one at the table joining in the song (such is the power of normative environments). It was difficult to tell from the looks on their faces why they stayed silent. The reasons might have differed for each. Perhaps the ritual was unfamiliar to some, in which case the scene could have easily struck them as bizarre. Perhaps some were uncomfortable with religious observance. I knew Evan's ambivalences because he had made them clear. Misha, too, had offered hints of his own feelings. Days later on a tour of a British detention camp for "illegal" Jewish immigrants in the 1940s, Misha, Mickey, and I stood off on our own, not paying attention to Ravit's presentation.

Out of the blue, Mickey said to us, "You know what's weird? I can't wait for it to be Shabbat again. I'm looking forward to it."

Misha's muttered response was a dismissive, "I can wait." Whether this informed his silence at the table, though, I cannot be sure.

"I Love Jews!"

Although the primary purpose of a tour is to enable people to encounter places, a by-product of this is that the tour itself ends up serving as a container for social interactions among travelers. These interactions have the potential to become unusually intense due to tourism's liminal and sometimes total institutional character. As a result, they can forge tour groups into close-knit traveling communities whose collective life comes to exert a dominant force on individual experience and consciousness. For the sponsors of homeland tours, the communities created by tourism become valuable not only for their mediation of the gaze and for their creation of normative environments but also for their ability to give diasporans a firsthand experience of immersion in a fellowship of co-ethnics. Recognizing that participation in the tour group can be a socializing experience of ethnic community in its own right, organizers take pains to craft the groups' social dynamics so that they advance the trips' diaspora-building goals.

Concerned with creating group solidarity and inclined to see rifts and cliques as dysfunctional, trip organizers take a view of community that we could term Durkheimian. As expressed in Chazan's Israel experience manifesto:

Trips are group experiences. The good trip makes maximal use of the group experience as an educational force. The development of a positive climate among participants and between staff and participants is a powerful force in a good trip. Sharing and learning from each other can enrich the trip greatly; divisiveness and intra-group tensions can be tiresome and wasteful.[16]

Similarly, Hillel's staff manual presents the following scenarios among its case studies of problem situations:

> There is a group of six "snobby" students who always sit in the back of the bus and do not make an effort to befriend anyone. They are quite disruptive and talk a lot during programs. The others on the bus are quite intimidated by them.

> There is one student who is not treated well by the rest of the bus and no one wants to be his or her roommate.[17]

Under the heading, "Building Group Dynamics," the manual goes on to inform staff of their responsibility to "discourage *lashon hora* (speaking inappropriately or gossiping about others)," to "encourage students to meet and talk with many other students," and to "create a sense of responsibility toward each other."[18]

Although homeland tours possess certain Turnerian structural features that promote solidarity among tourists (e.g., liminality, equality of status, a common goal orientation), the I-Thou relationships of "communitas" they generate tend to be sporadic and directed in a restricted manner to select individuals, not to all members of the group. To the degree that they do emerge, feelings of identification with the group as a whole tend to treat the group as a symbolic construct.[19] On a day-to-day level, the group is just as likely to be experienced as a site of differentiation and status competition— something to be navigated, not communed with. On buses that mix ethnic subcommunities (e.g., New York groups that mix Persian American Jews with Russian American Jews; Canadian groups that mix second-generation Moroccan Francophones with third-generation Ashkenazi Anglophones), clear lines of demarcation are often maintained. Travelers who do not belong to fraternities and sororities often speak derisively of those who do. Other forces for differentiation are emergent rather than imported. I have mentioned competition among women for the attention of Israeli soldiers. One also can see efforts to navigate an uneven social terrain by looking at how people quickly assess seating options when entering a hotel dining room at mealtime or on boarding the bus each morning.

The microstrategies that tourists develop to place themselves alongside those with whom they want to be placed include entering settings already in the company of others, first claiming seats in dining rooms and only then going to the buffet line, and reserving seats for friends. Other strategies are designed to maintain distance from other people or groups. This includes claiming a region of the bus for one's circle of friends, passing over empty seats next to low-status group members, and overtly or subtly signaling to low-status members that their presence is not desired (such as by plugging into headphones when such a person approaches). The fact that such strategies are developed indicates that there are limits to tour group solidarity.

Social network analyses offer evidence of the interplay between differentiation and cohesion. On the seventh day of Ravit's group's tour, I fielded a one-question survey: "At this point in the trip, which people in our group would you say you are close with?" The responses of the 29 tourists enable us to map the contours of their social landscape (Figure 6.1).[20] In broad terms, the group was divided into two, with an 11-person "core" whose members were strongly tied to one another and an 18-member "periphery" who had far fewer ties with one another and even less with the core.[21] At a finer level of resolution, one could see a tripartite social structure that included (1) a large, cohesive group of nine people with three "hangers on"; (2) a dozen more people broken up into smaller cliques, dyads, and isolates, and who had almost no close ties to people in the large group; and (3) five popular "floaters" who easily crossed the lines separating the other two categories. The second category, those in the smaller cliques, can be further distinguished by whether or not they befriended the "floaters."[22] These social divisions became especially visible to group members as they became inscribed spatially in the seating arrangements on the bus.

In this arena for differentiation and competition, group cohesion tends to be more accomplished than emergent. Staff invest significant effort in group building, referring to it by the term *gibbush* (coalescence), drawn from the classical Zionist language of tiyul. Hillel's staff manual devotes a section to group building and suggests program activities for fostering cohesion. Tour leaders supplement these with ideas of their own. In addition to discussion circles, disco buses, and stuffed mascots, these include icebreakers, bus games ("brushes with fame," "most embarrassing moments," karaoke), Sabbath parties, group t-shirts, and bus anthems. Staff also mix and match roommates, assign numbers for a gamelike count off that indicates whether all are pres-

FIGURE 6.1. *Close friendships in Ravit's group—Day 7*

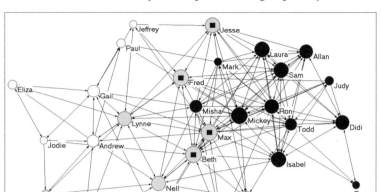

Shading indicates SEM Blocks:
○ Front of Bus 1 (Friendly with "floaters")
○ Front of Bus 2 (Not friendly with "floaters")
● Back of Bus
◉ Floaters

X → Y means that X named Y as a friend. Not all friendships are mutual. Size of circles represents popularity (normalized in-degree centrality, i.e., the number of times the person was named). For tabular or matrix view of the friendship network and its internal structure (the SEM block model), see the book's website.

ent, and delegate public responsibilities to students, including the responsibility for leading the count off.

Indications of the success (and lack thereof) of efforts to foster gibbush can be seen in the evolution of friendship networks in Ra'anan's and Michael's groups from Day 3 to Day 9 of their trips (Figures 6.2 to 6.5). Each group was comprised primarily of students from two different colleges. They were joined by a smattering of students from other schools and by the Israeli mifgash participants who stayed for only part of the tour. Over the course of the trips, bridges were built that connected initially discrete subgroups. Even so, for reasons that probably are related to weaker staff-participant rapport and sharper cleavages along social class lines, Michael's group ended up less unified than Ra'anan's, with more isolates, fewer connections between people, and fewer cross-university ties.[23]

FIGURE 6.2. *Reciprocated close friendships in Ra'anan's group—Day 3*

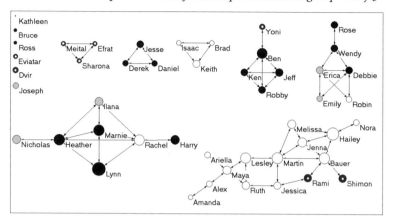

FIGURE 6.3. *Reciprocated close friendships in Ra'anan's group—Day 9*

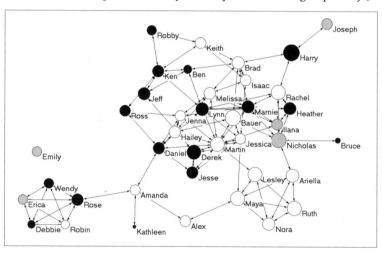

Shading indicates university:
- ● Private University #1
- ○ Private University #2
- ◐ Other universities
- ◉ Israeli mifgash soldiers

X ⇔ Y means that X and Y both named each other as friends. Size of circles represents popularity (normalized in-degree centrality, i.e., the number of times the person was named). Israeli mifgash soldiers had left the group by Day 9.

Encountering Community | 163

FIGURE 6.4. *Reciprocated close friendships in Michael's group—Day 3*

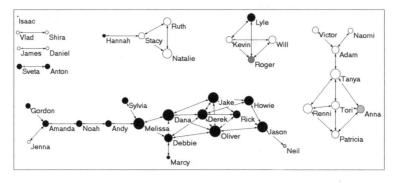

FIGURE 6.5. *Reciprocated close friendships in Michael's group—Day 9*

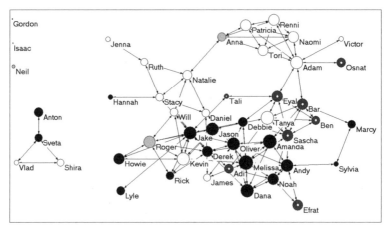

Shading indicates university:
- ● State College
- ○ Private University
- ◐ Other universities
- ◉ Israeli mifgash soldiers

X ⇔ Y means that X and Y both named each other as friends. Size of circles represents popularity (normalized in-degree centrality, i.e., the number of times the person was named). Israeli mifgash soldiers had not yet arrived in the group on Day 3.

Although efforts at gibbush can never fully overcome the forces of differentiation that exist within tour groups, even their partial success can significantly advance the homeland tour's diaspora-building work, liberating the potential for communitas relations that tourism's liminal environment makes possible. The relationship between communitas and liminality was first articulated by Victor Turner, who observed that when groups of people are temporarily removed from the structures and routines that ground their social identities (liminality), they become better able to see past the socially defined roles and statuses that divide them and, instead, encounter one another in a "direct, immediate, and total confrontation of human identities which tends to make those experiencing it think of mankind as a homogenous, unstructured, and free community" (communitas).[24] Communitas relations have an affective dimension alongside their cognitive one. They are typically experienced as an emotionally intense feeling of human connection. In the context of tourism, the "shipboard romance" can be viewed as an example of communitas.

The power of tour groups as socializing experiences of ethnic community lies in their ability to be perceived not merely as positive, but extraordinarily so. Tourism's liminality helps set the stage for this perception. Deliberate group-building work advances it, both by removing obstacles to its fruition and by positively fostering open, honest, and enjoyable relations among tourists. Sponsors and staff of diaspora Jewish homeland tours hope that the tour groups will be experienced emotionally as enriching sources of uplift and belonging. They accordingly build their group-related strategies around the production of repeated moments of Durkheimian collective effervescence, of which the disco bus and megaevent are typical examples,[25] and around the effort to foster an ever-deepening experience of Turnerian communitas. The two are not unrelated, as instances of the former contribute to the latter.

The efforts to foster communitas also involve work in two additional dimensions: the relational and the symbolic. To foster relations of intimacy, tour staff attempt to create embracing, nonjudgmental environments that encourage self-disclosure.[26] To foster mutual identification among tourists, they work to establish rich ritual environments that engage group members in shared performances toward unifying symbols. Some of these symbols are bus-specific, like Sababa the Cat, whereas others are rooted in Jewish or Israeli culture more broadly, such as the Shabbat dinner songs and the *shehechyanu* prayers recited on entry into Jerusalem.

This confluence of environment and effort typically produce powerful feelings of group belonging that lead a few to engage in tear-filled confessionals and more substantial numbers to make gushing testimonials about the sentiments generated by their membership in the group. In the midst of a Shabbat discussion circle about hopes and expectations for the trip, conducted in a hotel meeting room on the third day of one Canadian group's tour, one man had started choking up even before he had spoken his first words. "Sorry guys, I'm a little *farklempt*," Sean Berman said.

The Yiddishism, popularized by a sketch from the television show *Saturday Night Live*, elicited sympathetic laughter.

Sean was a chain-smoking art student who was generally well liked. He stood up, shook his limbs, collected himself and sat back down to continue: "The reason I came here. . . . In Canada we seem to have everything: loving parents, bars, women, television, rights, freedoms, etc. But I don't have happiness." At this point he burst into tears again. "Seeing Uri in the caves . . . so much emotion . . . it's the first experience [I have had] of this sort."

Others began crying, too, as Sean recalled their visit to the Roman-era catacombs of Beit Guvrin and the story their tour guide, Uri, had told of ancient Jews driven to cannibalism in order to survive—an example, Uri had said, of innumerable times Jews had been forced into dehumanizing situations. More tears flowed as Sean continued: "I feel so comfortable with you guys. . . . I was looking for direction and something to believe in. In Canada, I don't have a chance to really feel life. Being at the [Western] Wall . . . I put my head on the Wall and felt so alive. It was the best feeling. Being able to share this with people is really special. Thank you."

His groupmates responded with applause, then grew quiet. Some took out tissues to wipe their tears. Others embraced. Four women approached Sean, each offering a hug. One told him that she felt similarly. Another told him his words had made her cry.

This episode is not unique. Group discussion circles, particularly those surrounding visits to iconic places like Yad Vashem and the Western Wall, can at times elicit emotion-laden confessions about people's struggles with illness, loss, and the challenges of entering adulthood.[27] Travelers' willingness to bare their souls not merely to their few closest friends on the trip but to the entire assemblage points to the way the group can be imagined in idealized terms. Sean took a risk in making his tearful confession before a room of people who only three days before were strangers. Whether he had yet come to know all of them by name is doubtful. Yet his trust that such free self-disclosure would not expose him to ridicule by others indicates the sincerity of his assertion, "I feel so comfortable with you guys."

These paeans to the group become increasingly common as the trip wears on and are such dominant features of closing discussion circles that it would be astonishing were one to find a wrap-up session that did not include them. The following comments, voiced by members of two of Birthright Israel's earliest groups during their closing discussions, have since been echoed tens of thousands of times:

This trip meant so much to me. The best part was being with the group and not necessarily any of the experiences. . . . The trip has also renewed my faith with religion because of being in a place like this and being able to share it with other Jews.—*Male, crying*

I have the group to thank for making this experience special.—*Female, after telling the assembled that a friend of hers had been killed three days before she left on the trip*

I've never felt as comfortable and as accepted as I have here. There are no words to describe that sunrise on Masada, or singing [the hymn] "Adon Olam" with 6,000 Jewish kids.—*Female*

This will always be a place that I will envision that defines happiness. I've made friends for life here, and I know that we will always appreciate what we went through as a group to get to this point.—*Female*

I love Jews! That's all I can say right now. I just love Jews!—*Female*

I don't want to go home at all, but if I stayed none of you would be here with me.—*Male, getting the last word*

Clearly, the discussion circles are interaction rituals that elicit structured, rule-governed verbal performances. In the same interview in which she described the competition for the male soldiers' attentions (chapter 5 in this volume), Jenna Eisenstein commented on the dynamic in the closing discussion in Ra'anan's group:

What, are there 40 of us [in the group] going around [and taking turns speaking]? It just escalates. Like, I was noticing the talks got more and more extreme as it went on. The first person, like, "Oh, I really liked climbing Masada." [Then], "Oh, I really liked getting to know some new people." Then, like, "*I love everyone! This is the most amazing thing I've ever done in my life . . . and thank God I can share this with my best friends.*" Okay. "Hi. Not sure, like, if you know my name, but, whatever, we're best friends now."

Jenna's interpretation captures an important truth about the dynamics of self-presentation in the closing discussion circles. Yet we should not be too quick to dismiss the testimonials as only artifacts of a ritualized performance. At the level of the subgroup, people do experience communitas relations with specific others. There are even moments—often late at night, sometimes aided by alcohol—when such relations are experienced across lines of division in the group. Though isolated and fleeting, these instances of liminality within liminality are significant for the way they can reshape thinking about bus community. The declarations of love for the group can be understood on one level as generalizations from the experience of meaningfully intense relationships with one or two others—an imagining of the bus community based on the experience of a section of it. But they are more than this, for they occur in a context in which people are confronted with the imminent dissolution of the social group that has, as the "one constant" of the trip, been the primary grounding for their experience of the homeland and their experience of self-in-the-homeland.

There is a certain poetry in asserting that this confrontation with collective mortality is made especially poignant because it occurs on a tour that forces diaspora Jews to wrestle with the genocide of their ancestors, existential threats to their homeland, and fears of assimilation in the places where they live. But whether it is more than poetry is hard to say. What can be said is that the protestations of love for the group are laments in the face of its imminent demise, laments that already evince the nostalgia that will later characterize reflections on the trip.

For those who would use homeland tourism as a medium of diasporic socialization, this nostalgia is one of the crucial products of the group experience. Unlike the group itself, nostalgia can outlast the tour. Long after the El Al plane has deposited its passengers back at New York's Kennedy Airport, nostalgia can motivate the former tourists to try to recapture what they once had. The experience of being on a homeland tour with that particular group of people at that particular time in their lives can never fully be recaptured, though. The question then becomes, if feelings of nostalgia are to be acted on, to what will they be directed? Tour sponsors hope that the emotions generated by the group experience will attach to the symbols of homeland and ethnic community in which this group experience was embedded.[28] It will come as no surprise to students of Durkheim that this hope has been repeatedly vindicated over the years—not universally, but enough to sustain the sponsors' interest in a strategy they feel comfortable labeling a success.

Locating Self

"Yad Vashem." Translated literally, the words mean "a memorial" (*yad*) and "a name" (*shem*). "The Nazis wrote numbers on us," Ravit told her group at the Holocaust memorial as we sat beneath trees planted in honor of gentiles who had saved Jewish lives. "'Yad Vashem' means bringing the names back."

Ravit introduced our visit to the museum by speaking of the importance of names as markers of individuality and as links binding people to community. Her words began with reference to the Shoah but quickly came to focus on us, the tourists standing at a Holocaust memorial in an independent State of Israel six decades later. Ignoring our English names, she spoke about the Hebrew names many Jews are also given. In Hebrew, she said, every name has a meaning. Hers, she told us, means, "your thirst is quenched." Then she asked if we knew the meanings of our Hebrew names.

I thought about my name, Shaul, "prayed for" or "asked of God." As I considered this in silence, people called out their Hebrew names so that Ravit could translate their meanings.

"Shmuel," Sam Pollack, the shofar-blower, said.

"God hears," Ravit answered.

"Menachem?" Mark Gottlieb inquired.

"Comfort," came the reply.

"Avigayil," said Gail Jellinek.

"My father, God, is joyful."

"Bat-Ami," Beth Dolman announced.

"Daughter of my people."

"Yehoshua," both Evan Walsh and Jeffrey Shain said.

"That's Joshua. 'God is salvation,'" Ravit said. Then, in case people had not caught the point, she declared, "You can connect [to your Jewish heritage] through your name."

Not everyone had the same ability to forge such a connection. Misha Velinsky and Ellen Galperin had not been given Hebrew names. They had been born in the Soviet Union as the regime pursued its crusade to stamp out Jewish culture. Some American-born group members including children of interfaith marriages also did not have Hebrew names or did not know if their parents had given them one. Staff were prepared for this. One of them announced, "If you don't have a Hebrew name and you want one, come to us." They would help the travelers choose a fitting one. If sponsors hoped that the homeland tours would effect dramatic transformations of self, could they find a more powerful symbol than the traveler's adoption of a new name? And not just any name, but one in the language spoken by Israelis? On some buses, naming ceremonies conducted before the entire group ritualized the assumption of the new identities.

Ravit's introduction of Yad Vashem exemplified the way that Jewish homeland tours use the encounter with place to try to shape travelers' identities as diaspora Jews. She first directed the tourist gaze toward the Holocaust memorial, which she framed as a site where the nameless slaughtered have their names restored to them. As something that simultaneously individuates people and binds them to others, the act of naming returns to the victims their individual humanity even as it unites them with the community of the living who remembers them as their own and invokes their names. Then, remarkably, Ravit turned this frame onto the travelers themselves. She asked them to think about how naming—and Jewish naming in particular—makes each of them unique, as well as part of something larger than themselves: indeed, part of the same community to which those annihilated in the Shoah belonged. She took the lens that was used to reveal Israel and turned it onto the travelers to reveal them in a similar way. Moves such as these make homeland tourism a powerful medium of diasporic socialization.

By engaging diasporans in an activity that consists first and foremost of gazing on place and assigning it meaning within a defined interpretive frame, tourism's treatment of the homeland establishes the paradigmatic behavior that diasporans can then turn inward and apply to themselves. The Janus-faced character of this tourist gaze, simultaneously directed outward toward the toured objects and inward to the touring subjects, emerges informally as part of the natural dynamics of a group homeland tour. Yet like so many of tourism's other knowledge practices, it has been systematically mobilized to more fully realize its identity-shaping potential.

Schmoozing

In *Culture on Tour*, Edward Bruner asks a simple question: "What do the tourists talk about among themselves while on the tour?" His answer: All sorts of things. They discuss "the hotels, the food, the transportation, and the other specificities of the tour at hand." They discuss their previous travels. They talk to demonstrate familiarity with the places they are visiting. They also tell "tales about home and about themselves," including stories about family and work. Bruner reminds us that "all [these] tellings are situated and no story is told in a vacuum."[1]

In light of these findings about tourists in general, it is hardly surprising to observe that conversations among travelers on diaspora Jewish homeland tours often come around to the tourists' own Jewish backgrounds and beliefs. Indeed, it would be surprising if they did not. Sometimes the topic emerges as tourists try to get to know one another.

I followed the meanderings of one such conversation as it occurred on the bus on the second morning of my travels with Michael's group. Kevin Healy and Sylvia Levi-Soncino had only just met and were searching for common ground. Sitting across the aisle from one another, they first talked about the merits of different boxed wines. Kevin, a well-groomed Romeo who envisioned a future in finance, segued into a story from his recent semester in London. He and his friends would remove the bags from the wine boxes they had emptied, he said, blow them up, and use them as pillows as they slept on the lawn. The alcohol-abroad theme continued as the conversation spiraled to consider Spring Break in the Carribbean, favorite drinks, the flavor of vodka, getting carded, and drunken 13-year-olds in Cancun bars.

Somehow—I honestly don't know how—this discussion arrived at a point where Kevin began asking Sylvia about her Jewish upbringing. In a thick Long Island accent, she told him that she was raised "Conservadox," and when Kevin probed to find out what she meant, she told him that she went to a yeshiva high school, speaks Hebrew, keeps kosher, celebrates all the Jewish holidays, and dates only Jews.

Kevin told her that his father had converted to Judaism and that his family was not especially observant. Beyond this, he said little about his Jewish upbringing. Instead, he pressed Sylvia on her decision to date only Jews. Didn't it prevent her from making friends with people who were not Jewish?

Not at all, she said.

In other cases, discussion of people's Jewish lives emerges out of the encounter with Israel, particularly out of the semiotic of difference that structures the tourist gaze.

The day after Sylvia and Kevin's exchange, their groupmates Amanda Reese and Noah Mendelson sat together in the back seat of the bus, looking through the window at Israeli flags fluttering from people's homes. One said to the other that Israelis seemed to be more patriotic than Americans.

As they criticized their fellow citizens for not displaying a greater love of the United States, they also began criticizing American Jews for not caring enough about their Jewish heritage to learn about it. In Amanda's words (repeated into the recorder for my sake):

[A lot of Jews in the United States] don't know what it is to be Jewish. Like, they don't understand the religion so much. Like, even during Passover, I met some people who were Jewish, and I had no idea from before [that they were Jewish], and I was talking about, "Oh, are you going to have your seder? Like, where are you going to do it?" And they go, "Oh well, we don't really do that. You know like we only have like a family-made dinner." They don't do seder. They don't follow "no bread." *They don't even know that you can't have, like, flour.* They're like, "Oh, so I can't be eating crackers?" Like, I mean, "*No!*" Well, how do you really not know? . . . Most people don't, like, really understand kinda what, like, Judaism is like: How the culture is, and, like, what you do, and how you study. And they're just, like, "Oh, you know, you have to go to Hebrew school everyday." Like, I always *wanted* to. I wanted to go. And I wanted to go to confirmation class. . . . And I always want to go to temple, but I never have anyone to go with and it's so far away. . . . It's just difficult. People don't really understand. They're like, "Why do you have to go to temple? You can come out with us instead."

Other times, the discussion of Jewish lives emerges out of the recognition of the cultural divides separating Israeli and diaspora Jews. In one back-of-the-bus conversation between Israeli and American mifgash participants, one American tourist of mixed Jewish and Christian heritage took issue with an Israeli's suggestion that it is impossible to raise Jewish children in a multifaith household. "Yes, it is possible!" she declared. "We have a [Hanukah] menorah and Christmas tree. When we open the window, you see the menorah with the Christmas tree behind it."

Informal conversations like these help establish the salience of a Jewish interpretive frame that tourists can apply as much to themselves and to their traveling companions as they can to their destination. Viewing self, other, and place through a single conceptual filter asserts and reveals their essential commonality. The casual conversations also help establish a social context in which open discussion of Jewishness is felt to be so legitimate as to be unremarkable. The diaspora Jewish homeland tours open a private Jewish space that affirms tribalism and particularism and that is not constrained by etiquettes that elsewhere suppress public discussion of religion. Nor is it constrained by the self-censorship that can sometimes occur when people feel that they are speaking in "mixed company." (As the story of the traveler who grew up with a Hanukah menorah and a Christmas tree suggests, though, the notion of a clear dichotomy between Jew and gentile has eroded. Tourists sometimes offend their travelmates by failing to recognize that the tour groups include people who are simultaneously Jewish and some other religion.)

What the social context of the group homeland tour makes possible, tour organizers' efforts make common. One of the primary ways trip sponsors encourage and impose structure on public exchanges about private Jewish lives is by instituting group discussion circles as a regular feature of the Israel experience curriculum. These institutionalize a process in which tourists explicitly link their own stories to the collective Jewish and Zionist stories that are being used to frame Israel.

Sparse Narratives

The practice of linking individual and collective Jewish narratives has been explicitly codified by Hillel through its three-step method for staff-led group discussions. To recall, trained facilitators are supposed to start the conversations by "asking personal questions of the participants," then have them apply "that knowledge of individual experiences . . . to the collective experience of the Jewish people," and conclude by "bring[ing] that experience back to the participants to help individuals articulate where they stand in this new context."[2]

Over the course of the trips, discussion circles touch on a variety of topics. Participants may find themselves exchanging thoughts about American democracy, Yiddish, racism, or the value of tradition. They may speak about God, Israeli politics, the Holocaust, or assimilation. Irrespective of their content, the discussions are structured to encourage tourists to look to their own pasts. For example, in the conversation at Jaffa described in chapter 5, the staff person, Janet, asked explicitly, "What about being Jewish makes you feel special?" and Natalie Unger responded by telling of her experience denying Jesus' divinity in the third-grade classroom of her Episcopal elementary school.

In speaking to their personal histories, tourists also discuss aspects of family history that predate their birth. It is common in the discussions surrounding the visit to Yad Vashem, for instance, for grandchildren of survivors to talk about their grandparents' experiences in and after the Shoah.

Two aspects of the self-presentations that occur in discussion circles are especially noteworthy. The first regards their content and points to the relative ease of structuring the conversations to advance the diaspora-building goals of the trips. As tour sponsors might hope, discussants typically hew close to the themes set out by facilitators, confining themselves to addressing aspects of their lives that bear on their self-definitions as Jews. The second regards their form and points to the contradictions that complicate the use of discussion circles as mechanisms for engaging people in explicit acts of narrating identity. Narratives tend to be sparse and episodic, largely because the structure provides little opportunity for individuals to share extended life histories. For instance, a rabbi who met with members of a Reform movement–sponsored trip asked the tourists to introduce themselves and tell about their family backgrounds. She received formulaic responses in which the participants briefly identified their grandparents' or great-grandparents' countries of origin, noted the religious affiliations and Jewish organizational involvements of their parents, and then made some perfunctory statement asserting past Jewish commitment and expressing hope or expectation for its continuation in the future. The narratives were thin, consisting more of labeling and categorizing than actual storytelling.

On Ravit's bus, the initial presentation of Jewish backgrounds was less formulaic. This did not mean that people's stories resembled anything approaching fleshed-out autobiographies, however. For our first group conversation, held in a Jerusalem hotel, we gathered in a windowless meeting room decorated in forest green and earth tones. A hundred or so chairs had been set up auditorium style, but we pushed these against the walls so that we could sit on the floor in a large circle. It had been a long day—straight from the plane to the bus to the Old City of Jerusalem, King David's Tomb, the Jewish Quarter, the Western Wall, and then to the hotel to check in and eat dinner. Now, as the night wore on, people leaned back and stretched their legs straight. It felt good to sit, but the prospect of a group program was daunting to many of us, myself included, exhausted from the flight and from the day's activities.

The conversation began with a staff person introducing the discussion and asking us about our expectations for the trip. People at first answered the question directly, but soon the conversation evolved toward other matters.

Didi Sandler, a small, husky-voiced redhead, expressed frustration with her inability, even after years in her synagogue's afternoon Hebrew school, to make sense of the street life around her. "The Hebrew is so frustrating. We can't understand anything."

Her comment opened the floodgates for a mixture of Jewish autobiography and armchair sociology. Sam Pollack jumped in quickly: "Our elders did a piss-poor job of passing down the culture. Who [here] speaks Yiddish?! I feel cheated!"

Building on this comment, others discussed their feelings about Judaism as a cultural inheritance. In one of the few times he contributed to any of the group discussions, Evan Walsh, son of an Irish American father and a Jewish American mother, confessed, "I feel this pressure to dilute myself. Maybe it's just not really understanding my relationship to it [Jewish heritage]." No details, just a hint that there was a story he was not telling.

No one picked up on it. Another hand was raised, and the string of two-sentence monologues continued.

Mickey Goldman decided to tell about his "path to being the type of Jew" that he had become. He spoke in denominational labels: "I mean, I was raised Reformed [sic]. I'd like to leave here with a fuller Jewish identity. I'm definitely not Reformed. I'd like to move up to Conservative."

After Ellen elaborated on Mickey's comments, Eliza Rapp jumped in, engaging him directly, "Not to pick on you . . . but 'moving up' [in Judaism] . . . we should be careful with the terms we use." She was criticizing Mickey's colloquial ranking of the denominations according to how strictly they adhered to Eastern European traditions and Talmudic law.

Mickey's terminology was not picked up by others, but the discussion, or series of semiconnected statements, did respond to the line of questioning he had initiated. More and more people began speaking about their Jewish backgrounds:

MALE:[3] I want to experience my culture. My parents are not religious, but my grandmother is.

FEMALE: I don't know what I'm going to get [out of this trip]. In Hebrew school, I never had the drive. [It was] forced. [Now, I'm] looking for something to believe in.

Self-presentations indicative of some speakers' culturally rich Jewish backgrounds led others to assert that they felt at a disadvantage. Misha's comment at the end of the following conversational thread suggests a race to the bottom, as if people were competing to claim the title of "least Jewishly knowledgeable or connected." The four spoke in immediate succession:

NELL LOCURTO: I'm sure I'm not at the level you guys are at . . .

EVAN WALSH: I don't want to sound like a traitor, but I have a lot of . . . ambivalence.

LINDSEY ARNSTEIN: I don't have the Jewish background a lot of you guys have . . .

MISHA VELINSKY: Out of all of you, I have no idea what's going on. I have no idea because I grew up in a communist country.

Each time that the group was reconvened for a new discussion circle, tourists would reengage the process of reflecting publicly on their lives as Jews. Several days after the opening conversation in the Jerusalem hotel room, Ravit's group sat down for a conversation devoted to the topic, "Jewish Memory." As in the discussion circle that preceded it and in those that followed it, the self-representations that this conversation elicited showed more thematic consistency than narrative depth:

STAFF: What are your Jewish memories?
MICKEY GOLDMAN: Masada. Climbing it for the first time.
STAFF: It could also be something like seeing Coca-Cola written in Hebrew.
ISABEL PANKOW: After my brother was born, watching him grow up and be all into Hebrew and Judaism.
RON GELLER: Matzo ball soup. Whenever [my mom] made that, it was for something Jewish.
BETH DOLMAN: When I did the semester abroad, and I was abroad for Passover, we prepared a large seder . . .
JEFFREY SHAIN: The movie *Independence Day*. In the end they're praying. And also when [the actor] Will Smith says, "I'm not Jewish," and [his costar] Jeff Goldblum says, "Nobody's perfect," and nobody in the theater was laughing except me.
LINDSEY ARNSTEIN: I went to a boarding school that had a very small Jewish population. Every year there was an international fair, but there was never anything Jewish. I thought there should be Jewish food. I got all the recipes and spent all day cooking . . .

With their norm of giving everyone a chance to speak, discussion circles do not serve as venues for extended storytelling, much less for full-blown autobiographical narration. They provide opportunities for people to recall and invoke selected elements of their pasts, presents, and imagined futures. That these elements are drawn primarily from a single dimension of experience—the dimension that not coincidentally is the one also used to frame the homeland—is of crucial significance to the identity work that the tours effect. Moreover, the sparseness of the verbal narratives tells us more about the constraints of interaction than about any poverty of self-reflection. In our interview on the return flight, Kevin Healy called my attention to the gap between the little people say and the lot they might be thinking:

SK: What do they [the trip organizers] want to get out of it?

KEVIN: I feel the prime one, the obvious one, is they want to stimulate discussion. . . . On our trip that was a failure . . .

SK: I'll take it a step further. I think they are trying to stimulate discussion in order to stimulate personal reflection.

KEVIN: Yes. There you go. I definitely agree with that. And I think it definitely did, I think the personal reflection part it did stimulate, because I know a lot of people were probably thinking about what they wanted to say.

SK: Ah! Even if they don't say it!

KEVIN: Even if they don't say it. I mean, I always do.

Like Kevin, I had sat silent in the discussion circles (for different reasons), but I, too, had been thinking about what I would say if I were called on to speak, sifting memories, selecting ones that were topical, that would make a point I wanted to make, and that would allow me to present myself in a specific way. I had not been aware of the significance of this internal experience until Kevin pointed it out to me.

Especially in a structured group conversation where the turn-taking leads people to expect that they will at some point be expected to hold the floor, people often focus more on planning their own comments than on listening to others. This results in the tendency for the discussion circles to take the form of serial monologues rather than a sustained give and take. In the very disjointedness of the exchanges, we find evidence that people are looking inward and thinking more deeply than their words reveal.

Essentialized Identities

At first glance, tourist discussion circles appear to have much in common with the support groups that often feature in studies of identity narration.[4] Both include casts of recurring participants who periodically gather for structured conversations centered on thematically constrained presentations of self. Both are intended explicitly to inform self-understanding. If we seek to understand the nature of identity construction effected in the discussion circles, we would be wise to consider the research into support groups. This work is part of a broader body of scholarship that looks also to written autobiographies and life-history interviews to conceive of identity as a construct of narrative.[5] This conception of identity centers on the idea that people "make sense of their sometimes scattered lives by fashioning and internalizing stories that integrate their reconstructed past, perceived present, and anticipated future."[6] One might go further and say that, without the imposition of some meaningful framework to make sense of it all, people's lives are always and necessarily scattered. Only *emplotment*, the temporal ordering of events into a thematic whole, it is argued, transforms the welter of fleeting, fragmented moments into episodes that cohere in some meaningful fashion.[7]

The strength of narrative theories of identity rests in their recognition that the central problematic of identity is the question of coherence. In the face of a lived experience characterized by disjuncture, the ability to impose order on the chaos becomes a human imperative, and the salience of any particular ordering schema depends, in part, on the feelings of coherence it is able to generate. Narrative theories of identity acknowledge three primary ways in which narratives of the self generate a sense of autobiographical coherence. Coherence emerges through *sequencing*, which arranges life events into a meaningful order;[8] through *framing*, which by defining thematic relevance distinguishes information from noise and filters out the latter;[9] and through *grounding*, which roots individual stories in a collective narrative.[10]

For all their similarities to the support groups that commonly feature in studies of identity narration, diaspora Jewish homeland tour discussion circles offer travelers little opportunity to engage in the work of broad synthesis required for the creation of integrative life stories. Tourists do not typically sketch autobiographies that trace with any detail their lives as Jews from birth onward. Rather, they invoke episodes from their Jewish pasts and project forward their possible Jewish futures in a fragmentary and disjointed way. If the self-constructions that result from this process cohere in a compelling fashion, this coherence cannot be attributed to the act of sequencing life events into a meaningful order, for such sequencing is little in evidence. Rather, we should see it as a product of the narrow framing that governs processes of self-exploration on the tours and of the explicit grounding of these emergent identities in the collective Jewish narratives that saturate the tour.

When facilitators of Israel experience discussion circles direct diaspora Jews' gazes inward toward their own lives, they ask them to recall episodes and reflect on sentiments drawn from one narrow slice of their existence. Travelers are not asked to reflect on memories that speak to their self-understandings as men or as women, as students, as television viewers, as athletes, or as any of the other myriad selves around which they might construct their identities. They are asked only to select those aspects of experience that have something to do with their perceptions of themselves as Jews. Although little is done to piece these fragments together into coherent life narratives, the act of returning again and again to the same site to excavate the self heightens the relative salience of this locus of identity by temporarily marginalizing other possible constructions of self. In this sense, the process resembles the one being used to inscribe meaning on the homeland. As they bounce from place to place, tourists impose thematic coherence on the disparate objects of their gaze by consistently invoking a delimited Jewish nationalist frame to interpret them. This provides a sense of coherent place meaning, both by virtue of its breadth of applicability and by virtue of its marginalization of alternative interpretive frames. Something similar is accomplished through the processes of self-touring that the discussion circles encourage.

In ordinary circumstances, people's ongoing involvement in the diverse social contexts that bequeath them their multiple identities would work against a marginalization of alternative selves. The tours, however, are liminal spaces. Those who inhabit them have been removed from many of the roles, relationships, and status systems that ground their understandings of who they are. They find themselves in a separate social environment whose structure and discourse work hand in hand to both enable and encourage them to overlook the complexities of identity and, instead, construct radically simplified conceptions of self. The travelers are in their very essence and more than anything else, the tours suggest, Jews. This, it is said, is what connects them to Israel and what brings them to tour it. This is what brings those who travel with them. This is the shared identity that is said to unite them with each other and the basis on which they are encouraged to engage one another and forge bonds. This is also the basis on which they are encouraged to engage their own selves. The same frame that they apply to understand Israel is the one they should apply to understand their own pasts and anticipate their own futures.

In practice, other identities remain salient and, indeed, are made so by internal dynamics within tour groups. When getting to know one another, tourists come together first and foremost as Western youth, looking to generation-specific popular culture far more than Jewish heritage to find their common ground. Student identities are also very much on display as they discuss the particulars of their university experiences. Sorting into friendship networks shows evidence of divisions between those who have decided to join fraternities and sororities and those who have not. Mifgashim confront diaspora Jews with the cultural differences that separate them from Israelis, reinforcing awareness of national identities. Sexual orientation remains an important anchor of identity among gay and lesbian travelers, particularly in light of the tour groups' general heteronormativity.[11] Some who are out in their home communities closet themselves during the trips. Some are acutely aware of the absence of a dating market of their own to parallel the robust market enjoyed by their straight peers.

The activation of these other identities ensures that essentialist notions of a true Jewish self will not monopolize self-understandings during the trip. In spite of this, the tours do manage to heighten the salience of this more narrowly circumscribed construction of identity. This derives partly from the sense of coherence that its simplicity offers, partly from its situational relevance to the activities of the homeland tour, and partly from the situational irrelevance of some of the other potentially competing identities in that liminal environment. It also receives social reinforcement from the tour group itself, as tourists see their own representations of Jewish selves mirrored in the self-representations of their traveling companions.

Speaking in her group's closing discussion circle, Hailey Farber, who later that afternoon would tell me about the sexual dynamics of the mifgash (chapter 5 in this volume), spoke of the trip's influence on her own self-understanding:

I come from a family where my dad's side of the family is Jewish and my mom's side is Christian. And both my brother and I were raised Jewish. Like, we were both bar and bat mitzvahed, we were both confirmed. And people, like, as we are getting older, like, they'll ask us . . . "Oh, are you planning on raising your children Jewish?" and stuff like that. And, like, my brother . . . whenever people ask him, he always says, "Absolutely! Like, I'm raising my children Jewish, like no matter what." And when people ask me, I was kind of like, "Oh, like, I don't know. I guess it really just depends on, like, who I meet, who I marry." Like, it wasn't really that important to me. And I don't know if it's correlated with having come to Israel or not, but I have, like, absolutely no question in my mind that, like, I'm gonna raise my children Jewish. Like, I can't imagine not—*allowing*, I guess—my children to have this type of experience and to, like, to be around people just like you guys, like every other Jewish person. And it's just, like, this sense of, like, community and pride and tradition. So, I'm glad I came and I realize that now. It's really important to me.

The tours' implicit privileging of a Jewish self over other possible selves is also made compelling to travelers by virtue of the ability to ground them in a broader Jewish story. During our interview on the plane ride home, Patricia Portnoy imagined herself into the traumas of the Jewish past, first speaking of victims of the Holocaust ("I finally understood that there would be nothing that would have separated me from them. Had I been born however many years before I was. Nothing."), and then extending it to speak of the zealots on Masada:

Again, if that was me at Masada, as a Jewish person, I would have that choice and my, you know, father would have had to kill me for my faith. And that would have been *me*. . . . It's so easy to say, "Oh, *that* wouldn't have been me. Oh, the genocide in Darfur, *that's* not me, *that* wouldn't have been me." But if I was Jewish in those times, *that would have been me*.[12]

She could imagine herself out of her present time, but not out of her Jewish self.

Hailey's friend Brian Bauer spoke to the issue in a more conceptual, less-historically specific and also less-morbid way when it came his turn to speak in his group's final discussion circle. Bauer (no one called him Brian) was a towering man, whom I will best remember sitting stone-faced and silent at the bar of a Jerusalem hotel, wearing flippers and a diver's mask while puffing cigarette smoke out of a snorkel. He was sober, however, when he spoke in the discussion circle:

Like a lot of other people, I was fairly active in Judaism in high school. . . . And college came, and I completely lost much of it, skipped holidays, didn't really go to services. I was kind of unsure where I was in the Jewish religion. I didn't know where it fit in with me. And coming here has, I mean, not just reconnected me to Judaism, but *completely* changed my understanding of what it means to be Jewish. And I think what I've realized is, it's almost a *privilege* to be a part of Judaism. And being here and seeing and being in all the places which some of the historical events took place and sort of re-, relearning what happened made me realize how lucky I am to be Jewish and to be a part of this historical community, and also made me understand why a place like Israel is so important, because it connects all that. It connects the history to people now and it gives us a place to come. And I know that I'm going to take that with me from now on. It's defined me as a Jew.

This grounding of the self in a collective narrative that transcends the finite individual is especially important in light of the context in which it occurs. The homeland tours are immersive social environments that are thoroughly suffused with the metanarratives that are being used at every turn to inscribe meanings on Israel. Precisely at the time when these historical and mythic frameworks are made especially salient through their repeated invocation and application, tourists find themselves able to situate not only the country they are touring in terms of them but also themselves. Even as the collective narratives are being territorialized in the homeland, they are being internalized by the tourists. In the process, the link between person and place, diaspora Jew and Israel, is strengthened.

Affective Validation

Efforts to structure cognition only begin the identity work of diaspora Jewish homeland tours. Although discussion circles guide travelers through processes of self-excavation that enable them to represent themselves as Jewish selves, these discursive processes do not independently establish the subjective truth of these identities to those who articulate them. Any conviction that they are indeed authentic reflections of the self will rest less in how these identities are understood than in how they are felt.[13] Affect will be the ultimate validator of these cognitive constructs. And although the imaginings of an essentialized Jewish self find some of their validation in the feelings of coherence and rootedness that emerge by virtue of their narrow framing and of their grounding in the collective narratives that are even then being territorialized in an Israeli landscape, much of the emotional authority they command during the tour derives from the emotional and somatic states that attend their creation.

The power of tourism as a medium of socialization rests to a large extent in the fact that it is an embodied practice that fully engages people as actors in an immersive environment. Its semiotic and discursive work occurs not in a rarefied realm of pure thought but in the context of a situated, lived experience that generates affect and awareness of a self-in-context. Insofar as the experience of self is grounded socially and corporeally, the immediate experience of self on a tour is directly related to the interactional fields in which people participate and to the embodied behaviors they undertake. In their efforts to deploy the affective dimensions of tourism to validate the cognitive work of the tours, Israel experience programs seek to ensure that these environments and behaviors foster an experience of self that is uplifting and empowering in the extreme. Trip staff work to achieve a gibbush that will foster an uncommonly intense sense of community. Itinerary planners incorporate activities like hiking Masada, rafting the Jordan, and riding on camelback to ensure that tourists will engage in physical activities that are intense, challenging, and novel.

If one wanted to look for evidence that the social environments and embodied practices do, in fact, generate the types of inspiring feelings that sponsors hope for, one could find indicators in public behaviors and in verbal testimony. The environments surrounding hikes, rafting, and camel rides tend to be festive, with a lot of shouting and joking back and forth. Contributions to closing discussion circles typically include statements like the following, made in the conversation in which Hailey and Bauer also took part:

> LESLEY GOLD: I was just amazed by how close . . . you can become with somebody who you just meet, after four days or so.
>
> MELISSA BLUNT: I fell in love with this country within the first couple days of being here. I think that sharing it with all of you is something that made it an amazing experience rather than just a great experience.

As indicators, though, observations and testimonials are problematic. In the first instance, the observer imputes a relationship between subjective experience and visible behavior. In the second, the tourists themselves engage in a post hoc translation of subjective experience into language. Discussion circle testimony is additionally suspect because of the constraints governing its production.

Yet although we need not take it at face value, neither should we dismiss it as reflective only of its discursive context and not of the lived experience to which it refers. If discussants speak in superlatives, it is not simply because they believe they are supposed to speak in such terms. They are just as likely to speak this way in in-depth interviews, whose discursive context is governed by other norms.

Even Jenna Eisenstein, who dismissed the discussion circle pronouncements as hyperbole that "just escalate[d] . . . [and] got more and more extreme as it went on," asserted privately that she was "feeling extremes of feeling that I've never felt before."

A more compelling form of verbal testimony is the common assertion that the experience cannot be put into words. This follows Kirshenblatt-Gimblett's contention that the essence of Israel experience pedagogy is its ineffability. "These tours stress embodied experience over language," she writes: "For all the discussion and diary writing that take place on these tours, language will finally be inadequate to the task of communicating the youngsters' experience. . . . Feeling is the form that understanding will take, and language will fail to express it adequately."[14] What language will express, however, is the tourists' own inchoate awareness of Kirshenblatt-Gimblett's point.

In the same discussion circle mentioned above, one man introduced his remarks by saying, "Both my older siblings had come to Israel before me. They always talked about, like, 'This is an experience, you know, I can't just tell you about, you really have to go on it yourself.'"

Jenna made the same point in a more elaborate way during our interview. In her narrative, she positioned herself both as the recipient of such a message and the articulator of it to others:

JENNA: I just called my sister. She's two years younger. I just called her the other day. I said, "You know, you need to go. You need to go to Israel for Birthright. I can talk to you for hours and hours and try to explain to you what it's like. But there will be no way that you can fully *feel* what it is like to be here until you're actually here doing these things."

SK: Why?

JENNA: I could talk for hours . . . but I don't think I could fully, like, relay to her, like, *feelings*. Like, I could use words to describe, you know, "Oh, you know, when you go in the Dead Sea, it's really cool when your legs float up. It's nothing you've ever felt before." Or, you know, "You climb up Masada and you hear this story, and it makes you feel very proud of the heroic nature of the Jewish people." Or, "You go to the Western Wall and it's a really nice feeling knowing how many millions of people have been there to pray before, who you know share similar origins and, you know, ancestry." But, *words?* Like, I heard those words from other people who had been to Birthright before, had been to Israel. But they didn't stick. You know, I'd hear them, and I said, "Oh. That's, that's nice." I thought that would be a nice feeling. But there's nothing like actually feeling it for oneself.

Tourism creates an immediate experience of a self that is situated in the context of the tour. This experience is novel and unfamiliar by virtue of its setting. In Israel experience tourism, it is made even more exceptional by the fact that the tour environment is deliberately structured to intensify the positive sensations associated with the social group and the corporeal body, two pillars of the phenomenological experience of self. The nature of this experience is ineffable, yet the tours suggest a language that travelers can use to name it. This is the language of Jewish community, heritage, spirituality, pride, and connection to homeland that are offered in the discussion circles. As the tourists frame their immediate experiences of a subjective "I" with these very particular discursive constructions of an objective "me," they suggest to themselves and to each other that to feel the way they are feeling is to feel what it means to be Jewish, to be a part of a Jewish community, and to be at home in the State of Israel or anywhere else that they are with other Jews.

"It Changed My Life"

"Okay, I just need everyone's attention for one more minute," Gidi pleaded.

We shifted restlessly in our seats. It was the end of a long first day in Israel. The orientation meeting in the cramped hotel conference room was the last place we wanted to be. Gidi had established rapport with the group, though, which made people willing to bite their tongues and listen for a few minutes more.

"There is an idea that another university did [on Birthright Israel] . . . and I wanted to steal the idea and use it here," Gidi said:

> I'm going to start a bus journal. . . . Every day, everyone gets a chance to write in this bus journal. If you want to write once, you can write once. You can write twice. You can write one line. You can write 10 lines. . . . It can be anonymous. Just write something that strikes you. . . . I will take it home and I will make photocopies of this journal, and I will mail them to you as . . . a different kind of memento of your experience in Israel.

Gidi was accurate in calling this a "different kind of memento," for the bus journal was not simply a record of the trip's occurrences but also a record of the tourists' sentiments as they unfolded over the course of the 10 days. Clearly, it was a skewed record. We might fairly say that the entries tell us more about the norms governing contributions to this medium of public discourse than they do about the range of tourists' inner experiences. Still, in offering the journal as a souvenir, Gidi was sending an important message:

not only was Israel worthy of note, but so were the tourists' own feelings and reactions. This tour was as much about the tourists as it was about the place they had come to see.

Over the next week and a half, members of the group filled two books with entries that typically included some combination of declared enthusiasm, feel-good "remember whens," and earnest confession. Striking, however, was the fact that, as early as the third day of the trip, people were already writing journal entries in which they professed to be undergoing significant personal "change":

> Coming into this trip, I heard amazing stories of my friends' experiences and how much these 10 days changed the person they were. I thought at first that was a strange comment, but even within the first two days I realized what they said really is true.—*Entry 10, Day 3, anonymous female*[15]

> Coming into this thing people kept telling me this trip would change my life. I rolled my eyes at them. Change my life? Seeing SNL [*Saturday Night Live*] when it was good for the first time, that changed my life. But I can feel myself changing here. See, I'm not a very good Jew. I don't keep kosher. I don't go to services. I positively suck at keeping it in the tribe. But being here makes me so proud to be a Jew. I definitely feel like I'm gonna start doing those things (maybe not keep kosher though, because ham + pepperoni = crazy delicious). So being here makes me want to be a better Jew.—*Entry 5, Day 2, anonymous male*

The bus journal is its own genre, and its rhetoric of "life change" should be understood in that context. Yet the journals are by no means unique. The same rhetoric appears again and again in the many forms of literary expression that diaspora Jewish homeland tourism has spawned. One encounters claims of changed lives and profound self-discovery:

- *In group discussion circles*
  And coming here has not just reconnected me to Judaism, but completely changed my understanding of what it means to be Jewish.—*Bauer, see above*
  I really think I found myself here.—*Kathleen Bruder, in same discussion circle*

- *In op-eds for Jewish federation newspapers and websites*

  Words cannot describe how amazing and life-changing my Birthright Israel trip last spring with Livnot was for me. It was so much more than just a "free ride to Israel"; it was about discovering new things and overcoming my fears and making new friends. Most important, it was a spiritual journey to discover my Jewish roots.[16]

  I know it sounds cliché, but the truth is that this trip changed my life. In the midst of the bus rides and historical sites, I found a love for the state of Israel and its people. . . . I found something deep inside me I never knew existed. I now realize that the foundation of Israel is the foundation of the Jewish people. Strong in our convictions and faith we stand together proud as a community.[17]

- *In blog posts*

  I will warn you right now, there is NO WAY I can come close to doing justice to this trip. . . . Being in Israel has truly changed my life. It has changed the way I see myself and the context in which I fit into every aspect of my life. It is a very strange feeling to be in a place I have never been, on the other side of the world, and feel oddly at home. For many years now I have not been very connected to Judeism [sic]. In fact, at times I have even denied my association with it altogether. However, being in Israel has reminded me that Judeism in [sic] not just about religion. It's about tradition, values, and a shared history of fighting for what you believe in. I have never been more proud to be part of something in my life.[18]

- *In testimonials given for ad-copy*

  Israel and Oranim changed my life! I encountered my heritage and embraced it fully; I found myself![19]

  I came to Israel as a disconnected Jew—who didn't know what it meant to be Jewish. I left Israel with a sense of who I am, where I came from, and how to get there. My Mayanot experience has changed my life forever.[20]

- *In thank you speeches to program funders*

  I can honestly say that my experience with Birthright Israel changed my life. . . . I was born to parents of two religions . . . [but] became a member of neither religion. . . . From the moment I entered . . . Jerusalem, a profound feeling of coming home came upon me. I felt *Jewish* for the first time in my life.[21]

- *And in open-ended responses to program evaluation survey questions*
  Survey Question, asked three months posttrip: "Is there anything else you
    would like to tell us about your Birthright Israel experience?"
  I am so grateful. The trip reconnected me to Judaism. I felt accepted
    even though I am only Jewish on my father's side. This trip brought
    me home to myself and has changed my life. Thank You.
  THANK YOU. It was simply incredible—the best thing I've done in my
    entire life and I will be eternally grateful. It gave me a passion and
    a meaning to live and has literally changed my life. Thank you so
    much for providing this incredible opportunity and I am harassing
    each and every one of my Jewish friends to go.[22]

The notion that diaspora Jewish homeland tours can be and should be "life changing" is both a prevalent expectation among its participants and one of the central justifications for the massive investment of diaspora philanthropic dollars and Israeli tax sheqels in the enterprise. The question of whether it is so has been at the heart of over four decades of program evaluation research and forms the centerpiece of the most ambitious such effort, the $1.8 million evaluation of Birthright Israel.[23]

One of the paradoxes uncovered by this evaluation research is that travelers' declarations of profound change are, in the aggregate, not matched by corresponding changes in the concrete Jewish behaviors reported in the surveys.[24] This does not mean that the tourists' subjective experience of change is invalid or that their claims should be dismissed as hyperbole. On the contrary, it indicates emphatically that the type of life change of which the tourists speak is not that which the surveys typically measure.

Diaspora Jewish homeland tourists' assertions of life change are best understood as a discourse that draws on a generic rhetoric of self-actualization through travel, even as it has dimensions that are specific to the Israel experience field itself.[25] The fact that tourists embark on Israel experience programs having already been told by friends and sponsors that "this trip would change my life" indicates that this discourse is not emergent but learned. Travelers invoke it even at the outset of their trips, as we see in the journal entries, long before they return home to have a chance to see whether or not their claims will be borne out in the months and years to come. Because it appears, therefore, to bear no necessary relationship to the lives tourists will lead in the future, we might ask what it is that the phrase, as it is used contemporaneously during the tours and retrospectively afterward, is addressing?

During the tours themselves, the discourse of life change, although it sometimes bespeaks anticipations of future behavior, primarily points backward in time, not forward. The rhetorical convention is invoked by travelers to convey the emotionally powerful experience of reconstructing their understandings of their own pasts. Although the travelers do not weave complete autobiographies, they engage in partial acts of revision that are typically attended by feelings of life coherence, rootedness in history and place, affirmation in the eyes of respected others, and validation through the phenomenological experience of a social and embodied self. If we take the position that "personal narratives, in both facets of content and form, *are* people's identities . . . the story *is* one's identity," then we can say that the life that has been changed is not the life that will be led but the life that has been led.[26] By changing the stories that they tell themselves about themselves, people change not their futures but their pasts. In so doing, they create themselves in the present as different people. The rhetoric of life change expresses tourists' awareness of the fact that their self-understandings have been revised.

The inescapable fact of these tourist constructions of self is that they emerge in a liminal environment that must inevitably end. Insofar as identities are grounded in the social contexts that enable them to be enacted, the dissolution of the touring community and the cessation of the practices that constitute it strike at the foundations of the identities that the diaspora homeland tours create and sustain. Any self-understandings that emerge on these tours are necessarily fragile, and any intentions that they give rise to are necessarily provisional. The perpetuation of these identities and the realization of these intentions depend less on the tours than on the lives to which the travelers return. These later experiences can provide opportunities to reactivate and reground in new contexts the identities that were forged on the trips, but they will almost certainly also reaffirm the salience of alternative constructions of self that the tours had succeeded in temporarily marginalizing.

The final word on the life-changing effects of the trips remains with the tourists themselves, as they in future years incorporate their retrospections into their stories of self. As I, for example, reflect today on the United Synagogue Youth Israel Pilgrimage program in which I participated during the summer after I graduated from high school, I am aware that I position it in my own life story as the experience that planted in me both the idea and the desire to spend a year of college studying in Israel. As I commonly tell the story to myself and to others, the year I spent at the Hebrew University of Jerusalem led me to pursue an undergraduate major in Judaic studies, during which time I focused on the social scientific study of American Jews, which led me to pursue graduate work and an academic career in sociology and Judaic studies. Had I not gone on the high school Israel trip, would an alternate chain of events have led me to different career decisions? Perhaps, but it is senseless to argue the counterfactual. From a retrospective vantage point, the tour cannot logically be said to have *changed* a life, considering that none of the alternative possible futures were ever lived out.

Looking backward, we can speak of diaspora homeland tours as life changing only in a narrative sense, to the extent that former tourists position the trips as turning points in their stories of self. But the importance of this should not be underestimated. W. I. Thomas's dictum, "If men define situations as *real*, they are *real* in their consequences," applies to individuals, as well as to societies. If diasporans understand the homeland tours to have been life changing, they may just act as if they are.

---

8 ────

Building Diaspora

───────────────────────────────────

The past century and a half has seen the rise of modern mass tourism as a new way of engaging place. Although tourism was initially and still is largely a market-driven phenomenon, by the latter half of the 20th century, nation-states and nongovernmental organizations had discovered that they could systematically deploy this novel cultural form to influence political identities. The ethnic culture industries of many different countries and diaspora communities began applying rational planning, bureaucratic organization, and, in some instances, even ideological, philosophical, and theoretical articulation to develop tourism as a medium of diasporic political socialization. As suggested by the Israeli-Jewish case examined here, these efforts can demonstrate sophisticated understandings of tourism's many intersecting dimensions, teasing them apart so that they can be treated strategically as targets of intervention.

Ultimately, however, tourism's semiotic, interactional, embodied, and other dimensions all realize themselves simultaneously in a holistic manner. Tour operators generally recognize this, as we should, too. If it was useful for the sake of analytic clarity to devote separate chapters to different dimensions of tourism, it is also important to weave the separate strands of analysis back together when offering some overarching conclusions about the ways that the medium of tourism and the efforts to deploy it advance forms of diasporic socialization that bear on crucial questions of nationalism, transnationalism, and the politics of state-diaspora relations. In speaking to these issues, I also try to say something more broadly about the nature of tourism as a deployable medium of meaning construction.

This is hardly the first time that culture has been deployed to create political subjectivities. But the use of tourism to forge diasporic connections to homelands does not just mobilize a cultural practice; it mobilizes a *specific* cultural practice. This specificity is crucial for the types of outcomes that it makes possible. Like any medium, tourism has distinctive characteristics that shape how it can be used and what it can and cannot accomplish. If we

| 191

think of the attempts to manipulate this medium as a type of art, then we can recognize that the choice to use tourism rather than some other mode of socialization bears consequences, just as does an artist's choice to use clay instead of paint.

Tourism's unique powers and limitations as a medium stem from the fact that it is simultaneously bounded, emplaced, mobile, embodied, practice-based, symbol-rich, contrast-generating, social, collaborative, multifaceted, dynamic, and irreducibly complex. It is well suited for territorializing culture by inscribing meaning on place; for fostering intellectual and emotional engagement with the meanings that are being inscribed; for generating embodied behaviors that enact relationships with places and with their inscribed meanings; for incorporating these experiences of place into understandings of self; and for reinforcing the salience of these self-understandings by grounding them in a supportive social context, by attaching emotional valence to them, and by marginalizing alternative self-definitions. At the same time, the evanescence of the tour environment ensures the fragility of any constructions of self that are grounded in its social context. Likewise, to the degree that the practices of tourism are incommensurate with those of other contexts, the translation of a tourist experience into other types of behaviors after the tours will occur unevenly and inconsistently.

Although tourism can be crafted and deployed to great effect, it does not operate in any mechanistic or deterministic way. The medium will therefore always elude attempts to fully domesticate it. The control that its mobilizers can achieve over it, while substantial, will necessarily be partial and incomplete. One reason for this is that state-sponsored homeland tours do not operate *on* tourists but, rather, position them as active agents. This agency has been an important theme throughout these chapters. In addition, tourism's social dynamics have emergent properties that generate complexity and unpredictability. Perhaps most important, tourism—as a way of coming to know place, culture, community, self, and the connections among them all—relies not on a single form of knowing but on multiple, cross-cutting knowledge practices that are all occurring simultaneously. Some of these practices construct meaning through the semiotics of the gaze; others through narrative; and still others through dialogue, play, embodiment, emotion, and aesthetic appreciation. The intersection of these various practices also creates other forms of engaging or knowing place, including consumption (which draws on several elements of these) and performance (which draws together all of them, save, perhaps, dialogue).[1] The simultaneous use of so many different ways of knowing generates contradictions and encourages amplifier and canceling effects. These animate tourism, making it an open-ended, dynamic form of meaning-creation. Efforts to overcome tourism's contradictions never actually resolve them but simply introduce into the field of struggle additional forces of contention.

Politics of Nationalism

Diaspora homeland tours are political acts in the most mundane and most profound senses of the term. On one hand, the tours are efforts to garner diplomatic and material advantage for nation-states by mobilizing the support of foreign nationals; on the other hand, they are thoroughly implicated in the grand ideological work of imagining community and asserting relationships between people, cultures, and place. A transnational practice, they have the contradictory effects of furthering nationalist projects that territorialize culture in a single homeland and of subverting these projects by using tourism to ensure culture's portability and thereby insist that it not remain tethered in only one place. The politics of diaspora Jewish tourism to Israel are especially fraught, both because they bear on the clash of Jewish and Arab nationalisms and because they bear on Zionism's specific character as a critique of Jewish diasporic existence. As a mode of diasporic political socialization, Israel experience tours are anything but straightforward.

At the most prosaic level, if we can call it that, there are few grounds for concluding that the enterprise as a whole gives preference to one set of policy options vis-à-vis the Israeli-Palestinian conflict. The spectrum of mainstream Israeli Jewish opinion is given discursive expression on the tours. This spectrum ranges broadly from support for withdrawal from the Occupied Territories and the establishment of a free and independent Palestine, on one end, to support for retaining in perpetuity the biblical patrimony of Judea and Samaria, which was restored to Jewish sovereignty in 1967, on the other. Individual guides vary in the extent to which their presentations hew to an ambiguous center or skew toward either of the poles. Mifgash participants add a diversity of opinion and ensure that the guide's voice will not be the only one vested with the local's authority. Exposure to Israelis' contending conceptions of their national interest may have the effect of undercutting any tendency on the part of travelers to insist that an authentic "pro-Israel" stance demands support for one particular course of action.

As is emphasized throughout these pages, however, discursive representations are only one dimension of knowledge construction in tourism. To the extent that embodied experience and performative practice foster emotional attachments to land, one might expect that the tours will generate sentimental support for Israeli retention of areas over the Green Line and opposition to territorial concessions. Alternatively, to the extent that the tours primarily position Israel as a site of leisure and consumption, there is reason to doubt whether the tourists will end up translating this into any substantive conclusions on policy matters.

At present, it is unclear whether an enterprise such as Birthright Israel will substantially shift the spectrum of diaspora Jewish opinion to the right or the left. The program's official position is that the tours should remain nonpartisan in Israeli terms, and, indeed, it has maintained Israeli governmental support even as party control of the Knesset has passed from the right-leaning Likud to the left-leaning Labor to the centrist Kadima and back to Likud.[2] To date, program evaluators have not attempted to assess changes in tourists' positions regarding the best course of action for Israel to take with regard to the Palestinian question. Their survey questions focus mainly on changes in tourists' levels of political engagement, regardless of their particular stances. The closest indication that survey data provide of the tours' propensity to generate support for particular Israeli policies comes in the wake of the 2006 war in Lebanon and paints a mixed portrait. In a time of crisis regarding a different set of issues than those of the West Bank and Gaza, North American Jewish young adults who had taken part in Israel experience tours were more likely than those who had not "to have actively sought news of the war, to have sought news from an Israeli news source, to have supported Israel's position in the war, to have felt connected to Israel and Israelis, and to have taken action on Israel's behalf."[3] At the same time, the far stronger predictor of support for Israel's position was not tour participation but general political orientation on a scale from very conservative to very liberal. The tours encouraged a closing of ranks, but only partially.

At a deeper level of the political, the tours are powerful influences in the ideological conflict between rival nationalisms. This is not because the tours consistently ignore the claims of Palestinian nationalism or represent them only to subject them to critique. The tours commonly create a space where these perspectives can be conveyed and considered dispassionately. The point, however, is to generate understanding, not empathy. Limited to discursive presentations that are framed as the Other's narrative and that are filtered through the voices of Israeli guides, Arab nationalist narratives command little if any emotional weight on the tours. By contrast, tourists will not only hear Israel's ashes to redemption story but also experience it through sensation, dialogue, drama, display, and more. In addition, they will be guided through processes of self-exploration that will enable them to link their personal stories to collective Jewish narratives, which they can thereby embrace as their own. The fundamental asymmetry in the experience of Arab and Jewish narratives helps to accomplish the important ideological work of the tours in securing diaspora Jewish support for Zionism's claim of a right to Jewish self-determination in the ancestral land. By making these claims subjectively compelling and experientially self-evident, the tours work to win Jewish hearts and minds in the face of global campaigns to delegitimize Jewish assertions of national rights in Israel. In this sense, their ideological work is oriented primarily toward shoring up Zionism's own base of Jewish support and creating a bulwark against the ideological struggles being waged against it.

As pro-Zionist as the tours are vis-à-vis Palestinian nationalism's rival claims to the land, they are far less invested in Zionism's claims against the Jewish diaspora. This is largely because they originate in the efforts of diaspora organizations to respond to perceived problems of cultural identity in their own communities. If the tours can be said to be Zionist in any classical sense of the term, it is in an Ahad Ha'amian way that envisions the state not as a means of dismantling diaspora but as a spiritual center that can help sustain Jewish life around the world.[4] To some extent, the fact that tourism fosters a primarily aesthetic engagement with place serves to blunt the trips' ability to convey a critique of Jewish diasporic existence. The medium is structured to position Israel more as an object that exists for visitors' enjoyment and appreciation than as an agent that makes claims on them. Yet alongside this depoliticizing tendency, the semiotic of difference positions Israel relationally in a field of contrasts, such that its different model of Jewish collective existence is apparent to Jews visiting from abroad. This relativizes the models of diasporic Jewish existence familiar to the travelers, calling their inevitability into question. Drawing attention to and heightening this relativization is a key goal of tour educators, who use the confrontation with Israel's difference to unsettle tourists' taken-for-granted notions about what it means to be Jewish and to live Jewishly. Once unlearning occurs, new avenues of personal growth can be opened. Here, the humanistic orientation of the Deweyan model of experiential education that informs Israel experience tourism creates pressures on organizers to place a commitment to the learner at the center of their efforts, rather than a commitment to the prescription of any single path, such as aliyah or religious observance. Although the tours teach Zionism, they do not insist on it, and by virtue of this lack of insistence they take an ideology that presumes to make claims on all Jews and refashion it as a lifestyle choice. Rooted ultimately in a Western individualist ethos that seeks to expand rather than foreclose identity options, the Zionism of the Israel experience programs may be actualized by moving to Israel or by living a culturally rich and communally oriented Jewish life abroad.

That this is not Ben-Gurion's Zionism is already indicated in the choice to use tourism as a mode of diasporic interaction with the homeland, for tours are premised on the notion that those venturing forth will return to their home bases. (The word "tour" derives from the ancient Greek *tornos,* "a tool for describing a circle, a turner's wheel.")[5] The ticket that Birthright Israel provides is round-trip, not one-way. In this sense, although it is involved in bringing Jews to Israel, it is also very much in the business of flying them back out. Since the program's inception, it has funded the departures of almost 200,000 Jews from the Jewish state. Israel's government is a partner in this enterprise.

The exhortations to make aliyah voiced by cabinet ministers at Taglit megaevents must be understood against this backdrop. Although the program scores small wins for classical Zionism, opening a small trickle of new immigration (about 6% of alumni, most from the former Soviet Union) and bringing back a somewhat larger proportion for long-term programs in which aliyah is more explicitly held forth as the pinnacle of Jewish self-actualization, Birthright Israel's raison d'être is to ensure the continued existence of vibrant, Israel-oriented Jewish communities abroad. Israel's decision to devote state funds to such a project reflects a changing understanding of its own interests based on an evolving Zionism that is adapting to an era of transnationalism and globalization. Israel experience tourism is one of the forces helping to advance this evolution in state ideology.

Self and Place

As the first planeloads of Taglit participants were arriving at Ben-Gurion Airport in December 1999, the chairperson of the organization's North American branch published an op-ed in a popular Jewish news magazine in which she set forth the program's mission. Describing the program first and foremost as "an outreach to young [Jewish American] people who have not been drawn into existing Jewish frameworks and may therefore soon be lost to the Jewish people," she said it was also (but not exclusively) intended to "start the new century with a ringing affirmation of the centrality of Israel to Jewish life." That this centrality needed to be affirmed indicates that it was not something that could be taken for granted. There was a particular sense, the chairperson suggested, that young North American Jews did not conceive of Israel as central in or even necessarily relevant to their lives. Although "the reestablishment of Jewish sovereignty in the State of Israel is a fact in which Jews around the world can, and do, take pride," she asserted, such sentiments, she went on to lament, "do not embrace enough of our youth to compete with the powerful influence of assimilation."[6]

At issue deep below the surface was the very sense of at-homeness that Jewish Americans feel, for it strikes at traditional Jewish understandings of what it means to be in diaspora. The thrust of these understandings can be grasped by recognizing that Jewish religious discourse speaks less of diaspora (*pezurim, nefutzot*) than of *galut*—exile. To be living in galut is to feel not fully at home as a Jew in the place where one lives and, at the same time, to affirm that there *is* a place elsewhere where one *would* as a Jew feel fully at home. Rabbinic Judaism understands this "place" both spatially and temporally, as the land of Israel after the messianic redemption (although even before the redemption the land of Israel is considered more existentially home than anyplace else). Classical Zionism rejected the eschatological dimensions of the concept, reframed it in purely geographic and political terms, and thereby presented immigration to a Jewish state in Israel as the "solution" to the "problem" of diaspora.[7]

Israel experience tourism, particularly that emerging out of North America, can be understood as an effort to forestall an alternative solution to the problem of diaspora: the one that would allow people to escape it by not even recognizing that they should consider it a problem. In *New Jews: The End of the Jewish Diaspora*, Caryn Aviv and David Shneer argue that such an escape is increasingly evident. They claim that, unlike their elders, young generations of Jews outside Israel have little sense of being out of place as Jews and little sense that home lies elsewhere.[8] Leaders of diaspora Jewish organizations share this reading and are deeply troubled by it. In their embrace of programs like Birthright Israel, we can read an attempt to complicate easy notions of home—not only notions that would escape the problematics of diaspora by reducing home to one's place of residence or one's country of citizenship but also Zionist efforts to escape it by asserting that there is one and only one place that Jews truly can call home. In spite of their tetherings to Zionist practices, infrastructures, and ideologies, Israel experience programs are essentially efforts in *diasporic* political socialization, attempting to instill among non-Israeli Jews a sense that their existential condition is one of diaspora—multiply rooted and multiply uprooted, in which the relationship between self and place exists in ongoing tension.

Hence the efforts to encourage non-Israeli Jews to strike symbolic roots in a place where they do not live. Hence the efforts to complicate their identities by involving them in a transnational engagement with a foreign country that asserts a right to command some of their affections and loyalties. The basic nature of this engagement is to situate the non-Israeli Jews as acting agents in an Israeli space, where they join with others in applying the knowledge practices of tourism to their surroundings and to themselves. Through their actions, they inscribe place onto self and self onto place, recreating their understandings of themselves and of Israel in the meeting of the two.

One of the key themes running through these pages is the notion that tourism engages people in processes of active self-creation that are actually coproductions between social actors and their emplaced social contexts. There is nothing unique about tourism in this regard. Symbolic interactionism understands the basic nature of selfhood to be one of situated social coproduction. In sharp contrast to perspectives that would imagine the self to be a "thing" that is fundamentally bounded and separate from its environment, this approach understands selfhood to be an ongoing collaborative process that unfolds through time and is therefore always in the midst of being newly accomplished.[9]

Tourism does not change this nature of self-creation. It does, however, temporarily reground it, establishing a new context in which people can produce themselves through interactions with other people and with new material environments. As the diaspora Jewish tourists act *on* Israel and as they draw on the symbolic, interactional, and material resources that Israel provides to them to act *in* Israel, they are creating themselves anew, but this time in partnership *with* Israel. The place enters into the process of self-creation as coproducer, raw material, and context, such that it cannot be deemed separate from the self that is being accomplished with and through it. Once accomplished, these place-incorporating selves become facts of biography that serve as starting points and resources for future open-ended acts of self-creation.

How much these resources are consciously put to use is another matter. Inherent in tourism are potentials for making the experience of self-creation in its context feel more compelling than comparable experiences of self-creation outside of it. The sponsors of homeland tours work to bring these potentials to fruition out of a hope that these "Made in Israel" selves will remain salient long after the tours. Their ability to succeed to the extent that they do derives from the fact that they situate tourists' processes of self-construction in liminal group environments that are saturated with meaning, emotion, communitas, and extraordinary embodied sensation. The liminality is key, because it makes possible all the rest. By removing people temporarily from their ordinary environments, the tours create a new container for situated social action, changing the grounds of self-construction, creating new possibilities, marginalizing competing identities, constraining the nature of the meanings that will inform the emerging selves, enabling the meaning-ascribing gaze to become the dominant organizing principle of daily activity, creating the possibility for intense and uplifting communitas relations, and establishing the contrast between this experience of self and those that occur in nonliminal settings. In the liminal context of the tour, the programs can engage travelers in explicit, public, structured processes of self-reflection and self-representation whose thematic constraints—constraints that receive support and reinforcement from their social context—impose a compelling sense of coherence and rootedness to the self-understandings that emerge. That the themes used to ascribe meaning to the self are also those used to ascribe meaning to the place helps encourage the tourists not merely to *act* as Jewish-selves-in-Jewish-Israel but come to some discursive awareness of themselves as such.

The corollary to the inscription of place on self is the inscription of self on place. Although the discourse of diaspora Jewish homeland tourism speaks of the "Israel experience," the tours do not foster an experience of place, per se. Rather, they foster an experience of self-in-place. Even more precisely, we could say that they foster an emotionally compelling experience of a particular type of self-in-place, that of the touring self. This has implications for travelers' understandings of Israel. Regardless of the meanings they may have ascribed to it before their tours and may still ascribe to it afterward, their own actions will ensure that the country will also come to symbolize for them *their own personal experience of being a tourist in Israel.* For most, it will be remembered in an immediate way as a place where they themselves experienced certain extraordinary physical sensations, some intensely felt emotions, and not a few shipboard romance–like friendships; a place where the identities to which they gave voice had a degree of coherence, thematic unity, and rootedness in a broader collective story; a place where "everything seems to have meaning, *everywhere*," as Tanya Muller from Michael's group said. None of these experiences of self are rooted in Israel as such but, rather, in the modalities of controlled tourism that lead the country to be encountered in this particular way. Tanya's sense that everything in Israel is saturated with meaning, for example, does not reflect the thousands of years of history there as much as the fact that her tourist gaze was constantly treating the things she saw as signifiers. Like most of the tourists, she did not recognize that this was actually a product of social practices that she was helping to generate; instead, she ascribed the power to create such an experience to some inherent properties of the place itself. Marx would call this fetishism; Durkheim, totemism. Whatever we choose to label it, this misrecognition is a powerful form of symbolization that does much to create long-lasting attachments to Israel, for it leads people to remember the country not only as a place of extraordinary personal experience but also as a place *capable* of generating and regenerating such an experience.

As a medium for meditating on the relationship among self, community, culture, and place, diaspora homeland tourism resolves nothing. Rather than providing an answer to the question of home, the tours open the question further and introduce new dimensions of complexity that may not previously have been experienced or recognized. They juxtapose citizenship-based and ethnicity-based notions of political community, undermining them in some ways even while reinforcing them in others. Intended to foster feelings of connection to the homeland, they simultaneously generate among tourists a consciousness of their own outsiderness. Programs like Taglit bring diaspora Jews to Israel as co-ethnics, yet from passport control to the mifgashim and in many other situations throughout the trip, they reinforce tourists' awareness that they are engaging the country as foreign nationals. Alongside this, however, these programs call travelers' attention to their own feelings of otherness in the countries where they live, and generate feelings of ownership, belonging, implication, and responsibility to a country where they do not.

Although the shouts of "Welcome home!" that often greet the tourists would seem to suggest that the tours are trying to offer a ready-made solution to diaspora's central problematic, these declarations compete with, and ultimately founder on, the array of tourist experiences and practices that testify against the possibility of any easy resolution. As a medium for shaping the ways that diasporans imagine political community, homeland tourism is ultimately destabilizing. Herein lies its power. It operates against the monopolizing claims of both homelands and "host" countries, affirming a form of belonging that is constituted by multiple rootedness and multiple otherness. In this, it also breaks from diasporist ideologies that envision diaspora primarily as a state of homelessness and uprooting. The homeland tours suggest, by contrast, that rootedness—explicitly qualified and proudly multiple—is essential to the diasporic condition.

Politics of Diasporism

It is a point of no small significance that the term "diasporic" is not an indigenous category in these tours of Israel. Program organizers speak of strengthening "Jewish peoplehood." They speak, too, of building "Jewish identity." But they do not attach to this the modifier that would make clear that they are speaking of a different form of Jewish identity than that which Israelis can claim. Even as the tours function as agents of diaspora building by creating feelings of belonging and otherness in multiple places, they accomplish this in the context of a cultivated disregard that enables sponsors and staff to comfortably ignore the fact that the tours' implicit model of Jewish existence challenges the claim that the proper place of all Jews is in the State of Israel.

In their determined insistence not to position themselves oppositionally vis-à-vis Zionism, Israel experience programs avoid framing their work in ways that would elevate diaspora to a matter of principle. There are certainly no efforts made on the tours to articulate diaspor-*ism* as an ideological stance. One will hear no claims on the trips that, collectively, the deliberate eschewal of sovereignty is a preferable way of organizing Jewish life, or that, individually, Jews given the choice to live in Israel or outside it should choose the latter. At most, one may hear some affirmations of the legitimacy of the choice most Jews make to live outside of Israel, but this is more assumed than pressed. The tours mount no concerted effort to rebut classical *shelilat hagolah* (negation or rejection of diaspora). Instead, they avoid the argument, letting their general stance of tolerance and nonjudgmentalism mute any assertions of *shelilat hagolah* that are voiced.

The reluctance to take a principled stand touting the virtues of diasporic existence against Israeli claims to the contrary can be traced to a number of sources. The involvement of the Israeli government (especially of its state-sponsored NGO, the Jewish Agency) in planning and conducting Israel experience tours means that key partners have no stake in advocating ideological alternatives to state nationalism. Further, many aspects of the Israel experience trace their roots directly to the Zionist nation-building practice of tiyul. Perhaps most important is the strong support that the Jewish national project in Israel enjoys among the Jewish communities that use Israel experience programs as a form of diaspora Jewish education. This includes a conviction among diaspora-based tour sponsors that, notwithstanding its limitations, the Zionist critique of the perils and constraints of diaspora life contains important elements of truth. Coupled with this is also a firm belief that the collective empowerment that comes with national sovereignty is crucial for

Jews' security and for their ability to project power around the world (including the ability of diaspora communities to project power). For these reasons, there is little interest in taking deliberate steps to challenge Zionism on ideological grounds. The principled antinationalism of diasporist ideologies such as that articulated by Daniel and Jonathan Boyarin finds little sympathy in these circles.[10] Not that tour organizers are necessarily familiar with these ideologies. Still largely confined to academia (discussed below), these antinationalist ideologies have not spawned a broader Jewish political movement worthy of the name. To the extent that they have filtered into popular Jewish discourse, they have done so primarily as an artistic and literary movement.[11]

To these reasons we might add another two. For tours coming from places where physical threats to Jewish security are to some extent pertinent concerns (e.g., France and Hungary), the incentives for tour organizers to challenge Zionism with a diasporist alternative are few. For tours coming from more hospitable environments, organizers feel no real need to press the ideological point, either vis-à-vis the societies out of which they operate or vis-à-vis Israel, for doing so would simply affirm reality. Especially in the United States, where about 40% of the world's Jews live, it is generally taken for granted that Jews are free, if they wish, to lead culturally rich Jewish lives that include the maintenance of transnational connections with Israel. Jews have done this and have established a model of diasporic existence that uses a relationship with Israel to mutual advantage. In exchange for material and political resources, Jews in the United States and in other Western democracies gain the ability to use Israel's symbolic resources to inform, inspire, and strengthen their communities in the countries where they live. Although frequently criticized by Israeli and non-Israeli Jews alike, this model of state-diaspora relations has so far proven a sustainable one that has lasted for over half a century. Rather than undermine the model or advocate alternatives to it, Israel experience tours simply enact it.

The nondiasporist diasporism that emerges through the Israel experience enterprise conceptualizes diaspora in pronationalist, state-engaged terms. In this, it can be seen as continuing the past century's revolutionary transformation in the structure, practice, and imagining of the Jewish diaspora. For centuries, prayers and longing streamed toward an imagined Jerusalem much more than economic, political, and human resources were exchanged with the real city. Modern Zionism shifted the practice of Jewish diaspora from the rabbis' symbolically centered model to one that has been materially state centered and symbolically state informed. The Israel experience tours reinforce the material centrality of Israel by directing to it flows of diaspora tourists and diaspora philanthropic dollars. On the level of public culture, the tours affirm the symbolic centrality of Israel, not only through the performative act of sending hundreds of thousands of Jews there but through the political act of making diaspora homeland tourism a funding priority that precludes the expenditure of communal funds for alternative uses.

For the participants in Israel experience programs, the diasporic subjectivities that the tours advance are better described as state informed, state engaged, or territorialized rather than state centered. First, by using signifiers of place-transcending Jewish culture to inscribe meaning onto the geographies of Israel, the tours simultaneously inscribe the geographies of Israel onto these aspects of Jewish culture. This infuses them with a place-specific character and enables them later to evoke Israel and its landscape, in addition to any other meanings they may call to mind. This does not necessitate that, after the tours, those meanings associated with Israel will be the ones that the former tourists will privilege. The salience of such Israel-informed meanings, however, is no doubt enhanced by the fact that these added contents are shared symbols that are now more or less common to all who have participated in Israel experience tours. Whether the inscription of these territorialized meanings on extant Jewish symbols ends up narrowing or augmenting the range of meanings that the symbols can evoke is an open question. It may be that both will occur, particularly if it is true that every act of regarding is simultaneously an act of disregarding.

The second reason that the diasporic subjectivities advanced by the tours are better described as state engaged or state informed than state centered has to do with the particular nature of the knowledge practices being applied during the tours. If one wanted to argue that Israel experience programs foster an Israel-centered diasporic identity, one might point to the fact that trip leaders discursively affirm the centrality of the homeland while simultaneously engaging travelers in symbolically saturated ritual performances of identification with it. This focus highlights the official program and asserts that the self-aware intentions of program organizers are carried off in an essentially unproblematic manner. It misses the emergent dynamics that work to counter these efforts, however. The disjunctures that make tourists aware of their outsiderness in Israel work against the establishment of diasporic identities that are premised only on feelings of identification with the homeland. So, too, does the tourist gaze's semiotic of difference, which is continually constructing tourists' understandings of their own Jewish spaces by treating Israel as a foil. The terms of the comparison are set by Israel, which assigns it a crucial power in shaping diasporic self-understandings, but the nature of the comparison is one that emphasizes contrast. What emerges from this is a diasporic subjectivity that is conscious of its own difference and distance from Israel. It is this awareness that is not captured in the language of state-centeredness, a language that smoothes over disjunctures and forecloses the ability to speak of the ruptures that are an integral part of the orientations toward Israel that the homeland tours produce.

Diasporic Imagination and Practice

In the efforts to deploy homeland tourism as a medium of transnational political socialization, we find a form of diasporic practice that important theorizations of diaspora have a difficult time accounting for. From the perspectives of transnational migration studies, postcolonial diaspora studies, and neodiasporist Judaic studies, Israel experience tourism can only be deemed anomalous.[12] Yet this anomalous character can draw our attention to those points where our conceptual frameworks fail us and can suggest ways of revising them. We conclude, then, with some reflections on the ways that this consideration of Israel experience tourism can help us rethink fundamental aspects of contemporary diaspora and transnationalism.

When interest in diaspora and transnational studies began to coalesce in sociology in the 1980s and 1990s, it was spurred, in part, by the observation that not only were migrants striking roots in the places to which they had moved but also they were engaging in grassroots practices that involved them on a regular basis in the political, economic, social, and cultural affairs of their countries of origin. A notion among researchers that this involvement was unprecedented both in intensity and in scope led them to frame inquiry into transnationalism in terms that emphasized migrants' involvements in "occupations and activities that require regular and sustained social contacts over time across national borders for their implementation."[13] Transnational diaspora, as it came to be understood in this line of scholarship, was characterized largely as a phenomenon in which "transmigrants" were essentially finding ways to live back and forth between two countries that were equally home.[14] Within this conceptual framework, a one-time transnational practice applied from the top down to create diasporic connections between people who have no direct migration-based links to the country that is claiming them would have to be relegated to the margins. The theory cannot encompass it.

By the early 1990s, postcolonial cultural studies had also turned its lens onto the question of diaspora. Unlike the sociology of transnationalism, this line of scholarship developed a conceptualization in which "place" became almost incidental. It reconceived diaspora as an existential condition, a mode of relating to a fragmented world, at once a description of the postmodern experience and simultaneously an authorization to embrace the multiplicities of the ever-hybrid cultures that exist inside and around each one of us.[15] In this conception, the paradigmatic diasporan is not the new migrant but the postcolonial subject—anywhere—who experiences those "specific forms of double consciousness" that come from being rooted in antagonistic yet inextricable cultural traditions.[16]

As is often the case, the core aspects of a conceptual framework are most compellingly articulated by its critics. Sander Gilman characterized the postcolonial framing of diaspora as follows:

> Today we have seen a radical transvaluation of the meaning ascribed to the periphery. Diaspora has come to mean deterritorialized; homeless; rootless; displaced; dispersed; nomadic; discontinuous; hybrid; plural. . . . In a world defined as multicultural, they have reversed their traditional meanings and have come to mark the desirability of life at the margins rather than its failure. This romanticization of the periphery is just as deadly dangerous as it presents only the margins as a space for cultural success.[17]

A diasporic practice that places geography at its center and that is premised on an engagement with place and on the maintenance of an affectionate relationship with a nation-state, no less, would seem to belong to another class of objects. This is not the diaspora of which postcolonial theory speaks. The boundaries of the conceptual frame do not extend in ways that might include it.

In Judaic studies, what I am calling the "neodiasporist" position[18] is most clearly articulated in a 1993 piece in which Daniel and Jonathan Boyarin argue that only diaspora's "dissociation of ethnicities and political hegemonies" offers a nonoppressive means of affirming cultural particularism.[19] In an argument that represents almost a mirror image of classical Zionist *shelilat hagolah*, they stake a claim for diaspora as a more authentic Jewish political stance than Zionist nationalism by declaring Zionism both unfaithful to Jewish tradition ("not a continuation of Judaism but its final betrayal") and an alien implant ("the substitution of a Western, European cultural-political formation for a traditional Jewish one").[20] Other branches of neodiasporist scholarship emphasize the importance of abandoning the reigning state-centered core-periphery paradigms of thought in favor of other models that are noncentered or multiply centered.[21] A diasporic practice that continues to direct people, resources, and priority to the State of Israel would seem to represent nothing more than the persistence of this older paradigm. Either it testifies against neodiasporism, or it exists as something to be testified against.

In each of these cases, the inability to comfortably incorporate a transnational practice that more and more states and diasporas are adopting stems from a failure to recognize something essential about diaspora: a diaspora is, like the nation, an "imagined community."[22] As such, it can be imagined in many different ways, through many different practices. These imaginings and practices will necessarily inform one another, because they are each created through the other and because practice constructs meanings in ways that are specific to it. Diasporas are imagined as they are done, and they are done as they are imagined. They may be grounded in different legitimizing ideologies, the migration narrative being but one. Indeed, the nonessentiality of an immediate migration narrative to the creation of diasporic relationships is testified to by the case we have considered here: the Jewish adoption of the modern State of Israel as a symbolic homeland.

If we take seriously the idea of extending Benedict Anderson's notion of imagined communities beyond the national group to the transnational group, then we have to inquire into the reciprocal relationships between diasporic practice and diasporic imaginings. This imperative has guided my analysis here.

Just as national identities and communities are forged by collective practices of nation-building, diasporic identities and communities are constructed through collective acts of diaspora-building. One of the reasons that the transnationalism of contemporary diaspora-building efforts has not undermined state nationalism in the way that some had initially predicted is because in these efforts states can take leading roles. Recognizing that state-diaspora alliances confer advantages to both parties that are greater than the sum of their parts, states and their co-ethnic NGOs around the world have begun working in partnership to forge transnational community. Together, they are deploying cultural practices that cross geographies of division to effect diasporic political socialization. Culture, however, is contradictory. States and diasporas do not always see eye to eye. Human beings retain agency. And transnational spaces, although they can be influenced, can never be fully controlled. In the efforts to mobilize tourism, these contradictions of culture result in a type of diaspora-building that ultimately is open-ended and even in some ways destabilizing—undermining any attempts to offer easy answers to the question, "Where is home?" By complicating matters in this way, diaspora homeland tours create options for selves, for community, for culture, and for place.

Methodological Appendix

This book includes secondary analyses of data from pretrip and post-trip web-based surveys of participants in the winter 2000–2001 Taglit-Birthright Israel tours and of a control group of nonparticipant applicants to this round of trips. The surveys were conducted by Brandeis University's Cohen Center for Modern Jewish Studies (CMJS) in the context of a program evaluation.

In autumn 2000, all 24,371 American and Canadian applicants to Birthright Israel's winter 2000–2001 trips were e-mailed an invitation to participate in an online survey. The pretrip survey inquired into demographic and religious characteristics of the applicants, their decision to apply to Taglit, their activities, and their values and opinions. In April and May 2001, these program applicants were again invited to complete an online survey. The posttrip survey asked about Taglit, Jewish identity and practice, and feelings about Israel, among other things. Completion rates are presented in the appendix table A.1.

TABLE A.1
Survey Completion Rates, Taglit-Birthright Israel Tours, Winter 2000–2001

| | | Completed Surveys | | | |
| | Total | Pretrip Survey | | Posttrip Survey | |
	Population	N	%	N	%
Tour Participants	6,255	3,602	58%	2,476	40%
Non-Participants[1]	18,116	5,620	31%	2,717	15%
Total (All Applicants)	24,371	9,222	38%	5,193	21%

[1]Nonparticipants were applicants to the program who did not actually go on the tour.

Panel

A total of 1,862 Taglit participants responded to both the pretrip and post-trip surveys. This panel is used here for all analyses that address relationships between items measured before departure and after return.

Weighting

CMJS produced poststratification weights to facilitate generalization from the survey sample to the population of all winter 2000–2001 Taglit participants and nonparticipants. The weighting uses iterative proportional fitting (i.e., simultaneously applying all weights) so that the sample will reflect the population in terms of country of home residence (United States and Canada), age, sex, and participant status. Targets for each of these four variables were adjusted, based on the proportion of missing values in each. Weights were computed separately for those who responded to both surveys, for those who responded only to the pretrip survey, and for those who responded only to the posttrip survey.

Glossary

ahavat ha'aretz: love for the land of Israel

aliyah: Jewish immigration to Israel (lit., "ascent")

Ashkenazim: Jews of Central and Eastern European descent

gibbush: coalescence, group cohesion

goyim: non-Jews, often with a derogatory connotation (lit., "nations")

Haganah: the largest pre-state Jewish militia; affiliated with the socialist Labor Zionists (lit., "defense")

hamsa: amulet representing the hand of God

Hano'ar Ha'oved: The Working Youth; a socialist Zionist youth movement

Histadrut: General Federation of Labor; the federation of labor unions established in the Yishuv

kabbalah: Jewish mystical tradition, refined by Rabbi Isaac Luria and his followers in 16th-century Safed

kibbutz: a socialist Zionist agricultural commune

Knesset: Israeli parliament

lahuhe: Yemenite style pizza

madrich/ah (pl. *madrichim/madrichot*): counselor, tour guide

mifgash (pl. *mifgashim*): structured cross-cultural encounters between tourists and locals

Mizrachim: Jews of Middle Eastern and North African descent

moreh derech: educator-guide (lit., "teacher of the way")

moshav (pl. *moshavim*): kibbutz-like settlement that combines collective and private ownership

Palmach: elite "strike force" of the Haganah

sabra: the first generation of Jews to be born in the Yishuv and in Israel

Sephardim: Jews of Spanish and Mediterranean descent

shelilat hagolah: classical Zionism's ideological negation or rejection of diaspora

Shoah: the Holocaust

Taglit: the Hebrew name for the Birthright Israel program (lit., "discovery")

tefillin: phylacteries, traditionally worn by males in Jewish prayer

tiyul (pl. *tiyulim*): hiking; here, especially, as a ritualized sanctification of space

Tzfat: Safed

Tzofim: Scouts; a nonpartisan Zionist youth movement

yedi'at ha'aretz: knowing the land of Israel; also the field of scholarship and educational practice focusing on that knowledge

Yishuv: the pre-state Jewish community in Palestine, established by the Zionist movement

Notes

PREFACE

1. United Nations World Tourism Organization, *World Tourism Barometer* 6(2) (Madrid: UNWTO, 2008), 3, at http://unwto.org/facts/eng/pdf/barometer/UNWTO_ Baromo8_2_en_Excerpt.pdf (accessed August 8, 2008); World Trade Organization, *International Trade Statistics 2007* (Geneva: WTO, 2007), 112, at http://www.wto.org/english/ res_e/statis_e/its2007_e/its2007_e.pdf (accessed August 8, 2008).

2. In trying to strike this balance I follow Christian Smith, who argues for "taking a strong position on the power and importance of socialization in social reproduction, without conceiving of those socialized as passive recipients of cultural norms, values, and ends—since they are always both the objects and subjects of their own socialization." Christian Smith, *Moral, Believing Animals: Human Personhood and Culture* (Oxford: Oxford University Press, 2003), 30.

3. Staples of Sociology 101 courses, breaching experiments were popularized by Harold Garfinkel as a way of revealing taken-for-granted social rules. In them, a researcher deliberately violates a norm and studies others' reactions. Common examples are standing backward in elevators or eating food off others' plates.

4. This can be seen as consonant with Ahad Ha'am's Zionist philosophy, which saw Israel serving as a spiritual center to sustain Jewish life in diaspora. See, e.g., "Shelilat ha-golah," "Medinat ha-yehudim ve-tzarat ha-yehudim," and other essays in Ahad Ha'am, *Al Parashat Drachim*, 4 vols. (Tel Aviv: Dvir, 1979).

5. A critical view might label this a form of state-worship. Alternatively, it might be read as an affirmation of faith in traditional Judaism in that it asserts the continued validity of the biblical paradigms and affirms the rabbinic notion that God effects revelation through the unfolding of Jewish history.

CHAPTER 1

1. The term "homeland" is laden with assumptions and assertions. I place it in quotation marks here as I introduce it; for subsequent uses, I avoid the quotation marks. I trust the reader not to interpret this as a reification of the term.

2. David Timothy Duval, "Conceptualizing Return Visits: A Transnational Perspective," in *Tourism, Diasporas and Space,* edited by Tim Coles and Dallen Timothy (London: Routledge, 2004), 50–61; Thu-Huong Nguyen and Brian King, "The Culture of Tourism in the Diaspora: The Case of the Vietnamese Community in Australia," in *Tourism, Diasporas*

and Space, edited by Tim Coles and Dallen Timothy (London: Routledge, 2004), 172–87; Alejandro Portes, Luis Guarnizo, and Patricia Landolt, "The Study of Transnationalism: Pitfalls and Promise of an Emergent Research Field," *Ethnic and Racial Studies* 22(2) (1999): 217–37.

3. Susan Fainstein and Dennis Judd, "Global Forces, Local Strategies, and Urban Tourism," in *The Tourist City*, edited by Dennis Judd and Susan Fainstein (New Haven, Conn.: Yale University Press, 1999), 3.

4. United Nations Population Division, *International Migration Report 2002* (New York: UNPD, 2002), 2, at www.un.org/esa/population/publications/ ittmig2002/2002ITTMIGTEXT22–11.pdf (accessed August 8, 2008).

5. Michèle Lamont and Virág Molnár, "The Study of Boundaries in the Social Sciences," *Annual Review of Sociology* 28 (2002): 183.

6. Linda Basch, Nina Glick Schiller, and Cristina Szanton Blanc, *Nations Unbound: Transnational Projects, Postcolonial Predicaments, and Deterritorialized Nation-States* (Langhorne, Penn.: Gordon and Breach, 1994); Stuart Hall, "Cultural Identity and Diaspora," in *Identity: Community, Culture, Difference*, edited by Jonathan Rutherford (London: Lawrence and Wishart, 1990), 222–37; Paul Gilroy, *The Black Atlantic: Modernity and Double-Consciousness* (Cambridge, Mass.: Harvard University Press, 1993); Michael Kearney, "The Local and the Global: The Anthropology of Globalization and Transnationalism," *Annual Review of Anthropology* 24 (2004): 547–65; Yossi Shain, *Kinship and Diasporas in International Affairs* (Ann Arbor: University of Michigan Press, 2007).

7. Steven Vertovec, "Conceiving and Researching Transnationalism," *Ethnic and Racial Studies* 22(2) (1999): 447–62.

8. Hence the title of Basch et al.'s (1994) work on the subject, *Nations Unbound.*

9. Zygmunt Bauman, "From Pilgrim to Tourist—or a Short History of Identity," in *Questions of Cultural Identity*, edited by Stuart Hall and Paul du Gay (London: Sage, 1996), 18.

10. David Munir Nabti, "Conference Explores Diaspora's Relations to Homeland," *Daily Star* (Lebanon) (July 21, 2004), at http://www.dailystar.com.lb/article.asp?edition_ ID=1&article_ID=6465&categ_id=3 (accessed July 22, 2004).

11. The quote is taken from a press release: Birthright Armenia, "Birthright Armenia Celebrates Its Inaugural Year," press release (July 30, 2004), at http://www.armenian-diaspora.com/forum/showthread.php?t=7453 (accessed July 22, 2009). See also Linda Yepoyan, telephone interview, November 18, 2003; Barbara Aronson, personal correspondence, September 10, 2003.

12. Randy Cohen, "The Ethicist," *New York Times Magazine* (March 7, 2004), 22; Rachel Shabi, "Come, See Palestine!" *Salon* (June 5, 2006), at http://www.salon.com/news/feature/2006/06/05/birthright/print.html (accessed April 6, 2007).

13. Jackie Feldman, *Above the Death Pits, Beneath the Flag: Youth Voyages to Poland and the Construction of Israeli National Identity* (Oxford: Berghahn, 2008); Oren Baruch Stier, "Lunch at Majdanek: The March of the Living as a Pilgrimage of Memory," *Jewish Folklore and Ethnology Review* 17(1–2) (1995): 57–65; Jack Kugelmass, "The Rites of the Tribe: The Meaning of Poland for American Jewish Tourists," *YIVO Annual* 21 (1993): 395–453.

14. Emily Noelle Ignacio, *Building Diaspora: Filipino Cultural Community Formation on the Internet* (New Brunswick, N.J.: Rutgers University Press, 2005).

15. Don Rolnik, "A Study of Attitudes towards Israel of American Jewish Youth Participating in a Summer Institute," Ed.D. dissertation, New York University, 1965.

16. For a review of this literature, see Barry Chazan, *Does the Teen Israel Experience Make a Difference?* (New York: Israel Experience, Inc., 1997).

17. Caryn Aviv and David Shneer, *New Jews: The End of the Jewish Diaspora* (New York: New York University Press, 2005); Jasmin Habib, *Israel, Diaspora, and the Routes of National Belonging* (Toronto: University of Toronto Press, 2004); Pnina Steinberg, "Eizor-maga ba-tenuah: Leumiut va-etniut ba-derekh li-yisrael" [Contact zone en route: Nationalism and ethnicity on a voyage to Israel], Ph.D. dissertation, Tel Aviv University, 2002. A related literature also emerged in the 1990s around the other major systematically deployed form of Jewish identity tourism, Holocaust pilgrimages.

18. Harvey Goldberg, "A Summer on a NFTY Safari 1994: An Ethnographic Perspective," in *The Israel Experience: Studies in Jewish Identity and Youth Culture,* edited by Barry Chazan (Jerusalem: Andrea and Charles Bronfman Philanthropies, 2002), 21–140; Samuel Heilman, "A Young Judea Israel Discovery Tour: The View from Inside," in *The Israel Experience: Studies in Jewish Identity and Youth Culture,* edited by Barry Chazan (Jerusalem: Andrea and Charles Bronfman Philanthropies, 2002), 141–265; Barbara Kirshenblatt-Gimblett, "Learning from Ethnography: Reflections on the Nature and Efficacy of Youth Tours to Israel," in *The Israel Experience: Studies in Jewish Identity and Youth Culture,* edited by Barry Chazan (Jerusalem: Andrea and Charles Bronfman Philanthropies, 2002), 267–331; Shaul Kelner, Leonard Saxe, Charles Kadushin, Rachel Canar, Matthew Lindholm, Hal Ossman, Jennifer Perloff, Benjamin Phillips, Rishona Teres, Minna Wolf, and Meredith Woocher, *Making Meaning: Participants' Experience of Birthright Israel* (Waltham, Mass.: Brandeis University, Cohen Center for Modern Jewish Studies, 2000); Shaul Kelner, "The Impact of Israel Experience Programs on Israel's Symbolic Meaning," *Contemporary Jewry* 24 (2003): 124–54; Leonard Saxe and Barry Chazan, *Ten Days of Birthright Israel: A Journey in Young Adult Identity* (Waltham, Mass.: Brandeis University Press, 2008); Faydra Shapiro, *Building Jewish Roots: The Israel Experience* (Montreal: McGill-Queen's University Press, 2006).

19. The primary exception is Kirshenblatt-Gimblett, "Learning from Ethnography."

20. Mary Kelly, "Born Again Lithuanians: Ethnic Conversions and Pilgrimages and the Resurgence of Lithuanian-American Ethnic Identity," Ph.D. dissertation, University of Kansas, 1996.

21. Alan Morinis (editor), *Sacred Journeys: The Anthropology of Pilgrimage* (Westport, Conn.: Greenwood, 1992), 4.

22. Cf. Fainstein and Judd, "Global Forces, Local Strategies, and Urban Tourism," 6–7.

23. Sara Lipka, "Eyes on the Past," *Chronicle of Higher Education*, February 9, 2007, A48.

24. Erik Cohen, "Pilgrimage and Tourism: Convergence and Divergence," in *Sacred Journeys: The Anthropology of Pilgrimage,* edited by Alan Morinis (Westport, Conn.: Greenwood, 1992), 50.

25. Daniel Boorstin, *The Image: A Guide to Pseudo-Events in America* (New York: Atheneum, [1961] 1985), 77, 79.

26. Nelson Graburn, "Tourism: The Sacred Journey," in *Hosts and Guests: The Anthropology of Tourism,* edited by Valene Smith (Philadelphia: University of Pennsylvania Press, [1977] 1989), 28.

27. John Urry, *The Tourist Gaze* (London: Sage, 1990).

28. Chris Rojek and John Urry (editors), *Touring Cultures: Transformations of Travel and Theory* (London: Routledge, 1997).

29. Urry, *Tourist Gaze*, 3.

30. Dean MacCannell calls sightseeing "a ritual performed to the differentiations of society." Dean MacCannell, *The Tourist: A New Theory of the Leisure Class* (New York: Schocken, [1976] 1989), 13.

31. Fainstein and Judd, "Global Forces, Local Strategies, and Urban Tourism."

32. Edward M. Bruner, "Tourism in Ghana: The Representation of Slavery and the Return of the Black Diaspora," *American Anthropologist* 98(2) (1996): 290–304.

33. Tim Coles and Dallen Timothy, "'My Field Is the World': Conceptualizing Diasporas, Travel and Tourism," in *Tourism, Diasporas and Space,* edited by Tim Coles and Dallen Timothy (London: Routledge, 2004), 1–29; Keith Hollinshead, "Tourism and Third Space Populations: The Restless Motion of Diaspora Peoples," in *Tourism, Diasporas and Space,* edited by Tim Coles and Dallen Timothy (London: Routledge, 2004), 33–49; Andrea Louie, *Chineseness across Borders: Renegotiating Chinese Identities in China and the United States* (Durham, N.C.: Duke University Press, 2004).

34. Richard Alba, *Ethnic Identity: The Transformation of White America* (New Haven, Conn.: Yale University Press, 1990), 157.

35. Paul Basu, *Highland Homecomings: Genealogy and Heritage Tourism in the Scottish Diaspora* (London: Routledge, 2007); Louie, *Chineseness across Borders;* Kevin Meethan, "'To Stand in the Shoes of My Ancestors': Tourism and Genealogy," in *Tourism, Diasporas and Space,* edited by Tim Coles and Dallen Timothy (London: Routledge, 2004), 139–50.

36. Lydia Polgreen, "Ghana's Uneasy Embrace of Slavery's Diaspora," *New York Times,* December 27, 2005, 1, at http://query.nytimes.com/gst/fullpage.html?sec=travel&res=9B0 0E0DA1230F934A15751C1A9639C8B63 (accessed July 14, 2006).

37. Portes et al., "Study of Transnationalism," 219; emphasis added.

38. Louie, *Chineseness across Borders,* 7.

39. Russian-speaking Jewish émigrés might be an exception, with a grassroots transnationalism linking communities in the former Soviet Union, Israel, the United States, Germany, and elsewhere.

40. Alan Lew and Alan Wong, "Sojourners, *Guanxi* and Clan Associations: Social Capital and Overseas Chinese Tourism to China," in *Tourism, Diasporas and Space,* edited by Tim Coles and Dallen Timothy (London: Routledge, 2004), 202–14; Andrea Louie, "When You Are Related to the 'Other': (Re)Locating the Chinese Homeland in Asian American Politics through Cultural Tourism," *Positions* 11(3) (2003): 735–63; Louie, *Chineseness across Borders.*

41. Vanessa Hua, "A Cultural Awakening: Program Lets Young Chinese Americans Discover Their Identity," *Los Angeles Times,* July 6, 1998, 1, at http://huaren.org/diaspora/n_america/usa/docs/0798-04.html (accessed July 17, 2005).

42. Alison Dakota Gee, "The Love Boat," *South China Morning Post,* August 14, 1994, 12, at http://web.lexis-nexis.com/universe/ (accessed July 14, 2006).

43. Kelly, "Born Again Lithuanians," 196.

44. Sean Carter, "Mobilizing *Hrvatsko:* Tourism and Politics in the Croatian Diaspora," in *Tourism, Diasporas and Space,* edited by Tim Coles and Dallen Timothy (London: Routledge, 2004), 188–201.

45. Kevin Hannam, "India and the Ambivalences of Diaspora Tourism," in *Tourism, Diasporas and Space,* edited by Tim Coles and Dallen Timothy (London: Routledge, 2004), 246–60.

46. This theme commonly emerges when tourism is being promoted by diaspora organizations. Linda Yepoyan, interview by telephone, November 18, 2003; Taryn Harrison, Irish-American Cultural Institute's "Irish Way" (www.iaci-usa.org /irishway.html), interviews, Lackawanna, N.J., October 28, 2002 and January 6, 2003; Richard Santoro and Serena Cantoni, National Italian-American Foundation "Gift of Discovery" (www.niaf.org/ giftofdiscovery/index.asp), interview by telephone, January 6, 2004. On trips to China, see Louie, *Chineseness across Borders*. On the discussion about offering organized diaspora trips to Lebanon, see Nabti, "Conference Explores Diaspora's Relations to Homeland." On trips to South Korea, see Nazli Kibria, "Of Blood, Belonging, and Homeland Trips: Transnationalism and Identity among Second-Generation Chinese and Korean Americans," in *The Changing Face of Home: The Transnational Lives of the Second Generation*, edited by Peggy Levitt and Mary C. Waters (New York: Russell Sage Foundation, 2002), 295–311. On trips to Lithuania, see Kelly, "Born Again Lithuanians"; Mary Kelly, "Ethnic Pilgrimages: People of Lithuanian Descent in Lithuania," *Sociological Spectrum* 20 (2000): 65–91; Mary E. Kelly and Joane Nagel, "Ethnic Re-Identification: Lithuanian Americans and Native Americans," *Journal of Ethnic and Migration Studies* 28(2) (2002): 275–89. On trips to Taiwan, see Gee, "Love Boat"; Hua, "Cultural Awakening"; Kibria, "Of Blood, Belonging, and Homeland Trips." On Jewish trips to Israel, see chapter 2 in this volume.

47. This can be seen as part of a broader phenomenon of diasporas trying to influence the policies of homelands. Shain, *Kinship and Diasporas in International Affairs*.

48. Ann Swidler, "Culture in Action: Symbols and Strategies," *American Sociological Review* 51(2) (1986): 273–86.

49. Kelly and Nagel, "Ethnic Re-Identification," 277.

50. Coles and Timothy, "'My Field Is the World,'" 13.

51. Louie, *Chineseness across Borders;* Kibria, "Of Blood, Belonging, and Homeland Trips."

52. Kelly, "Born Again Lithuanians"; Kelly, "Ethnic Pilgrimages."

53. Louie, *Chineseness across Borders*, 71, 76, 81, 170.

54. The term "knowledge practices" has the ring of sociological jargon, but compared with its colloquial equivalent, "ways of knowing," it does a better job conveying (1) the knower's active role in the process and (2) the notion that a whole set of activities is involved, producing a certain type of knowledge.

55. Benedict Anderson, *Imagined Communities* (London: Verso, 1991).

CHAPTER 2

1. Pseudonyms are used to mask the identities of all tourists and tour staff.

2. Oz Almog, *The Sabra: The Creation of the New Jew,* translated by Haim Watzman (Berkeley: University of California Press, 2000).

3. Joseph Braslavi (Braslavsky), *Bi-netivot lo-selulot el yediat ha-arets* [On unpaved paths to knowing the land of Israel] (Tel Aviv: Am Oved, 1973); Zev Vilnay, *Ha-tiyul ve-erko ha-hinukhi* [The *tiyul* and its educational value] (Jerusalem: World Zionist Organization, Youth and Pioneer Department, [1945], 1953).

4. Eric Hobsbawm and Terence Ranger, *The Invention of Tradition* (Cambridge: Cambridge University Press, 1983).

5. Howard Sachar, *A History of Israel: From the Rise of Zionism to Our Time* (New York: Knopf, 1979), 130.

6. Quoted in Mordechay Naor (editor), *Tenuot ha-noar 1920–1960* [Youth movements, 1920–1960] (Jerusalem: Yad Yitshak Ben-Tsevi, 1989), 248. Unless otherwise noted, all translations from the Hebrew are my own.

7. Vilnay, *Ha-tiyul ve-erko ha-hinukhi,* 22.

8. Tamar Katriel, "Touring the Land: Trips and Hiking as Secular Pilgrimages in Israeli Culture," *Jewish Folklore and Ethnology Review* 17(1–2) (1995): 7.

9. Almog, *Sabra,* 160. Almog's work remains the most thorough history of tiyul in print.

10. Zali Gurevich and Gideon Aran, "Al ha-makom" [About the place], *Alpayim* 4 (1991): 10–11.

11. Braslavi, *Bi-netivot lo-selulot el yediat ha-arets;* Katriel, "Touring the Land"; Vilnay, *Ha-tiyul ve-erko ha-hinukhi.*

12. Orit Ben-David, "*Tiyul* (Hike) as an Act of Consecration of Space," in *Grasping Land: Space and Place in Contemporary Israeli Discourse and Experience,* edited by Eyal Ben-Ari and Yoram Bilu (Albany: State University of New York Press, 1997), 129–45; Katriel, "Touring the Land." Samuel Heilman makes a similar point about *lernen,* the devotional study of Talmud, in *The People of the Book: Drama, Fellowship, and Religion* (Chicago: University of Chicago Press, 1983), 245–49.

13. Katriel, "Touring the Land," 8.

14. Almog, *Sabra,* 176–81.

15. On Israeli civil religion, see Charles S. Liebman and Eliezer Don-Yehiya, *Civil Religion in Israel: Traditional Judaism and Political Culture in the Jewish State* (Berkeley: University of California Press, 1983).

16. Almog, *Sabra,* 164; Yael Zerubavel, *Recovered Roots: Collective Memory and the Making of Israeli National Tradition* (Chicago: University of Chicago Press, 1995), 64.

17. Shaul Katz, "The Israeli Teacher-Guide: The Emergence and Perpetuation of a Role," *Annals of Tourism Research* 12(1) (1985): 52–55, 61.

18. Almog, *Sabra,* 161–68.

19. Braslavi, *Bi-netivot lo-selulot el yediat ha-arets,* 41–42, 237–38, 263.

20. Nachman Ben-Yehuda, *The Masada Myth: Collective Memory and Mythmaking in Israel* (Madison: University of Wisconsin Press, 1995), 71–82; Braslavi, *Bi-netivot lo-selulot el yediat ha-arets,* 39; Katz, "Israeli Teacher-Guide," 57–60. The term "educator-guide" is adapted from Katz.

21. On the differences between the two approaches, see Rivka Ben-Yosef's comments in Naor, *Tenuot ha-noar 1920–1960,* 4–5.

22. Ibid., 6–9, 246.

23. Almog, *Sabra,* 171.

24. The quotations are taken, respectively, from a 1944 guide manual produced by the nonpartisan Tzofim, a 1950 article in the journal of the socialist Ha-Tenuah Ha-Me'uchedet, and a 1957 collection of writings from the Orthodox nationalist B'nei Akiva. Naor, *Tenuot ha-noar 1920–1960,* 247–50.

25. Ben-Yehuda, *Masada Myth,* 71–126; Naor, *Tenuot ha-noar 1920–1960,* 251–53; Zerubavel, *Recovered Roots,* 64.

26. Ben-Yehuda, *Masada Myth,* 71–75, 86–88, 96.

27. Ibid., 129.

28. Almog, *Sabra,* 176–81.

29. Tiyul was also adopted in the Kookian Religious Zionist and Jabotinskyite Revisionist Zionist youth movements, although the Revisionist paramilitary forces Etzel and Lehi were less likely than the Laborite Haganah and Palmach to use tiyul as a training exercise, primarily because they were forced to operate further underground. Ben-Yehuda, *Masada Myth*, 116–23, 145.

30. Ben-David, "*Tiyul* (Hike) as an Act of Consecration of Space," 131–32; Ben-Yehuda, *Masada Myth*, 147–62; Katz, "Israeli Teacher-Guide," 65–68.

31. Ben-Yehuda, *Masada Myth*, 90, 200–205, 254; Katriel, "Touring the Land," 11–12; Zerubavel, *Recovered Roots*, 137.

32. Katriel, "Touring the Land," 9–10; Ben-Yehuda, *Masada Myth*, 152.

33. Katriel, "Touring the Land," 10–11.

34. American Jews wishing to travel to Palestine before 1948 could join university study programs and youth movement *hachsharah* programs that prepared members for permanent resettlement in Israel. The development of long-term programs for diaspora Jews in Israel is a separate story that has not been adequately documented. Firsthand accounts abound, such as those in J. J. Goldberg and Elliot King (editors), *Builders and Dreamers: Habonim Labor Zionist Youth in North America—A Century in Memoir* (Cranbury, N.J.: Cornwall Books, 1993). One of the few works to attempt a partial history is M. Herbert Danzger, *Returning to Tradition: The Contemporary Revival of Orthodox Judaism* (New Haven, Conn.: Yale University Press, 1989), which addresses the emergence in the 1960s and 1970s of Israeli religious seminaries (*yeshivot*) for non-Orthodox diaspora Jewish youth.

35. Erik H. Cohen and Eynath Cohen, *Ha-hawaya ha-yisreelit* [The Israel experience] (Jerusalem: Jerusalem Institute for Israel Studies, 2000), 6–7. The Jewish Agency has been central to the implementation of Israel experience programs from their inception to the current day.

36. Rolnik, "Study of Attitudes towards Israel," 47, 302; "Our Israel Tour," *Senior* (May 1951), 4, in Hadassah Archives, American Jewish Historical Society, Center for Jewish History, New York (hereafter, cited as HA/AJHS): RG 17/publications/Young Judaea/"The Senior," Box 1; Young Judaea, *Young Judaea Course in Israel: Summer—1951* (1951), 9, 13, in HA/AJHS: RG 8, Box 12A/Israel Programs/Summer Programs.

37. "1957 Can Be Your Israel Year," *News and Views* (February, 1957), 1, in United Synagogue Youth Archives, United Synagogue of Conservative Judaism, Rapaport House, New York (hereafter, cited as USYA/RH): News and Views Bound Vols. I–X; Albert Lewis, "Looking Back at USY Israel Pilgrimage," *Hamadrich: A Journal of Jewish Education* 8(1) (1991): 13–15; Dr. Morton K. Siegel, interview, New York, May 8, 2002. The congregational and clerical arms of Conservative Judaism each ran separate programs: USY Israel Pilgrimage and Ramah Seminar, respectively.

38. Various sources have reported the programs' years of origin as anywhere from 1954 to 1959. Samuel Cook, "Four Decades," *Visions*, Union of American Hebrew Congregations (UAHC) Youth Division, Winter, 1979, 8–9; "NFTY at Fifty: Looking Back," *Ani V'atah*, 1989, 4–5. Rabbi Henry Skirball, interview by telephone, April 29, 2002. UAHC annual reports through 1955 do not report any such programs. Union of American Hebrew Congregations, *Proceedings of the Union of American Hebrew Congregations: Seventy-Seventh–Eightieth Annual Reports, July 1, 1950 to June 30, 1955,* (Cincinnati, Ohio: Union of American Hebrew Congregations,1956).

39. Riv-Ellen Prell, "Summer Camp, Post-War American Jewish Youth and the Redemption of Judaism," in *The Jewish Role in America: An Annual Review*, edited by Bruce Zuckerman and Jeremy Schoenberg (West Lafayette, Ind.: Purdue University Press, 2007), 77–106; Jack Wertheimer, "Jewish Education in the United States," in *American Jewish Year Book*, vol. 99, edited by David Singer and Ruth R. Seldin (New York: American Jewish Committee, 1999), 3–115.

40. Thomas Hine, *The Rise and Fall of the American Teenager* (New York: Bard Books, 1999).

41. Judith Kramer and Seymour Leventman, *Children of the Gilded Ghetto: Conflict Resolutions of Three Generations of American Jews* (New Haven, Conn.: Yale University Press, 1961); Deborah Dash Moore, *To the Golden Cities: Pursuing the American Jewish Dream in Miami and L.A.* (Cambridge, Mass.: Harvard University Press, 1994).

42. "Israel Summer Program," *Senior* (February 1951), 1, in HA/AJHS: RG 17/publications/Young Judaea/"The Senior," Box 1; "1957 Can Be Your Israel Year"; United Synagogue Youth, "1957 Israel Pilgrimage" [program brochure] (New York: USY, 1957), in USYA/RH: Assorted papers; Rabbi Paul Freedman, interview by telephone, May 7–8, 2002; Siegel interview; Skirball interview.

43. "Summer Israel Scholarship Plan with Tsofim Announced," *Senior* (December 1949), 1, in HA/AJHS: RG 17/publications/Young Judaea/"The Senior," Box 1; "Our Israel Tour"; "1957 Can Be Your Israel Year"; Freedman interview; Siegel interview; Skirball interview.

44. Young Judaea, *Young Judaea Course in Israel: Summer—1951*, 4–5, 9. Other means of diffusion included contact with Israeli youth movements, independent hiring of Israeli staff, the use of state-licensed Israeli guides, and, later, curriculum development undertaken by transnational Jewish educators who integrated Israel's tiyul culture with philosophies of experiential education.

45. Ibid.

46. Freedman interview; Siegel interview.

47. Hillel: The Foundation for Jewish Campus Life, "Israel 2001," at http://www.israel2001.com (accessed October 12, 2001).

48. United Synagogue Youth, "1957 Israel Pilgrimage," 3.

49. Cohen and Cohen, *Ha-hawaya ha-yisreelit*, 14–15; David Mittelberg, *The Israel Connection and American Jews* (Westport, Conn.: Praeger, 1999), 137–38. Because of discrepancies in these books' reports of winter and long-term program enrollment, I present figures only for participation in short-term summer programs.

50. Birthright Israel North America, *Israel Experience 2001: Your Complete Guide to Programs for College, Post-College and High School Students* (New York: Birthright Israel North America, 2001).

51. Ibid.

52. Feldman, *Above the Death Pits, Beneath the Flag*, 3.

53. Barry Chazan, "The Israel Trip: A New Form of Jewish Education," in *Youth Trips to Israel: Rationale and Realization* (New York: CRB Foundation and the Mandell L. Berman Jewish Heritage Center at JESNA, 1994), A1.

54. Ibid., A5–A7.

55. Ibid., A7–A8.

56. Cf. Charles Kadushin, "The Motivational Foundation of Social Networks," *Social Networks* 24(1) (2002): 77–91.

57. Chazan, "Israel Trip," A13–A14.

58. Steven M. Cohen and Susan Wall, "Excellence in Youth Trips to Israel," in *Youth Trips to Israel: Rationale and Realization* (New York: CRB Foundation and the Mandell L. Berman Jewish Heritage Center at JESNA, 1994), B1–B66.

59. Chazan, "Israel Trip," A15–A18.

60. Rolnik, "Study of Attitudes towards Israel."

61. For example, Gerald Bubis and Lawrence Marks, *Changes in Jewish Identification: A Comparative Study of a Teen Age Israel Camping Trip, a Counselor-in-Training Program, and a Teen Age Service Camp* (Los Angeles: Florence G. Heller–JWB Research Center in cooperation with the Jewish Community Centers Association, 1975); Erik H. Cohen and Ariela Keysar, *The 1992 Summer Israel Experience Educational Programs* (Jerusalem: CRB Foundation and Mandel Associated Foundations, 1993); Erik H. Cohen, *Toward a Strategy of Excellence: The Participants of the Israel Experience Short-Term Programs Summer/1993–Winter/1994* (Jerusalem: JAFI, Youth and Hechalutz Department, and Joint Authority for Jewish Zionist Education, 1994); Steven M. Cohen, *Committed Zionists and Curious Tourists: Travel to Israel among Canadian Jewish Youth* (Jerusalem: CRB Foundation, 1991); Steven M. Cohen, *Israel Travel Program for Canadian Youth: Levels of Participation and Cost for 1989 and 1990* (Jerusalem: CRB Foundation, 1991); Perry London and Alissa Hirshfeld, "Youth Programs in Israel: What the Findings Mean," *Journal of Jewish Communal Service* 66 (1989): 87–91; R. R. Kafka, Perry London, S. Bandler, and Naava Frank, *The Impact of "Summer in Israel" Experiences on North American Jewish Teenagers* (Montreal: CRB Foundation, 1990); Amy Sales, *Israel Experience: Is Length of Time a Critical Factor?* (Waltham, Mass.: Brandeis University, Cohen Center for Modern Jewish Studies, 1998); Leonard Saxe, Charles Kadushin, Juliana Pakes, Shaul Kelner, Bethamie Horowitz, Amy Sales, and Archie Brodsky, *Birthright Israel Launch Evaluation: Preliminary Findings* (Waltham, Mass.: Brandeis University, Cohen Center for Modern Jewish Studies, 2000); Leonard Saxe, Charles Kadushin, Shaul Kelner, Mark Rosen, and Erez Yereslove, *A Mega-Experiment in Jewish Education: The Impact of Birthright Israel* (Waltham, Mass.: Brandeis University, Cohen Center for Modern Jewish Studies, 2002); Meryle Weinstein, *An Assessment of the Koret Israel Teen Trip and Summer in Israel Youth Program* (Waltham, Mass.: Brandeis University, Cohen Center for Modern Jewish Studies, 1998).

62. Mittelberg, *Israel Connection and American Jews.*

63. Sherry Israel and David Mittelberg, *The Israel Visit—Not Just for Teens: The Characteristics and Impact of College-Age Travel to Israel* (Waltham, Mass.: Brandeis University, Cohen Center for Modern Jewish Studies, 1998); David Mittelberg, *The Israel Visit and Jewish Identification* (New York: Institute on American Jewish–Israeli Relations of the American Jewish Committee, 1994).

64. Charles Kadushin, Shaul Kelner, and Leonard Saxe, *Being a Jewish Teenager in America: Trying to Make It* (Waltham, Mass.: Brandeis University, Cohen Center for Modern Jewish Studies, 2000); Tamar Levinson and Susan Zoline, "Impact of Summer Trip to Israel on the Self-Esteem of Jewish Adolescents," *Journal of Psychology and Judaism* 21(2) (1997): 87–119.

65. For a review of this literature, see Chazan, *Does the Teen Israel Experience Make a Difference?*

66. Goldberg, "A Summer on a NFTY Safari"; Lisa Grant, "Planned and Enacted Curriculum Stories on a Congregational Israel Trip," *Conservative Judaism* 53(3) (2001): 63–81; Lisa Grant, "The Role of Mentoring in Enhancing Experience of a Congregational Israel

Trip," *Journal of Jewish Education* 67(1/2) (2001): 46–60; Habib, *Israel, Diaspora, and the Routes of National Belonging;* Heilman, "Young Judea Israel Discovery Tour"; Kelner, "Impact of Israel Experience Programs"; Kelner et al., *Making Meaning;* Kirshenblatt-Gimblett, "Learning from Ethnography."

67. Orit Avivi, *Birthright Israel Mifgashim: A Summary of the Planning, Implementation and Evaluation of Mifgashim during Birthright Israel Programs. Executive Report: Winter Launch 1999–2000* (Jerusalem: Bronfman Mifgashim Center, 2000); Yehuda Bar-Shalom, *Encounters with the Other: An Ethnographic Study of Mifgashim Programs for Jewish Youth, Summer 1997* (Jerusalem: Bronfman Centre for the Israel Experience–Mifgashim, 1998); Elan Ezrachi and Barbara Sutnick, *Israel Education through Encounters with Israelis* (Jerusalem: CRB Foundation, Joint Authority for Jewish Zionist Education, and Bronfman Centre for the Israel Experience–Mifgashim, 1997).

68. Jonathan Woocher, *Sacred Survival: The Civil Religion of American Jews* (Bloomington: Indiana University Press, 1986).

69. Jack Wertheimer, *A People Divided: Judaism in Contemporary America* (New York: Basic Books, 1993).

70. Robert Putnam, *Bowling Alone: The Collapse and Revival of American Community* (New York: Simon and Schuster, 2000).

71. Barry Kosmin, Sidney Goldstein, Joseph Waksberg, Nava Lerer, Ariela Keysar, and Jeffrey Scheckner, *Highlights of the CJF 1990 National Jewish Population Survey* (New York: Council of Jewish Federations, 1991).

72. Mary Waters, *Ethnic Options: Choosing Identities in America* (Berkeley: University of California Press, 1990).

73. This list includes Charles Bronfman, Edgar Bronfman, Morton Mandel, Lynn Schusterman, Steven Spielberg, Michael Steinhardt, and Leslie Wexner, among others. Debra Nussbaum Cohen, "The Feminine (Giving) Mystique," *New York Jewish Week,* June 14, 2002, 10–12; Norman Eisenberg, "Foundations for Change," *New York Jewish Week,* June 14, 2002, 6–9; Michael Massing, "Should Jews Be Parochial?" *American Prospect,* November 6, 2000, 30–35.

74. CRB was later reconstituted as the Andrea and Charles Bronfman Philanthropies.

75. For example, Chazan, "Israel Trip"; Cohen and Keysar, *1992 Summer Israel Experience Educational Programs;* Cohen, *Committed Zionists and Curious Tourists;* Cohen, *Israel Travel Program for Canadian Youth;* Cohen and Wall, "Excellence in Youth Trips to Israel"; Steven M. Cohen and Susan Wall, *The Good Trip* (Montreal: CRB Foundation, 1992); Goldfarb Consultants, *Attitudes towards Travel to Israel among Jewish Adults and Jewish Youth* (Jerusalem: CRB Foundation, 1991); Kafka et al., *Impact of "Summer in Israel" Experiences;* Jay Levenberg, *Marketing Trips to Israel: Recommendations of the Israel Experience Marketing Project* (Jerusalem: CRB Foundation, 1992).

76. Chazan, *Does the Teen Israel Experience Make a Difference?* 4.

77. The partners were the United Jewish Appeal (UJA), United Israel Appeal (UIA), Council of Jewish Federations (CJF), Jewish Agency for Israel, World Zionist Organization, and Israeli Ministry of Tourism.

78. *Contact: The Journal of Jewish Life Network / Chaverim Kol Yisrael* (Spring 2002), 2.

79. Yossi Beilin, *His Brother's Keeper: Israel and Diaspora Jewry in the Twenty-First Century* (New York: Schocken, 2000), 122.

80. Ibid., 122–24.

81. Birthright Israel, "Birthright Israel Gives American Jewish Youth Largest, Most Meaningful Hanukah Gift Ever," *PR Newswire,* press release (November 22, 1999), at web. lexis-nexis.com/universe (accessed May 22, 2002).

82. These bodies were the UJA, UIA, and CJF (which merged in 2000 to become United Jewish Communities, or UJC), Keren Hayesod, and the Jewish Agency for Israel.

83. Joel Greenberg, "Trips to Renew Jewish Ties Set Off Debate about Costs," *New York Times,* January 8, 2000, 6, at http://web.lexis-nexis.com/universe/ (accessed October 25, 2004); Isi Leibler, "Birthright Israel: Too Quick and Superficial," *New York Jewish Week,* November 19, 1999, at www.thejewishweek.com/top/editletcontent.php3?artid=554 (accessed August 3, 2000); Jonathan Rosenblum, "Misplaced Generosity," *Jerusalem Post,* January 7, 2000, B9, at web.lexis-nexis.com/universe (accessed June 17, 2002); Ruthi Sinai, "Ha-noar ha-yehudi ba lehapes shorashim: Hashkaah mishtalemet?" [The Jewish youth come to seek roots: a worthwhile investment?], *Ha'aretz* (Tel Aviv), January 20, 2000, at http://www.haaretz.co.il (accessed January 31, 2007).

84. I found no evidence that ideological sensitivities explicitly informed the decision not to employ a Hebrew equivalent of the term "birthright." One official involved in the decision recalled in an interview with me that the choice of the Hebrew name was guided by marketing considerations, especially by the desire to find an exciting name for use in Israeli radio ads. The power of the English word was lost in translation, the person said, as the Hebrew equivalents *zchut leidah* and *bchorah* sounded antiquated.

85. Stewart Ain, "Free Heritage Trip on the Runway," *New York Jewish Week,* July 31, 1999, at www.thejewishweek.com/news/newscontent.php3?artid=1668 (accessed May 20, 2002).

86. Cited in Stuart Elliott, "The Media Business: Advertising—Addenda; Accounts," *New York Times,* August 2, 1999, C12, at web.lexis-nexis.com/universe (accessed May 20, 2002); Gary Rosenblatt, "Is It Hard Being Jewish?" *New York Jewish Week,* October 8, 1999, at shamash.org./listarchives/jweek/960306 (accessed May 20, 2002).

87. Birthright Israel, "Birthright Israel Announces Successful Enrollment for Inaugural Season of Free Trips to Israel Signaling Youth Interest in Jewish Heritage; Overwhelming Response to 5,000 Free Winter Break Trips Offered by Birthright Israel," *PR Newswire,* press release (October 12, 1999), at web.lexis-nexis.com/universe (accessed May 20, 2002); Birthright Israel, "Largest, Most Meaningful Hanukah Gift Ever."

88. "Birthright Booms as Terror Sinks Tourism," *Ha'aretz* (Tel Aviv), January 26, 2001, at http:// web.lexis-nexis.com/universe/ (accessed June 17, 2002); Richard Joel, "Birthright Is Born" (op-ed), *Jerusalem Post,* January 3, 2000, at http:// web.lexis-nexis.com/ universe/ (accessed October 25, 2004); Julie Gruenbaum Fax, "Birthright Israel Launches $50 Million Campaign, Cuts Trips," *Los Angeles Jewish Journal,* February 11, 2009, at http://www.jewishjournal.com/articles/item/birthright_launches_50m_campaign_cuts_ trips_20090211/ (accessed July 31, 2009).

89. For example, Jason Nielsen, "Hillel Introduces Israel Advocacy," *Boston Jewish Advocate,* January 11, 2002, 5.

90. Paul Reichenbach, interview, New York, June 19, 2002.

91. Marlene Post, "Don't Bash Birthright," *Jerusalem Report,* December 20, 1999, 54.

92. Feldman, *Above the Death Pits, Beneath the Flag;* Karen Sinclair, "Mission to Waitangi: A Maori Pilgrimage," in *Sacred Journeys: The Anthropology of Pilgrimage,* edited by Alan Morinis (Westport, Conn.: Greenwood, 1992), 233–56; Zerubavel, *Recovered Roots.*

93. Marion Bowman, "Drawn to Glastonbury," in *Pilgrimage in Popular Culture*, edited by Ian Reader and Tony Walter (London: Macmillan, 1993), 29–62; Peter W. Wood, "Pilgrimage and Heresy: The Transformation of Faith at a Shrine in Wisconsin," in *Sacred Journeys: The Anthropology of Pilgrimage*, edited by Alan Morinis (Westport, Conn.: Greenwood, 1992), 115–34.

94. Victor Turner, "Pilgrimages as Social Processes," in *Dramas, Fields and Metaphors: Symbolic Action in Human Society*, edited by Victor Turner (Ithaca, N.Y.: Cornell University Press, [1974] 1987), 166–230; Victor Turner and Edith Turner, *Image and Pilgrimage in Christian Culture* (New York: Columbia University Press, 1978); John Eade and Michael Sallnow, *Contesting the Sacred: The Anthropology of Christian Pilgrimage* (London: Routledge, [1991] 2000).

95. Michael Costen, "The Pilgrimage to Santiago de Compostela in Medieval Europe," in *Pilgrimage in Popular Culture*, edited by Ian Reader and Tony Walter (London: Macmillan, 1993), 137–54; Richard West Sellars and Tony Walter, "From Custer to Kent State: Heroes, Martyrs and the Evolution of Popular Shrines in the USA," in *Pilgrimage in Popular Culture*, edited by Ian Reader and Tony Walter (London: Macmillan, 1993), 179–200.

96. Alan Morinis, "Introduction: The Territory of the Anthropology of Pilgrimage," in *Sacred Journeys: The Anthropology of Pilgrimage*, edited by Alan Morinis (Westport, Conn.: Greenwood, 1992), 1–28.

97. Eade and Sallnow, *Contesting the Sacred.*

98. Paul Lazarsfeld and Robert K. Merton's Columbia School sociology was built on this model. Their approach guided CMJS, which designed the qualitative and quantitative data-gathering processes for its Taglit evaluation in sufficiently broad a manner to enable secondary analyses that extend beyond the evaluative dimension.

CHAPTER 3

1. Leonard Saxe, Theodore Sasson, and Shahar Hecht, *Israel at War: The Impact of Peer-Oriented Israel Programs on the Responses of American Jewish Young Adults* (Waltham, Mass.: Brandeis University, Steinhardt Social Research Institute, 2006), 8. Note that opposition to Israel's position in the war does not necessarily indicate lack of identification with Israel. By the war's end, support for it had eroded even among Israeli Jews.

2. On a much smaller scale than Birthright Israel, two political tours known as Birthright Unplugged and Birthright Re-Plugged seek to convey this narrative. The former brings diaspora Jews to encounter Palestinian life on the West Bank. The latter brings Palestinian youth across the Green Line into Israel proper. The tours retain the nationalist terminology of "birthright" but frame the Jewish and Palestinian claims to it as mutually exclusive while affirming it only for Palestinians. One may ask of these the same type of question asked above, "But what about the Israeli counternarrative?" Jodi Melamed, "Creating Cultures of Solidarity: American Jews Redefine Birthright," Nerve House, at http://www.birthrightunplugged.org/html/brup12press.html#nerve (accessed May 7, 2007).

3. For example, during the second intifada, controversy erupted when international NGOs working in the West Bank and Gaza Strip to oppose the occupation began seeing Birthright Israel as a potential way of bringing over diaspora Jewish volunteers, and Birthright Israel, in response, began disqualifying applicants who expressed an intention to use

the free airfare for the purpose of joining these groups. Daphna Berman, "I.S.M. Activists Use Birthright Program to Get to Israel," *Haaretz* (Tel Aviv), July 16, 2004, at http://www.haaretz.com/hasen/pages/ShArt.jhtml?itemNo=452230&contrassID=1&subContrassID=5&sbSubContrassID=0&listSrc=Y (accessed April 2, 2009); Shabi, "Come, See Palestine!"

4. After the outbreak of the second intifada in September 2000, Taglit tour providers came to include organizations devoted explicitly to political advocacy for Israel, whose recruitment materials promised, "When it's over, you will be an ambassador for Israel, able to make her case and promote peace for Israel and her neighbors." Stand With Us International, "StandWithUs Free Trip to Israel," at http://www.standwithus.co.il/birthright/index.htm (accessed March 7, 2007).

5. Some journalistic and scholarly critiques paint a scenario in which socialization is effected through imposition and misrepresentation. Tour guides are said to address the challenge posed by Palestinian claims by erasing the presence of all but the Jewish experience, neglecting to mention rival perspectives, attacking those who ask challenging questions, and selectively representing Israelis and the Palestinians to emphasize the heroism of the former and the iniquity of the latter. It is claimed that such portrayals manage to convince because (save for those whose preexisting political opinions lead them to resist) the majority of tourists are passive and uncritical. Habib, *Israel, Diaspora, and the Routes of National Belonging,* 73, 79, 82, 101, 114–15; Shabi, "Come, See Palestine!"

6. Kibria, "Of Blood, Belonging, and Homeland Trips"; Louie, *Chineseness across Borders.*

7. Encouraging guide worship can be seen as a variant of the strategy of role modeling in which emotional ties to trip staff are used to foster feelings of connection to the homeland. See chapter 5.

8. The Israeli human rights group B'Tselem reports 176 civilians and 8 soldiers killed by Palestinian suicide bombers in West and East Jerusalem during the time period in question, with an additional 280 civilians and 56 soldiers killed by suicide bombers elsewhere in Israel proper. Data compiled from B'Tselem, "Casualties List," at http://www.btselem.org/english/Statistics/Casualties.asp (accessed April 2, 2009).

9. Habib, *Israel, Diaspora, and the Routes of National Belonging.*

10. On the simultaneously challenging and reaffirming character of joking, and on the ways in which successful jokes give symbolic expression to real contradictions in the social order, see Mary Douglas, "The Social Control of Cognition: Some Factors in Joke Perception," *Man* 3(3) (1968): 361–76.

11. Shapiro, *Building Jewish Roots,* 64–67.

12. This distinction is informed by Goffman's discussion of fabrications. Erving Goffman, *Frame Analysis: An Essay on the Organization of Experience* (Cambridge, Mass.: Harvard University Press, 1974).

13. Ben-Yehuda, *Masada Myth;* Zerubavel, *Recovered Roots.*

14. Theodore Sasson and Shaul Kelner, "From Shrine to Forum: Masada and the Politics of Jewish Extremism," *Israel Studies* 13(2) (2008): 146–63.

15. Habib, *Israel, Diaspora, and the Routes of National Belonging;* Shabi, "Come, See Palestine!" Neither Habib nor Shabi represents the Palestinian narratives as politicized representations themselves. Although they are inconsistent in applying the principle that politicized terrains should be represented as politicized, the principle itself can be derived from their writings.

16. This compliance assessment, conducted by an Israeli firm, is separate from the impact evaluation conducted by Brandeis University's CMJS. It also addresses other aspects of quality control. In Taglit's parlance, missionizing has both political and religious connotations, and political bias refers to a failure to represent the spectrum of Israeli Jewish opinion, left to right, religious and secular.

17. Some 16% strongly disagreed, 32% slightly disagreed, 37% slightly agreed, and 15% strongly agreed, $N = 2,390$. The 48%–52% split between disagreers and agreers is not statistically significant at the .05 level. Unless otherwise noted, all survey data presented here are based on analyses of Leonard Saxe, Charles Kadushin, Shaul Kelner, and Erez Yereslove, *Taglit-Birthright Israel Evaluation Survey, Winter 2000–2001 Cohort* [Computer data file] (Waltham, Mass.: Brandeis University, Cohen Center for Modern Jewish Studies, 2001). For details, see the appendix to this volume.

18. The proportion rating the Israeli guides as "sensational" drops steadily from 78% to 67% to 55% to 45% as we move from respondents who felt strongly that the guides were not "preaching" to those who felt strongly that they were. When rating the American bus staff, these proportions drop from 59% to 46% to 39% to 26%. *Tau-c* (Israeli guide) = −.164, *tau-c* (North American staff) = −.171, $p < .001$.

19. Chazan, "Israel Trip."

20. Taglit-Birthright Israel, *Revised Educational Standards 2001* (Jerusalem: Taglit-Birthright Israel, 2001).

21. Hillel: The Foundation for Jewish Campus Life, *Hillel's Birthright Israel: The Tour* (Washington, D.C.: Hillel, 2000), 71–124.

22. Clare Goldwater, "Constructing the Narrative of Authenticity: Tour Educators at Work in the Israel Experience," M.A. thesis, Hebrew University of Jerusalem, 2002, 72.

23. Again, I am following Christian Smith: "One of the central and fundamental motivations for human action is to act out and sustain moral order." Smith, *Moral, Believing Animals*, 8.

24. Chazan, "Israel Trip," 15–16.

25. I distinguish here between a critique that treats a country's problems as imperfections capable of being fixed and one that considers them inevitable products of a fundamentally flawed system.

26. Interviews were conducted in Hebrew. Translations into English are my own.

27. Katz, "Israeli Teacher-Guide," 63.

28. There is no inherent reason that the separation barrier needs to be read politically. So strong is the "preferred reading" of the separation barrier as a signifier of Israeli-Palestinian politics, however, that it essentially crowds out any alternative readings. Stuart Hall, "Encoding/Decoding," in *Culture, Media, Language: Working Papers in Cultural Studies, 1972–79*, edited by Stuart Hall, Dorothy Hobson, Andrew Lowe, and Paul Willis (London: Hutchinson, 1980), 128–38.

29. A subtext was that Israel is a society worthy of emulation, one whose environmentally conscious innovations outpace those of the United States. A similar theme also frequently arises in discussions of counterterrorism measures.

30. The Dan River is actually below the Golan Heights in an area that has been part of Israel proper since 1948. Raʾanan used it as a stand-in for the other two sources, which are located on the Heights and which we did not visit.

31. No one raised a question about the reference to a goddess in an Israelite city.

32. The students were of legal drinking age in Israel.

33. This is one of the contradictions of the medium, insofar as the tourism industry's place promotion efforts depend on marketing coherent and iconic place narratives. See chapter 4 in this volume.

34. Taglit's website addresses concerns about the safety of traveling to Israel. Satisfaction of these concerns is an important factor in people's decisions to participate. Enrollment levels have fluctuated inversely with the severity of the violence in the region.

35. Pierre Bourdieu, *Distinction: A Social Critique of the Judgement of Taste,* translated by Richard Nice (Cambridge, Mass.: Harvard University Press, 1984).

CHAPTER 4

1. Left unstated was the idea that, had they not bowed at that moment, the shrapnel would have hit the worshippers.

2. In neither case was this representation so pervasive as to crowd out other meanings; the totality of this encounter encompassed the same type of hodgepodge of interactions that characterized the visit to Tel Dan (chapter 3 in this volume).

3. On bohemianism as a cultural ideal, see Richard Lloyd, *Neo-Bohemia: Art and Commerce in the Post-Industrial City* (New York: Routledge, 2006).

4. Such mutually referencing iconic representations are the essence of "urban branding." Kevin Fox Gotham, *Authentic New Orleans: Tourism, Culture and Race in the Big Easy* (New York: New York University Press, 2007), 135.

5. Jonathan Culler, "Semiotics of Tourism," *American Journal of Semiotics* 1(1–2) (1981): 140.

6. The term "semiotic relationship" is typically used to refer to relations among symbols, independent of the human beings to whom the symbols are meaningful. My use differs, emphasizing the relationship between symbol readers and the objects of their contemplation.

7. Edward M. Bruner, *Culture on Tour: Ethnographies of Travel* (Chicago: University of Chicago Press, 2005), 13, 17–19, 191–210.

8. Mark Gottdiener, *The Theming of America: American Dreams, Media Fantasies, and Themed Environments,* 2nd ed. (Boulder, Colo.: Westview, 2001); Gotham, *Authentic New Orleans,* 133–41; David Grazian, *Blue Chicago: The Search for Authenticity in Urban Blues Clubs* (Chicago: University of Chicago Press, 2003), 197–227.

9. Gotham, *Authentic New Orleans,* 135, 137.

10. Lamont and Molnár, "Study of Boundaries in the Social Sciences," 181.

11. Taglit-Birthright Israel, *Revised Educational Standards 2001,* 5.

12. Gottdiener, *Theming of America.*

13. Chazan, "Israel Trip," A15–A18; Goldwater, "Constructing the Narrative of Authenticity," 24.

14. Grant Wiggins and Jay McTighe, *Understanding by Design,* 2nd ed. (Alexandria, Va.: Association for Supervision and Curriculum Development, 2005).

15. The Jewish leaders at Masada chose death over compromise, whereas the rabbis at Yavneh chose to reconfigure Judaism to make it viable in a post-Temple period.

16. Barbara Kirshenblatt-Gimblett writes, "It is simply not possible to provide chrono-logical coherence to itineraries that are, by necessity, determined by spatial relation-ships. . . . An itinerary is not a textbook. . . . Even if the elements in a single day are more closely related, the contrasts from day to day contribute much to the pleasure of the trip and to the sense of its fullness and completeness." Kirshenblatt-Gimblett, "Learning from Ethnography," 302.

17. Goldwater, "Constructing the Narrative of Authenticity."

18. Clare Goldwater, interview, New York, February 7, 2005.

19. Goldwater, "Constructing the Narrative of Authenticity," 24–25.

20. Taglit-Birthright Israel, *Educational Standards and Program Requirements* (Jerusalem: Taglit-Birthright Israel, 2005), 5.

21. Saxe and Chazan, *Ten Days of Birthright Israel*, 43–49; Taglit-Birthright Israel, *Revised Educational Standards 2001*, 6. Habib's treatment shows how this essentialist representation of Israel as a Jewish space is accomplished not only positively, by associating it with Jews, but also negatively, by dissociating it from the Palestinians who also lay claim to it. Habib, *Israel, Diaspora, and the Routes of National Belonging*.

22. On the development of Masada for tourism, see Ben-Yehuda, *Masada Myth*. Itinerar-ies, reports, and testimonials from Israel experience programs before 1968 make virtually no reference to Masada.

23. Kelner et al., *Making Meaning*, 11–15, 29.

24. Goldwater, "Constructing the Narrative of Authenticity," 24.

25. The site-sacralization process can extend to include developing the framing material as an attraction in itself (*enshrinement*), making *mechanical reproductions* of the attraction (e.g., souvenir postcards), and making *social reproductions* of it (e.g., naming the town of Niagara Falls after its star attraction). MacCannell, *Tourist*, 44–48.

26. In this reconstruction, I follow the approach taken by Goldwater, the educator most responsible for bringing MacCannell's model of site sacralization to conscious deploy-ment in the Israel experience field. Goldwater, "Constructing the Narrative of Authentic-ity." See also Elizabeth Fine and Jean Haskell Speer, "Tour Guide Performances as Sight Sacralization," *Annals of Tourism Research* 12(1) (1985): 73–95.

27. MacCannell, *Tourist*, 41–42, 109–11, 117–20, 131–33. Following MacCannell, I use the term "marker" to refer only to the information conveyed, not to the vehicle of its convey-ance (such as a plaque, inscription, speech, or video).

28. Swidler, "Culture in Action."

29. MacCannell, *Tourist*, 131–33.

30. Bourdieu, *Distinction*.

31. Urry, *Tourist Gaze*, 12.

32. This list is hardly comprehensive, but it will suffice to convey the point.

33. Edward M. Bruner, "Abraham Lincoln as Authentic Reproduction: A Critique of Postmodernism," *American Anthropologist* 96(2) (1994): 400.

34. Ibid., 399.

35. Editorial, "Language and History," *Guardian* (London), February 7, 2009, 40, at http://www.guardian.co.uk/commentisfree/2009/feb/07/race-judaism-antisemitism (accessed May 5, 2009); Simon Romero, "Venezuela's Jews, Already Uneasy, Are Jolted by Attack," *New York Times*, February 13, 2009, A8, at http://www.nytimes.com/2009/02/13/

world/americas/13venez.html (accessed May 5, 2009); Henry Samuel, "Gaza Killing Sparks Attacks on Jews across Europe," *Daily Telegraph* (London), January 6, 2009, at http://www.telegraph.co.uk/news/worldnews/europe/4142583/Gaza-killing-sparks-attacks-on-Jews-across-Europe.html (accessed May 5, 2009).

36. Goldberg, "Summer on a NFTY Safari," 89; Harold Lovy, "Searching for God in Israel," *Jewish Telegraphic Agency*, January 18, 2000, at http://www.jta.org/cgi-bin/iowa/news/article/20000118SearchingforGodin.html (accessed August 12, 2008). For a discussion of this discourse, see Kirshenblatt-Gimblett, "Learning from Ethnography," 307–9.

37. Gottdiener, *Theming of America*; Sharon Zukin, *Point of Purchase: How Shopping Changed American Culture* (New York: Routledge, 2004), 197.

38. Antonella Carù and Bernard Cova, "Consuming Experiences: An Introduction," in *Consuming Experience,* edited by Antonella Carù and Bernard Cova (London: Routledge, 2007), 3–16; Gottdiener, *Theming of America;* Zukin, *Point of Purchase,* 197–225.

39. Gottdiener, *Theming of America,* 171.

40. Goldwater, "Constructing the Narrative of Authenticity," 24–25.

41. On the history of the Western Wall's use as a synagogue, see Stuart Charmé, "The Construction of Gender Traditions at the Western Wall in Jerusalem," paper presented at the 33rd Annual Meetings of the Association for Jewish Studies, Washington, D.C., December 18, 2001.

42. Before traveling on Taglit, 56% of tourists on the winter 2000–2001 trips did not rank "caring about Israel" highly when asked what being Jewish meant to them. Afterward, four in 10 (41%) of these non-Israel-oriented Jews changed their positions. If we consider actions rather than mindsets, by contrast, we find that, before the trips, 80% of tourists were not participating "often" in on-campus or off-campus Jewish activities, and, afterward, only one in 10 of these nonactivists said they had started to do so. These newly engaged represented 7% of the total cohort. See also chapter 7 in this volume.

43. For a review of this literature, see Sharon Zukin and Jennifer Smith MacGuire, "Consumers and Consumption," *Annual Review of Sociology* 30 (2004): 173–97.

44. For a rich social history of the market's role in American Christianity, see Leigh Eric Schmidt, *Consumer Rites: The Buying and Selling of American Holidays* (Princeton, N.J.: Princeton University Press, 1995). Schmidt argues that the commercial exploitation of Christmas and Easter gave both holidays "new cultural prominence . . . [by] provid[ing] the relatively austere liturgical culture of evangelical Protestantism with lush new corporeal forms for celebration" (14). See also Jenna Weissman Joselit, *The Wonders of America: Reinventing Jewish Culture, 1880–1950* (New York: Hill and Wang, 1994); George Sanders, "*Late* Capital: Negotiating a New American Way of Death," Ph.D. dissertation, Vanderbilt University, 2008.

45. Bauman, "From Pilgrim to Tourist," 33.

46. This conceptualization began to gain a hearing in the 1990s as historians of the American Jewish immigrant experience revisited the acculturation-through-work narrative and found it lacking. Andrew R. Heinze, *Adapting to Abundance: Jewish Immigrants, Mass Consumption, and the Search for American Identity* (New York: Columbia University Press, 1990); Joselit, *Wonders of America.*

CHAPTER 5

1. The interviews from which these quotations are drawn are examined further in Sasson and Kelner, "From Shrine to Forum."

2. Kibria, "Of Blood, Belonging, and Homeland Trips"; Louie, *Chineseness across Borders*, 30, 169–70; Kelly, "Born Again Lithuanians," 219–20.

3. Lamont and Molnár, "Study of Boundaries in the Social Sciences," 183.

4. The extent to which tourists embrace or reject this dependency on mediating agents informs Erik Cohen's distinction between institutional and noninstitutional tourists. Erik Cohen, "Toward a Sociology of International Tourism," *Social Research* 39(1) (1972): 164–82.

5. Urry, *Tourist Gaze*, 11.

6. Walker Percy, "The Loss of the Creature," in *The Message in the Bottle: How Queer Man Is, How Queer Language Is, and What One Has to Do with the Other* (New York: Farrar, Straus and Giroux, [1954] 1982), 47.

7. Boorstin, *Image*.

8. The seminal critique was made in Culler, "Semiotics of Tourism," 138.

9. Yehuda Amichai, "Tourists," in *The Selected Poetry of Yehuda Amichai*, translated and edited by Chana Bloch and Stephen Mitchell (Berkeley: University of California Press, 1996), 137–38.

10. Culler, "Semiotics of Tourism."

11. Goldwater, "Constructing the Narrative of Authenticity," 53, 57.

12. $N = 989$. People in the same group might have similar responses because they are referring to the same tour guide. A variance components analysis shows that 10% of the variance in responses to this question is explained by the group with which the respondent traveled. The remaining 90% is explained by other (presumably individual) factors and by random error.

13. Crosstabulations of "too much 'preaching'" (strongly disagree, slightly disagree, slightly agree, strongly agree) with the posttrip question, "To what extent do you feel connected to Israel" (not at all, a little, somewhat, very much), controlling for the pretrip question on connection, identically worded and coded: not at all and a little connected pretrip: chi square = 24.532, d.f. = 6, p = .000; somewhat connected pretrip: chi square = 7.621, d.f. = 6, p = .267; very connected pretrip: chi square = 2.295, d.f. = 6, p = .891.

14. *Tau-c* = –.260, asymp. SE = .059, approx. T = –4.419, p = .000.

15. Peter L. Berger and Thomas Luckmann, *The Social Construction of Reality: A Treatise in the Sociology of Knowledge* (New York: Anchor Books, 1967).

16. On the sexual othering of American Jewish women, see Riv-Ellen Prell, *Fighting to Become Americans: Jews, Gender, and the Anxiety of Assimilation* (Boston: Beacon Press, 1999).

17. By 2006, of the approximately 100,000 Taglit alumni, an estimated 6,000 (mostly from the former Soviet Union, but including about 1,000 North Americans) had moved to Israel. Daphna Berman, "Number of Single Immigrants from N. America Leaps by 40% in 2006," *Ha'aretz* (Tel Aviv), October 21, 2006, at http://www.haaretz.com/hasen/spages/777251.html (accessed September 28, 2008).

18. Ann Swidler, *Talk of Love: How Culture Matters* (Chicago: University of Chicago Press, 2001), 5–6, 11–23.

19. Erik H. Cohen, Maurice Ifergan, and Eynath Cohen, "A New Paradigm in Guiding: The Madrich as a Role Model," *Annals of Tourism Research* 29(4) (2002): 926. See also Goldwater, "Constructing the Narrative of Authenticity," 62.

20. Cohen et al., "New Paradigm in Guiding," 927.

21. Taglit-Birthright Israel, *Revised Educational Standards 2001,* 2; emphasis added.

22. Hillel, *Hillel's Birthright Israel.*

23. Hillel: The Foundation for Jewish Campus Life, *Taglit-Birthright Israel: Hillel Journal* (Washington, D.C.: Hillel, 2006), 32–50.

24. Hillel, *Hillel's Birthright Israel,* 72.

25. Kirshenblatt-Gimblett, "Learning from Ethnography," 314.

26. Goldwater interview.

27. Goldwater, "Constructing the Narrative of Authenticity."

28. This section builds on Kirshenblatt-Gimblett's work, which offers the only sustained consideration of the embodied character of Israel experience pedagogy. Kirshenblatt-Gimblett, "Learning from Ethnography," 312.

29. Ibid., 315–18.

30. Ibid., 305.

31. Heilman, "Young Judea Israel Discovery Tour," 253–59.

32. On Orthodox Jewish English, see Sarah Bunin Benor, "*Talmid Chachams* and *Tsedeykeses:* Language, Learnedness, and Masculinity among Orthodox Jews," *Jewish Social Studies* 11(1) (2004): 147–69.

33. There is no equivalent on the women's side of the Western Wall.

34. Theodore Sasson, David Mittelberg, Shahar Hecht, and Leonard Saxe, *Encountering the Other, Finding Oneself: The Taglit-Birthright Israel Mifgash* (Waltham, Mass.: Brandeis University, Cohen Center for Modern Jewish Studies, 2008).

35. Tammi Hendel and Sherry Steinberg, "Our Israeli Adventure," *Senior,* October 1951, 4, in HA/AJHS: RG 17/publications/Young Judaea/"The Senior," Box 1.

36. Saxe and Chazan, *Ten Days of Birthright Israel,* 73.

37. Heilman, "Young Judea Israel Discovery Tour," 263.

38. Bar-Shalom, *Encounters with the Other;* Ezrachi and Sutnick, *Israel Education through Encounters with Israelis;* Jackie Feldman and Neta Katz, *The Place of the Jewish Agency in Mifgashim between Israeli and Diaspora Youth: Cultural Differences, Administrative Practices and Hidden Ideological Positions* (Jerusalem: Jewish Agency for Israel, Department of Jewish Zionist Education, 2002); Gabriel Horenczyk and Zvi Bekerman, "The Effects of Intercultural Acquaintance and Structured Intergroup Interaction on In-Group, Out-Group and Reflected In-Group Stereotypes," *International Journal of Intercultural Relations* 21(1) (1996): 71–83; Ezra Kopelowitz, "Between *Mifgash* and *Shlichut:* Paradigms in Contemporary Zionist Education and the Question of the Ideological Relationship between Israel and Diaspora," paper presented at the Research Seminar of the Department of Jewish Zionist Education, Jewish Agency for Israel, Jerusalem, March 12, 2003.

39. Avivi, *Birthright Israel Mifgashim;* Saxe and Chazan, *Ten Days of Birthright Israel,* 74–75.

40. Sasson et al., *Encountering the Other.*

41. Denise Brennan, "When Sex Tourists and Sex Workers Meet: Encounters within Sosúa, the Dominican Republic," in *Tourists and Tourism: A Reader,* edited by Sharon Bohn Gmelch (Long Grove, Ill.: Waveland Press, 2004), 303–15; Deborah Pruitt and Suzanne LaFont, "Romance Tourism: Gender, Race and Power in Jamaica," in *Tourists*

and Tourism: A Reader, edited by Sharon Bohn Gmelch (Long Grove, Ill.: Waveland Press, 2004), 317–35.

42. Boorstin, *Image.*

43. Culler, "Semiotics of Tourism," 138.

CHAPTER 6

1. Being fruitful and multiplying, and observing the Sabbath are each in their own right a religious commandment (*mitzvah*). Together they are sometimes called a "double *mitzvah.*" The joke refers to the Sabbath copulation taking place at a holy site.

2. This response was removed from the social network dataset.

3. Heilman, "Young Judea Israel Discovery Tour," 209.

4. Ibid., 203. The body can also be seen as another constant.

5. Erving Goffman, *Asylums: Essays on the Social Situation of Mental Patients and Other Inmates* (Garden City, N.Y.: Anchor Books, 1961), 6. See also Kelner et al., *Making Meaning,* 22.

6. Consider, for example, water canteens filled with alcohol for the hike up Masada and a fire ignited by throwing coals from a hookah water pipe off a hotel balcony.

7. This also creates a countervailing drive to encourage less-structured encounters as a form of experiential education. The willingness to act on this in Birthright Israel diminished substantially after the outbreak of the second intifada. Chazan, "Israel Trip," A14–A16.

8. Dean MacCannell, "Staged Authenticity: Arrangements of Social Space in Tourist Settings," *American Journal of Sociology* 79(3) (1973): 589–603.

9. Kelner et al., *Making Meaning.*

10. Kirshenblatt-Gimblett, "Learning from Ethnography," 314.

11. The principal exceptions are (1) those convinced that the group impedes an "authentic" encounter, (2) those negotiating with or purchasing from shopkeepers, and (3) those in transition from one group to another.

12. Erik Cohen, "The Tourist Guide: The Origins, Structure and Dynamics of a Role," *Annals of Tourism Research* 12(1) (1985): 5–29.

13. Cynthia Lightfoot, quoted in Judith Rich Harris, *The Nurture Assumption: Why Children Turn Out the Way They Do* (New York: Free Press, 1998), 281.

14. In spite of her class background and Jewish education, Isabel had never been to Israel in the context of a "peer-educational program" and hence was eligible for Taglit.

15. Hillel, *Hillel's Birthright Israel,* 39.

16. Chazan, "Israel Trip," A17.

17. Hillel, *Hillel's Birthright Israel,* 24.

18. Ibid., 39.

19. This idea is developed later in this chapter. For Turner's discussion of pilgrims' communitas, see Turner, "Pilgrimages as Social Processes." The concept of an "I-Thou relationship" is Buber's, not Turner's.

20. Network analyses were performed using Steven P. Borgatti, M. P. Everett, and Linton C. Freeman, *Ucinet 6 for Windows: Software for Social Network Analysis* (Analytic Technologies: Harvard, 2002), and Vladimir Batagelj and Andrej Mrvar, *Pajek: Program for Large Network Analysis,* Ver. 1.23 (Ljubljana, Slovenia, 1996–2008).

21. This core consisted of Allan, Beth, Didi, Isabel, Laura, Max, Mickey, Misha, Ron, Sam, and Todd. The density of ties within this block was 0.78 (i.e., of all possible friendship pairs, 78% were realized). Only 22% of the core's possible ties to the periphery were present. Those in the periphery were even less likely to claim friendship with members of the core (15%). The periphery did not form a cohesive group of its own, with a block density of only 0.21. Final fitness (correlation fit function): 0.530.

22. Structural equivalence models (SEMs) arrange people not around their connections to one another but around their connections to third parties. Hence, the "floaters" are not a cohesive group among themselves. This SEM was produced with a CONCOR procedure. Stanley Wasserman and Katherine Faust, *Social Network Analysis: Methods and Applications* (Cambridge: Cambridge University Press, 1998), 348–49.

23. Tourists were asked, "Of the people in the group, who do you feel closest to at this point, when we are 3 [or 9] days into the trip? . . . You are free to name anyone who is a member of our tour group, whether student or non-student, American or Israeli. You may name as many or as few people as you want." Analysis of reciprocated ties found that in Ra'anan's bus, the number of components shrank from 12 to 1, the number of isolates dropped from 6 to 1, and density increased from 0.05 to 0.12. In Michael's group, components dropped from 8 to 2, isolates increased from 1 to 3, and density rose from 0.06 to 0.09. Ra'anan's bus more successfully integrated its two primary university groups. Its Day 9 ratio of within-university ties to cross-university ties was 3.7:1, contrasted to 6.7:1 for the two main university groups on Michael's bus. Randomization tests of autocorrelation show that, in all cases, the patterning of friendships by university is statistically significant.

24. Whereas "liminality" refers to the positional relationship to social structures (the state of in-betweenness), "communitas" refers to the interactional relationship with other people (the intimacy undiminished by social roles and statuses). Turner, "Pilgrimages as Social Processes," 169.

25. The embedding of physical challenges and other extraordinary embodied experiences into a group setting is also commonly used to foster a sense of uplift. Rafting, hiking, rappeling, and camel riding excursions are typically undertaken with chatter, laughter, and good feeling.

26. Hillel, *Hillel's Birthright Israel,* 39, 73.

27. Kelner et al., *Making Meaning.*

28. Emile Durkheim, *The Elementary Forms of Religious Life,* translated by Karen E. Fields (New York: Free Press, [1912] 1995); Kelner, "Impact of Israel Experience Programs."

CHAPTER 7

1. Bruner, *Culture on Tour,* 16.

2. Hillel, *Hillel's Birthright Israel,* 72.

3. Because it was the first day of the trip, I still had not learned everyone's name.

4. Jaber Gubrium, *Oldtimers and Alzheimer's: The Descriptive Organization of Senility* (Greenwich, Conn.: JAI Press, 1986); Jaber Gubrium and James Holstein, "Narrative Practice and the Coherence of Personal Stories," *Sociological Quarterly* 39(1) (1998): 163–87; Robert Wuthnow, *Sharing the Journey: Support Groups and America's New Quest for Community* (New York: Free Press, 1994).

5. For example, Joy Webster Barbre, Amy Farrell, Shirley Nelson Garner, Susan Geiger, Ruth-Ellen Boetcher Joeres, Susan M. A. Lyons, Mary Jo Maynes, Pamela Mittlefehldt, Riv-Ellen Prell, and Virginia Steinhagen, *Interpreting Women's Lives: Feminist Theory and Personal Narratives* (Bloomington: Indiana University Press, 1989); Douglas Ezzy, "Theorizing Narrative Identity: Symbolic Interactionism and Hermeneutics," *Sociological Quarterly* 39(2) (1998): 239–43; Anita Plath Helle, "Reading Women's Autobiographies: A Map of Reconstructed Knowledge," in *Stories Lives Tell: Narrative and Dialogue in Education,* edited by Carol Witherell and Nel Noddings (New York: Teachers College Press, 1991), 48–66; Dan McAdams, Ann Diamond, Ed de St. Aubin, and Elizabeth Mansfield, "Stories of Commitment: The Psychosocial Construction of Generative Lives," *Journal of Personality and Social Psychology* 72(3) (1997): 678–94. For reviews of this literature, see David Maines, "Narrative's Moment and Sociology's Phenomena: Toward a Narrative Sociology," *Sociological Quarterly* 34(1) (1993): 17–38; Terri Orbuch, "People's Accounts Count: The Sociology of Accounts," *Annual Review of Sociology* 23 (1997): 455–78.

6. McAdams et al., "Stories of Commitment," 678.

7. Donald Polkinghorne, *Narrative Knowing and the Human Sciences* (Albany: State University of New York Press, 1988).

8. Handler and Saxton speak of "the satisfying *configurational* unity that a good plot provides." Richard Handler and William Saxton, "Dyssimulation: Reflexivity, Narrative, and the Quest for Authenticity in 'Living History,'" *Cultural Anthropology* 3 (1988): 251; emphasis added. See also Jerome Bruner, *Actual Minds, Possible Worlds* (Cambridge, Mass.: Harvard University Press, 1986), 7; Polkinghorne, *Narrative Knowing,* 6, 53.

9. The term "framing" is Goffman's. Gubrium and Holstein speak of "editing" and "substantive monitoring." Goffman, *Frame Analysis;* Gubrium and Holstein, "Narrative Practice and the Coherence of Personal Stories," 8–13.

10. Others refer to this as "linkage." Gubrium and Holstein, "Narrative Practice and the Coherence of Personal Stories," 4–8.

11. Birthright Israel tours for LGBT Jews include Young Judaea's "Pride in Israel" tour and the Jewish Agency's "Rainbow" tour. Michal Lando, "Gays, Lesbians Take Pride in Their Own Israeli Birthright," *Jerusalem Post,* May 19, 2008, 6.

12. Discussions of the Holocaust often layered universalistic and particularistic interpretations onto one another. It was not uncommon for travelers to refer to the genocides in Darfur, Rwanda, and the former Yugoslavia.

13. Kirshenblatt-Gimblett writes that the pedagogy of Israel experience tours "appeals to the truth of the senses. . . . [The tourists] will feel, not understand." Kirshenblatt-Gimblett, "Learning from Ethnography," 313.

14. Ibid.

15. I am imputing gender based on the handwriting.

16. Livnot U'Lehibanot is a Birthright Israel trip provider. Jessica Sibelman, "Israeli Trip an 'Eye-Opening' Experience," *New Jersey Jewish News,* September 4, 2008, at http://www.njjewishnews.com/njjn.com/090408/ltIsraeliTrip.html (accessed November 11, 2008).

17. Adelle Gomelsky, "10 Days That Changed My Life," Jewish Federation of Greater Los Angeles, at http://www.jewishla.org/10_Days_That_Changed_My_Life.cfm (accessed November 11, 2008).

18. Alyson Teich, "Israel in a Nutshell," Travelblog, at http://www.travelblog.org/Middle-East/Israel/blog-294902.html (accessed November 11, 2008).

19. Oranim is a Birthright Israel trip provider. Oranim Educational Initiatives, "See What Some of Our 35,000 Alumni Are Saying about the Taglit-Birthright Israel: Oranim Program," at http://www.oranimcanada.com/returnees.asp (accessed November 11, 2008).

20. Mayanot is a Birthright Israel trip provider. Mayanot, "Testimonials," at http://www. mayanotisrael.com/testimonials2.asp (accessed November 11, 2008).

21. Sarah Glick, quoted in Masha Leon, "Birthright Israel: A Voyage of Change," *Forward*, January 26, 2007, at http://www.forward.com/articles/9953/ (accessed November 11, 2008).

22. These examples are illustrative. Between 5% and 10% of respondents used both the terms "life" and "change/changed/changing" in their replies to this question. Saxe et al., *Taglit-Birthright Israel Evaluation Survey, Winter 2000–2001 Cohort.*

23. Leonard Saxe, Charles Kadushin, Shahar Hecht, Mark Rosen, Benjamin Phillips, and Shaul Kelner, *Evaluating Birthright Israel: Long-Term Impact and Recent Findings* (Waltham, Mass.: Brandeis University, Cohen Center for Modern Jewish Studies, 2004); Leonard Saxe, Theodore Sasson, and Shahar Hecht, *Taglit-Birthright Israel: Impact on Jewish Identity, Peoplehood, and Connection to Israel* (Waltham, Mass.: Brandeis University, Cohen Center for Modern Jewish Studies, 2006).

24. The evaluation uses a quasi-experimental design in which surveys of participants and a control group of nonparticipants are compared, both before and after the intervention. It finds that the trips strengthen positive feelings about Israel and make Israel and Jewish heritage more salient to travelers' identities. Longitudinal tracking finds that these effects persist at least four years after the trip. In spite of the attitudinal change, alumni do not engage in Jewish behaviors at higher rates than the control group, except for a greater propensity to participate in on-campus Jewish activities, which include activities that Hillel organizes specifically for Birthright Israel alumni. Saxe et al., *Taglit-Birthright Israel: Impact on Jewish Identity*, 11; Saxe et al., *Evaluating Birthright Israel*, 17–30; Saxe and Chazan, *Ten Days of Birthright Israel*, 147–49.

25. Edward M. Bruner, "Transformation of Self in Tourism," *Annals of Tourism Research* 18(2) (1991): 238–50; Chaim Noy, "This Trip Really Changed Me: Backpackers' Narratives of Self-Change," *Annals of Tourism Research* 31(1) (2004): 78–102.

26. Amia Lieblich, Rivka Tuval-Mashiach, and Tamar Zilber, *Narrative Research: Reading, Analysis and Interpretation* (Thousand Oaks, Calif.: Sage, 1998), quoted in Noy, "This Trip Really Changed Me," 84.

CHAPTER 8

1. Dialogue here refers not to a script but to the creation of meaning through conversation and verbal exchanges of ideas. Edward M. Bruner and Phyllis Gorfain, "Dialogic Narration and the Paradoxes of Masada," in *Text, Play and Story: The Construction and Reconstruction of Self and Society,* edited by Edward M. Bruner (Washington, D.C.: American Anthropological Society, 1984), 56–75.

2. Benjamin Netanyahu's Likud-led coalition pledged funding in principle in 1998, but the first state moneys were allocated after Ehud Barak's Labor-led government came to power in 2000. Stewart Ain, "Bibi Pledges $20m," *New York Jewish Week,* July 31, 1998, at www.thejewishweek.com/news/newscontent.php3?artid=441 (accessed May 20, 2002); Saxe and Chazan, *Ten Days of Birthright Israel*, 11.

3. Saxe et al., *Israel at War,* 8.

4. For example, see "Shelilat ha-golah," "Medinat ha-yehudim ve-tzarat ha-yehudim," and other essays in Ahad Ha ʿam, *Al Parashat Drachim.*

5. "Tour, *n.*" *The Oxford English Dictionary,* 2nd ed., OED Online (Oxford: Oxford University Press, 1989), at http://dictionary.oed.com.proxy.library.vanderbilt.edu/cgi/entry/50255209 (accessed November 28, 2008).

6. Post, "Don't Bash Birthright."

7. For American Jewish meditations on existential and geopolitical dimensions of *galut,* see Arnold Eisen, *Galut: Modern Jewish Reflections on Homelessness and Homecoming* (Bloomington: Indiana University Press, 1986); Jacob Neusner, *Stranger at Home: "The Holocaust," Zionism and American Judaism* (Chicago: University of Chicago Press, 1981).

8. Hence, their subtitle, "The End of the Jewish Diaspora." Aviv and Shneer, *New Jews.*

9. For a classic statement, see Erving Goffman, *The Presentation of Self in Everyday Life* (New York: Anchor Books, 1959).

10. Daniel Boyarin and Jonathan Boyarin, "Diaspora: Generation and the Ground of Jewish Identity," *Critical Inquiry* 19(4) (1993): 693–725.

11. One might cite novels like Philip Roth's 1993 *Operation Shylock* and perhaps Michael Chabon's 2007 *The Yiddish Policeman's Union,* as well as the klezmer revival that gained strength in the 1990s.

12. For an analogous critique of the treatment of diaspora in the fields of political science and international relations, see Shain, *Kinship and Diasporas in International Affairs.*

13. Portes et al., "Study of Transnationalism," 219.

14. Basch et al., *Nations Unbound;* Nancy Foner, "What's New about Transnationalism? New York's Immigrants Today and at the Turn of the Century," *Diaspora* 6(3) (1997): 355–75. See also all the articles in volume 22(2) (1999) of *Ethnic and Racial Studies.*

15. Hall, "Cultural Identity and Diaspora"; James Clifford, *Routes: Travel and Translation in the Late Twentieth Century* (Cambridge, Mass.: Harvard University Press, 1997).

16. Gilroy, *Black Atlantic,* 1.

17. Sander L. Gilman, *Jewish Frontiers: Essays on Bodies, Histories, and Identities* (New York: Palgrave Macmillan, 2003), 8–9.

18. I use the term "neodiasporist" rather than simply "diasporist" to acknowledge previous Jewish affirmations of diaspora from ancient times to the modern period and to distinguish the current wave of theorizing as a product of this particular historical moment.

19. This article also centrally informs postcolonial discourse on diaspora. Boyarin and Boyarin, "Diaspora," 723.

20. Ibid., 712, 717.

21. Aviv and Shneer, *New Jews;* Charlotte Elisheva Fonrobert and Vered Shemtov, "Introduction: Jewish Conceptions and Practices of Space," *Jewish Social Studies* 11(3) (2005): 1–8; Gilman, *Jewish Frontiers.*

22. Anderson, *Imagined Communities.*

Bibliography

ARCHIVAL SOURCES

Hadassah Archives, American Jewish Historical Society, Center for Jewish History, New York (cited as HA/AJHS): RG 17/publications/Young Judaea/"The Senior" and RG 8, Box 12A/Israel Programs/Summer Programs.
United Synagogue Youth Archives, United Synagogue of Conservative Judaism, Rapaport House, New York (cited as USYA/RH)

REFERENCES

Ahad Ha'am. *Al Parashat Drachim*. 4 vols. Tel Aviv: Dvir, 1979.
Ain, Stewart. "Bibi Pledges $20m." *New York Jewish Week,* July 31, 1998. At www.the jewishweek.com/news/newscontent.php3?artid=441 (accessed May 20, 2002).
———. "Free Heritage Trip on the Runway." *New York Jewish Week*, July 31, 1999. At www. thejewishweek.com/news/newscontent.php3?artid=1668 (accessed May 20, 2002).
Alba, Richard. *Ethnic Identity: The Transformation of White America.* New Haven, Conn.: Yale University Press, 1990.
Almog, Oz. *The Sabra: The Creation of the New Jew.* Translated by Haim Watzman. Berkeley: University of California Press, 2000.
Amichai, Yehuda. "Tourists," pp. 137–38 in *The Selected Poetry of Yehuda Amichai,* translated and edited by Chana Bloch and Stephen Mitchell. Berkeley: University of California Press, 1996.
Anderson, Benedict. *Imagined Communities.* London: Verso, 1991.
Aviv, Caryn, and David Shneer. *New Jews: The End of the Jewish Diaspora.* New York: New York University Press, 2005.
Avivi, Orit. *Birthright Israel Mifgashim: A Summary of the Planning, Implementation and Evaluation of Mifgashim during Birthright Israel Programs. Executive Report: Winter Launch 1999–2000.* Jerusalem: Bronfman Mifgashim Center, 2000.
Bar-Shalom, Yehuda. *Encounters with the Other: An Ethnographic Study of Mifgashim Programs for Jewish Youth, Summer 1997.* Jerusalem: Bronfman Centre for the Israel Experience–Mifgashim, 1998.
Barbre, Joy Webster, Amy Farrell, Shirley Nelson Garner, Susan Geiger, Ruth-Ellen Boetcher Joeres, Susan M. A. Lyons, Mary Jo Maynes, Pamela Mittlefehldt, Riv-Ellen Prell, and Virginia Steinhagen. *Interpreting Women's Lives: Feminist Theory and Personal Narratives.* Bloomington: Indiana University Press, 1989.

Basch, Linda, Nina Glick Schiller, and Cristina Szanton Blanc. *Nations Unbound: Transnational Projects, Postcolonial Predicaments, and Deterritorialized Nation-States.* Langhorne, Penn.: Gordon and Breach, 1994.

Basu, Paul. *Highland Homecomings: Genealogy and Heritage Tourism in the Scottish Diaspora.* London: Routledge, 2007.

Batagelj, Vladimir, and Andrej Mrvar. *Pajek: Program for Large Network Analysis.* Ver. 1.23. Ljubljana, Slovenia, 1996–2008.

Bauman, Zygmunt. "From Pilgrim to Tourist—or a Short History of Identity," pp. 18–36 in *Questions of Cultural Identity,* edited by Stuart Hall and Paul du Gay. London: Sage, 1996.

Beilin, Yossi. *His Brother's Keeper: Israel and Diaspora Jewry in the Twenty-First Century.* New York: Schocken, 2000.

Ben-David, Orit. "*Tiyul* (Hike) as an Act of Consecration of Space," pp. 129–45 in *Grasping Land: Space and Place in Contemporary Israeli Discourse and Experience,* edited by Eyal Ben-Ari and Yoram Bilu. Albany: State University of New York Press, 1997.

Ben-Yehuda, Nachman. *The Masada Myth: Collective Memory and Mythmaking in Israel.* Madison: University of Wisconsin Press, 1995.

Benor, Sarah Bunin. "*Talmid Chachams* and *Tsedeykeses:* Language, Learnedness, and Masculinity among Orthodox Jews." *Jewish Social Studies* 11(1) (2004): 147–69.

Berger, Peter L., and Thomas Luckmann. *The Social Construction of Reality: A Treatise in the Sociology of Knowledge.* New York: Anchor Books, 1967.

Berman, Daphna. "I.S.M. Activists Use Birthright Program to Get to Israel." *Ha'aretz* (Tel Aviv). July 16, 2004. At http://www.haaretz.com/hasen/pages/ShArt.jhtml?itemNo=452 230&contrassID=1&subContrassID=5&sbSubContrassID=0&listSrc=Y (accessed April 2, 2009).

———. "Number of Single Immigrants from N. America Leaps by 40% in 2006." *Ha'aretz* (Tel Aviv). October 21, 2006. At http://www.haaretz.com/hasen/spages/777251.html (accessed September 28, 2008).

"Birthright Booms as Terror Sinks Tourism." *Ha'aretz* (Tel Aviv). January 26, 2001. At http://web.lexis-nexis.com/universe/ (accessed June 17, 2002).

Birthright Israel. "Birthright Israel Announces Successful Enrollment for Inaugural Season of Free Trips to Israel Signaling Youth Interest in Jewish Heritage; Overwhelming Response to 5,000 Free Winter Break Trips Offered by Birthright Israel." *PR Newswire.* Press release (October 12, 1999). At web.lexis-nexis.com/universe (accessed May 20, 2002).

———. "Birthright Israel Gives American Jewish Youth Largest, Most Meaningful Hanukah Gift Ever." *PR Newswire.* Press release (November 22, 1999). At web.lexis-nexis.com/universe (accessed May 22, 2002).

Birthright Israel North America. *Israel Experience 2001: Your Complete Guide to Programs for College, Post-College and High School Students.* New York: Birthright Israel North America, 2001.

Boorstin, Daniel. *The Image: A Guide to Pseudo-Events in America.* New York: Atheneum, [1961] 1985.

Borgatti, Steven P., M. P. Everett, and Linton C. Freeman. *Ucinet 6 for Windows: Software for Social Network Analysis.* Analytic Technologies: Harvard, 2002.

Bourdieu, Pierre. *Distinction: A Social Critique of the Judgement of Taste.* Translated by Richard Nice. Cambridge, Mass.: Harvard University Press, 1984.

Bowman, Marion. "Drawn to Glastonbury," pp. 29–62 in *Pilgrimage in Popular Culture,* edited by Ian Reader and Tony Walter. London: Macmillan, 1993.

Boyarin, Daniel, and Jonathan Boyarin. "Diaspora: Generation and the Ground of Jewish Identity." *Critical Inquiry* 19(4) (1993): 693–725.

Braslavi (Braslavsky), Joseph. *Bi-netivot lo-selulot el yediat ha-arets* [On unpaved paths to knowing the land of Israel]. Tel Aviv: Am Oved, 1973.

Brennan, Denise. "When Sex Tourists and Sex Workers Meet: Encounters within Sosúa, the Dominican Republic," pp. 303–15 in *Tourists and Tourism: A Reader,* edited by Sharon Bohn Gmelch. Long Grove, Ill.: Waveland Press, 2004.

Bruner, Edward M. "Abraham Lincoln as Authentic Reproduction: A Critique of Postmodernism." *American Anthropologist* 96(2) (1994): 397–415.

———. *Culture on Tour: Ethnographies of Travel.* Chicago: University of Chicago Press, 2005.

———. "Tourism in Ghana: The Representation of Slavery and the Return of the Black Diaspora." *American Anthropologist* 98(2) (1996): 290–304.

———. "Transformation of Self in Tourism." *Annals of Tourism Research* 18(2) (1991): 238–50.

Bruner, Edward M., and Phyllis Gorfain. "Dialogic Narration and the Paradoxes of Masada," pp. 56–75 in *Text, Play and Story: The Construction and Reconstruction of Self and Society,* edited by Edward M. Bruner. Washington, D.C.: American Anthropological Society, 1984.

Bruner, Jerome. *Actual Minds, Possible Worlds.* Cambridge, Mass.: Harvard University Press, 1986.

B'Tselem. "Casualties List." At http://www.btselem.org/english/Statistics/Casualties.asp (accessed April 2, 2009).

Bubis, Gerald, and Lawrence Marks. *Changes in Jewish Identification: A Comparative Study of a Teen Age Israel Camping Trip, a Counselor-in-Training Program, and a Teen Age Service Camp.* Los Angeles: Florence G. Heller–JWB Research Center in cooperation with the Jewish Community Centers Association, 1975.

Carter, Sean. "Mobilizing *Hrvatsko:* Tourism and Politics in the Croatian Diaspora," pp. 188–201 in *Tourism, Diasporas and Space,* edited by Tim Coles and Dallen Timothy. London: Routledge, 2004.

Carù, Antonella, and Bernard Cova. "Consuming Experiences: An Introduction," pp. 3–16 in *Consuming Experience,* edited by Antonella Carù and Bernard Cova. London: Routledge, 2007.

Charmé, Stuart. "The Construction of Gender Traditions at the Western Wall in Jerusalem." Paper presented at the 33rd Annual Meetings of the Association for Jewish Studies, Washington, D.C., December 18, 2001.

Chazan, Barry. *Does the Teen Israel Experience Make a Difference?* New York: Israel Experience, Inc., 1997.

———. "The Israel Trip: A New Form of Jewish Education," pp. A1–A26 in *Youth Trips to Israel: Rationale and Realization.* New York: CRB Foundation and the Mandell L. Berman Jewish Heritage Center at JESNA, 1994.

Clifford, James. *Routes: Travel and Translation in the Late Twentieth Century.* Cambridge, Mass.: Harvard University Press, 1997.

Cohen, Debra Nussbaum. "The Feminine (Giving) Mystique." *New York Jewish Week,* June 14, 2002, 10–12.

Cohen, Erik. "Pilgrimage and Tourism: Convergence and Divergence," pp. 47–61 in *Sacred Journeys: The Anthropology of Pilgrimage,* edited by Alan Morinis. Westport, Conn.: Greenwood, 1992.

——. "The Tourist Guide: The Origins, Structure and Dynamics of a Role." *Annals of Tourism Research* 12(1) (1985): 5–29.

——. "Toward a Sociology of International Tourism." *Social Research* 39(1) (1972): 164–82.

Cohen, Erik H. *Toward a Strategy of Excellence: The Participants of the Israel Experience Short-Term Programs Summer/1993–Winter/1994.* Jerusalem: JAFI, Youth and Hechalutz Department, and Joint Authority for Jewish Zionist Education, 1994.

Cohen, Erik H., and Eynath Cohen. *Ha-hawaya ha-yisreelit* [The Israel experience]. Jerusalem: Jerusalem Institute for Israel Studies, 2000.

Cohen, Erik H., and Ariela Keysar. *The 1992 Summer Israel Experience Educational Programs.* Jerusalem: CRB Foundation and Mandel Associated Foundations, 1993.

Cohen, Erik H., Maurice Ifergan, and Eynath Cohen. "A New Paradigm in Guiding: The Madrich as a Role Model." *Annals of Tourism Research* 29(4) (2002): 919–32.

Cohen, Randy. "The Ethicist." *New York Times Magazine,* March 7, 2004, 22.

Cohen, Steven M. *Committed Zionists and Curious Tourists: Travel to Israel among Canadian Jewish Youth.* Jerusalem: CRB Foundation, 1991.

——. *Israel Travel Program for Canadian Youth: Levels of Participation and Cost for 1989 and 1990.* Jerusalem: CRB Foundation, 1991.

Cohen, Steven M., and Susan Wall. "Excellence in Youth Trips to Israel," pp. B1–B66 in *Youth Trips to Israel: Rationale and Realization.* New York: CRB Foundation and the Mandell L. Berman Jewish Heritage Center at JESNA, 1994.

——. *The Good Trip.* Montreal: CRB Foundation, 1992.

Coles, Tim, and Dallen Timothy. "'My Field Is the World': Conceptualizing Diasporas, Travel and Tourism," pp. 1–29 in *Tourism, Diasporas and Space,* edited by Tim Coles and Dallen Timothy. London: Routledge, 2004.

Cook, Samuel. "Four Decades." *Visions,* Union of American Hebrew Congregations Youth Division, Winter 1979, 8–9.

Costen, Michael. "The Pilgrimage to Santiago de Compostela in Medieval Europe," pp. 137–54 in *Pilgrimage in Popular Culture,* edited by Ian Reader and Tony Walter. London: Macmillan, 1993.

Culler, Jonathan. "Semiotics of Tourism." *American Journal of Semiotics* 1(1–2) (1981): 127–40.

Danzger, M. Herbert. *Returning to Tradition: The Contemporary Revival of Orthodox Judaism.* New Haven, Conn.: Yale University Press, 1989.

Douglas, Mary. "The Social Control of Cognition: Some Factors in Joke Perception." *Man* 3(3) (1968): 361–76.

Durkheim, Emile. *The Elementary Forms of Religious Life.* Translated by Karen E. Fields. New York: Free Press, [1912] 1995.

Duval, David Timothy. "Conceptualizing Return Visits: A Transnational Perspective," pp. 50–61 in *Tourism, Diasporas and Space,* edited by Tim Coles and Dallen Timothy. London: Routledge, 2004.

Eade, John, and Michael Sallnow. *Contesting the Sacred: The Anthropology of Christian Pilgrimage.* London: Routledge, [1991] 2000.

Editorial. "Language and History." *Guardian* (London). February 7, 2009, 40. At http://www.guardian.co.uk/commentisfree/2009/feb/07/race-judaism-antisemitism (accessed May 5, 2009).

Eisen, Arnold. *Galut: Modern Jewish Reflections on Homelessness and Homecoming.* Bloomington: Indiana University Press, 1986.

Eisenberg, Norman. "Foundations for Change." *New York Jewish Week,* June 14, 2002, 6–9.

Elliott, Stuart. "The Media Business: Advertising—Addenda; Accounts." *New York Times,* August 2, 1999, C12. At web.lexis-nexis.com/universe (accessed May 20, 2002).

Ezrachi, Elan, and Barbara Sutnick. *Israel Education through Encounters with Israelis.* Jerusalem: CRB Foundation, Joint Authority for Jewish Zionist Education, and Bronfman Centre for the Israel Experience–Mifgashim, 1997.

Ezzy, Douglas. "Theorizing Narrative Identity: Symbolic Interactionism and Hermeneutics." *Sociological Quarterly* 39(2) (1998): 239–43.

Fainstein, Susan, and Dennis Judd. "Global Forces, Local Strategies, and Urban Tourism," pp. 1–17 in *The Tourist City,* edited by Dennis Judd and Susan Fainstein. New Haven, Conn.: Yale University Press, 1999.

Fax, Julie Gruenbaum. "Birthright Israel Launches $50 Million Campaign, Cuts Trips." *Los Angeles Jewish Journal.* February 11, 2009. At http://www.jewishjournal.com/articles/item/birthright_launches_50m_campaign_cuts_trips_20090211/ (accessed July 31, 2009).

Feldman, Jackie. *Above the Death Pits, Beneath the Flag: Youth Voyages to Poland and the Construction of Israeli National Identity.* Oxford: Berghahn, 2008.

Feldman, Jackie, and Neta Katz. *The Place of the Jewish Agency in Mifgashim between Israeli and Diaspora Youth: Cultural Differences, Administrative Practices and Hidden Ideological Positions.* Jerusalem: Jewish Agency for Israel, Department of Jewish Zionist Education, 2002.

Fine, Elizabeth, and Jean Haskell Speer. "Tour Guide Performances as Sight Sacralization." *Annals of Tourism Research* 12(1) (1985): 73–95.

Foner, Nancy. "What's New about Transnationalism? New York's Immigrants Today and at the Turn of the Century." *Diaspora* 6(3) (1997): 355–75.

Fonrobert, Charlotte Elisheva, and Vered Shemtov. "Introduction: Jewish Conceptions and Practices of Space." *Jewish Social Studies* 11(3) (2005): 1–8.

Gee, Alison Dakota. "The Love Boat." *South China Morning Post,* August 14, 1994, 12. At http://web.lexis-nexis.com/universe/ (accessed July 14, 2006).

Gilman, Sander L. *Jewish Frontiers: Essays on Bodies, Histories, and Identities.* New York: Palgrave Macmillan, 2003.

Gilroy, Paul. *The Black Atlantic: Modernity and Double-Consciousness.* Cambridge, Mass.: Harvard University Press, 1993.

Goffman, Erving. *Asylums: Essays on the Social Situation of Mental Patients and Other Inmates.* Garden City, N.Y.: Anchor Books, 1961.

———. *Frame Analysis: An Essay on the Organization of Experience.* Cambridge, Mass.: Harvard University Press, 1974.

———. *The Presentation of Self in Everyday Life.* New York: Anchor Books, 1959.

Goldberg, Harvey. "A Summer on a NFTY Safari 1994: An Ethnographic Perspective," pp. 21–140 in *The Israel Experience: Studies in Jewish Identity and Youth Culture,* edited by Barry Chazan. Jerusalem: Andrea and Charles Bronfman Philanthropies, 2002.

Goldberg, J. J., and Elliot King (editors). *Builders and Dreamers: Habonim Labor Zionist Youth in North America—A Century in Memoir.* Cranbury, N.J.: Cornwall Books, 1993.

Goldfarb Consultants. *Attitudes towards Travel to Israel among Jewish Adults and Jewish Youth.* Jerusalem: CRB Foundation, 1991.

Goldwater, Clare. "Constructing the Narrative of Authenticity: Tour Educators at Work in the Israel Experience." M.A. thesis, Hebrew University of Jerusalem, 2002.

Gomelsky, Adelle. "10 Days That Changed My Life." Jewish Federation of Greater Los Angeles. At http://www.jewishla.org/10_Days_That_Changed_My_Life.cfm (accessed November 11, 2008).

Gotham, Kevin Fox. *Authentic New Orleans: Tourism, Culture and Race in the Big Easy.* New York: New York University Press, 2007.

Gottdiener, Mark. *The Theming of America: American Dreams, Media Fantasies, and Themed Environments.* 2nd ed. Boulder, Colo.: Westview, 2001.

Graburn, Nelson. "Tourism: The Sacred Journey," pp. 21–36 in *Hosts and Guests: The Anthropology of Tourism,* edited by Valene Smith. Philadelphia: University of Pennsylvania Press, [1977] 1989.

Grant, Lisa. "Planned and Enacted Curriculum Stories on a Congregational Israel Trip." *Conservative Judaism* 53(3) (2001): 63–81.

———. "The Role of Mentoring in Enhancing Experience of a Congregational Israel Trip." *Journal of Jewish Education* 67(1/2) (2001): 46–60.

Grazian, David. *Blue Chicago: The Search for Authenticity in Urban Blues Clubs.* Chicago: University of Chicago Press, 2003.

Greenberg, Joel. "Trips to Renew Jewish Ties Set Off Debate about Costs." *New York Times,* January 8, 2000, 6. At http://web.lexis-nexis.com/universe/ (accessed October 25, 2004).

Gubrium, Jaber. *Oldtimers and Alzheimer's: The Descriptive Organization of Senility.* Greenwich, Conn.: JAI Press, 1986.

Gubrium, Jaber, and James Holstein. "Narrative Practice and the Coherence of Personal Stories." *Sociological Quarterly* 39(1) (1998): 163–87.

Gurevich, Zali, and Gideon Aran. "'Al ha-makom" [About the place], *Alpayim* 4 (1991): 9–44.

Habib, Jasmin. *Israel, Diaspora, and the Routes of National Belonging.* Toronto: University of Toronto Press, 2004.

Hall, Stuart. "Cultural Identity and Diaspora," pp. 222–37 in *Identity: Community, Culture, Difference,* edited by Jonathan Rutherford. London: Lawrence and Wishart, 1990.

———. "Encoding/Decoding," pp. 128–38 in *Culture, Media, Language: Working Papers in Cultural Studies, 1972–79,* edited by Stuart Hall, Dorothy Hobson, Andrew Lowe, and Paul Willis. London: Hutchinson, 1980.

Handler, Richard, and William Saxton. "Dyssimulation: Reflexivity, Narrative, and the Quest for Authenticity in 'Living History.'" *Cultural Anthropology* 3 (1988): 242–60.

Hannam, Kevin. "India and the Ambivalences of Diaspora Tourism," pp. 246–60 in *Tourism, Diasporas and Space,* edited by Tim Coles and Dallen Timothy. London: Routledge, 2004.

Harris, Judith Rich. *The Nurture Assumption: Why Children Turn Out the Way They Do.* New York: Free Press, 1998.

Heilman, Samuel. "A Young Judea Israel Discovery Tour: The View from Inside," pp. 141–265 in *The Israel Experience: Studies in Jewish Identity and Youth Culture,* edited by Barry Chazan. Jerusalem: Andrea and Charles Bronfman Philanthropies, 2002.

———. *The People of the Book: Drama, Fellowship, and Religion.* Chicago: University of Chicago Press, 1983.

Heinze, Andrew. *Adapting to Abundance: Jewish Immigrants, Mass Consumption, and the Search for American Identity.* New York: Columbia University Press, 1990.

Helle, Anita Plath. "Reading Women's Autobiographies: A Map of Reconstructed Knowledge," pp. 48–66 in *Stories Lives Tell: Narrative and Dialogue in Education,* edited by Carol Witherell and Nel Noddings. New York: Teachers College Press, 1991.

Hillel: The Foundation for Jewish Campus Life. *Hillel's Birthright Israel: The Tour.* Washington, D.C.: Hillel, 2000.

———. "Israel 2001." At http://www.israel2001.com (accessed October 12, 2001).

———. *Taglit-Birthright Israel: Hillel Journal.* Washington, D.C.: Hillel, 2006.

Hine, Thomas. *The Rise and Fall of the American Teenager.* New York: Bard Books, 1999.

Hobsbawm, Eric, and Terence Ranger. *The Invention of Tradition.* Cambridge: Cambridge University Press, 1983.

Hollinshead, Keith. "Tourism and Third Space Populations: The Restless Motion of Diaspora Peoples," pp. 33–49 in *Tourism, Diasporas and Space,* edited by Tim Coles and Dallen Timothy. London: Routledge, 2004.

Horenczyk, Gabriel, and Zvi Bekerman. "The Effects of Intercultural Acquaintance and Structured Intergroup Interaction on In-Group, Out-Group and Reflected In-Group Stereotypes." *International Journal of Intercultural Relations* 21(1) (1996): 71–83.

Hua, Vanessa. "A Cultural Awakening: Program Lets Young Chinese Americans Discover Their Identity." *Los Angeles Times,* July 6, 1998, 1. At http://huaren.org/diaspora/n_america/usa/docs/0798-04.html (accessed July 17, 2005).

Ignacio, Emily Noelle. *Building Diaspora: Filipino Cultural Community Formation on the Internet.* New Brunswick, N.J.: Rutgers University Press, 2005.

Israel, Sherry, and David Mittelberg. *The Israel Visit—Not Just for Teens: The Characteristics and Impact of College-Age Travel to Israel.* Waltham, Mass.: Brandeis University, Cohen Center for Modern Jewish Studies, 1998.

Joel, Richard. "Birthright Is Born" (op-ed). *Jerusalem Post.* January 3, 2000. At http:// web.lexis-nexis.com/universe/ (accessed October 25, 2004).

Joselit, Jenna Weissman. *The Wonders of America: Reinventing Jewish Culture, 1880–1950.* New York: Hill and Wang, 1994.

Kadushin, Charles. "The Motivational Foundation of Social Networks." *Social Networks* 24(1) (2002): 77–91.

Kadushin, Charles, Shaul Kelner, and Leonard Saxe. *Being a Jewish Teenager in America: Trying to Make It.* Waltham, Mass.: Brandeis University, Cohen Center for Modern Jewish Studies, 2000.

Kafka, R. R., Perry London, S. Bandler, and Naava Frank. *The Impact of "Summer in Israel" Experiences on North American Jewish Teenagers.* Montreal: CRB Foundation, 1990.

Katriel, Tamar. "Touring the Land: Trips and Hiking as Secular Pilgrimages in Israeli Culture." *Jewish Folklore and Ethnology Review* 17(1–2) (1995): 6–13.

Katz, Shaul. "The Israeli Teacher-Guide: The Emergence and Perpetuation of a Role." *Annals of Tourism Research* 12(1) (1985): 49–72.

Kearney, Michael. "The Local and the Global: The Anthropology of Globalization and Transnationalism." *Annual Review of Anthropology* 24 (2004): 547–65.

Kelly, Mary. "Born Again Lithuanians: Ethnic Conversions and Pilgrimages and the Resurgence of Lithuanian-American Ethnic Identity." Ph.D. dissertation, University of Kansas, 1996.

———. "Ethnic Pilgrimages: People of Lithuanian Descent in Lithuania." *Sociological Spectrum* 20 (2000): 65–91.

Kelly, Mary E., and Joane Nagel. "Ethnic Re-Identification: Lithuanian Americans and Native Americans." *Journal of Ethnic and Migration Studies* 28(2) (2002): 275–89.

Kelner, Shaul. "Almost pilgrims: Authenticity, Identity and the Extra-ordinary on a Jewish Tour of Israel." Ph.D. dissertation, City University of New York, 2002.

———. "The Impact of Israel Experience Programs on Israel's Symbolic Meaning." *Contemporary Jewry* 24 (2003): 124–54.

Kelner, Shaul, Leonard Saxe, Charles Kadushin, Rachel Canar, Matthew Lindholm, Hal Ossman, Jennifer Perloff, Benjamin Phillips, Rishona Teres, Minna Wolf, and Meredith Woocher. *Making Meaning: Participants' Experience of Birthright Israel.* Waltham, Mass.: Brandeis University, Cohen Center for Modern Jewish Studies, 2000.

Kibria, Nazli. "Of Blood, Belonging, and Homeland Trips: Transnationalism and Identity among Second-Generation Chinese and Korean Americans," pp. 295–311 in *The Changing Face of Home: The Transnational Lives of the Second Generation,* edited by Peggy Levitt and Mary C. Waters. New York: Russell Sage Foundation, 2002.

Kirshenblatt-Gimblett, Barbara. "Learning from Ethnography: Reflections on the Nature and Efficacy of Youth Tours to Israel," pp. 267–331 in *The Israel Experience: Studies in Jewish Identity and Youth Culture,* edited by Barry Chazan. Jerusalem: Andrea and Charles Bronfman Philanthropies, 2002.

Kopelowitz, Ezra. "Between *Mifgash* and *Shlichut:* Paradigms in Contemporary Zionist Education and the Question of the Ideological Relationship between Israel and Diaspora." Paper presented at the Jewish Agency for Israel, Research Seminar of the Department of Jewish Zionist Education, Jerusalem, March 12, 2003.

Kosmin, Barry, Sidney Goldstein, Joseph Waksberg, Nava Lerer, Ariela Keysar, and Jeffrey Scheckner. *Highlights of the CJF 1990 National Jewish Population Survey.* New York: Council of Jewish Federations, 1991.

Kramer, Judith, and Seymour Leventman. *Children of the Gilded Ghetto: Conflict Resolutions of Three Generations of American Jews.* New Haven, Conn.: Yale University Press, 1961.

Kugelmass, Jack. "The Rites of the Tribe: The Meaning of Poland for American Jewish Tourists." *YIVO Annual* 21 (1993): 395–453.

Lamont, Michèle, and Virág Molnár. "The Study of Boundaries in the Social Sciences." *Annual Review of Sociology* 28 (2002): 167–95.

Lando, Michal. "Gays, Lesbians Take Pride in Their Own Israeli Birthright." *Jerusalem Post,* May 19, 2008, 6.

Leibler, Isi. "Birthright Israel: Too Quick and Superficial." *New York Jewish Week,* November 19, 1999. At www.thejewishweek.com/top/editletcontent.php3?artid=554 (accessed August 3, 2000).

Leon, Masha. "Birthright Israel: A Voyage of Change." *Forward,* January 26, 2007. At http://www.forward.com/articles/9953/ (accessed November 11, 2008).

Levenberg, Jay. *Marketing Trips to Israel: Recommendations of the Israel Experience Marketing Project.* Jerusalem: CRB Foundation, 1992.

Levinson, Tamar, and Susan Zoline. "Impact of Summer Trip to Israel on the Self-Esteem of Jewish Adolescents." *Journal of Psychology and Judaism* 21(2) (1997): 87–119.

Lew, Alan, and Alan Wong. "Sojourners, *Guanxi* and Clan Associations: Social Capital and Overseas Chinese Tourism to China," pp. 202–14 in *Tourism, Diasporas and Space,* edited by Tim Coles and Dallen Timothy. London: Routledge, 2004.

Lewis, Albert. "Looking Back at USY Israel Pilgrimage." *Hamadrich: A Journal of Jewish Education* 8(1) (1991): 13–15.

Lieblich, Amia, Rivka Tuval-Mashiach, and Tamar Zilber. *Narrative Research: Reading, Analysis and Interpretation.* Thousand Oaks, Calif.: Sage, 1998.

Liebman, Charles S., and Eliezer Don-Yehiya. *Civil Religion in Israel: Traditional Judaism and Political Culture in the Jewish State.* Berkeley: University of California Press, 1983.

Lipka, Sara. "Eyes on the Past." *Chronicle of Higher Education,* February 9, 2007, A48.

Lloyd, Richard. *Neo-Bohemia: Art and Commerce in the Post-Industrial City.* New York: Routledge, 2006.

London, Perry, and Alissa Hirshfeld. "Youth Programs in Israel: What the Findings Mean." *Journal of Jewish Communal Service* 66 (1989): 87–91.

Louie, Andrea. *Chineseness across Borders: Renegotiating Chinese Identities in China and the United States.* Durham, N.C.: Duke University Press, 2004.

———. "When You Are Related to the 'Other': (Re)Locating the Chinese Homeland in Asian American Politics through Cultural Tourism." *Positions* 11(3) (2003): 735–63.

Lovy, Harold. "Searching for God in Israel." *Jewish Telegraphic Agency,* January 18, 2000. At http://www.jta.org/cgi-bin/iowa/news/article/20000118SearchingforGodin.html (accessed August 12, 2008).

MacCannell, Dean. "Staged Authenticity: Arrangements of Social Space in Tourist Settings." *American Journal of Sociology* 79(3) (1973): 589–603.

———. *The Tourist: A New Theory of the Leisure Class.* New York: Schocken, [1976] 1989.

Maines, David. "Narrative's Moment and Sociology's Phenomena: Toward a Narrative Sociology." *Sociological Quarterly* 34(1) (1993): 17–38.

Massing, Michael. "Should Jews Be Parochial?" *American Prospect,* November 6, 2000, 30–35.

Mayanot. "Testimonials." At http://www.mayanotisrael.com/testimonials2.asp (accessed November 11, 2008).

McAdams, Dan, Ann Diamond, Ed de St. Aubin, and Elizabeth Mansfield. "Stories of Commitment: The Psychosocial Construction of Generative Lives." *Journal of Personality and Social Psychology* 72(3) (1997): 678–94.

Meethan, Kevin. "'To Stand in the Shoes of My Ancestors': Tourism and Genealogy," pp. 139–50 in *Tourism, Diasporas and Space,* edited by Tim Coles and Dallen Timothy. London: Routledge, 2004.

Melamed, Jodi. "Creating Cultures of Solidarity: American Jews Redefine Birthright." Nerve House. At http://www.birthrightunplugged.org/html/brup12press.html#nerve (accessed May 7, 2007).

Mittelberg, David. *The Israel Connection and American Jews.* Westport, Conn.: Praeger, 1999.

————. *The Israel Visit and Jewish Identification.* New York: Institute on American Jewish–Israeli Relations of the American Jewish Committee, 1994.

Moore, Deborah Dash. *To the Golden Cities: Pursuing the American Jewish Dream in Miami and L.A.* Cambridge, Mass.: Harvard University Press, 1994.

Morinis, Alan. "Introduction: The Territory of the Anthropology of Pilgrimage," pp. 1–28 in *Sacred Journeys: The Anthropology of Pilgrimage*, edited by Alan Morinis. Westport, Conn.: Greenwood, 1992.

——— (editor). *Sacred Journeys: The Anthropology of Pilgrimage.* Westport, Conn.: Greenwood, 1992.

Nabti, David Munir. "Conference Explores Diaspora's Relations to Homeland." *Daily Star* (Lebanon), July 21, 2004. At http://www.dailystar.com.lb/article.asp?edition_ID=1&article_ID=6465&categ_id=3 (accessed July 22, 2004).

Naor, Mordechay (editor). *Tenuot ha-noar 1920–1960* [Youth movements, 1920–1960]. Jerusalem: Yad Yitshak Ben-Tsevi, 1989.

Neusner, Jacob. *Stranger at Home: "The Holocaust," Zionism and American Judaism.* Chicago: University of Chicago Press, 1981.

"NFTY at Fifty: Looking Back." *Ani V'atah,* 1989, 4–5.

Nguyen, Thu-Huong, and Brian King. "The Culture of Tourism in the Diaspora: The Case of the Vietnamese Community in Australia," pp. 172–87 in *Tourism, Diasporas and Space,* edited by Tim Coles and Dallen Timothy. London: Routledge, 2004.

Nielsen, Jason. "Hillel Introduces Israel Advocacy." *Boston Jewish Advocate.* January 11, 2002, 5.

Noy, Chaim. "This Trip Really Changed Me: Backpackers' Narratives of Self-Change." *Annals of Tourism Research* 31(1) (2004): 78–102.

Oranim Educational Initiatives. "See What Some of Our 35,000 Alumni Are Saying about the Taglit-Birthright Israel: Oranim Program." At http://www.oranimcanada.com/returnees.asp (accessed November 11, 2008).

Orbuch, Terri. "People's Accounts Count: The Sociology of Accounts." *Annual Review of Sociology* 23 (1997): 455–78.

Percy, Walker. "The Loss of the Creature," pp. 46–63 in *The Message in the Bottle: How Queer Man Is, How Queer Language Is, and What One Has to Do with the Other.* New York: Farrar, Straus and Giroux, [1954] 1982.

Polgreen, Lydia. "Ghana's Uneasy Embrace of Slavery's Diaspora." *New York Times,* December 27, 2005, 1. At http://query.nytimes.com/gst/fullpage.html?sec=travel&res=9B00E0DA1230F934A15751C1A9639C8B63 (accessed July 14, 2006).

Polkinghorne, Donald. *Narrative Knowing and the Human Sciences.* Albany: State University of New York Press, 1988.

Portes, Alejandro, Luis Guarnizo, and Patricia Landolt. "The Study of Transnationalism: Pitfalls and Promise of an Emergent Research Field." *Ethnic and Racial Studies* 22(2) (1999): 217–37.

Post, Marlene. "Don't Bash Birthright." *Jerusalem Report,* December 20, 1999, 54.

Prell, Riv-Ellen. *Fighting to Become Americans: Jews, Gender, and the Anxiety of Assimilation.* Boston: Beacon Press, 1999.

————. "Summer Camp, Post-War American Jewish Youth and the Redemption of Judaism," pp. 77–106 in *The Jewish Role in America: An Annual Review,* edited by Bruce Zuckerman and Jeremy Schoenberg. West Lafayette, Ind.: Purdue University Press, 2007.

Pruitt, Deborah, and Suzanne LaFont. "Romance Tourism: Gender, Race and Power in Jamaica," pp. 317–35 in *Tourists and Tourism: A Reader,* edited by Sharon Bohn Gmelch. Long Grove, Ill.: Waveland Press, 2004.

Putnam, Robert. *Bowling Alone: The Collapse and Revival of American Community.* New York: Simon and Schuster, 2000.

Rojek, Chris, and John Urry (editors). *Touring Cultures: Transformations of Travel and Theory.* London: Routledge, 1997.

Rolnik, Don. "A Study of Attitudes towards Israel of American Jewish Youth Participating in a Summer Institute." Ed.D. dissertation, New York University, 1965.

Romero, Simon. "Venezuela's Jews, Already Uneasy, Are Jolted by Attack," *New York Times,* February 13, 2009, A8. At http://www.nytimes.com/2009/02/13/world/americas/13venez.html (accessed May 5, 2009).

Rosenblatt, Gary. "Is It Hard Being Jewish?" *New York Jewish Week,* October 8, 1999. At shamash.org./listarchives/jweek/960306 (accessed May 20, 2002).

Rosenblum, Jonathan. "Misplaced Generosity." *Jerusalem Post,* January 7, 2000, B9. At web.lexis-nexis.com/universe (accessed June 17, 2002).

Sachar, Howard. *A History of Israel: From the Rise of Zionism to Our Time.* New York: Knopf, 1979.

Sales, Amy. *Israel Experience: Is Length of Time a Critical Factor?* Waltham, Mass.: Brandeis University, Cohen Center for Modern Jewish Studies, 1998.

Samuel, Henry. "Gaza Killing Sparks Attacks on Jews across Europe." *Daily Telegraph* (London), January 6, 2009. At http://www.telegraph.co.uk/news/worldnews/europe/4142583/Gaza-killing-sparks-attacks-on-Jews-across-Europe.html (accessed May 5, 2009).

Sanders, George. "*Late* Capital: Negotiating a New American Way of Death." Ph.D. dissertation, Vanderbilt University, 2008.

Sasson, Theodore, and Shaul Kelner. "From Shrine to Forum: Masada and the Politics of Jewish Extremism." *Israel Studies* 13(2) (2008): 146–63.

Sasson, Theodore, David Mittelberg, Shahar Hecht, and Leonard Saxe. *Encountering the Other, Finding Oneself: The Taglit-Birthright Israel Mifgash.* Waltham, Mass.: Brandeis University, Cohen Center for Modern Jewish Studies, 2008.

Saxe, Leonard, and Barry Chazan. *Ten Days of Birthright Israel: A Journey in Young Adult Identity.* Waltham, Mass.: Brandeis University Press, 2008.

Saxe, Leonard, Charles Kadushin, Juliana Pakes, Shaul Kelner, Bethamie Horowitz, Amy Sales, and Archie Brodsky. *Birthright Israel Launch Evaluation: Preliminary Findings.* Waltham, Mass.: Brandeis University, Cohen Center for Modern Jewish Studies, 2000.

Saxe, Leonard, Charles Kadushin, Shahar Hecht, Mark Rosen, Benjamin Phillips, and Shaul Kelner. *Evaluating Birthright Israel: Long-Term Impact and Recent Findings.* Waltham, Mass.: Brandeis University, Cohen Center for Modern Jewish Studies, 2004.

Saxe, Leonard, Theodore Sasson, and Shahar Hecht. *Israel at War: The Impact of Peer-Oriented Israel Programs on the Repsonses of American Jewish Young Adults.* Waltham, Mass.: Brandeis University, Steinhardt Social Research Institute, 2006.

Saxe, Leonard, Charles Kadushin, Shaul Kelner, Mark Rosen, and Erez Yereslove. *A Mega-Experiment in Jewish Education: The Impact of Birthright Israel.* Waltham, Mass.: Brandeis University, Cohen Center for Modern Jewish Studies, 2002.

Saxe, Leonard, Theodore Sasson, and Shahar Hecht. *Taglit-Birthright Israel: Impact on Jewish Identity, Peoplehood, and Connection to Israel.* Waltham, Mass.: Brandeis University, Cohen Center for Modern Jewish Studies, 2006.

Saxe, Leonard, Charles Kadushin, Shaul Kelner, and Erez Yereslove. *Taglit-Birthright Israel Evaluation Survey, Winter 2000–2001 Cohort* [Computer data file]. Waltham, Mass.: Brandeis University, Cohen Center for Modern Jewish Studies, 2001.

Schmidt, Leigh Eric. *Consumer Rites: The Buying and Selling of American Holidays.* Princeton, N.J.: Princeton University Press, 1995.

Sellars, Richard West, and Tony Walter. "From Custer to Kent State: Heroes, Martyrs and the Evolution of Popular Shrines in the USA," pp. 179–200 in *Pilgrimage in Popular Culture,* edited by Ian Reader and Tony Walter. London: Macmillan, 1993.

Shabi, Rachel. "Come, See Palestine!" *Salon,* June 5, 2006. At http://www.salon.com/news/feature/2006/06/05/birthright/print.html (accessed April 6, 2007).

Shain, Yossi. *Kinship and Diasporas in International Affairs.* Ann Arbor: University of Michigan Press, 2007.

Shapiro, Faydra. *Building Jewish Roots: The Israel Experience.* Montreal: McGill-Queen's University Press, 2006.

Sibelman, Jessica. "Israeli Trip an 'Eye-Opening' Experience." *New Jersey Jewish News,* September 4, 2008. At http://www.njjewishnews.com/njjn.com/090408/ltIsraeliTrip.html (accessed November 11, 2008).

Sinai, Ruthi. "Ha-noar ha-yehudi ba lehapes shorashim: Hashkaah mishtalemet?" [The Jewish youth come to seek roots: a worthwhile investment?], *Ha'aretz* (Tel Aviv), January 20, 2000. At http://www.haaretz.co.il (accessed January 31, 2007).

Sinclair, Karen. "Mission to Waitangi: A Maori Pilgrimage," pp. 233–56 in *Sacred Journeys: The Anthropology of Pilgrimage,* edited by Alan Morinis. Westport, Conn.: Greenwood, 1992.

Smith, Christian. *Moral, Believing Animals: Human Personhood and Culture.* Oxford: Oxford University Press, 2003.

Stand With Us International. "StandWithUs Free Trip to Israel." At http://www.standwithus.co.il/birthright/index.htm (accessed March 7, 2007).

Steinberg, Pnina. "Eizor-maga ba-tenuah: leumiut va-etniut ba-derekh Li-yisrael" [Contact zone en route: nationalism and ethnicity on a voyage to Israel]. Ph.D. dissertation, Tel Aviv University, 2002.

Stier, Oren Baruch. "Lunch at Majdanek: The March of the Living as a Pilgrimage of Memory." *Jewish Folklore and Ethnology Review* 17(1–2) (1995): 57–65.

Swidler, Ann. "Culture in Action: Symbols and Strategies." *American Sociological Review* 51(2) (1986): 273–86.

———. *Talk of Love: How Culture Matters.* Chicago: University of Chicago Press, 2001.

Taglit-Birthright Israel. *Educational Standards and Program Requirements.* Jerusalem: Taglit-Birthright Israel, 2005.

———. *Revised Educational Standards 2001.* Jerusalem: Taglit-Birthright Israel, 2001.

Teich, Alyson. "Israel in a Nutshell." Travelblog. At http://www.travelblog.org/Middle-East/Israel/blog-294902.html (accessed November 11, 2008).

"Tour, n." *The Oxford English Dictionary,* 2nd ed. OED Online (Oxford: Oxford University Press, 1989). At http://dictionary.oed.com.proxy.library.vanderbilt.edu/cgi/entry/50255209 (accessed November 28, 2008).

Turner, Victor. "Pilgrimages as Social Processes," pp. 166–230 in *Dramas, Fields and Metaphors: Symbolic Action in Human Society,* edited by Victor Turner. Ithaca, N.Y.: Cornell University Press, [1974] 1987.

Turner, Victor, and Edith Turner. *Image and Pilgrimage in Christian Culture*. New York: Columbia University Press, 1978.

Union of American Hebrew Congregations. *Proceedings of the Union of American Hebrew Congregations: Seventy-Seventh–Eightieth Annual Reports, July 1, 1950 to June 30, 1955*. Cincinnati, Ohio: Union of American Hebrew Congregations, 1956.

United Nations Population Division. *International Migration Report 2002*. New York: UNPD, 2002. At www.un.org/esa/population/publications/ittmig2002/2002ITTMIGTEXT22–11.pdf (accessed August 8, 2008).

United Nations World Tourism Organization. *World Tourism Barometer* 6(2). Madrid: UNWTO, 2008. At http://unwto.org/facts/eng/pdf/barometer/UNWTO_Barom08_2_en_Excerpt.pdf (accessed August 8, 2008).

Urry, John. *The Tourist Gaze*. London: Sage, 1990.

Vertovec, Steven. "Conceiving and Researching Transnationalism." *Ethnic and Racial Studies* 22(2) (1999): 447–62.

Vilnay, Zev. *Ha-tiyul ve-erko ha-hinukhi* [The *tiyul* and its educational value]. Jerusalem: World Zionist Organization, Youth and Pioneer Department, [1945] 1953.

Wasserman, Stanley, and Katherine Faust. *Social Network Analysis: Methods and Applications*. Cambridge: Cambridge University Press, 1998.

Waters, Mary. *Ethnic Options: Choosing Identities in America*. Berkeley: University of California Press, 1990.

Weinstein, Meryle. *An Assessment of the Koret Israel Teen Trip and Summer in Israel Youth Program*. Waltham, Mass.: Brandeis University, Cohen Center for Modern Jewish Studies, 1998.

Wertheimer, Jack. *A People Divided: Judaism in Contemporary America*. New York: Basic Books, 1993.

———. "Jewish Education in the United States," pp. 3–115 in *American Jewish Year Book*, vol. 99, edited by David Singer and Ruth R. Seldin. New York: American Jewish Committee, 1999.

Wiggins, Grant, and Jay McTighe. *Understanding by Design*. 2nd ed. Alexandria, Va.: Association for Supervision and Curriculum Development, 2005.

Woocher, Jonathan. *Sacred Survival: The Civil Religion of American Jews*. Bloomington: Indiana University Press, 1986.

Wood, Peter. "Pilgrimage and Heresy: The Transformation of Faith at a Shrine in Wisconsin," pp. 115–34 in *Sacred Journeys: The Anthropology of Pilgrimage*, edited by Alan Morinis. Westport, Conn.: Greenwood, 1992.

World Trade Organization. *International Trade Statistics 2007*. Geneva: WTO, 2007. At http://www.wto.org/english/res_e/statis_e/its2007_e/its2007_e.pdf (accessed August 8, 2008).

Wuthnow, Robert. *Sharing the Journey: Support Groups and America's New Quest for Community*. New York: Free Press, 1994.

Zerubavel, Yael. *Recovered Roots: Collective Memory and the Making of Israeli National Tradition*. Chicago: University of Chicago Press, 1995.

Zukin, Sharon. *Point of Purchase: How Shopping Changed American Culture*. New York: Routledge, 2004.

Zukin, Sharon, and Jennifer Smith MacGuire. "Consumers and Consumption." *Annual Review of Sociology* 30 (2004): 173–97.

INTERVIEWS AND CORRESPONDENCE

Aronson, Barbara. Personal correspondence. September 10, 2003.

Freedman, Rabbi Paul. Telephone interview. May 7–8, 2002.

Goldwater, Clare. Interview. New York. February 7, 2005.

Harrison, Taryn. Interviews. Lackawanna, N.J. October 28, 2002 and January 6, 2003.

Reichenbach, Paul. Interview. New York. June 19, 2002.

Santoro, Richard, and Serena Cantoni. Telephone interview. January 6, 2004

Siegel, Dr. Morton K. Interview. New York. May 8, 2002.

Skirball, Rabbi Henry. Telephone interview. April 29, 2002.

Yepoyan, Linda. Telephone interview. November 18, 2003.

Index

Adelson, Sheldon, 6
adventure tourism, 14
African Americans, 11, 12, 14
Ahad Ha'am, 195, 211n4
ahavat ha'aretz (loving the land of Israel), 25, 123
air travel: interactions in airports, 44, 45–46, 137; interactions on airplanes, 146–147, 153, 181
aliyah (immigration to Israel): diaspora Jewish tourism, xxiii, 33–34, 44, 122; from France, 119; Taglit tourists, 109–110, 117, 196, 228n17
Almog, Oz, 29, 216n9
American Israel Public Affairs Committee (AIPAC), 106
Amichai, Yehuda, 114
Anderson, Benedict, 20, 206
antisemitism: experiences of, 119–122; French, 119
"applied tourism," xviii
Arab-Israeli conflict: Gaza Strip, war in (2009), 99; intifadas (*see* intifadas); Lebanon, war in (2006), 47–48, 194; Six-Day War (1967), 31, 35, 70–71, 124; Taglit tour guides' representations of, 48, 49–50, 51, 75, 76, 78, 79–80, 81, 193. *See also* Israeli-Palestinian conflict; Israeli-Syrian conflict
Arafat, Yasser, xxi
authenticity, 113, 150
Aviv, Caryn, 197
Avshalom Institute for Yedi'at Ha'aretz, 30

Baden-Powell, Lord, 28
Baedeker, 27

Bar Kokhba revolt, 115
Bauman, Zygmunt, 4
Bedouin, 29, 79, 103
Beilin, Yossi, 41–42
Ben-Gurion, David, 130, 196
Birthright Armenia / Depi Hayk, 6
Birthright Israel. *See* Taglit-Birthright Israel
Birthright Re-Plugged tour, 222n2
Birthright Unplugged tour, 222n2
B'nai Brith Youth Organization, 35
Boorstin, Daniel, 8–9, 140
borderzone. *See* "touristic borderzone"
Boy Scouts, 28
Boyarin, Daniel and Jonathan, 202, 205
branding of products, 102
Braslavi, Joseph, 27, 29
bridging strategies, 114–140; cross-cultural peer-to-peer encounters (see *mifgashim*); discourse of belonging and home, 115–117, 125; discourse of Jewish otherness outside Israel, 117–123, 197; fostering embodied experience, action, 132–134; group discussion circles, 125–127, 151, 166–167, 173; linking individual and collective Jewish narratives, 173–178; site-specific rituals, 128–132; tour leaders as role models, 123–125, 134
Bronfman, Charles R., 40, 42, 122–123
Bruce, Lenny, 126
Bruner, Edward, 11, 16, 88, 170–171
bus. *See* tour buses

Carlebach, Shlomo, 86, 104
Central Europe, diaspora tourism in, 14, 35–36

Chazan, Barry, 36–38; CRB Foundation, 41; "The Israel Trip: A New Form of Jewish Education" (Chazan), 36–38, 65, 69, 159–160

Chien-Tan Overseas Chinese Youth Language Training and Study Tour, 14, 16, 146

China, diaspora tourism in, 11, 13–14, 17, 50, 111–112

Church of Loaves and Fishes, 92

Cohen, Eli, 124

Cohen, Erik, 8–9, 152

Cohen Center for Modern Jewish Studies (CMJS, Brandeis University), xxiv, 19, 46

Coles, Tim, 16

collective effervescence, 145, 165

communitas relationships, fostering of, 160, 165, 168, 231n24

Conservative Judaism, 32, 33, 175

consumerism, 8–9, 105–108

consumption of symbols, 87, 89, 102–105, 113–114. *See also* consumption of themed environments; semiotic of diasporic difference; sight-marker transformations

consumption of themed environments, 96, 101–105

Council of Jewish Federations, 41, 42

CRB Foundation, 40–41, 44

Croatia, diaspora tourism in, 14–15

cross-cultural encounters: with Bedouin, 79; with Druze, 79; interactions with other tourists compared to, 113; with Israeli children, 150; with Israelis working on behalf of other Jews, 99; with Palestinians, 79–80; with religiously committed Jews, 101; in "touristic borderzone," 88–89. See also *mifgashim* (cross-cultural peer-to-peer encounters)

Culler, Jonathan, 87, 140

Culture on Tour (Bruner), 170–171

Dallen, Timothy, 16

Dan (Biblical city), 73–74

Dan River, 69–70, 75

dancing, 141–143

Depi Hayk / Birthright Armenia, 6

depoliticization by Taglit tour guides, 60, 62–63

Dewey, John, educational theory of, 38, 64, 65–66, 124, 195

diaspora: as assumed category, xx; globalization and, 3; Holocaust, relevance of, 118–119; Jewish identity, strengthening of, xx; in Jewish religious discourse, 197; maintenance of, xix; migration, nonessentiality of, 206; nation state-diaspora relationship, 2–4, 13; in neodiasporist scholarship, 205–206; in postcolonial cultural studies, 204–205; rootedness essential to, 200; *shelilat hagolah* (negation of diaspora), 122, 201; in sociology of transnationalism, 204; tourism and (*see* diaspora Jewish tourism; diaspora tourism); Zionist critique of, 34, 193, 197, 201–202

diaspora difference, semiotic of, 96–101, 195, 203–204

diaspora Jewish tourism: 1950s, 31–32; *aliyah* (immigration to Israel) following, xxiii, 33–34, 44, 122; annual enrollments, 35; asymmetry in experience of Arab and Jewish narratives, 195; bridging strategies (*see* bridging strategies); central challenge to, 49; changes in Jewish behaviors, 188; citizenship check on arrival, 112, 117; common denominator of, 77; conflict as primary interpretive frame, 75–76; consciousness-raising discussions during, 77; consumerism and, 105–108; context for, xviii–xix; core themes, 37, 92–93; cost per trip, 32; credibility as education, 78; cross-cultural peer-to-peer encounters (*see* cross-cultural encounters); diaspora, maintenance of, xix; as diaspora-building enterprise, xx, 24; diaspora communities, strengthening of, 122; diasporic identities, strengthening of, 31, 34, 78, 92, 105–108, 203; diasporic political socialization and, 197; disjunction between formal program and informal interactions, 76; educational dimensions of, 31, 36–38, 64–66,

91; educational institutions and, 64; ethnic identity, privileging of, 34, 178–181; experience of Israel, 80; fostering of, systematic approaches to, 18; framing of, 32–33; funding for, 42, 203; growth/ expansion, 34–35; home trope, 110–112; identity formation and, 37, 38, 45, 77, 170, 178–179; informal activities in, 38; itinerary as curriculum, 38; Jewish messianism in graffiti, 94–95; Jewish mysticism commodified, 83–88, 95, 103; Jews worldwide as stakeholders in Israeli state-building, 49; justification for, 122, 133, 188; knowledge practices applied during tours, 203; as life-changing experience, 185–190; long-lasting attachments to Israel, creation of, 200; mappings of place and culture, 87; meaning making and, 96–100, 105; mediating encounters with place during, 145–153; "megadonors" to, 40, 42; metatheme of Jewish culture, 103; mission/purpose, 34; nondiasporist diasporism of, 201–203; offshoots of, 35–36; organizational structure, 42; origins, 31–34; Palestinian counternarratives, acknowledgment of, xix, 58, 78, 81, 222n2; participant observations of, xxiv, 19; pedagogical framework for, 36–38; place differentiation in, 89–91, 93–94; political conversations during, 77; political identities, effect on, 50–51; political socialization, effect on, xx–xxi, 6, 34, 51, 57–59, 67–74, 75–76, 193–194; politics of, 62–63; privileging of aesthetic over moral engagement, 107, 195; rationale for, 36–38; ritual dimensions of, 31; scope of, xvi–xvii; security and liability concerns, 148; self-discovery during, 38; sites always visited, 93, 148–149; sites not visited, 92; socialization by, 34; sponsors, 32–33, 34; studies of, 7, 40–41; symbolic consumption, 87, 89, 102–105 (*see also* consumption of themed environments; semiotic of diasporic difference; sight-marker transformations); territorialization of

Jewish heritage, 106; thematizing of itineraries, 87, 90–96, 103; *tiyul* (hiking as sanctification of space), effect of, 33; tour guide's role, 38; Young Judaea youth movement, 32, 33, 35, 44; Zionism and, xix–xx, 31–32, 195–196

diaspora Jewish tours, organized: Antiquities Tour (NFTY), 32; author's participation in, xxii–xxv, 19, 44, 45, 189–190; Bible Tour (NFTY), 32; Birthright Israel (*see* Taglit-Birthright Israel); Birthright Unplugged tour, 222n2; Etgar! The Ultimate Israel Challenge tour (USY), 35; Holocaust pilgrimages, 6, 36 (*see also* Yad Vashem Holocaust memorial museum); Israel and Safari Kenya tour (B'nai Brith Youth Organization), 35; Israel Experience, Inc. (IEI), 41–42; Israel Pilgrimage tour (USY), xxii, 32, 44, 189; Italy and Israel tour (USY), 35; Kivvunim (Directions) program, 44; March of the Living tour (to Poland), 6; Masa (Israel Journey), 44; Summer-in-Israel Course (Young Judaea), 32; Taglit-Birthright Israel (*see* Taglit-Birthright Israel)

diaspora tour groups, 147–168; anger amongst, 153; baring of souls among, 166–168; bus groups as "total institutions," 147–150; bus journals, 185–186; cliques among, 161; collective effervescence during, 145, 165; communitas relationships among, 160, 165, 168, 231n24; conversations among members of, 77, 170–173, 183; discussion circles among, 125–127, 151, 166–167, 173; dissent, channeling of, 157–159; free time, use of, 151–152; *gibbush* (group-building, coalescence), 161–167, 183; hedonism of, 153; heteronormativity of, 180; interplay between differentiation and cohesion, 160–162; liminality and, 165, 168, 179–180, 199, 231n24; normative environments, creation of, 153–157; paeans to, 166–168; politics, avoidance of, 153–154; post-tour nostalgia for, 168; socialization by, xviii; sorting into friendship networks, 179–180 diaspora tourism, 10–18; by African Americans, 11, 12, 14; as an intersection, xvii; as antidote to cultural illiteracy, 15; as "applied tourism," xviii; at-homeness in America, sense of, 111–112, 197; "brainwashing" by, xxi–xxii; collective identity, strengthening of, xvi; communitas relationships, fostering of, 160, 165, 168, 231n24; contrasting ethnic spaces in, 97; cultural incompetencies, 112–113, 117; destinations (*see* diaspora tourism in); as diaspora-building enterprise, xx; difference and similarity in, 10–11; diversity of, 3; economic considerations, 14; effect on identity, 16–17, 185–190; effectiveness of programs, 15–16, 185–190; familiarity and strangeness in, 17; government sponsorship of, xvi, xx–xxi, 12, 192, 206; imagined communities, 193, 200, 206; immersion in a fellowship of co-ethnics, 159; ineffability of, 184–185; inherent contradictions in, 50; justification for, 89; language barriers, 112, 117; limitations of, xvii; linguistic and cultural differences, effect of, 16; meaning making and, xviii, 89, 93–101, 105; as medium of transnational political socialization, 204; mobilization of, 15; multiculturalism, favoring of, xx–xxi; nation-building and, 14; nation-state, fostering of identification with, xvi, xx; nationalism and, 48–49, 193–196; by native-born American whites, 11–12; normative environs, creation of, 153–157; pilgrimage framing of, 7–8; place differentiation in, 89–91, 93–94; political considerations, 14; political socialization, effect on, xvii, 16, 18, 76–77; politics of, 77; post-tour nostalgia, 168; primary target for, 146; as a roots-seeking phenomenon, 12; socialization and, 16; sponsors of, 7; standardization of experience, 147–150; structural features promoting solidarity among tourists, 160; support for sponsors' official goals, 153–154; Taglit-Birthright Israel as model for, 5, 6, 12; tourism compared to, 8; tourism framing of, 7–8; transnationalism and, 13, 48–49, 110, 193, 198

diaspora tourism in: Central Europe, 14, 35–36; China, 11, 13–14, 17, 50, 111–112; Croatia, 14–15; Ghana, 11, 12, 14; India, 15; Israel (*see* diaspora Jewish tourism); Lebanon, 5; Lithuania, 14, 16–17, 111–112; Poland, 6, 35; South Korea, 16, 50, 111–112; Taiwan, 14, 50

diasporic Jewish identity, 49

diasporic political socialization, 191, 197

diasporism, politics of, 201–204

Discover Your Roots program (India), 15

Disneyland metaphor (for Israel), 102–103

Druze, 79

Durkheim, Emile, 145, 200

Eastern Europe, diaspora tourism in, 14, 35–36

"El Adon" ("God Is Master of All His Works") (hymn), 86

Elementary Forms of Religious Life (Durkheim), 145

Etzel, 217n29

eucalypti, bombing of, 124

Exodus (Uris), 96

Feldman, Jackie, 36

fetishism, 200

Foucault, Michel, 9

galut (exile), 197

Garfinkel, Harold, 211n3

Gaza Strip, 1, 31

Gaza Strip, war in (2009), 99

Ghana, diaspora tourism in, 11, 12, 14

gibbush (group-building, coalescence), 161–167, 183

Gilman, Sander, 205

globalization, 3, 4, 11

Goffman, Erving, 148

Goldwater, Clare, 91–92, 115, 130

Gottdiener, Mark, 102–103

Graburn, Nelson, 8–9

graffiti, Jewish messianism in, 94–95

Grand Canyon, 113
Guttman, Shmaria, 29
Gymnasia Hertzliya, 26

hachsharah programs, 217n34
Haganah, 27, 217n29
Hamas, 56
Hano`ar Ha`oved ("Working Youth"), 28, 29
"Hatikvah" ("The Hope"), 130
Hebrew botanic nomenclature, 71–72
Hebrew names, 169–170
Heilman, Samuel, 146, 147
Herzl, Theodor, 110, 118, 126
heteronormativity of diaspora tour groups, 180
Hezbollah, 83
Hillel: "Educational Model of Our Ten-Day Experience" program, 125–126; group-building among diaspora Jews, 145; group discussion circles sponsored by, 125–127; "How I Relate to Israel—How Israel Relates to Me" program, 126; method for group discussions, 173; nonjudgmental environments, policy supporting, 157; ritual on arrival in Jerusalem, 131; staff manual, 33, 160, 161; Taglit-Birthright Israel and, 5, 33, 64, 114; training for tour guides, 39
Histradrut (General Federation of Labor), 27, 30
Holocaust: ashes-to-redemption narrative, 37, 93, 118, 194; diaspora and, 118–119
Holocaust pilgrimages, 6, 36. *See also* Yad Vashem Holocaust memorial museum
homeland tours. *See* diaspora tourism
hotels: dinners at, 68, 159–159; discussion circles at, 166, 174, 176, 181; Hebrew signage in, 98; as homes away from home, 88; hotel workers, encounters with, 80; as infrastructure for tourist borderzone, 147; irresponsible behavior at, 230n6; as meeting places, 150; orientation meetings at, 185; in Safed, 82; seating arrangements at, 161; as topic of discussion, 170; in tourism industry, 3

identity, 177–190; affective validation of, 182–184; American Jewish identity crisis, 39–41, 42, 196–197; at-homeness of Jewish Americans, 111–112, 197; changes in Jewish behaviors, 188; coherence in, 178, 199; collective identity, strengthening of, xvi; diaspora tourism's effect on, 16–17, 185–190; diasporic identities, strengthening of, 31, 34, 78, 92, 105–108, 203; diasporic Jewish identity, 49; diasporic Jewish identity, and Israel, 33, 78, 92, 105–108, 203–204; ethnic identity, privileging of, 34, 178–181; Jewish identity, strengthening of, xx; Jewishness as a consumer identity, 108; life-changing experiences, 185–190; liminality and, 165, 168, 179–180, 231n24; narrative theories of, 177–178; political identity, 50–51, 191; self-creation, 198–199; state informed/engaged diasporic subjectivities, 203–204; transnational engagement, 198
identity formation: diaspora Jewish tourism and, 37, 38, 45, 77, 170, 178–179; Taglit-Birthright Israel and, 45, 77; tourism and, 192
imagined communities, 20, 193, 200, 206
India, diaspora tourism in, 15
ineffability of diaspora tourism, 184–185
international tourism, 2, 117
intifadas: joking about, 59; second, 43, 222n3, 223n4; Taglit tour guides' representations of, 53–57
Israel: as backdrop, 146; commercial tourism, 26; diaspora tourism in (*see* diaspora Jewish tourism); experience of, 80; as forum for reflecting on existential questions, 36, 37; Hebrew signage in, 98; "homeland" trope, 88; iconic attractions, 148–149; immigration to (see *aliyah*); Jewishness of, 97–101; landscape of, 98; meanings ascribed to, 96–101, 105; as microcosm of Jewish world, 36–37; as model for empowerment, 36; to North American Jews, 197; as site of safety, 100; as spiritual center of diaspora life, 211n4; as a symbolic homeland, 13;

mass migration, 3, 13
"megadonors," 40, 42
Merton, Robert, xxiv
mifgashim (cross-cultural peer-to-peer encounters), 135–140; as boundary-crossing strategy, 20, 38–39; diversity of opinion provided by, 193; hooking up between tourists and Israelis, 137–139, 146–147; intention, 135; with Israeli soldier co-tourists, 47–48, 60, 74, 79, 100, 101, 104, 122, 136, 137–139; post-tour contacts between tourists and Israelis, 136; sexual relations, 137–139; success of, 136
migration, 3, 13, 206
Mount of Beatitudes, 92
multiculturalism, diaspora tourism's favoring of, xx–xxi
music: dancing by tourists, 141–143; "El Adon" ("God Is Master of All His Works") (hymn), 86; Shabbat dinner songs, 158–159, 165
mysticism, commodification of, 83–88, 95, 103

Nachman of Breslov, 86, 94, 126
narrative theories of identity, 177–178
nation-building: diaspora tourism and, 14; *tiyul* (hiking as sanctification of space), 25–26, 28, 29; tourism and, 6–7
nation state-diaspora relationship, tourism and, 2–4, 13
nation states, globalization and territoriality and, 4
National Council of Synagogue Youth, 35
National Federation of Temple Youth (NFTY): Antiquities Tour, 32; Bible Tour, 32; Reform Judaism, 39
nationalism: Arab, 24, 194–195; diaspora tourism and, 48–49, 193–196; Jewish, xxi, 24; Palestinian, xxi (*see also* Zionism); tourism and, xvi
neodiasporist scholarship, 205–206
Nesiya Institute, 35
New Jews (Aviv and Shneer), 197
nostalgia, 168

Obetsebi-Lamprey, J. Otanka, 12
Oslo Accords (1993), xxi, 61

Palestine: commercial tourism in, 26–27; population (1923), 24; pre-1948 travel to, 217n34
Palestinian Authority, 61
Palestinian nationalism, xxi
Palestinians: counternarratives, acknowledgment of their, xix, 58, 78, 81, 222n2; cross-cultural encounters with, 79–80; intifada, second, 43, 222n3, 223n4; sympathy for, 80; Taglit tour guides' representations of, 53, 55–56, 57–60, 80–81, 194, 223n5
Palmach, *tiyul* and, 27, 29–30, 31, 217n29
passport control, 112, 200
Percy, Walker, 113
Peres, Shimon, 29
photography / picture taking: as alternative to listening to guides, 53; as consumption of themed environments, 103; identification with Jewish homeland, development of, 107; of a lahuhe chef, 86–87; at Masada, 129; of soldiers, 100; of synagogues, 104–105; at Tel Dan Nature Reserve, 72, 76; in tourism industry, 3; tourists' use of space, 9–10
pilgrimage studies, 45–46
places: ascription of meaning to, 89, 93–96, 96–101, 105; mediating encounters with, 145–153; place differentiation, 89–91. *See also* territoriality
Poland, Jewish tourism in, 6, 35
political identity, 50–51, 191
political socialization: decentering of conflict narrative, 75–76; depoliticization by Taglit tour guides, 60, 62–63; diaspora Jewish tourism and, xx–xxi, 6, 34, 51, 57–59, 67–74, 75–76, 193–194; diaspora tourism and, xvii, 16, 18, 76–77; diasporic political socialization, 191, 197; normalization of the political, 75; politicization of the normal, 75; during Taglit tours, 67–76;

political socialization (*continued*): through nondiscursive practices, 77; *tiyul* (hiking as sanctification of space), 24–31; tourism and, xvii, 4–5, 8, 51, 182; transnational political socialization, 204

prayer: *shehechyanu*, 131, 165; *Sh'ma*, 155; during Taglit tours, 104–105, 106, 128, 134–135, 157

Rabin, Yitzhak, xxi, 127
Reform Judaism, 32, 175
Reichenbach, Paul, 44–45
Rosh Pinah, Israel, 83

Saturday Night Live (television series), 186
Seinfeld (television series), 72
self-creation, 198–199
Self/Other dialectic, 10–11, 20
semiotic of diasporic difference, 96–101, 195, 203–204
Shabbat dinner songs, 158–159, 165
Sharansky, Natan (Anatoly), 42
Sharon, Ariel, 1–2, 5–6
shehechyanu, 131, 165
shelilat hagolah (negation of diaspora), 122, 201
Shimon bar Yochai, 21
Shneer, David, 197
Shoah. *See* Holocaust, diaspora and
Shorashim, 35
sight-marker transformations, 95–96
site sacralization, 93–94, 130
Six-Day War (1967), 31, 35, 70–71, 124
Smith, Christian, 211n2, 224n23
socialization: by diaspora Jewish tourism, 34; diaspora tourism and, 16; peer group as socializing agent, 145; political socialization (*see* political socialization); shared stories in, 151; in societal reproduction, 211n2; by *tiyul* (hiking as sanctification of space), 25; by tour groups, xviii
Society for the Protection of Nature (Israel), 30
South Korea, diaspora tourism in, 16, 50, 111–112

souvenirs: bus journals as, 185; consumption-based engagement with the ethnic homeland, 87; identification with Jewish homeland, development of, 107; peer pressure in selecting, 151, 153; postcards, 226n25; ritual objects and religious art, 85–86, 105; in Safed, 83, 85–86; shofars as, 128; t-shirts as, 89, 100, 104, 108; in tourism industry, 3
Steinhardt, Michael, 41–42, 45–46
Strawberry Fields (New York City), 9–10
Summer-in-Israel Course (Young Judaea), 32
Swidler, Ann, 123
symbolic consumption, 87, 89, 102–105, 113–114. *See also* consumption of themed environments; semiotic of diasporic difference; sight-marker transformations
Syria, 71, 75

Taglit-Birthright Israel: advertising for, 43; American Jewish identity crisis, 39–41, 42, 196–197; annual enrollment in, 5–6, 43; conflict as primary interpretive frame, 75–76; CRB Foundation's contributions, 40–41; disjunction between formal program and informal interactions, 76; educational frame, 64–66, 91; educational standards, 91; evaluations of, 45–46, 48, 188, 194; Fordist character of, 148; funding for, 42, 45; group discussion circles, 119–122, 125–127, 151, 154–157, 166–167, 173, 181, 183–184; Hillel and, 5, 33, 64, 114; identity formation and, 45, 77; intifada and, second, 43, 222n3, 223n4; Israel Experience, Inc. (IEI) and, 41–42; Israeli-Palestinian conflict's effect on, 43; Jewish Life Network (JLN) and, 41; mission/purpose/goals, 5, 23, 43–46, 196–197; missionizing and, 63–64, 224n16; as model for diaspora tourism, 5, 6, 12; naming of, 23, 43, 221n83; NGOs and, 222n3; origins, context of, 39–43; participant observations of, 19; pilgrimage compared to, 46; as pilgrimage instrumentalized, 45; political bias of tour guides, monitoring of, 51, 63–64;

national tourism, 2, 117; as knowledge practices, 9, 17–18, 215n54; limitations and powers as a medium, 192; as ludic practice, 127, 134–135; materiality of, 133; meaning construction, as a process of, xviii, 51, 89, 93–101, 105; mobilization of, 16; nation-building and, 6–7; nation state-diaspora relationship and, 2–4, 13; objectification of locals, 135; the Other, movement toward, 8–9; place differentiation in, 89–91, 93–94; political socialization and, xvii, 4–5, 8, 51, 182; politics of, 48–49; predictability as desideratum, 90; as a resource to nation-states, 4; self-creation, 198–199; self-knowledge and, 20; Self/Other dialectic, 10–11, 20; semiotic of, 95–96; *sights vs. markers* in, 95–96; symbolic ties, mobilization of, 13; transnationalism and, 13–14; volunteer tourism, 14, 111; as way of knowing a place, xviii, 3, 10, 18, 192–193; as way of traveling, 3, 8–9; Zionism and, 6–7

tourism studies, xv, 7

"tourist gaze": ascribing meaning to place, 88–89, 93–96, 96, 170; group dynamics on, effect of, 145; Janus-faced character of, 170; in Self/Other dialectic, 10, 113; as a semiotic relationship with surroundings, 9; sight-marker transformation in, 96; treating things seen as signifiers, 200; turned inward, 20, 147, 178–179

The Tourist (MacCannell), 93–94, 95

"touristic borderzone," 88–89, 112, 147, 150

tourists: agency of, xvii–xviii, 76; anxieties about validity of their experiences, 113; definition of, hospitality industry's, 3; diaspora tourism (*see* diaspora Jewish tourism; diaspora tourism); guidance for one another, 152–153; nationalism and, xvi; passivity of, xvii; politics of, xvi; population flow from, xv; as readers of symbols, 9; self-awareness of, 133–134; social interactions among, 159; transnationalism and, xvi, 4; uses of space by, 9–10; as way to achieve effects, xviii. *See also* Taglit tourists

"Tourists" (Amichai), 114

transnationalism: diaspora tourism and, 13, 48–49, 110, 193, 198; globalization and, 11; mass migration and, 13; sociology of, diaspora in, 204; tourism and, xvi, 4, 13–14; transnational political socialization, 204

Turner, Victor, 45, 165

Twain, Mark, 126

Tzofim ("Scouts"), 28, 33

United Jewish Appeal, 36

United Nations, 71

United Nations Partition Plan (1947), 53

United Synagogue Youth (USY): Etgar! The Ultimate Israel Challenge tour, 35; Israel-centered diasporic identity, 33; Israel Pilgrimage tour, xxii, 32, 44, 189; Italy and Israel tour, 35; staff training for tour guides, 39; USY on Wheels tour, xxii

Uris, Leon, 96

Urry, John, 9, 97

Vilnay, Zev, 24–25, 27

volunteer tourism, 14, 111

Wandervogel, 28

water shortage, Israel's, 68–71

West Bank: future of, 31; Taglit tours to, 51–62

Western Wall: plaza in front of, 94; Taglit tours to, 93, 104, 134–135, 144, 148, 166

Wiesel, Elie, 126

Yad Vashem Holocaust memorial museum: Jewish otherness outside Israel, emphasis on, 118; Taglit tours to, 90, 100, 118, 121, 127, 132, 148, 166, 169–170, 173

yedi`at ha'aretz, 25–26, 27, 30

Yishuv, 24–26, 27–28

Yom Kippur War (1973), 67

Yossi and Jagger (film), 61

Young Judaea youth movement, 32, 33, 35, 44

youth movement culture, 28–30

Zionism: cemetery for Zionist pioneers, tours to, 92; delegitimization of anti-Zionism, 81; diaspora, critique of, 34, 193, 197, 201–202; diaspora Jewish tourism and, xix–xx, 31–32, 195–196; enjoyment of, 107; Etzel and, 217n29; evolution of, 196; Israel as spiritual center of diaspora life, 211n4; Jabotinsky, Ze'ev, and Revisionist Zionism, 217n29; Jewish self-determination n ancestral lands, right to, 195; Kook, Rabbi Abraham Isaac, and Religious Zionism, 217n29; Labor Zionism, 27, 30; Lehi and, 217n29; liberal critique from within, 65; Masada, pilgrimages to, 29; purpose, 24; state-building, 24; *tiyul* (hiking as sanctification of space), 21–31, 34, 217n29; tourism and, 6–7; as unfaithful to Jewish traditions, 205; youth pilgrimages, 29

Zogby, James, 5–6

Zohar, 82, 83

About the Author

SHAUL KELNER is Assistant Professor of Sociology and Jewish Studies at Vanderbilt University.